Framing Class

Framing Class

Media Representations of Wealth and Poverty in America

Second Edition

Diana Kendall

ROWMAN & LITTLEFIELD PUBLISHERS, INC.
Lanham • Boulder • New York • Toronto • Plymouth, UK

Published by Rowman & Littlefield Publishers, Inc.
A wholly owned subsidiary of The Rowman & Littlefield Publishing Group, Inc.
4501 Forbes Boulevard, Suite 200, Lanham, Maryland 20706
http://www.rowmanlittlefield.com

Estover Road, Plymouth PL6 7PY, United Kingdom

British Library Cataloguing in Publication Information Available

Library of Congress Cataloging-in-Publication Data
Kendall, Diana Elizabeth.
  Framing class : media representations of wealth and poverty in America / Diana Kendall. — 2nd ed.
     p. cm.
  Includes bibliographical references and index.
  ISBN 978-1-4422-0223-8 (cloth : alk. paper) — ISBN 978-1-4422-0224-5 (pbk. : alk. paper) — ISBN 978-1-4422-0225-2 (electronic)
  1. Mass media—Social aspects—United States. 2. Social classes—United States. 3. United States—Social conditions. I. Title.
  HN90.M3K46 2011
  302.23086'2—dc22

                                                                                    2010047438

♾™ The paper used in this publication meets the minimum requirements of American National Standard for Information Sciences—Permanence of Paper for Printed Library Materials, ANSI/NISO Z39.48-1992.

Printed in the United States of America

Contents

Acknowledgments

I am solely responsible for the contents of this book; however, in the eight years in which I have researched and written the first two editions of *Framing Class*, I have incurred many debts to people who have provided me with encouragement and assistance. First of all, I wish to thank Jessica Farrar, a former graduate student at Baylor University, who has worked untiringly, helping me to update statistics and find newer and better examples of the media framing approaches that I describe in this book. Second, I would like to honor the memory of the late Alan D. McClare of Rowman & Littlefield, with whom I had a wonderful friendship and a long working relationship as editor-author before his untimely death in 2009. Alan helped me to bring several books to fruition with Rowman & Littlefield, and he was a constant encouragement on my other research and writing projects as well. Third, I am extremely grateful to Sarah Stanton, my current acquisitions editor, for the energy and enthusiasm that she has brought to the task of publishing the second edition of *Framing Class*. Jin Yu, editorial assistant, has been most helpful in working with the technical aspects of this manuscript, and the copyeditor, Jennifer Kelland, and production editor, Janice Braunstein, have helped to make this a far better book than it otherwise might have been.

Chapter 1

Class Action in the Media

San Francisco, California:

> They live—and die—on a traffic island in the middle of a busy downtown street, surviving by panhandling drivers or turning tricks. Everyone in their colony is hooked on drugs or alcohol. They are the harsh face of the homeless in San Francisco.
>
> The traffic island where these homeless people live is a 40-by-75 foot triangle chunk of concrete just west of San Francisco's downtown. . . . The little concrete divider wouldn't get a second glance, or have a name—if not for the colony that lives there in a jumble of shopping carts loaded with everything they own. It's called Homeless Island by the shopkeepers who work near it and the street sweepers who clean it; to the homeless, it is just the Island. The inhabitants live hand-to-mouth, sleep on the cement and abuse booze and drugs, mostly heroin. There are at least 3,000 others like them in San Francisco, social workers say. They are known as the "hard core," the people most visible on the streets, the most difficult to help. . . .
>
> Every effort to help the Islanders—from family, probation officers, drug counselors, homeless aid workers—has failed. They have been in and out of hospitals or methadone programs and jails . . . so many times even they have lost count. "We want to get off the street, but I got to tell you true," [Tommy, a homeless man, said], "Unless they take people like us and put us somewhere we can't keep f——ing up, we're going to keep f——ing up."[1]

How does this excerpt from a newspaper article make you feel about homeless people? Based on this news account, most newspaper readers would have a hard time feeling sympathy for the inhabitants of Homeless Island. To the contrary, they typically react to the situation depicted above, as reported in a *San Francisco Chronicle* series "Shame of the City," with disgust, thinking,

1

"Yeah, that's the sort of homeless people who are the problem"—bums who sleep on the cement, abuse drugs and alcohol, and panhandle for the money it takes to support their habit.

Compare that media-generated account of San Francisco's homeless population with this one, also from a newspaper article:

> "He's OK," Michelle, 48, said of San Francisco Police Officer Matt Maciel one afternoon after he gently told them to move their carts and then asked if they had enough to eat. "He's just doing his job."
>
> Michelle remembers when she might have been the one calling the cops on people leaving needles outside her house. She was born . . . in Colorado . . . and was sexually abused as a child. Her dad was shotgunned to death young, and her mother was a drug addict gone to cancer. But before Michelle crash-landed at the Island five years ago, she worked as a home health aide and wore smart, pressed dresses.
>
> She dreams of getting back to that life. "That cop might be the guy who helps me, or maybe the jail people—it could be anybody," she said, giving Maciel a smile as he drove off. "I just need another chance."[2]

Based on this article, readers might feel some degree of sympathy for the homeless—especially for homeless people like Michelle. Surprisingly, both of these depictions of the homeless were written by the same reporter and ran in the same newspaper. Together, they show how media framing of a particular news story or television program often influences how we feel about the people described, especially when the subject relates to wealth, poverty, or the future of the middle class. The manner in which the media frame class has a major impact on how people feel about class and inequality. For example, most people in the United States are not really middle class (since that would be statistically impossible); yet, most of us think that we belong in this category—at least partly because the media define the middle class in such a way that most of us can easily self-identify with it.

WHY "FRAMING CLASS"?

In writing *Framing Class* I aim to demonstrate how newspaper articles and television entertainment programs contribute to the social construction of reality about class in the United States, including the manner in which myths and negative stereotypes about the working class and the poor create a reality that seemingly justifies the superior positions of the upper-middle and upper classes and establishes them as entitled to their privileged position in the stratification system. Although I started this chapter with an example of how the media frame stories about homeless people—those at the bottom of the class hierarchy—the interest in class-based media research that led me to write this book initially related to the upper and upper-middle classes. When conducting research for *The Power of Good Deeds: Privileged Women and the Social Reproduction of the Upper Class*,[3] I became aware of how little has been written about media representations of class, particularly the U.S. upper or privileged class. Though some scholars have examined media content in relation to race and gender, class remains largely overlooked or deeply enmeshed in the larger race/class/gender sociological paradigm in these studies. *Framing Class* specifically focuses on class to fill in the gap pertaining to media representations of class; however, I am not suggesting that class is more important than race or gender in studying inequality. Rather, this volume reflects my belief that we must consider class as the media frame it, especially in television entertainment programs and national newspapers, in its own right as a form of reality construction and maintenance.

Even a cursory look at the media reveals that class clearly permeates media content.[4] Regardless of whether journalists and scriptwriters or entertainment writers consciously acknowledge the importance of framing class in their analysis of everyday life, it continually imbues the millions of articles and television shows written and produced each year.

Prior to writing this book, I had studied the media for a number of years, and I must admit to being an avid reader and a frequent viewer of television and films. Previously, I have focused on the ways in which the media discuss social problems and how the political economy of media industries contributes to media content. On a more personal level, my interest in the upper classes and media emerged as I worked with the "high-society" media in various cities, performing volunteer public relations work for several prestigious nonprofit organizations. In that role, I provided "fact sheets" and other information to columnists and television reporters about major charity fundraisers such as debutante presentations, society balls, designer show houses, and other gala events. While observing a variety of society columnists who wrote about social elites, I became aware of the complex relationship between privileged people and the paid journalists who work on the political, business, and philanthropy beats covering their activities. I noticed that for journalists to maintain their "inner-circle" access, they must typically take care with what and how they write about the wealthy and powerful members of their communities.

Based on these observations, I began to compare information provided by the media about the upper classes with media representations of the working class and the poor. It was evident that journalists and television writers hold elites and their material possessions in greater awe—and encourage their audiences to do likewise—than they do the poor or homeless, who are portrayed, at best, as in need of our pity and, at worst, as doomed by their own shortcomings. I became convinced, in the words of sociologist Herbert Gans, that "the news especially values the order of the upper-class and upper-middle class sectors of society."[5] Consequently, although my investigation into media representations of class began with a desire to learn more about how journalists and television entertainment writers portray the rich and famous, over time my area of interest expanded. As I began systematically to gather data about the upper and upper-middle classes in the media, I saw how other socioeconomic dimensions (such as a person's school affiliation or the cost and location of his or her residence) often become proxies for class. I realized that I should compare the framing of media stories across class lines to demonstrate fully the prevailing themes used to write about social class in this country. My primary focus remains on how the media glorify the upper classes, even when they are accused of wrongdoing, but I also demonstrate how the framing of stories about the middle, working, and poor classes may maintain and justify larger class-based inequalities in the United States.

"ALL MEDIA, ALL THE TIME" AND OUR IDEAS ABOUT CLASS

How the media portray class in the United States is a crucial issue because the typical individual spends so many of his or her waking hours with some form of media. In the past the average American spent an estimated three hours a day watching television, or the equivalent of forty-five days per year.[6] When overall electronic media—including television and radio programs, televised sports events, movies, video and audio tapes, CDs and DVDs, video games, and website materials—were added to the mix, the typical person spent over three thousand hours per year consuming media products.[7] However, these figures do not take into account the rapid expansion of all forms of media usage, including social media networking by people of all ages. American children and teens spend almost eight hours a day watching TV, playing video games, and surfing the Internet. This adds up to more than fifty-three hours a week—more time than many adults spend at work.[8] Nielson Company reports, for example, show that individuals of all ages spend more than 5.5 hours a day on social-networking sites. People continue to increase the number of hours they spend in front of television sets and on computers, especially using such sites. A Pew study found that 72 percent of young adults and teens between the ages of eighteen and twenty-nine use social-networking sites, and the number of adults over age thirty using these sites continues to grow at a rate that will soon reach 50 percent of all respondents.[9] As media use continues to grow, so does the necessity and importance of systematically studying media representations of wealth and poverty.

Understanding how the media portray the different social classes in our society is important because studies have shown that how the media frame certain issues may affect audiences' attitudes and judgments.[10] Although some may argue that how media depict class does not matter because we can each use our own experiences to balance any inaccurate portrayals that we see on television or read in newspapers or magazines, this contention assumes unrealistically that we can distinguish between the realities of the U.S. class structure as it actually exists and the fictionalized version of a perceived class reality as depicted by the mass media.

Framing is an important way in which the media emphasize some ideological perspectives and manipulate salience by directing people's attention to certain ideas while ignoring others. As such, a frame constitutes a story line or an unfolding narrative about an issue.[11] These narratives organize experience and bring order to events. As such, they wield power because they influence how we make sense of the world.[12] By the time readers and viewers such as ourselves gain access to media products, they customarily have undergone an extensive process of review and filtration. In the news industry, for example, the joint efforts of reporters, writers, producers, camera operators, photographers, and many others have framed the available information and produced a construction of social reality that does not necessarily accurately reflect the real conditions of social life. Words like "spin" describe the framing of stories based on organizational constraints, professional judgments, and the targeted audience for the media product. Surveying print, television, and Internet news, we find that lead stories and their coverage of particular events are quite similar. The details are often interchangeable, and headlines and leads use ready-made clichés. According to media scholar Gaye Tuchman, "The news frame organizes everyday reality and the news frame is part and parcel of everyday reality. . . . [It] is an essential feature of news."[13] Both conscious and unconscious motives on the part of media framers play into how the news is framed.

As in the news industry, the story lines, or frames, in television entertainment shows are standardized and frequently repetitive. Similar plots are found across a variety of situation comedies, the primary differences being the location and the characters who act out the various events. Each year during the holiday season, for example, numerous sitcoms portray a lead character who attempts to help poorer individuals by giving them a handout or who performs some other act of kindness toward someone less fortunate.

With regard to the portrayal of class in the media, all of this means that we are not receiving "raw" information or "mere" entertainment that accurately reflects the realities of life in different classes; in fact, audiences are receiving formulaic products that have been previously sanitized and schematized so that readers and viewers do not have to think for themselves or deal with the underlying problems of our society.[14] Today, we must consider media framing as a process in which frame building and frame setting form important components of what we think of as reality. By this I mean that the framing of news articles and television story lines does not necessarily realistically portray class and how it affects our daily lives. We should not assume that what we see in the media accurately reflects class and class-based inequalities. In fact, contemporary media messages about class have a limited basis in reality. At the extreme, French social theorist Jean Baudrillard argues that media images have replaced reality to an extent that we are unable to distinguish between a media image of reality and reality itself.[15] Other scholars join him, arguing that for many people the media constitute "reality" as much as anything that actually happens in the real world.

Consider, for example, how people have, for days after episodes of such popular television shows as *The Office*, *Gossip Girl*, *The Bachelor* and *The Bachelorette*, and the *Real Housewives* franchise, discussed what happened to the characters or participants, often referring to them by their first names as if they were friends or neighbors. "Did you see who Ali sent home last night at the rose ceremony on *The Bachelorette*?" is a typical question. Media scholar Todd Gitlin explains this sociologically:

> Of all the institutions of daily life, the media specialize in orchestrating everyday consciousness—by virtue of their pervasiveness, their accessibility, their centralized symbolic capacity. They name the world's parts, they certify reality as reality—and when their certifications are doubted and opposed, as they surely are, it is those same certifications that limit the terms of effective opposition. To put it simply: the mass media have become core systems for the distribution of ideology.[16]

As Gitlin points out, media products not only are pervasive and widely accessible in our society but have the symbolic capacity to define the world for people and to limit the terms of debate if someone challenges ideologies implicitly or explicitly set forth in the media product.

By analyzing how the media socially construct meanings about class, we can more clearly see how ideology and everything that passes for knowledge in our society can affect our thinking about inequality and our personal identity in regard to the class structure. Based on a theoretical approach referred to as the social construction of reality, I argue that we use the information we gain from the media to construct a picture of class and inequality that we come to accept as reality. In the words of sociologists Peter L. Berger and Thomas Luckmann, "Human reality [is] socially constructed reality."[17] Accordingly, we learn about our world through primary and secondary socialization, which collectively serves as our induction into participation in the larger societal dialectic. According to Berger and Luckmann, we learn a class-oriented view of society by looking through the lens of the class-related perspectives of significant others—those people whose care, affection, and approval we especially desire and who are most important in the development of the self:

> The significant others who mediate this world to [us] modify it in the course of mediating it. They select aspects of it in accordance with their own location in the social structure, and also by virtue of their individual, biographically rooted idiosyncrasies. The social world is "filtered" to the individual through this double selectivity. Thus the lower-class child not only absorbs a lower-class perspective on the social world, he [or she] absorbs it in the idiosyncratic coloration given it by his [or her] parents (or whatever other individuals are in charge of his [or her] primary socialization). The same lower-class perspective may induce a mood of contentment, resignation, bitter resentment, or seething rebelliousness. Consequently, the lower-class child will not only come to inhabit a world greatly different from that of an upper-class child, but may do so in a manner quite different from the lower-class child next door.[18]

In addition to the coloration given to class through the socialization process in the family, people also experience class-related coloration in the secondary socialization process when social institutions such as schools, churches, and the media present a highly selective (and sometimes distorted) view of how class works. Along with primary agents of socialization in the family and close friendship units that help to maintain the individual's subjective reality of class, a number of "less significant others" reaffirm a person's class location and serve as a "chorus in reality-maintenance."[19] The media are crucial agents in this chorus.

MEDIA FRAMING AND SOCIAL REALITIES

Framing is the process by which sense is made of events.[20] When we read a newspaper or watch television or a movie, we live vicariously: we do not actually experience firsthand the event that we are reading about or seeing. Instead, we experience a mediated form of communication in which images and words supply us with information that shapes our perceptions of the world around us. The media selectively frame the world,[21] and these frames manipulate salience, meaning media direct audiences to consider certain features or key points and to ignore or minimize others. The term *media framing* describes the process by which the media (newspapers, magazines, radio and television networks and stations, and the Internet) package information and entertainment before presenting it to an audience. This process includes factors such as the amount of exposure given to a story, where it is placed, the positive or negative tone it conveys, and the nature of any accompanying headlines, photographs, or other visual and auditory effects.

Although various analysts have defined and applied the concept of framing differently,[22] early sociological views of framing by the media were often based on Erving Goffman's *Frame Analysis: An Essay on the Organization of Experience*, in which he states,

> I assume that definitions of a situation are built up in accordance with principles of organization which govern events—at least social ones—and our subjective involvement in them; frame is the word I use to refer to such of these basic elements as I am able to identify. My phrase "frame analysis" is a slogan to refer to the examination in these terms of the organization of experience.[23]

According to Goffman, frames serve as cognitive structures that guide perception and the representation of reality. Frames denote schemata of interpretation that make it possible for people "to locate, perceive, identify, and label" occurrences within their life space and the world at large.[24] However, Goffman did not believe that individuals consciously manufacture frames; he thought that we unconsciously adopt them in the course of communication so that we can deal with reality and attempt to choose appropriate repertories of cognition and action.[25] Thus, a key argument of Goffman's frame analysis is that individuals make sense of their everyday lives by devising frames that shape and compartmentalize their experiences and help them explain the realm of objects and events around them.

Goffman's frame analysis has been applied to a wide range of studies examining issues including social movements,[26] gender politics,[27] and news coverage of terrorism.[28] For the most part, these studies shift his use of frame analysis from a focus on an individual's personal approach to reality to a larger view of how other people or entities, especially the media, devise frames that influence our interpretation of reality. For example, in their examination of the framing process and social movements, sociologists Robert D. Benford and David A. Snow describe how social movement actors serve as agents who actively engage in the production and maintenance of meaning for other people through processes such as frame amplification, which involves "accenting and highlighting some issues, events, or beliefs as being more salient than others."[29] According to Benford and Snow, by punctuating or accenting certain elements, the frame-amplification process creates a conceptual handle or peg that links together various events and issues, and "these punctuated issues, beliefs, and events may function much like synecdoches that come to symbolize the larger frame or movement of which it is a part."[30] The movement slogan "Homeless, Not Helpless" illustrates this function. Other synecdoches—such as "angry white males" and "soccer moms"—have taken on a political reality after journalists created pervasive gendered frames to describe social phenomenon, such as using the term *gender gap* to refer to differences between women and men in political preferences and voting behavior.[31]

Framing helps us make sense of social life because facts have no intrinsic meaning. Facts "take on their meaning by being embedded in a frame or story line that organizes them and gives them coherence, selecting certain ones to emphasize while ignoring others."[32] Out of the many facts or bits of information that the news media might report on class-related issues, for example, frames are used to highlight or privilege certain items over others, thereby elevating them in salience—making them more noticeable, meaningful, or memorable to the audiences receiving those bits of information.[33] Factors that make bits of information more salient are their placement within a text, how often the same information is repeated, and the extent to which bits of information are associated with other symbols familiar to readers or viewers.[34]

Although most often discussed with regard to the news media, the concept of framing also applies to the processes television entertainment writers use to create story lines for dramas and situation comedies. According to Gitlin, "Frames are principles of selection, emphasis and presentation composed of little tacit theories about what exists, what happens, and what matters."[35] As we watch a television entertainment show, we are influenced by the tacit theories that guided the writers of that program, whether we are aware of them or not. Like news reports, television entertainment programming provides "symbolic representations of society rather than literal portrayals thereof."[36]

Although aware that they are living vicariously as they watch fictionalized versions of life, media audiences may identify with the characters and the events depicted, coming to experience the emotions of individuals whom they have never met and will never actually know. For example, media blur the line between fact and fiction when viewers come to identify strongly with fictional characters or cast members on reality shows. Consider, for example, the now-classic television show *Marcus Welby, M.D.*, in which actor Robert Young played the title role. So convincing was Young's portrayal that many viewers came to view the actor as an actual doctor and sent letters asking him for medical advice. These viewers could not distinguish the real actor Young from the unreal Dr. Welby. Further blurring the line between the real and unreal, the actor Robert Young later played a doctor in television ads, recommending medical products to potential patients.[37] Since 2004, real-life physicians have reported that TV series such as *House M.D.* have become so real to media audiences that these programs have impacted health care: Viewers/real-life patients have accepted as reality the medical cases diagnosed by the actor (Hugh Laurie) who plays Dr. House, and the real-life patients self-diagnose (usually incorrectly) their own condition as being a rare, life-threatening illness they saw on the show. Consequently, some patients expect their real-life doctors to order costly medical tests to determine if they have the rare condition shown on the TV series.[38] Reality miniseries such as *Hopkins* and *Boston Med* contribute to media reality creation because they are quasidocumentary programs presented in an entertainment format for television. In these programs, doctors, nurses, and patients at major hospitals go about their daily routines, as if not being followed by a television camera crew, while they perform unusual surgical procedures such as face transplants.[39] The line between what is real and what is fake becomes further blurred in the media as a wide variety of sources become more adept at gaining access to all aspects of people's personal and social lives.

The framing of news and entertainment shows is not accidental. A basic premise of framing analysis holds that the process of framing is an active endeavor involving patterns of selection, emphasis, and exclusion on the part of journalists and writers who determine what material might be entertaining or newsworthy for readers and viewers. In the process of selecting some topics as important, they discard others. Once a topic has been chosen, determining the aspects to be emphasized, minimized, or excluded is largely left up to the journalist or scriptwriter. In news stories about the middle class, for example, journalists may frame articles to show how the middle class is victimized by the rich (for instance, if wealthy individuals receive a special tax break) or by the working class (for instance, if workers demand higher wages that will increase prices). In framing articles to suggest that middle-class people are victims, journalists may ignore how members of the middle class themselves victimize people in other classes, such as the low-paid house cleaners and yard workers who help them maintain their middle-class lifestyles.

Viewers and listeners often take for granted class-based media representations when they see or hear the same ideas repeated frequently.[40] Take, for example, the annual media coverage that accompanies holiday charity toward those who are down on their luck. This coverage typically receives a homogeneous media interpretation as journalists and television entertainment writers give their annual nod to the poor and homeless by writing news stories[41] or television scripts calling for leading characters to serve a Thanksgiving or

Christmas meal to the homeless at the local soup kitchen. These media representations suggest that Americans are benevolent people who do not forget the less fortunate. Ironically, the rest of the story line for the holiday episode of major television situation comedies typically shows the characters fretting over their own extensive Christmas lists and overindulging at holiday parties, conveying a message widely divergent from the one about unselfishly helping the poor and homeless.

Images of wealth and poverty repeatedly depicted by the media may either reinforce or challenge readers' and viewers' beliefs about inequality.[42] This can be true even with regard to a situation comedy or other television program that viewers know is fiction. As communications scholar Linda Holtzman states, "We may say of television, music, or film, 'I know it's not real,' and yet with heavy consumption of the media the repetition of the images will influence us in spite of that understanding."[43] Positive images of the wealthy may make us believe that they are deserving of their wealth; negative images of the poor and homeless may make us believe that they deserve their wretched condition.

Beliefs and attitudes can influence behaviors. In regard to wealthy celebrities who are constantly featured in media culture, philosopher and media critic Douglas Kellner writes, "The celebrities of media culture are the icons of the present age, the deities of an entertainment society, in which money, looks, fame, and success are the ideals and goals of the dreaming billions who inhabit Planet Earth."[44] If we accept this dream of fame and fortune, we may engage in voyeurism, vicarious living, and unduly high levels of consumerism, all the while concluding that there is nothing wrong with our society and that our primary concern should be to get rich and avoid being poor—or at least to be solidly middle class but able to show that we can live as the wealthy and famous do. Media analysts suggest that audiences are strongly influenced by constant media bombardment about the lives of high-profile, rich celebrities and that many everyday people seek to model their appearance and behavior on cultural icons they have never met. According to Kellner, for example,

> The stars of the entertainment industry become fashion icons and models for imitation and emulation. In a postmodern image culture, style and look become increasingly important modes of identity and presentation of the self in everyday life, and the spectacles of media culture show and tell people how to appear and behave.[45]

In sum, the melding of information and entertainment in the media has created an "infotainment society," in which many people cannot get enough media spectacle and are willing to participate in everything from appearing on reality TV shows as contestants to engaging in excessive consumerism that may bankrupt them.

For all these reasons, I became fascinated with the study of how the media have represented class in the United States. As you read this book, I hope that you will share my interest in this important topic.

CONDUCTING THE RESEARCH

Because little prior research had examined media and class, I began my study with newspaper databases, searching for key words and phrases like "working class," "elites," and "middle class" to identify a range of articles containing some specific acknowledgment of class location or socioeconomic status. I watched thousands of hours of television entertainment shows, looking specifically for such class-related identifiers as the occupational status of characters and the types and locations of their residences. I also examined media publicity about shows that emphasized economic characteristics, such as *Life of Luxury* and *Rich Kids*. Since the first edition of this book, I have continued my research and found many more programs with overt class overtones, such as *90210*, the *Real Housewives* franchise, *Modern Family*, *My Name Is Earl*, and numerous criminal-investigation/forensic-science television dramas.

Although my research includes articles from many newspapers, I found that the *New York Times* best reflected what was being printed in newspapers throughout the country; many other papers are affiliated with the *Times* syndicate and publish the same articles within a day or two. Reliance on the *New York Times* as a major source for my research is in keeping with the work of journalism scholar Jack Lule, who has stated,

> But more than any other U.S. news medium, the *New York Times* has become crucial reading for those interested in the news, national politics and international affairs. Understanding the *Times* has become a necessary part of understanding the times. Though not the biggest, it may well be the most significant newspaper in the world.[46]

As Lule points out, stories are not necessarily truer if they are in the *Times*, but those that do appear in the *Times* carry great weight and are often widely cited by television reporters and others because they were initially published there.

I narrowed my research to newspaper articles and television entertainment shows because both are taken for granted as a form of either information or entertainment. Although reality series have become increasingly popular since the late 1980s and early 1990s, I have limited my observation of such shows to those that overtly employ the idea of class, such as Bravo's multi-city *Real Housewives* franchise, which follows the lives of affluent women and their families in places like New York City; Franklin Lakes, New Jersey; Orange County, California; Atlanta, Georgia; and Washington, DC. Regardless of the setting, *Real Housewives* programs focus on material possessions, expensive cosmetic surgery, and class-based distinctions such as whether a person may have money but still have no "class." This series appears less staged than some others, but it cannot accurately be described as a show about how affluent women actually live.

Many "reality" shows are indeed staged and do not indicate the true class position of cast members. For instance, in the finale of the first season of ABC's *The Bachelorette*, middle-class participants Trista Rehn (a physical therapist) and Ryan Sutter (a firefighter) enjoy a fully televised, multi-million-dollar wedding extravaganza paid for by the television network and the show's sponsors. Beginning in 2009, a reality show on the WEtv Network has provided free, lavish weddings for middle- and working-class women. One competition on the network offered viewers the opportunity to win a $100,000 dream wedding by participating in a watch-and-play giveaway.

Regarding newspapers and class representations, I have attempted to gain a historical perspective on how newspapers have covered class-related issues over time. I found the archives of the *New York Times* particularly useful, as its articles dating back to the 1850s have been systematically organized by headline or key words and can be easily retrieved (for a fee) for full-text analysis. I carried out research on more recent newspaper and television news reports, as well as television entertainment shows, through Internet database searches. I recorded many of the television shows mentioned in this book and watched the episodes numerous times, looking each time for subtle nuances of class that I previously might have missed.

I divided all of the materials that I had gathered into categories reflecting the different components of the U.S. class structure and the divisions set forth by well-known sociologists in the field of social stratification. Despite the variety of views of the American class system, I find a fairly traditional model most useful for explaining the objective view of class because it reflects more closely than some other models what most media typically purport to show about class divisions in this country. According to sociologists, a class system is a type of social stratification based on the ownership and control of resources and on the type of work people do.[47] One resource is income—the economic gain derived from wages, salaries, income transfers (governmental aid), and ownership of property. Income is most important to those in the middle and lower tiers of the class structure because, without it, they would not have the means for economic survival. By contrast, wealth is the value of all a person's or family's economic assets, including income, personal property, and income-producing property. Some wealthy people do not need to work because they possess sufficient economic resources—derived from ownership of property, including buildings, land, farms, factories, stocks, bonds, and large bank accounts—to live very well for the duration of their lives and to pass on vast estates to their children and grandchildren.

Because the media frequently use terms like *working class* and *upper-middle class*, I employed the model developed by Dennis Gilbert and Joseph A. Kahl,[48] which divides the United States into six classes—the upper class (or capitalist class), the upper-middle class, the middle class, the working class, the working poor, and the poor and homeless (or underclass)—as a basis for analyzing my data. The Gilbert-Kahl model identifies economic variables (such as occupation, income, and wealth), status variables (prestige, association, and socialization), and political variables (power and class consciousness), which I used to divide my data into categories for analysis. In regard to status variables, for example, the media often use prestige as a concept to differentiate between people on the basis of how much deference or, alternatively, condescension they receive from others. Similarly, the concept of association helps to peg a person's class location with respect to the individuals or groups with whom he or she associates. Socialization is the process through which we learn the skills, attitudes, and customs of a particular class. In regard to the political variables of power and class consciousness, power is the ability of individuals or groups to achieve their goals despite opposition from others,[49] whereas class consciousness is the degree to which people at a similar location in the class system think of themselves as a distinctive group sharing political, economic, and social interests. All of these variables either contribute to or limit opportunity for social mobility—the extent to which people can move up or down in the class system.[50]

At the top of the social-class hierarchy is the upper (capitalist) class, which constitutes about 1 percent of the U.S. population and comprises the wealthiest and most powerful people, who control the majority of the nation's (and, in some cases, the world's) wealth. The investment decisions of people in this class shape national and international economies. Typical household income is about $1 million annually. The upper class includes "owners of substantial enterprises, investors with diversified wealth, heirs to family fortunes, and top executives of major corporations."[51]

Distinctions are sometimes made between "old-money" (upper-upper) and "new-money" (lower-upper) classes in the sociological literature.[52] Members of the old-money category come from prominent families that have possessed great wealth for several generations. On a national level, names like Astor, Rockefeller, Mellon, Du Pont, and Kennedy come to mind. However, many regional elites also have immense wealth and pass its benefits on to children and grandchildren through gifts and legacies. By contrast, families with new money have accumulated vast economic resources during the lifetime of people in the current generation. Since the 1980s and 1990s, this money has come from high-tech industries, investment and banking, top-earning professions, and high-profile careers in sports and entertainment. Often new-money individuals' net wealth exceeds that of people with old money. An example of new-money wealth is that held by Dr. Patrick Soon-Shiong, a surgeon, who added to his $4 billion fortune when he sold his company, Abraxis Bio-Science, to Celgene for $2.9 billion in cash and stock. Previously, Dr. Soon-Shiong gained $3.7 billion when he sold a generic-drug company he founded. The two sales together made him the wealthiest man in Los Angeles.[53]

Like the upper class, the upper-middle class (about 14 percent of the U.S. population) is identified as privileged in comparison to the middle and working classes, working poor, and underclass in that the upper-middle class primarily consists of professionals with college and postgraduate degrees. This group includes many top managers of large corporations, business owners, lawyers, doctors, dentists, accountants, architects, and others who earn incomes far above the national average. People in the upper-middle class are often portrayed as having achieved the American Dream. Unlike many in the upper class, however, members of the upper-middle class work to earn a living, and their children must acquire the requisite education if they are to enter well-paid employment; they cannot simply assume that they will inherit family-owned businesses or diversified stock and bond portfolios. Typical annual household income for people in the upper-middle class is about $150,000.

By comparison, people in the middle of the middle class (about 30 percent of the U.S. population) typically hold two-year or four-year college degrees, have more supervision at work, and experience less job stability than those in the upper-middle class. Occupational categories include lower-level managers, semiprofessionals, and nonretail sales workers. About $70,000 is a typical annual household income for people in this segment of the middle class. In the past, middle-class occupations were considered relatively secure and thought to provide opportunities for advancement if people worked hard, increased their level of education, and gained more experience on the job. Today, however, a number of factors—including the recession of the 2000s, the housing crisis and high mortgage-foreclosure rates, occupational insecurity and long-term job loss, and the continual cost-of-living squeeze—are subjects of major concern and increasing analysis in various media sources.

The working class (about 30 percent of the U.S. population) comprises semiskilled workers such as machine operators in factories (blue-collar jobs) and some service-sector workers, including clerks and salespeople whose jobs involve routine, mechanized tasks that require little skill beyond basic literacy and brief on-the-job training. Typical household pay is $40,000 a year or less among the working class. Few people in this group have more than a high school diploma, and many have less, making job opportunities for them scarcer in the second decade of the 2000s. Jobs in fast-food restaurants and "big-box" chains such as Walmart have been the largest employment growth area for the working class; the segment made up of semiskilled blue-collar workers in construction and manufacturing has shrunk since the 1950s. The working class has been hard hit by everything from natural disasters such as Hurricane Katrina and other major weather events to human disasters such as the vast BP oil spill off the southern U.S. coastline. For example, current estimates suggest that as a direct result of the 2010 oil-spill crisis, thousands of working-class jobs may be lost in the fishing industry, tourism, and the oil-drilling and oil-service businesses.

Below the working class in the social hierarchy is the working-poor category (about 13 percent of the U.S. population). Members of the working poor live just above or below the poverty line. Typical annual household income is about $25,000. Individuals identified as the working poor often hold un-skilled jobs, seasonal migrant jobs in agriculture, lower-paid factory jobs, and minimum-wage service-sector jobs (such as counter clerk in restaurants). As some people once in the unionized, blue-collar sector of the workforce have lost their jobs, they have faced increasing impoverishment. A large number of the working poor hold full-time jobs, and some hold down more than one job, but they simply cannot make ends meet. At the bottom end of the work-ing class, there is often a pattern of oscillating mobility in which people move back and forth between the working-class and the working-poor categories.

The poor and homeless, or the underclass (about 12 percent of the U.S. population), typically include unemployed individuals or part-time workers caught in a pattern of long-term deprivation that results from low educa-tion and income levels and high unemployment rates. In this category are unskilled workers, many single parents, members of subordinate racial and ethnic groups, people with mental or physical disabilities, recent immigrants with low levels of educational attainment, and individuals who depend on public assistance and other government transfers. Household income in the underclass typically is $15,000 or less each year.[54]

By using these objective criteria for class established by Gilbert and Kahl, I began to look for recurring frames used over time to describe the lifestyles of people in the upper, middle, and lower classes. It was interesting to see the extent to which these recurring themes could be found not only over decades but also over centuries in media portrayals. For example, although the harsh representations of the poor and homeless have been mitigated by the more respectful terms of political correctness since the 1990s, many of the same themes and framing devices are still used to describe the plight of those at the bottom of our society's social, economic, and political ladder. Over the years, there has also been an almost fawning acceptance of the rich and famous, even when they are accused of wrongdoing, that is not found in representations of the working class. And though most people choose to identify themselves as members of the good, solid middle class, for the past 150 years the media have portrayed this group as fragile and caught perilously between the rich and the poor. Media representations of the upper class seldom suggest that its members' favored location in the class structure might be short-lived, but depictions of the middle class often portray its members as holding on by a thin thread.

ORGANIZATION OF THE CHAPTERS

Because most of us think of ourselves as being in the middle class, that might seem the logical place to start; however, I have organized the chapters in a different manner, one that places the framing of stories about the rich and famous next to those of the poor and homeless so that readers can more closely compare the sharply contrasting images of wealth and poverty that continually influence our attitudes and perceptions about class. In this way, I hope to demonstrate the sharp contrast between the often flattering descriptions of the rich and the pitying or derogatory descriptions of those at the bottom of the class heap.

Chapter 2, "Twenty-Four-Karat Gold Frames: Lifestyles of the Rich and Famous," describes the history of media framing of the upper class, showing how discussions of the rich and famous have captured the interest of journalists from the days of the earliest newspapers up to today, with our Internet websites. Changes in the "society page" over time reflect larger societal transformations and new information technologies, but they do not indicate a diminished interest in the doings of the wealthy and famous. If anything, just the contrary is true: audiences can increasingly feed around the clock on gossip about those at the top of the economic pyramid. For this reason, chapter 2 analyzes four positive media frames and their messages: (1) the consensus frame: the wealthy are like everyone else; (2) the admiration frame: the wealthy are generous and caring people; (3) the emulation frame: the wealthy personify the American Dream; and (4) the price-tag frame: the wealthy believe in the gospel of materialism.

Not all media representations of the top class are positive, however, and chapter 3, "Gilded Cages: Media Stories of How the Mighty Have Fallen," sets forth negative framing devices sometimes used to portray the upper class: (1) the sour-grapes frame: the wealthy are unhappy and dysfunctional; and

(2) the bad-apple frame: some wealthy people are scoundrels and downright criminals. Chapter 3 specifically looks at media coverage of the downfall of some top corporate executives and people in the financial industry, showing how media audiences find these individuals' excessive consumption of great interest even as they decry the greedy actions of these captains of industry. The extent to which some wealthy people believe they can buy anything, including their way out of trouble, is a recurring media frame discussed in this chapter. Media framing of articles about the wealthy showing them to be more interesting and more deserving of what they have stands in sharp contrast to portrayals of the poor as living tedious and less worthy lives.

In chapter 4, "Fragile Frames: The Poor and Homeless," I show that although some framing of impoverished and homeless people is sympathetic, much media coverage offers negative images of individuals in such circumstances, showing them as dependent on others (welfare issues) or as deviant in their behaviors and lifestyles. A favorite media device employs exceptionalism framing: if this person escaped poverty, why can't anyone else? This approach tells inspirational stories about people who have risen from poverty or homelessness to find greater economic solvency and happiness in the working or middle classes. The media use another device, charitable framing, to show how we can help the poor at holidays and after disasters. Articles and television entertainment story lines using charitable framing focus on the need to lend a helping hand on special occasions, but they do not suggest that we should make a more focused effort on a daily basis to help alleviate the larger societal problems that contribute to individual problems of poverty, hunger, and homelessness.

Chapter 5, "Tarnished Metal Frames: The Working Class and the Working Poor," discusses five framing devices used by the media to portray the working class: (1) shady framing: greedy workers, unions, and organized crime; (2) heroic framing: working-class heroes and victims; (3) caricature framing #1: white-trashing the working class; (4) caricature framing #2: television's buffoons, bigots, and slobs; and (5) fading blue-collar framing: out of work or unhappy at work. As these frames show, media representations of the working class typically do not provide a positive image.

In chapter 6, "Splintered Wooden Frames: The Middle Class," I identify three key frames that I found frequently employed in media representations of the middle class: middle-class-values framing, squeeze framing, and victimization framing. The first of these—middle-class-values framing— emphasizes that the core values held by people in the middle class should be the norm for this country and that these values remain largely intact over time despite economic, political, and cultural changes. Within that frame, the middle class becomes not only the nation's frame of reference but the ideal model to which people in the United States should aspire, particularly those in the working and poor classes. However, the media also employ the other two (seemingly contradictory) frames that I identified to represent the middle class. Squeeze framing sends the message to media audiences that the middle class is perilously caught between the cost of a middle-class lifestyle and the ability to pay for it, whereas victimization framing suggests that many middle-class problems stem from actions of the upper and lower classes, actions that potentially endanger the middle-class way of life.

Chapter 7, "Framing Class, Vicarious Living, and Conspicuous Consumption," looks at how the media may affect our behavior, particularly in regard to how we think of other people and what we purchase. It also suggests that changing economic times influence how the media frame articles and entertainment shows involving the wealthy, the middle and working classes, and the poor. The chapter suggests that we, as readers and viewers, must be more aware of class realities in our everyday lives and have a responsibility to ourselves and our children to develop a greater awareness of how news and entertainment programming and social networking color our views about our own class location and about wealth, poverty, and inequality in the larger society. Since print media, television, the Internet, and social media have become the twenty-first century's primary storytellers, we should be concerned about the kinds of stories being told as well as how these socially constructed representations of reality contribute to the way we think of ourselves, fostering an unhealthy ideology that supports the ever-widening chasm between the haves and have-nots in the United States and around the world. The chapter concludes with a discussion of how old-media representations (in newspapers, magazines, and television) of wealth and poverty are replicated in new-media sources, despite the fact that some people believe that technology is completely changing the news and entertainment that we receive via new media, such as the Internet and social networking sites.

Chapter 2

Twenty-Four-Karat Gold Frames
Lifestyles of the Rich and Famous

Like Prada handbags and Hermes scarves, a spot on one of New York City's most prestigious cultural boards never goes on sale, even in a recession.

Looking to join the power set at the Metropolitan Museum of Art? Be ready with a check for as much as $10 million. The price of admission can reach that high at the Museum of Modern Art, and remains roughly $5 million at the New York Public Library, according to people involved in the process.

"For those who can, we have an expectation and we try to be very clear about that expectation," said Reynold Levy, the president of Lincoln Center, whose board members are generally asked to contribute $250,000 upfront and on an annual basis. . . .

The pressure to raise money from volunteer boards has intensified as the economy slumped and broader charitable giving declined. Yet even with weakened portfolios, many people of means remain willing to answer the call because a spot on a cultural board is among the most coveted prizes in a city of strivers and mega-achievers. And spots are limited: the New York City Ballet, for example, has 40 voting members; the Museum of Natural History has 56. . . . "People want to be part of winners," said Sanford I. Weill, Carnegie Hall's chairman and a former chairman at Citigroup. . . . "Give, get or get off," is a motto many in the cultural world know well.[1]

Although they have played down the glittering lifestyles of the superrich since 2007 because of the worldwide economic downturn, recent media representations of the wealthy continue to show that the rich and superrich spend vast sums of money on $22 million residences, $1 million yachts, $250,000 automobiles, and even cultural and charitable pursuits such as "purchasing" a seat (only if invited to do so) on a prestigious cultural board. In the words of novelist F. Scott Fitzgerald, "Let me tell you about the very rich. They are different from you and me."[2]

To emphasize the differences between the rich and everyone else, media framers often provide elaborate descriptions of the ways the wealthy spend their money and the social events they attend to "do good deeds," or to have a good time and impress one another. This framing device conveys the message that the wealthy are not only different from other people but perhaps better than other people—or at least some of them may be better.

How media frame news stories about the wealthy and television writers develop story lines for entertainment shows that include affluent characters helps to shape our perceptions about the rich and famous. Communications scholars Robert M. Entman and Andrew Rojecki state that people have two paths to social information: personal experience from formal education, socialization, and conversation with others and mediated communication from sources such as television and newspapers.[3] Although some individuals in the top economic and social tiers may choose to be highly visible to others, their wealth and privileged lifestyle make it possible—if they so desire—to live completely away from the gaze of the masses except for the media coverage they receive. Accordingly, most of us do not really know how the "other half" lives. The manner in which news and entertainment sources frame information about the upper classes therefore helps shape how others view the wealthy and well connected, as well as how middle- and lower-income individuals perceive the U.S. class structure and larger issues of social inequality in general.

Media framing either reinforces or contradicts most people's previously held ideas about the wealthy because we use mental shortcuts such as schemas—sets of related concepts that allow us to make inferences about new information based on already organized prior knowledge—across many different situations. Entman and Rojecki give this example:

> For instance, mainstream U.S. culture includes a schema stored in many Americans' minds that associates the concept of success with other ideas such as wealth, hard work, educational attainment, intelligence, status, snobbery, fancy cars, and good looks. Images representing those related concepts readily come to mind when people hear the word or see a symbol that evokes the concept of success—a picture of a BMW, a mansion, a big executive office suite.[4]

By contrast, a television news story on welfare reform might summon schema about individuals on welfare as lazy or likely to be members of racial or ethnic minorities.[5]

The most popular media frames for news accounts and entertainment TV program story lines about the rich play on the preexisting schema within many people's minds that it is okay simultaneously to love and hate the rich. This is nothing new; fascination with the lifestyles and material possessions of the rich and well connected in the United States goes back several centuries, perhaps finding its apex during the Gilded Age, between the 1880s and 1920s, and it has always contained a mixture of both love and hate.

FROM THE SOCIETY PAGE TO THE INTERNET: A BRIEF HISTORY OF MEDIA FRAMING OF THE UPPER CLASSES

Today, news stories about the top classes appear throughout the newspaper in sections ranging from "Top News Stories" and "Business" to "Entertainment and Leisure," "Fashion and Travel," "Food," and "Book Reviews." However, some of the earliest visible media framing of stories about the rich and famous found its way into specifically designated portions of major newspapers typically referred to as the society or women's page.

The first society pages performed a useful function for journalists and editors who wanted to sell newspapers, but they also played a latent role for some of the rich and those who hoped to reach the top tiers of society. Writing during the Great Depression, social historian Dixon Wecter described the society page as a useful tool for the wealthy with social aspirations:

> It is seldom realized how greatly the Society Page has helped create social consciousness in the United States. . . . The Society Page, which is flowered with peculiar luxuriance in American journalism, has often been sufficient to confer leadership on individuals or groups simply by printing their names, day in and day out, or ascribing to them a dictatorship which is accepted first by the gum-chewing typist and finally by the enthroned dowager.[6]

Among the first journalists in the United States to print personal notes about individuals in high society were James Gordon Bennett Sr. and his staff at the *New York Herald* in the 1830s. No news item was too inconsequential if the participants included "people we know," a designation used by many of the wealthy and well connected to refer to others whom they considered part of their in-group. According to social historians, plenty of individuals in the "people we don't know" category read excitedly about such trivial matters as the comings and goings of the privileged class on luxury ocean liners or their parties at big New York City hotels, even when the economic fates of the masses were dismal by comparison.[7]

Experienced journalists frequently advised junior members of the profession on the importance of covering the wealthy. Social historian Wecter reported that one well-known journalist told a class of college students, "Only the rich man is interesting."[8] Before the advent of television and other electronic media, newspapers and magazines provided people in the lower classes opportunities to see "magic phantoms," such as the very wealthy Mrs. Cornelius Vanderbilt, and to gain entry to her residence by way of tabloid reporters who routinely covered her activities and described her lifestyle in intricate detail. For those within the top class, sneaking a peak at the society page afforded an opportunity to keep score of one's position in relation to other elites. For the newly rich, being included in the society page was a reason for celebration. For people outside the top class, the society page afforded a chance to live vicariously: "The society editor rejoices in barriers, cliques, snobberies, and invidious implications, knowing that these things make news and give the humble reader a sense of being 'in the know' even though he may never dream of impinging upon that holy sphere."[9]

Although the society page reached the apex of its power and readership during the Gilded Age and early to mid-twentieth century, its history reaches back several centuries. It is believed that the idea was borrowed from the European custom of reporting on the comings and goings of royalty, who at the time received dignified, low-key treatment, unlike in the tabloid formats that later emerged and brought great embarrassment to many royal families.[10] In the United States, however, the *New York Herald*'s Bennett adopted a tell-all tabloid format in his reporting on high society in America:

> No one ever attempted till now to bring out the graces, the polish, the elegancies, the bright and airy attributes of social life. . . . Our purpose has been, and is, to give to the highest society of New York a life, a variety, a piquancy, a brilliancy, an originality that will entirely outstrip the worn out races of Europe.[11]

By 1840, Bennett had successfully infiltrated high society by smuggling a society reporter into a famous Fifth Avenue fancy dress ball in New York City, with the host's reluctant approval. Following that event, the barriers between "society" columnists and upper-crust hostesses began to crumble. As Wecter notes, journalism began to "break down the old exclusiveness of a clique which once regarded its balls and dinners as no more the public's business than its bankruptcies and adulteries."[12] Eventually, the privileged class went from "anger to tolerance and thence to secret pleasure in seeing itself written up."[13]

After Bennett successfully launched the society page in the *New York Herald*, a number of other newspapers in New York and other major cities copied the idea of Society (with a capital *S*) as news and began to "dish up social soufflé" to the public.[14] The job of the society reporter often went to a widow or an unmarried woman with the right connections and easy entrée into elite social circles.[15] Perhaps the media received greater acceptance because many reporters shifted the framing of their stories from derision and mockery to admiration for the pomp and grandeur of the rich and famous.[16]

Despite journalists' greater praise for the upper class and its lavish lifestyle in the late nineteenth and early twentieth centuries, the typical story framing suggested deep-seated contradictions in attitudes toward the way the privileged class lived. For example, in recording his impressions of a famous ball given in 1897 by the Bradley-Martins, one journalist stated, "The power of wealth with its refinement and vulgarity was everywhere."[17] This ball—costing almost $370,000 for the party itself and the work to transform the ballroom of the Waldorf Astoria into a replica of a hall in the palace at Versailles (outside Paris)—was considered quite excessive for its time. Ironically, the Bradley-Martins allegedly threw this lavish costume ball to stimulate the U.S. economy during a time of severe economic depression, stating that they believed the event would "give an impetus to trade."[18] The extensive media coverage of the ball's excesses resulted not in praise for the Bradley-Martins' charitable endeavors but in their decision to relocate permanently to England, outside the glare of negative publicity.

While some early newspaper accounts of the rich came from correspondents who entered the homes of the wealthy by getting jobs as butlers, chambermaids, or musicians, hangers-on who were never quite accepted into the magic circle of society were the main informants, dishing dirt on people who had snubbed them.[19] Although little has been written about how people in other classes viewed earlier media reporting of the upper class, social historian Mary Cable states,

> Annoying though this publicity may have been to its subjects, it was certainly adulation. For Society people, the nightmare was when the papers got hold of some scandalous event in their lives—a separation or divorce, a murder, an assault, a swindle, a paternity suit, a breach of promise, grand larceny, or some display of total absence of taste or common sense. The public wanted its idols to at least appear to behave well, and when they were found wanting, they were savaged by the process. "You can do anything you like," was the famous dictum of the actress Mrs. Patrick Campbell, "as long as you don't do it in the streets and frighten the horses." Rumors might fly, but as long as no one admitted to anything, they simply flew, like Fourth of July rockets, and fell to earth harmlessly.[20]

However, Cable notes, when the horses did stampede and an uproar ensued, newspaper sales were guaranteed to soar.

Although society scandals may have sparked a temporary upswing in sales, regular readers thrived on stories of society brides and debutantes, especially the coming-out parties that accompanied their debuts. Even among debutantes, there were inner and outer circles, and the public became enamored with young women who received such titles as "Debutante of the Year." In addition to stories about debutantes from families with "old money" (families that had possessed great wealth for several generations), many people with "new money" became the favorite topic of a new breed of society reporter who covered "café society" by hanging around nightclubs. The use of women to sign endorsements and advertise such products as cosmetics, cigarettes, pianos, and whiskey further blurred the lines between the truly wealthy and the celebrity set.[21]

Newspaper articles about the wealthy proliferated whether or not members of the media had official entrée into the lives and social functions of the privileged class, and these articles began to show up in other parts of the newspaper, such as the fashion, travel, and business sections and the women's page. In *The Private World of High Society*, Lucy Kavaler describes how press agents in the 1950s became liaisons between the upper classes and the media because they had both society and newspaper contacts and did not hesitate to use the former on behalf of their clients.[22] Press agents not only influenced what the media reported about the privileged class but helped to frame the settings in which media events took place. Some press agents held parties for their clients, which members of the media attended; others made sure that journalists and society columnists were invited to prestigious openings and charity events where their clients were sure to be present. Public relations people also facilitated publicity tie-ins between individuals and products, as Kavaler explains:

> I was in Mr. Davis' office one day when he got a telephone call from a man who is a favorite with both the international set and society columnists. He had been approached by a lipstick manufacturer eager for a publicity tie-in. The firm was introducing a new shade, to be called "Continental," and it wanted the gentleman to be named "our favorite Continental" by a group of debutantes. They could then all be photographed together at a society hotel. Although this sounds pretty obvious, pictures of this type do appear regularly in the afternoon newspapers. Mr. Davis, of course, was expected to produce the debutantes—getting publicity in turn for his clients or their daughters.[23]

Although the daughters of old-line families might have had no interest in this type of publicity, many of the newly wealthy families jumped at the chance. Eventually, the combined efforts of public relations agents, debutante-ball organizers, party planners, and others who wanted to capture the attention of the media further blurred the lines between old guard society, the nouveau riche, and the media. According to Kavaler, in her discussion of high society in the 1950s,

> The society pages are taken seriously in small towns and big cities alike. People will go to great lengths to be mentioned. . . . Even in society's inner circle very few pay more than lip service to the still much-quoted cliché: "A lady's name

should appear in the newspapers three times—when she is born, when she is married, and when she dies."[24]

In the decades following Kavaler's writing, sociologists like G. William Domhoff turned to the society or women's page as "a window on the ruling class." Although no longer strictly considered a society page, the women's page of daily newspapers became one of the central places where readers could learn about the ruling class.[25] Some papers referred to this section as the people's page, but it still contained society news, gossip, and other trivia about the wealthy and famous. Based on research in the women's pages of various newspapers in the 1960s and 1970s, Domhoff asserted that there indeed existed a cohesive culture of the richest people and the top U.S. managers in high society. Domhoff deemed the women's page not only useful in studying connections among people in the ruling class but informative about their lifestyle and shared ideology:

> It is on the women's page we learn that our business, cultural, and government leaders, for all their public differences on specific issues, share in a deeper social community that keeps them as one on essential questions concerning the distribution of wealth and the system of property, questions that seldom become issues, questions that rarely receive attention on the straight news pages. Only on the women's page does the newspaper tell us each and every day that there is a ruling class in America.[26]

Since Domhoff's study, daily newspapers have largely replaced the women's page with sections on lifestyle, food, fashion, and travel, thereby slightly reframing the stories they contain. For example, a 2003 article ("Tacos, Stir-Fries and Cake: The Junior League at 102") in the *New York Times* food section not only gave a sales pitch for the Junior League cookbook and included several of its recipes but featured an interview with Deborah C. Brittain, an African American woman and former president of the Association of Junior Leagues International. In addition to being the official spokeswoman for the cookbook, Brittain was in charge of dispelling myths about the Junior League, historically known as an organization that "doubled for decades as an exclusive social club where the blood was blue and the gloves were as white as the members."[27] According to journalist Alex Witchel,

> As for its stringent social qualifications, Ms. Brittain said, the Junior League relaxed them years ago. Not only had African Americans been discouraged from joining, but Jews, Italians, middle-class women and older women were as well. She dispatched this unappetizing bit of history briskly. "The Junior League is good at changing, which is why we still survive," [Ms. Brittain] said. "Particularly in the 70's, they realized their history had a little baggage. But for

the majority of our chapters, we've been there, done that, and it's over. Now our membership is open to all women who want to contribute to their community."[28]

Even with the changes so described in the Junior League, most middle- and working-class and minority-group women remain unlikely candidates for membership in this prestigious organization. However, placing the story in the "Dining In/Dining Out" section of the *New York Times* gave it a more egalitarian frame than it would have received on the society page. As we examine contemporary media framing of the wealthy and social elites, we see that the top classes are now the subjects of news reports and other accounts throughout virtually all sections of major daily newspapers.

In the twenty-first century, television and the Internet are increasingly becoming avenues by which elites keep informed of the activities of other elites. These media outlets also provide a window through which middle- and upper-middle-class individuals can vicariously participate in the comings and goings of the wealthy and famous. One example is New York Social Diary (www.newyorksocialdiary.com), a website maintained by David Patrick Columbia, a society writer with access to many in the subcultures of international wealth and celebrity. This website provides party pictures of social and charity benefits attended by the rich, a calendar of "society" events, and a social diary describing Columbia's interactions with members of the top tiers at parties and other exclusive events. Such websites have also become popular in cities like San Francisco (see www.nobhillgazette.com), and they are perhaps one of the closest equivalents to the old society page in newspapers.

Along with society websites, local magazines and neighborhood newspapers in affluent sections of major cities have become popular ways in which well-to-do people keep up with each other. In New York City, *AVENUE* magazine provides party pictures and stories about well-known socialites and elite volunteers, who typically live on Manhattan's Upper East Side. Such magazines can be found in affluent enclaves throughout the country. Weekly newspapers for the privileged also serve the function of the old society page. In Dallas, Texas, for example, newspapers and magazines sold specifically in Highland Park and University Park (among the most affluent zip codes in the central Dallas area) and available on the Internet (see www.parkcitiespeople .com) carry stories about society events in that area. Some stories highlight children's school accomplishments or neighborhood issues, but most resemble the old society page, publishing party photos and articles about society events, debutante presentations, and elite weddings in the community. Although available to anyone who wants to purchase them, they serve as the virtual "in-house" publications of affluent groups, making it possible for elites to read about each other and keep up with social events regardless of whether major newspapers or television stations carry information about their activities. In this sense, the old society page is not dead; it has been reincarnated in newer technologies and more specialized publications read primarily by the affluent and well connected as well as those who aspire to join their ranks.

Most people, however, do not get their information about the upper classes from publications like these. Rather, their information comes primarily from the daily newspaper, any magazines they read, and the television programs they watch. It is therefore important to examine the framing mechanisms that these media sources use in depicting the various social classes in order to understand their effect on our perceptions of social class in the United States.

POSITIVE DEPICTIONS OF THE
WEALTHY IN THE UNITED STATES TODAY

An examination of routine journalistic practices is important to determine what stories are covered and how, as well as what dominant cultural meanings they convey. According to media scholars, although each day's news is unique in some ways, the framing of similar events in the past greatly influences how journalists observe and report a specific occurrence.[29] As a result, information about the very wealthy is often framed similarly whether it appears in newspaper, broadcast, or Internet news sources or in the story lines of television entertainment shows. I have identified six dominant media frames and their messages used in articles and story lines about the rich and famous that I believe influence how people in other classes view the wealthy:

• The consensus frame: the wealthy are like everyone else.
• The admiration frame: the wealthy are generous and caring people.
• The emulation frame: the wealthy personify the American Dream.
• The price-tag frame: the wealthy believe in the gospel of materialism.
• The sour-grapes frame: the wealthy are unhappy and dysfunctional.
• The bad-apple frame: some wealthy people are scoundrels.[30]

This chapter discusses the first four of these frames, while chapter 3 addresses the fifth and sixth.

Consensus Framing: The Wealthy Are Like Everyone Else

The consensus frame tends to obscure inequalities between the classes by highlighting ways in which very wealthy people are similar to people in other classes and by downplaying key differences between the wealthy and everyone else. An article or story that utilizes this frame makes it is easy to believe that the very rich are just ordinary people who happen to have more money than the rest of us and, further, that if we just earned or saved a little bit more, we could be just like them—if we wanted to be. If we are all alike, perhaps the concept of social class is outdated: the differences between us are simply gradations of accumulated wealth.

Consensus framing largely ignores, however, vast differences in lifestyles and life chances—the extent to which individuals have access to such important societal resources as food, clothing, shelter, education, and health care—between the rich and the poor. According to sociologist Dennis Gilbert, if income were a national pie sliced into portions, the wealthiest 20 percent of U.S. households would receive almost 50 percent of the total pie, whereas the poorest 20 percent would receive only 3 percent.[31] In fact, the income share received by the wealthiest fifth of households is seventeen times that received by the poorest 20 percent.[32] The average pretax income of people in the top 1 percent of households was $1,743,700 in 2006 as compared with an average pretax income of $17,200 in the bottom 20 percent of households.[33] These figures look only at income inequality; they do not take into account wealth inequality, which has also increased dramatically in the twenty-first century. It is estimated, for example, that the top 1 percent of wealth holders in this country owned about 34 percent of net worth in 2007. As Gilbert explains, "The concentration of wealth at the top is so great that the top 1 percent now holds more net worth than the bottom 90%."[34] Consensus framing ignores the fact that few people in the top tiers of the upper class derive their income from a paycheck for hours worked, that the wealthy are not likely to experience the economic and psychological hardships of the unemployed or homeless, and that wealth may afford some people more leisure time, better security, better health care, and better connections and opportunities for their children than are available to people with less wealth.

Despite the vast differences in income and wealth across the United States, consensus framing of media stories serves the purpose of portraying the very rich as similar to everyone else or showing how the affluent and nonaffluent should agree on certain pressing issues or social problems. Articles about the Great Recession beginning in 2008 and disasters such as hurricanes and the BP oil spill in the Gulf of Mexico often use this framing device to show that rich and poor alike suffer from devastating events. An example is the Reuters .com article "Recession, Bear Markets Hit the Rich, Too," which states, "Turns out the rich may not be so different from you and me: They, too, are falling behind on their mortgages." However, the article primarily discusses the delinquency rate on multimillion-dollar mortgages, such as one month when there were two hundred foreclosures nationwide on mortgages of $5 million or more.[35]

Consensus ("we are all alike") framing is compatible with the ideological perspective of scholars who believe that class is no longer a meaningful analytical concept for studying social life in the United States. For example, Jan Pakulski and Malcolm Waters argue that advanced or postmodernist consumer culture has shifted the focus from class-based relations to relations based on "taste," "fashion," and "lifestyle," which have become key sources of social differentiation and affiliation, thereby displacing old identity packages like class.[36] Pakulski and Waters contend that key groupings in contemporary society are organized not around class per se but rather around noneconomic, nonclass bases, including "ethnicity, gender, value-commitment, life-style, and consumption."[37] Some analysts refer to this idea as the class-convergence thesis based on the assumption that differences in lifestyle between the wealthy, capitalist class and the working class have largely diminished or disappeared.[38]

Previous assessments of how the media report on the wealthy have not examined the consensus approach to news reporting as much as they have analyzed existing media content to determine the topics most frequently presented and to assess whether they are class specific or not. Many media scholars believe that news media content focuses almost exclusively on issues of concern to middle- and upper-class readers and viewers. News items of concern to the wealthy, such as stock market and other business reports, are routinely presented with a pressing urgency, suggesting that most American families own stock and cannot wait for the latest reports from Wall Street and about other financial markets.[39] However, the popularity of such reports primarily rests with the more affluent members of society because, as previous studies have shown, "most American families do not own any type of stock and four out of five families do not own stock directly. In fact, 86 percent of the nation's stock is owned by just 10 percent of the nation's families."[40] "Thus," as media scholars David Croteau and William Hoynes state, "the vast majority of the public is unlikely to be interested in stock reports. Most Americans do not even understand stock listings and reports. Yet stock market reports are a prominent feature of news programs and newspapers."[41] According to Croteau and Hoynes, stock market reports vastly outnumber news stories on topics such as how to apply for welfare benefits or workers' rights to form a union.

Although he does not refer to it as media framing, sociologist Gregory Mantsios argues that the media often send the message that "the wealthy are us."[42] He notes that everything from business reports to fashion and sporting news, wedding announcements, and obituaries often has a built-in class bias not detected by ordinary readers and viewers. According to Mantsios, although the news as reported may have practical value to the wealthy, it has a strong ideological value in that it sends the message that "the concerns of the wealthy are the concerns of us all."[43]

Political reporting is a key area of news coverage that sometimes portrays the rich as being like everyone else. Obviously, this framing technique has the approval of wealthy politicians and their spokespersons, who hope, at least for the duration of an election, to show that even though wealthy, the candidate shares important concerns and lifestyle elements with people in other classes. *New York Times* articles offer numerous examples of the consensus framing of political reporting. For example, the media often feature wealthy candidates and elected officials, such as New York City's mayor, Michael R. Bloomberg, when they are doing something that might endear them to the masses. In a 2002 article titled "Bloomberg's Salon, Where the Powerful Mix over Meatloaf," for instance, journalist Jennifer Steinhauer emphasized that multibillionaire Mayor Bloomberg, who owns not only a $17 million, five-story, 7,500-square-foot limestone beaux arts mansion in Manhattan but sprawling homes in North Salem (New York), Vail (Colorado), Bermuda, and London,[44] likes to serve "common folk" food, including meatloaf and mashed potatoes, potpie, scrambled eggs, and grilled hotdogs to people he invites to his Manhattan mansion.[45] The article begins, "A few times a month, 20 or so New Yorkers open their closets and contemplate what to wear to eat meatloaf at the Beaux-Arts town house of the 108th mayor of New York."[46] Of course, as the article states, most people invited to come eat meatloaf with the mayor are celebrities, executives, and socialites who arrive for "an evening of comfort food, highbrow chitchat and networking."[47]

Articles like this typically appeal to middle- and upper-middle-class readers, the primary purchasers of the *New York Times*. The framing of the article appears democratic because the very wealthy mayor is acting like an ordinary person, and the meatloaf and potpie have middle- to working-class connotations. However, the menu served by the mayor's staff also includes cocktail hors d'oeuvres, a first course of asparagus with lemon butter, a main course of meatloaf and potatoes, a dessert of berry cobbler with ice cream, an assortment of wines served throughout dinner, and after-dinner cookies decorated to reflect the interests of individual diners, including "a Labrador retriever for the dog lover, the insignia from Yale's rowing team for an alumnus, or the seal of a hospital for a generous donor."[48] Although this front-page article is framed using the consensus approach ("we're all the same; even rich people eat meatloaf"), it brings into sharp contrast both the commonalities and differences between people in divergent class locations. Media portrayals of the wealthy as just like everyone else ("good ole boys") obscure vast differences in economic conditions in the United States. If the very wealthy are viewed as down-home people who just have more money than everyone else, the invidious distinctions inherent in the capitalist economy are obscured and class-based oppression is downplayed, or appears to be nonexistent, in news accounts and entertainment programming.

As the Bloomberg example shows, one technique of consensus framing presents extremely wealthy people as basically like people in other classes but then sets them apart from others by emphasizing their wealth or "ruling-class" social position. Using this hook to catch the interest of media audiences, the newspaper or television journalist initially leads readers or viewers to perceive the wealthy individual as just an average person, perhaps no different from someone in the middle class, on the basis of the individual's lifestyle or appearance. However, this down-home image is juxtaposed with an elaborate description of the person's material possessions or net worth, clearly setting the wealthy subject apart from ordinary people. Consider, for example, this paragraph about S. I. Newhouse Jr., the octogenarian family ruler of the Condé Nast media empire:

> The lights of Midtown Manhattan still twinkle in the early-morning darkness as a man walks toward 4 Times Square, a huge office tower. He is short and moves with a shuffle, a gait that suggests he may be a bit old for punching a clock at 5 A.M. With his khakis, loafers, and a green sweatshirt that seems too big on him, he could be one of the kitchen staff showing up to prep food at the vaunted Condé Nast cafeteria, four floors up.
>
> But look closer at the sweatshirt and the outline of the New Yorker logo emerges. Peer closer at the man and S. I. Newhouse, Jr., is revealed, one of the world's richest men and the owner, along with the rest of his family, of a far-flung and immensely profitable media empire. As chairman of Condé Nast Publications, he presides over magazines like *Vogue, Vanity Fair* and yes, *The New Yorker*—shiny totems built to assemble wealthy readers and the advertisers who covet them.[49]

This is a typical introduction for an article about a business empire and the wealthy people who control it. When a very wealthy individual does not appear to embrace overtly the trappings of great wealth, reporters often see in this a newsworthy beginning for a story even if the majority of the article concerns the holdings of the person's business empire and personal wealth. By starting the article in this manner, members of the media build a tension or internal contradiction into the story line—juxtaposing appearance and reality—thereby showing media audiences that things are not always as they seem. This framing device allows journalists to reveal significant discrepancies between appearance and reality without questioning economic inequality, particularly the source of wealth and how it is otherwise spent. Journalists who use this approach are more likely to get interviews and personality profiles from wealthy individuals, many of whom are leery of publications that do not always show them in a favorable light. For this reason, images of the wealthy as generous and caring people who engage in acts of philanthropy are among the most common forms of media coverage for individuals and families in the top economic tiers of society.

Admiration Framing: The Wealthy Are Generous and Caring People

The media also tend to serve the interests of the wealthy when they engage in admiration framing, showing the rich as generous and caring people who share their vast resources with other people and organizations. Although philanthropy, which involves a spirit of goodwill toward others as demonstrated in efforts to promote their welfare, takes place at all levels of the class structure, major contributions of money to worthy causes are uniquely identified with the upper classes, whose members can make larger financial contributions (even extremely large ones) than those in the lower tiers of the class structure.[50] In this case, the media may serve as a public relations outlet for the wealthy, helping to smooth the rough edges of their business dealings and (sometimes) unscrupulous acts by letting others know about their good deeds. Of course, some wealthy donors prefer to remain anonymous; however, taken as a whole, these individuals number far fewer than those who desire to see their names on the buildings of well-known hospitals and universities or on the major donor lists of high-prestige nonprofit organizations.

Admiration framing is often used to publicize a high-society social event that raises money for a good cause. This type of coverage includes lavish descriptions of charity galas and other black-tie events, such as balls sponsored by hospital foundations or arts organizations. Events that collect money for the symphony or opera not only serve as fund-raisers but provide opportunities for the wealthy and well connected to socialize; media reports typically describe the duality between raising money for the cause and spending vast amounts of money to stage the event or attend it. French sociologist Pierre Bourdieu used opera performances as an example, stating that such performances "are the occasion or pretext for social ceremonies enabling a select audience to demonstrate and experience its membership in high society in obedience to the integrating and distinguishing rhythms of a 'society' calendar."[51] Similarly, charity events provide elites and wannabe elites with such venues.

Extensive media coverage of high-priced charity parties may gain the admiration (or the disdain) of the general public. When the media record these prestigious, by-invitation-only events, they provide people in other classes glimpses of how key players at high-society social events conduct their lives. The typical tone of such reports can be seen in a 2009 article, "After the Polo Match, in the Tented Pavilion," describing a New York event to raise money for Sentebale, the charity started by Prince Harry of Wales in memory of his late mother Princess Diana, to help vulnerable village children and nomadic shepherd boys in Lesotho, South Africa:

> His Royal Highness Prince Harry of Wales had finished his Champagne and found a seat. His small joke about falling off his polo horse had actually gone over rather well: warm applause from the jowly dons and willowy social beauties at his feet.
>
> His guests at Table 1, at the Veuve Clicquot Manhattan Polo Classic, were in fact still smiling brightly, though it might have been less the prince's sense of humor than the ravishing midspring day. . . . In the Royal Enclosure, the prince's area, things were as they should be: The waiters brought the porterhouse with fingerling potatoes; there were sodden models, daffy heiresses. Michelle Paige Paterson [wife of New York governor David Paterson] sat to the royal left; Mark Cornell, president of Moet Hennessy USA, was opposite her on the right.
>
> "I dare say," said Mr. Cornell, an Englishman in a dashing khaki suit, "one thinks of Champagne, polo and princes, and it gives one a sense of exclusivity. But today . . . is about inclusivity. Fun yes. Exclusivity, no." Such are the prerogatives of privilege, the license given the rich to construe their own good fortune as part of the Great Democracy.[52]

Using admiration framing in its introduction, the article follows with a description emphasizing the elaborateness of the event itself rather than the worthiness of the cause being benefited. Based on admiration framing, the fact that the event raises a large sum of money for a worthy cause justifies the behavior of those who spend tens of thousands of dollars on tickets (in this case, the fee was $50,000 per table) and clothing to wear to the event.

As some journalists point out, however, not all charity fund-raising is so glamorous. Some big-ticket fund-raisers benefit causes such as AIDS research, homes for abused and neglected children, or schools for the disadvantaged. In this case, high-profile organizers and donors are important for the success of the event because they will capture more media coverage than less well-known individuals. For example, media sources—ranging from websites to news magazines and daily papers—carry lead stories about very wealthy and well-known people like Bill and Melinda Gates when they give away billions of dollars for such nonelite causes as bringing better health care to the world's poorest children[53] or providing better schools for the disadvantaged in the United States.[54] Rather than emphasizing opulent events, these media reports focus on the down-home nature of foundations like the one started by Gates.

According to one media report, the Gates Foundation, unlike the posh old-line charities, operates in the bare-bones environment of a refurbished check-processing plant that abuts a working dock on Lake Union (in Seattle) and has no imposing nameplate on the building, just a street number.[55] Similarly, Paul Allen, who founded the Microsoft Corporation with Bill Gates, announced in 2010 that he will donate half of his estimated $13.5 billion fortune to philanthropy, particularly to benefit the Allen Institute for Brain Science, which is linked to the Paul G. Allen Family Foundation, and the Experience Music Project/Science Fiction Museum in Seattle, Washington. Although Gates supports projects around the world, Allen's charitable contributions go primarily to programs in the Pacific Northwest and tend to produce less international media coverage.

The seemingly low-profile, no-publicity-please approach of some contemporary philanthropists may diffuse public frustration over current economic crises and the excesses of contemporary capitalism. Philanthropy, when set in an admiration frame by the media, may help soften the rough edges of the capitalist economy in much the same way that Domhoff suggests the charitable work of privileged women volunteers helps to offset the negative public image of their elite husbands' sometimes unsavory business practices.[56]

Although some media reports may focus on the down-home nature of certain philanthropists, many other articles and television shows highlight the activities of the rich and famous in expensive surroundings, enjoying lavish food and entertainment in the name of charity fund-raising. From Manhattan to Houston and San Francisco to Atlanta, media descriptions of these parties typically resemble this one about the charity events organized by Houston's social organizer Becca Cason Thrash:

> Some of Becca's parties looked like they cost a small fortune. At one Venetian-themed fete for [the] Houston Grand Opera, she had an authentic gondola shipped from St. Louis, lowered by a crane through a skylight, and placed in her swimming pool. At another party for Best Buddies, which she called "Shanghai in the Spring," she transformed her home into . . . a Far East still life filled with Asian statuary, golden parasols, and dangling lanterns.[57]

According to journalists, organizers of lavish charity events like these argue that such expenditures and visible signs of conspicuous consumption are necessary for successful major fund-raising endeavors because they inspire rich donors to contribute to a good cause. Often a few high-society socialites, such as Becca Cason Thrash, plan major top-dollar fund-raisers. Since the above description of Thrash's parties was written, she has also planned major events to raise big bucks for UNICEF and the American Friends of the Louvre, as described here:

> When Houston's Becca Cason Thrash sends out an invitation with a dress code of "High Black Tie," you better follow directions, and the guests attending her

gala benefiting American Friends of the Louvre did not disappoint. Fans and friends of Becca—a group ranging from Princess Napoleon to Charlie Rose—flew in from Miami, San Francisco, Los Angeles, Washington, D.C., New York, Toronto, Paris, and all over Texas to raise funds and glasses of Dom Pérignon in her spectacular 20,000-square-foot, glass-walled home. The highlight: a re-creation of last month's Christian Lacroix Haute Couture show that was presented on a mirrored runway built on top of an indoor swimming pool. Said Becca: "I had to take out a wall of my house to accommodate everyone!"[58]

The privileged women who frequently plan these social or charitable events for the wealthy and well connected also believe that this sort of media coverage is crucial for the success of the event.[59] Evidence of this is found in columns like "Boldface Names" in the *New York Times*, in the lifestyle sections of local newspapers, and in neighborhood newspapers (such as *Park Cities People* in Dallas) and on numerous websites (such as Style.com).

The media also use admiration framing to describe situations in which naming rights have been purchased. The term *naming rights* describes a practice whereby universities, hospitals, and other charitable organizations offer, for a large fee, to name a building or a portion of a structure (such as the surgical wing of a hospital, a theater within an arts complex, or even a stone paver) after an individual, family, or corporation. Some colleges, universities, hospitals, museums, and arts venues bear the names of corporations—such as Comcast Center (at the University of Maryland), Save Mart Center (at Fresno State University), or Value City Arena (at Ohio State University). Other buildings are named for individuals or families who have made significant financial contributions. The McCombs School of Business at the University of Texas at Austin, for example, is named for Red McCombs, a major university donor who owns car dealerships and the former owner of the Minnesota Vikings National Football League franchise. Media framing of stories about very wealthy philanthropists like McCombs frequently employs humor. For example, media accounts of the McCombs naming event often mention a comment by also-very-wealthy Southwest Airlines founder Herb Kelleher: "For $50 million, I'll change my name to Red McCombs."[60]

Not all media reports of naming events describe acknowledgments on such a grand scale as placing major donors' names on the sides of coliseums or academic buildings. Some stories relate how people who give $50,000 or $100,000 in charitable donations receive little recognition other than having their names placed on a small stone paver or donors' wall. Media reports of philanthropy at Disney Hall in Los Angeles are an example. According to one journalist, Disney Hall came in at nearly double the original projected construction budget; consequently, the project "became a rare naming opportunity, a kind of permanent billboard for wealthy people to have their names inscribed."[61] Newspaper and television accounts of this naming event showed that donors giving $50,000 were honored with stone pavers (their names were two inches tall) in the concert hall's terrace garden, while those contributing $100,000 were honored with inch-and-a-half-letter names inscribed on the donors' wall (located in a more visible interior position). According to media reports, many people seized upon this naming opportunity and gave much more: "Every atrium, every staircase, every reception room, even every escalator in and around Disney Hall carries the name of a benefactor."[62]

Even when a major naming-rights donor is later involved in a scandal or crime, media representations continue to speak about him or her with a degree of admiration. What happens when the name of a major donor who has bought naming rights becomes tarnished? A typical example arises in the *New York Times* article "If a Name Is Tarnished, but Carved in Stone," which describes the problem experienced by administrators and regents at the University of Michigan, Ann Arbor, when A. Alfred Taubman, an extremely generous donor, was convicted of price fixing:

> Valets were parking cars and assisting patients at the A. Alfred Taubman Health Care Center here last Wednesday when a federal jury in Manhattan convicted Mr. Taubman, principal owner of Sotheby's, in a price-fixing scheme. Just down the hill, University of Michigan students were entering the A. Alfred Taubman Medical Library to study for exams. Nearby, aspiring designers were completing end-of-term projects at the A. Alfred Taubman College of Architecture and Urban Planning. . . . Mr. Taubman, who attended Michigan but left before graduating, has given more than $35 million to the university. His generosity does not stop there. His name is on institutes at Harvard and Brown, he leads a list of the most generous donors at Michigan State University, and he has given millions to Detroit area charities.[63]

In articles about the Taubman scandal and how it might affect naming-rights issues at universities and medical centers, media writers chronicled Taubman's good works and frequently concluded with statements such as this: "Mr. Taubman's philanthropy, rather than his conviction, could still prove to be his legacy."[64] And, indeed, it appears that this prediction has come true: a number of university business schools celebrate Taubman as "one of America's most successful entrepreneurs," and his involvement in business and philanthropic initiatives was widely praised as he continued to reside in Michigan in 2010.[65]

Admiration framing by the media typically includes informing ordinary people about how much it costs to be considered a real philanthropist. Journalists place price tags on donations and discuss what contributors receive in return. Admiration framing sends a mixed message to audiences about philanthropy. On one hand, by informing readers and viewers about the large sums of money contributed by wealthy individuals, the media suggest that the average person cannot make a difference; on the other hand, editorials may urge each of us to learn from the good deeds of others and follow their example. At this point admiration framing becomes blurred with emulation framing, which suggests that ordinary people should be like rich people.

Emulation Framing: The Wealthy Personify the American Dream

The most obvious examples of emulation framing of the rich and famous crop up on the editorial pages of major newspapers or in television commentaries about their charitable contributions. Although news articles about philanthropists extol the generosity of those who give money for a good cause and typically include photographs of those individuals, editorial comments further edify readers and viewers with the significance of major charitable contributions and tend to suggest that ordinary people should also be philanthropists.

Two editorials are instructive on this point. The first concerns the Long Center for the Performing Arts in Austin, Texas. Banker and lawyer Joe R. Long and his wife, Teresa, had given an initial gift of $20 million to start the fund-raising campaign for transforming an old city auditorium (previously named for Lester E. Palmer, a former mayor) into a state-of-the-art performing arts venue. Long is quoted as saying, "It gives us a great deal of satisfaction in seeing something done with our money while we're still alive. . . . [This project] could have an impact on lives in this community for the next 50 years." The editorialist comments, "In the coming years, that kind of thinking and generosity will be important not only for maintaining, but advancing, the quality of life Austinites revere."[66] Although other wealthy donors, including Michael and Susan Dell, have reached into their pockets to give $10 million to help complete the project,[67] average citizens do not see themselves as playing in the same financial league as these individuals, and funds have been slow to come in long after the construction project should have commenced.[68]

The second editorial, from the *Dallas Morning News* and also reported on its affiliated television station, WFAA, concerns philanthropist Margaret McDermott's $8 million contribution for the design of two Trinity River bridges to enhance the appearance of roadways entering the city of Dallas. The editorial, quotes McDermott: "If I'm a small catalyst in bringing this goal—this dream to reality, I'm thrilled. Also, I feel it might be the most meaningful thing I have been able to do for my city." The editorial comments, "This is the kind of philanthropy that turns a good city into a great one. . . . Ms. McDermott shows us how it is done. Let's all follow her lead."[69] Neither editorial makes clear what the average individual might do to equal such largesse, and editorialists typically do not suggest that small contributions are as valuable to the public good as multimillion-dollar gifts from the wealthy.

Individuals on the lower rungs of the class system may be able to ignore the philanthropy of the rich and famous, but it is more difficult to ignore media stories about people who move from "rags to riches" through hard work and determination. This kind of emulation framing raises the question, If they can do it, why can't you? It portrays the United States as the land of opportunity, where anyone who works hard and plays by the rules can achieve the American Dream.[70] Basic tenets of this dream include the notions that each generation should have a higher standard of living than the previous[71] and that all people, regardless of race, creed, color, national origin, gender, or religion, stand on a level playing field with an equal opportunity to get ahead. According to the political scientist Jennifer Hochschild, four key beliefs are associated with the American Dream: everyone can participate equally and can always start over if he or she needs to; it is reasonable to anticipate success; success results from individual actions and traits that are under the individual's control; and success stems from virtue and merit, whereas failure corresponds to lack of talent or will.[72] The emulation framing of stories about the rich, particularly those who came from working-class or impoverished origins, incorporate these beliefs.

The old Horatio Alger rags-to-riches stories of the late nineteenth century inspire contemporary media framing of stories about individuals from humble origins who make fortunes during their lifetimes. Horatio Alger–type stories perpetuate the American Dream by relating sagas about people who rise from poverty to wealth through hard work, individual initiative, and merit. Although belief in the American Dream may give working- and lower-class people some degree of hope for a better future, this ideology hides structural barriers to upward mobility. Ironically, some American Dream stories in the media contradict the notion that hard work and traditional values are important by telling of individuals who get rich through nothing more than good luck in games of chance. According to television, Internet, and newspaper accounts, the contemporary American Dream may be achieved through winning the lottery (see the TLC network's *Lottery Changed My Life*) or winning TV reality shows like *American Idol, America's Got Talent, America's Next Top Model,* or *The Next Food Network Star.*

Stories about people who win multimillion-dollar lotteries like Powerball typically include at least these three points: the humble origins of the winners; their extreme luck, which might also come to others who purchase lottery tickets; and their hardworking nature, even after their windfall. The story "School Cooks Win over $95 million in Powerball" contains all three ingredients:

> They waited until the students got their lunch, then 15 school cooks and one janitor who each put a quarter into a lottery pool came forward Monday night as the holders of a Powerball ticket worth more than $95 million.
>
> The women started their first Monday as millionaires back on the school lunch line where they fed the students in the tiny Holdingford School District before hopping a bus to the state lottery headquarters to claim their prize.[73]

This media report tells of the persistence of the school workers, in that they put a quarter from each paycheck toward the purchase of four Powerball tickets for more than a decade before acquiring one of the two winning tickets for the $190.9 million Powerball jackpot. The journalist emphasized the women's continuing dedication to their school lunch jobs, pointing out that they did not plan to quit immediately because, as one of the winners stated, "The kids come first."[74]

Although some rags-to-riches media stories concern onetime windfalls like winning the lottery, others employing emulation framing describe how an individual rose from poverty to wealth through entrepreneurship. Media sources around the world have told the inspiring story of Oprah Winfrey, one of the world's wealthiest women, because she is seen as personifying the American Dream. Since the often-repeated theme of her television program, books, and lectures is the importance of self-empowerment, she serves as a media role model for success among the downtrodden. Here is a typical example of media framing about her humble origins and her rise to wealth: "Somewhere en route from dirt-poor Mississippi schoolgirl to TV news anchor to talk-show empress to award-winning actress to therapist for an anxious nation, Oprah Winfrey became a businesswoman."[75] Journalism accounts of Winfrey's success carefully regale audiences with the fortune she has amassed from *The Oprah Winfrey Show*, which airs in 145 countries and brings in about $300 million each year. Her net worth is estimated to be in the range of $2.3 billion, a figure calculated before she launched her own television network. Winfrey's message—you are responsible for your own life—is in keeping with the ideal of the American Dream, making it all the easier for journalists to frame stories about her using the emulation model.

Winfrey herself has never suggested that anyone can be Oprah, but media accounts of her success suggest that others could do as well. According to one journalist, "By making herself and her struggles central to her message, [Winfrey] taps deeply into the American psyche and its desire for self-reliance."[76] According to "The Church of O" (an article in *Christianity Today*), Winfrey has become one of the most influential spiritual leaders in America by seeking to empower others.[77] Her gospel includes the belief that people can change and that they are responsible for their own destinies. Members of media audiences who see Winfrey as a role model may gain the unrealistic expectation that they too can become successful if they only work harder or change some negative aspect of their lives. This is a central message of emulation framing: You too can get ahead (like that person) if you try hard enough. If you are not successful, you have no one to blame but yourself.

Emulation framing involves not only class but race and gender. As an African American woman, Winfrey becomes the model for economic, gender, and racial/ethnic empowerment. She is not alone, however, in receiving praise for her ability to rise above inequalities based on race and class. In 2009 *Forbes* magazine compiled for the first time a list of the wealthiest black Americans (based on net worth, not income), a number of whom came from working-class families. Don Peebles, worth $350 million, is the grandson of a hotel doorman but now runs one of the country's largest minority-owned real estate development companies. Quintin Primo III had an estimated net worth of $300 million in 2009 but grew up in more modest circumstances as the son of a minister.[78]

Emulation framing in news stories about wealthy individuals of color suggests that two barriers can be broken down relatively easily in our society: class-based inequality and historical patterns of racism. This type of framing suggests that low-income people, even those who historically have been the objects of discrimination, can rise up and achieve the American Dream of success and wealth. Given the long odds against such an outcome, emulation framing not only creates unrealistic expectations given economic and social realities in the 2000s but provides an excuse for those who are better off financially to deride those who are not. Emulation framing of stories about self-made millionaires and billionaires, particularly those who have demonstrated business acumen or talent as entrepreneurs, entertainers, or athletes, perpetuates the myth of the American Dream. Beyond descriptions of how the rich and famous attain that dream, media stories also suggest that a part of living it entails the continuous consumption of expensive goods and services in accordance with a gospel of materialism.

Price-Tag Framing: The Wealthy Believe in the Gospel of Materialism

Price-tag framing describes the practice of making the cost of luxury items a key feature in media stories about the rich and famous. While straight news accounts typically provide information about the basic who, what, when, where, why, and how, price-tag framing focuses on how much. Notwithstanding the old saying "If you have to ask how much it costs, you can't afford it," price-tag framing informs media audiences of the cost of luxury items and who owns them. Whether on the Internet and television or in newspapers and magazines, price-tag framing is an extremely popular storytelling device because it both entertains and shocks media audiences with the expensive spending habits of the very wealthy. Media descriptions of the power-lunch hamburger (stuffed with foie gras and short ribs) for $29, the $6,000 shower curtain in the maid's room, or the $20 million mansion inform audiences about how at least some of the wealthy spend their money. As the recession continues in the second decade of the twenty-first century, power lunches and high-priced dinners are still served in the finest, most expensive restaurants. Media reports such as "No Recession Special on the D.C. Power Lunch Menu"[79] and "Expensive New York Restaurants," which describes high-end restaurants like Masa in New York City's Time Warner Center where the fixed-price menu starts at $400 per person,[80] still abound.

Publicizing the price of goods and services, however, sets the wealthy apart from other people and in the process raises a barrier between the lifestyles of the rich and those of other classes. According to one journalist's account of power lunches in New York's finest restaurants, "[Prices] can act as a kind of velvet rope to keep out tourists and people paying their own way, allowing a big hitter to tuck in a napkin secure in the belief that no one who works for him can afford to walk in the door."[81] Price-tag framing provides "outsiders" with information about what luxury items cost, but it also establishes the notion that people in other classes are categorically excluded from many elite settings by their inability or unwillingness to pay such prices.

Journalists employing price-tag framing in their stories typically use the concept of conspicuous consumption,[82] formulated by economist Thorstein Veblen (who wrote at the turn of the twentieth century), to describe the excessive and extravagant purchases of the wealthy. According to Veblen, conspicuous consumption is one of many signs of the superfluous lifestyle of the rich. Although some contemporary media reports condemn them, others glorify the excessive spending and "gracious lifestyles" of the wealthy in order to gain media audiences and advertising revenue.

If one tenet of the American Dream is that individuals can rise from humble origins to great wealth, another is that, given great wealth, a person can spend extravagantly and enjoy the "good life." Returning to the American Dream saga of Oprah Winfrey, for example, media reports about her not only mention stories of her childhood, youth, and rise to fame but also how much it costs to be Oprah. For example, a *Chicago* magazine article titled "The

Richest Chicagoans" (which was also carried by the Associated Press, CNN, and FOX News International, among others), said,

> If the economic downturn is worrying some, it's not stopping the world's most famous woman, who in April dropped $50 million for a 10,000-square-foot estate on 40 acres in Montecito, near Santa Barbara, California. She retains her homes in Colorado and downtown Chicago, and a farm in LaPorte, Indiana. *Forbes* estimates her wealth at around $900 million.[83]

In two brief sentences, the article makes readers aware of Winfrey's owner-ship of multiple residences, the latest of which cost an amount equaling what the United Nations might spend to feed several million Colombian refugees.

Disclosure of the cost of luxury residences and the identities of the rich and famous people who live in them underlies one of the most widely used forms of price-tag framing in the media. Homes that cost more than $10 million of-ten gain media attention when they are for sale, even when a well-known ce-lebrity does not live there. The proliferation of shows about residences, such as those on the popular house and garden network HGTV, Bravo, and other cable networks, has contributed to a public awareness that millions of single-family residences and high-end, luxury condominiums sell for amounts ex-ceeding the lifetime earnings of most families in the United States. Reports about the most expensive gated communities in the United States provide another example of emphasis on the cost and exclusivity of residences. Ac-cording to Forbes.com, the most expensive are located in Hawaii and Califor-nia, for instance, in Beverly Park (Los Angeles), where homes ranging in size from eight to forty thousand square feet sell for between $10 and $34 million; in 2010 residents include media star Eddie Murphy and top executive Sumner Redstone, a global media businessperson.[84]

Price-tag framing of the homes of the wealthy is not limited to how large the residence is or where it is located; some stories emphasize intangible fac-tors. For example, in the *New York Times* article "How Much Is That View in the Window?" a key issue is the cost of residences with the best views of Central Park:

> "Central Park is the most expensive view," Frederick W. Peters, the president of Ashforth Warburg Associates, said, and the most expensive views of it are from Fifth Avenue. Even in the less fashionable 90's on Fifth, a full-floor apartment with a view of the park, he said, "will command 10 million bucks." The same apartment on Fifth Avenue and 73rd street, he added, can run to $14 million.[85]

In 2010, some apartments on Fifth Avenue with a view of the park run as high as $22 million in a city where the average sale price is over $2 million. The HGTV series *Selling New York* highlights some of the most expensive properties as real estate brokers show properties to wealthy and trendy potential buyers. The typical viewer of this TV program and its accompanying website is middle-class and probably lives in a residence that costs about $100,000 at most.

Although we might expect price-tag framing to focus on celebrities who are continually in the media spotlight, they are not the only subjects of this kind of publicity. Articles about residences of the wealthy are not limited to those of the superrich living in large urban centers such as New York City, San Francisco, and Chicago. Local and regional newspapers and television stations often report on sales of top-priced luxury real estate. An article in the *Austin American-Statesman*, "Austin Mansion Sale's a Stunner," is an example:

> Radio industry millionaire Steve Hicks and his wife, designer Donna Stockton-Hicks, are buying the most expensive existing house in Austin: a 13,362-square-foot estate in the heart of Pemberton Heights, West Austin's most exclusive neighborhood. The asking price: $8.5 million, down from $10 million. . . . The estate's property tax bill last year was $138,000, not much less than the current median home price in Austin of $158,900.[86]

This article makes a point of comparing the tax bill on this luxury estate with the current median home price in the area to show how utterly unaffordable this property is for most people.

Even more elaborate descriptions of luxury residences, interior design, and other material possessions of the rich and famous are found in specialty magazines like *Millionaire*, *Robb Report*, and *Worth*; in business publications such as *Forbes* and *Fortune*; in regional magazines like *Texas Monthly*; and in city magazines, such as *D Magazine* (Dallas) and *Chicago*—all of which print articles and copious advertisements showcasing the luxury acquisitions of the affluent. Articles in these publications are typically available on companion websites such as Millionaire.com and Billionaire.com, and their subjects receive additional coverage from the Associated Press and other news services, bringing this information via Internet, television, or newspaper into the homes of people who do not subscribe to these high-end publications.

Luxury magazines targeting upper-middle- to upper-class readers frequently have tie-ins (intentional or not) between published articles and advertisements. *Texas Monthly*, which frequently publishes articles such as "Who Wants to Be a Billionaire? Ten of the Richest Texans Tell You How," carries many residential ads that sell "class" as well as a piece of real estate. An ad for The Woodlands, a relatively expensive residential community (prices range from $400,000 to over $2 million) outside of Houston bears the headline "Move to the Head of Your Class." A portion of the ad copy reads,

"There is a class distinction that sets The Woodlands apart. An unparalleled class of living that you simply won't find anywhere else." After detailing such amenities as the six championship golf courses, the "peaceful, forested home sites," the lakefront estates, and the "unparalleled luxury and exclusivity of a private, gated community," the ad declares that the residences and the families who own them are "truly in a class of their own."[87]

As this advertisement suggests, the media use discussions of how to live like the rich as a continuing subplot in price-tag framing. Television networks such as E!, HGTV, MTV, the Food Network, and VH1 attempt to provide useful insights for middle- and working-class viewers into how the rich spend money. VH1's *The Fabulous Life* takes viewers on virtual tours in episodes like "Hollywood's High-End Homes." The Travel Channel offers programming like "How the Rich Stay Young" and "Ways to Vacation Like a Millionaire," suggesting that it might be possible for the ordinary viewer to achieve the lifestyle of the rich and famous—or at least to sample it. A central technique in price-tag framing is spreading this idea: you too can live like the wealthy, even on a more modest budget. Consider, for example, HGTV's programs that feature an expensive designer room re-created affordably for the average viewer. A decorating expert first analyzes the design principles used in the expensive original, then viewers see how they too might apply those principles to produce a satisfying version that is less expensive but "sensibly chic." Programs like these teach viewers what luxury items cost and that they can have the look without the price, giving them an opportunity to feel superior to people who spend excessively on material possessions.

It is not possible to provide examples of all the ways in which the media use price-tag framing; however, the following are frequent subjects: lavish residences and residential enclaves; rare and highly valuable items such as art collections; luxury cars, yachts, and airplanes; tuition and other expenses incurred at private schools and elite universities; expensive toys for rich children and adults; membership dues for private clubs; and luxury dining, travel, and other leisure pursuits. Of these, money spent on residences, lavish entertainment, and toys for the wealthy are particular favorites for media coverage. The Neiman Marcus department store chain receives millions of dollars in free advertising each year from the media through articles and news stories about the items for sale in its annual *Christmas Book*. In 2009, the book's most expensive item was a His & Hers Icon A5 Sports Aircraft priced at $250,000, with flight lessons included. The cost of the top item was down considerably from previous years because of the global economic recession: the previous year a Learjet 60 (with lessons included) had been priced at more than $12 million. In the past other "fantasy gifts" have included a one-of-a-kind 44.6-karat yellow diamond for $800,000; recently, a Jaguar XJL Supercharged Neiman Marcus Edition commanded only $105,000.[88] By informing everyday people of the prices of these luxury goods, the media make them aware of the conspicuous (or at least excessive) consumption of the wealthy and creditworthy. The department store is pleased to receive the free publicity about its merchandise, and media audiences have an inside view of how the rich might spend their money. According to a Neiman Marcus vice president of public relations, "Everybody is so jaded today, there's so little out there that makes you go, 'Oh, wow!' I like to think of the fantasy element as the equivalent of a Barbie dreamhouse for adults. There's nothing anyone really needs, but there's definitely things they can fantasize about having."[89]

Children's toys are another topic for media stories, particularly near Christmas. The old adage "The only difference between the men and the boys is the price of their toys" may have less meaning today than in the past because the cost of some children's toys has skyrocketed. Manufacturers and retailers of expensive lines rely on the media to carry stories about their products so as to fuel consumer desire for the latest playthings and gadgets for children. These "news" items typically have headlines like "Over-the-Top Gifts for Junior?" The Superplexus, a sphere that looks like a large globe, is a $30,000 example of this kind of toy:

> This is the three-dimensional spherical labyrinth that challenges the limits of your manual dexterity and spatial understanding as you maneuver a 5/8 inch wooden marble through its entire course. The Superplexus is a complex network of chicanes, multi-planar hairpin turns, spirals, and staircases—even a vortex. Handmade from 3- and 6-ply Finnish birch that form the track, over 400 hours are involved in its construction. The labyrinth is set inside a 36 inch diameter acrylic sphere affixed to a Jatoba base using a stainless steel gimbaled mount that allows you to tilt the sphere in any direction to guide the marble. The entire track laid out on a straight line is 31 feet longer than a football field. . . . Successful completion requires a minimum of 425 turns (plane changes) of the sphere—without letting the marble fall off the track.[90]

Ironically, the boy shown looking at this toy appears bored compared with the typical child who looks excited when playing with a much less expensive, handheld video game. Here are some other examples of expensive toys widely described in media reports: How about a $97,395 luxury vehicle for your six- to eleven-year-old? A red Ferrari Testaroessa two-seater might fill the bill. Another option is a $40,000 Junior Off Roader vehicle with an all-weather fiberglass body and three-speed transmission for the seven- to fifteen-year-old. Junior-sized residences are also popular: a ten-by-sixteen-foot minimansion that features ten flower boxes across the front, twenty-two working windows, four columns, a loft with ladder, a child-sized front door, and an adult-sized wooden porch across the back is available for only $5,875. An eightieth anniversary Winnie the Pooh, measuring thirty-two inches tall, was also available for $775 in 2010.[91]

Although fantasy toys such as junior-sized mansions and luxury cars do not show up under the Christmas trees in most homes, journalists frequently report on the rich and famous who actually purchase such items for their children. For example, one story told how actor Chris O'Donnell and NBA star Jason Kidd had purchased custom-built playhouses (with heat, insulation, and running water) for their children.[92] Based on media reports of wealthy parents' purchases for their children, some parents with average or lower-than-average incomes feel inadequate because they cannot afford even the far-less-expensive items they would like to buy for their own children.

Placing a price tag on exclusive residences, lavish toys, and other trappings of the rich and famous is not a recent media practice. In the 1980s, the television series *Lifestyles of the Rich and Famous* profiled the self-made members of that set, providing detailed reports of what they bought and how much it cost. Created and hosted by Robin Leach, himself a model for the American Dream who had risen from shoe salesman to wealthy television personality, *Lifestyles of the Rich and Famous* ran for thirteen seasons in over thirty countries and continues today in syndication and video games. Leach was the master of price-tag framing, showing viewers some of the lavish residences, luxury vehicles, and exotic travel destinations enjoyed by the world's wealthiest people.[93] At the end of each episode, Leach wished his viewers "champagne wishes and caviar dreams."

As that tag line suggests, the lifestyles of the rich and famous shown on Leach's program were nothing more than "wishes" or "dreams" for the typical viewer. However, the series supported one of the key tenets of the gospel of materialism—namely, "Greed is good," as stockbroker Gordon Gekko (played by Michael Douglas) declares in the 1980s film *Wall Street*. During the economic crisis of the 2000s, in *Wall Street 2: Money Never Sleeps*, Michael Douglas reprises his role as Gordon Gekko, who emerges twenty years later from prison and seeks to rebuild his career and repair his relationship with his daughter. She is engaged to a young, ambitious Wall Street trader with goals much like Gekko himself had when he became involved in chicanery resembling much of what has contributed to many of this country's financial problems in the twenty-first century.[94] Like the original *Wall Street* and other films such as the 1980s classic *Bonfire of the Vanities*, *Wall Street 2* highlights price-tag framing: everything (and everybody) has a price, and the higher the price, the greater the zeal with which people will pursue wealth and power at any cost.

Not only does price-tag framing tell media audiences how much the rich pay for their possessions, but it also may suggest that ordinary people can live like millionaires, even if on a reduced scale. For example, a promotional piece for the video game spun off from *Lifestyles of the Rich and Famous* says,

> You deserve to live the high life. The Lifestyles of the Rich and Famous® game gives you that rich feeling. . . . Limo, mansion and yacht symbols animate in amazing 3-D fashion when you land in winning combinations, adding adrenaline to the thrill of receiving a big payout. . . . With the Lifestyles of the Rich and Famous® game, you can get a taste of champagne wishes and caviar dreams.[95]

By looking behind the scenes at how the rich live, Lifestyles shows and games place price tags on the lavish material possessions of the rich and famous, offering viewers a chance either to pretend that they are part of that lifestyle or to ridicule it. Numerous other games, including The Sims, have taken up the theme of gaining the most wealth by correctly guessing the prices of some of the world's most luxurious items.

The story lines of reality TV shows constantly use price-tag framing. VH1's *The Fabulous Life* is an excellent example; in it the prices of a celebrity's lavish possessions pop up on the TV screen as the story of the well-known individual's life unfolds. Viewers get the "inside scoop" on the cost of birthday celebrations, clothes, residences, and private jet travel. The price of each item is carefully put into perspective for middle- and lower-class viewers.

THE TWENTY-FOUR-KARAT GOLD FRAME: EFFECTS OF FRAMING THE WEALTHY

The media's framing of stories about the wealthy influences the opinions of people in other classes. Lacking personal encounters with extremely wealthy individuals, people in the middle, working, and poor classes look to the media for an insider's view of how the "other half" lives. Television programs such as *E!*, *Entertainment Tonight*, *Inside Edition*, and *Access Hollywood* promise to take viewers behind the scenes to learn what goes on in the lives of the rich and famous. Vicarious living through the media helps ordinary people feel that they know about celebrities and other wealthy individuals. Be it celebrity gossip ("what's going on with Lady Gaga?") or news stories about scandals involving the rich ("can you believe that CEO got a $20 million buyout after he put the company into bankruptcy and left employees destitute?"), many people talk about the good deeds and misfortunes of the wealthy as if they had personal knowledge of them. Extensive media coverage of the rich and famous creates this illusion of familiarity over time. It is important for us to evaluate the framing, however, because, like rose-colored glasses, a frame used to tell a story may distort our perceptions. As an artist once suggested, "The frame you select can completely change the look and feel of my painting. Choose your frame very carefully."

Similarly, how the media, as powerful purveyors of information and entertainment, frame stories is a significant concern because we use these frames as mental shortcuts (schemas) in forming our thoughts both about the wealthy and about larger issues of social stratification and inequality. Media messages about the rich—for instance, the wealthy are more powerful and somehow better than other people—may influence our views not only about the affluent but about the poor and homeless.

This chapter has discussed four of the most frequently used frames for building news stories or entertainment story lines about the upper class. Consensus framing depicts the wealthy as being like people in other classes and suggests that "we all put on our pants one leg at a time" regardless of our location in the class hierarchy. This framing technique ignores invidious distinctions in material possessions and life chances, distinctions brought about by vast economic differences in society. Showing the wealthy dining on meatloaf ignores larger social realities about the exploitative nature of capitalism or such pressing social problems as poverty and hunger. Cropped out of the picture by this frame are the vast differences between the rich and poor regarding life expectancy, health care, police and other security protection, and many of the other factors that influence one's life chances. Consensus framing leaves media audiences with the impression that the concerns of the wealthy are the most important issues facing the nation.[96]

Admiration framing, which casts the wealthy as generous and caring people, provides media audiences with copious examples of how the rich help others. Based on the concept of noblesse oblige (those who have much should give to those who are less fortunate), admiration framing highlights the contributions of the rich to prestigious institutions like universities and hospitals. A central message of admiration framing holds that although the rich have so much money, they can afford to give away millions without diminishing their wealth, other people should follow their good example to whatever extent their finances allow. Admiration framing deflects criticism of the wealthy by portraying them as good citizens who put their money to work for others.

Emulation framing also casts the rich in a very positive light; however, this type of framing goes one step beyond admiration framing by suggesting to media audiences that they should be like the wealthy, not just admire them. Based on the ideology of the American Dream, emulation framing plays on the widely held belief that anyone can become rich through hard work and determination. This type of framing offers people in other classes suggestions about how to emulate the lifestyles of the celebrity wealthy in small ways, such as by purchasing a bar of luxury soap or designing a room to "look like a million."

Many media stories intertwine emulation framing with price-tag framing. Cost often becomes a central issue in news or entertainment accounts about the rich and famous. For example, the amount an individual spends on spa and beauty treatments and cosmetic surgery may become a major topic in a celebrity profile, overshadowing discussion of the person being interviewed. Although individuals are the purported subjects of news articles or television story lines, in actuality products and services are the stars. Audiences are left to ask, Can you believe how much that costs? Journalists and television writers realize that price-tag framing often produces ambivalent responses, but they also know it draws in viewers and readers from targeted age categories. Media audiences receive conflicting messages, one preaching the gospel of materialism and another disputing its worth. Preaching the gospel of materialism as practiced by the wealthy encourages some viewers to engage in excessive consumerism. Other audiences reject the idea that how much a person owns is a measure of his or her worth. Overall, price-tag framing—whether of middle- and working-class television shows like *The Price Is Right* or upscale lifestyle programs like the *Private Chefs of Beverly Hills*—sends the message that material possessions make some people happy and that a trip to the mall can, at least temporarily, help us forget our worries.

In sum, audiences receive mixed messages about the wealthy based on media portrayals of that group. The ancient Greek philosopher Aristotle (384–322 BC) suggested that human passions (emotions) are present in antagonistic pairs: love and fear, shame and shamelessness, pity and resentment, and envy and contempt. Our beliefs about the rich and famous, as framed by media depictions, may come in pairs as well. We may simultaneously pity them ("poor little rich girl") and resent them ("Life is unfair! Why do the rich have more than I do?"). We may not feel bad because a rich celebrity owns a particular possession (such as $250,000 sports car), but we may resent not being able to afford that item ourselves. Stories about the wealthy particularly evoke contradictory emotions in audiences when the media employ two additional kinds of framing—sour-grapes or bad-apple framing—as discussed in chapter 3.

Chapter 3

Gilded Cages

Media Stories of
How the Mighty Have Fallen

Beating up on the wealthy seems to be the order of the day. I suspected that. But a recent Wealth Matters column [in the *New York Times*] touched a particularly raw nerve. It looked at how even people with sizable fortunes were concerned about money in this recession and the impact that could have on the rest of us.

Readers rejected the attempt to understand the concerns of the rich.

"That's so stupid that you ought to be slapped for it," one woman wrote. My favorite began "Bowties and Reaganomics are for losers. You can cry for the rich all you want, the rest of us will be happy to see them get taxed."

The vehemence in these e-mail messages made me wonder why so many people were furious at those who had more than they did. And why are the rich shouldering the blame for a collective run of bad decision-making? After all, many of the rich got there through hard work. And plenty of not-so-rich people bought homes, cars and electronics they could not afford and then defaulted on the debt, contributing to the crash [in 2008]. But in this recession, anger flows one way.[1]

As this *New York Times* columnist suggests, editorials such as "Too Rich to Worry? Not in This Downturn" do not go over well with people who think the rich have it made and feel they personally are far from wealthy.[2] Certain types of media framing of stories and commentaries about the well-to-do and their problems produce schadenfreude, a feeling of malicious satisfaction in learning of the misfortune of others. However, the sour-grapes and bad-apple framing discussed in this chapter typically produce contradictory feelings of both schadenfreude and a desire to know more about—and perhaps possess—the premium-price goods and services enjoyed by the very wealthy, even when they are experiencing financial difficulties or legal trouble. Although media audiences may gain some gratification from learning about the problems of the rich, readers and viewers often believe that if they had as much money and all of the material possessions of the wealthy, they would do things differently: they would not be unhappy or get into trouble with the law because of excessive greed.

Media coverage of the downfall of top Wall Street financiers, mortgage executives, and other captains of industry has amply proven this point by emphasizing both the nature of their misconduct and the elaborate lifestyle to which they have become accustomed. Reports of their legal problems have cataloged their opulent residences, lavish lifestyles, and other forms of conspicuous consumption. For example, a 2010 *New York Times* article titled "Mortgage Executive Accused in Multibillion-Dollar Fraud" described how federal prosecutors accused Lee B. Farkas, former chairman of Taylor, Bean & Whitaker, one of the nation's largest mortgage lending firms, of "masterminding a fraud scheme that cheated investors and the federal government out of billions of dollars and led to the failure of Colonial Bank."[3] According to the article, Farkas perpetrated the fraud by setting up an elaborate shell game that involved covering up the lender's losses by creating fake mortgages and passing them along to private investors and government agencies: "Mr. Farkas pocketed at least $20 million from the fraud, which he used to finance a private jet and a lavish lifestyle that included five homes and a collection of vintage cars, prosecutors said."[4] Similarly, media sources have described R. Allen Stanford, a Texas financier who defrauded investors in a massive $8 billion Ponzi scheme, as a "billionaire inmate" with a net worth of $2.2 billion who possesses $100 million in private jets, a yacht he paid $100,000 a week to rent, and a fully stocked, professional kitchen in his company's Houston headquarters.[5]

Media descriptions of upper-class crime and the excessive patterns of consumption that typically accompany it may influence ordinary people's perceptions of how the rich live and the gratification they receive from acquiring more and more luxury possessions such as private jets, yachts, and mansions. Many middle- and lower-income people are simply unaware of the nature and extent of the opulent surroundings that very wealthy families enjoy on a daily basis. Television and Internet coverage of lavish residences and luxury cars brings home the point that the rich are very different from other people, and this may produce a variety of feelings about the most affluent individuals and families in a nation. When the rich have accumulated some, or all, of their material possessions through dishonest means, everyday people may initially assume that the wrongdoers will be punished by having wealth and other assets removed. However, the articles point out that wealthy individuals accused of crime often do not lose the lifestyles they have created, even after being sent to a country-club prison for a brief period. In other words, people who gain an opulent lifestyle though criminal endeavors or other means perceived to be unethical or immoral may not lose these rich gains even if it is proven that these persons acquired their possessions through dishonest means.

Sour-grapes and bad-apple framing focus on the problems of the rich as individual pathologies, not structural concerns rooted in larger economic, political, or social hierarchies, and these forms of framing often include detailed descriptions of the material possessions of the very wealthy. Sour-grapes framing portrays the rich as frequently unhappy and dysfunctional people; bad-apple framing suggests the rich have problems but still enjoy the good life. Since bad-apple framing typically focuses on the individual scoundrel rather than on harm done by many people or established corporate practices, media audiences typically view the problem as one of individual, rather than corporate, abuse. According to media scholar Michael J. Parenti, when we treat the wrongdoings of the rich as mere isolated deviations from the socially beneficial system of "responsible capitalism," we overlook the larger structural features of the system that produce these problems.[6] When the media portray the abuses of the wealthy as isolated problems rather than as predictable and frequent outcomes of the economic and political system, readers and viewers have little reason to question the status quo. Parenti states that viewing the misconduct of the wealthy as nothing more than an occasional individual aberration serves to legitimate, rather than challenge, existing systems of social inequality.[7]

SOUR-GRAPES FRAMING:
THE WEALTHY ARE UNHAPPY AND DYSFUNCTIONAL

One of Aesop's fables, "The Fox and the Grapes," tells the story of a fox who strolls through an orchard, finds a bunch of grapes ripening on a vine, and decides that they are just the thing to quench his thirst. After several unsuccessful attempts to run, jump, and grab the bunch, however, he walks away with his nose in the air, saying, "I am sure they are sour." The moral of this story is, "It is easy to despise what you cannot have."[8] Similarly, sour-grapes framing displays for media audiences the abundance of material possessions and opulent lifestyles of the rich and famous, then suggests that the grapes, which are out of reach for the typical reader or viewer, are not worth having—they are flawed, thus undesirable. A classic example of sour-grapes framing is the poor-little-rich-girl (or -boy) story. Books, television, and films have popularized stories about the problems of people who have inherited large sums of money, then lived lives of despair. Stories about, for example, Woolworth heiress Barbara Hutton[9] and tobacco heiress Doris Duke[10] tell of unhappy childhoods, personal traumas, and misfortunes among the wealthy. From best-selling biographies to media tabloids to television entertainment shows like *E!*, *Hard Copy*, and *Entertainment Tonight*, audiences learn about the supposed problems and heartaches of the rich and famous.

Many of these stories convey the message that ordinary people are better off because the rich and famous suffer as a result of their wealth and typically do stupid things because they cannot cope with the real world. This frame gives middle- and working-class media audiences a bird's-eye view of the lives of the wealthy, as well as delivers a cautionary tale about the problems associated with great wealth and notoriety. However, stories with this type of framing draw audiences by providing them with opportunities to feel good about themselves, even though they have not achieved the American Dream of success, wealth, and perhaps fame. Readers and viewers can conclude that being rich is not all it is cracked up to be ("the grapes are sour"); thus, they should feel content with their own lives. A website posting by "Grace" from Seattle, who reviewed C. David Heymann's *Poor Little Rich Girl: The Life and Legend of Barbara Hutton*, demonstrates this kind of thinking:

> I think I got a pretty good idea of what Ms. Hutton was about, and have a hard time sympathizing with her . . . *poor little rich girl* indeed! She popped into a Woolworth's once in her life, just to sign a few autographs. Her cheesy poetry netted her less than $200, the only money she truly earned of her own effort. Someone else handled all her financial matters (luckily for her, usually quite well), because she couldn't be bothered. . . . Spending money takes time, you know. She dropped husbands as soon as they no longer entertained her. Yes, she had exquisite taste in clothing and jewelry, and traveled incessantly to places I can only dream of ever seeing, but had no grasp on reality—she once sent one of her employees to the bank to change a bill because she had no change. . . . It was a $10,000 bill (I didn't even know those existed!). I enjoyed this book because it took me somewhere I could never go myself. It's hard to feel sorry for her though. . . . She dug her own grave!!![11]

Like many people who read biographies or see films portraying the lives of wealthy, typically unhappy individuals such as Barbara Hutton, this reviewer enjoyed living vicariously in that she is quick to point out Barbara Hutton's "exquisite taste in clothing and jewelry" and her ability to travel "incessantly to places I can only dream of ever seeing." However, the reviewer also emphasizes Hutton's individual character flaws, such as that she never worked a day in her life and spent her time and money frivolously. Comments like these are typical of media audiences who do not question the larger economic conditions that produced the Woolworth-Hutton family fortune or other macrolevel concerns associated with capitalism and excessive consumerism. The focus rests strictly on microlevel concerns through an emphasis on the activities and possessions of individuals, not of organizational and societal entities.

Another media message about the wealthy suggests that happiness would be within their reach if certain character flaws—such as greed—did not keep them from finding personal satisfaction with their great wealth. For some wealthy scions, inheriting millions of dollars simply is not adequate, so they attempt to gain even more from the estate of a wealthy relative. For example, following the death of his mother, New York socialite Brooke Astor, at age 105, Anthony D. Marshall waged a battle over her $180 million estate. Marshall and his wife, Charlene, were already wealthy and living in luxury, when he began to steal from his mother while she was still alive. Among other activities, he allegedly brought lawyers and financial advisers to her home to coerce her into changing her will, which previously bequeathed a large portion of her estate to the Metropolitan Museum of Art and New York Public Library. In that will, Marshall would receive payments to live on until his death, at which point the remainder of the estate would go to charity. The subsequent will, orchestrated by Marshall at a time when Mrs. Astor was probably not of sound mind, gave him a larger portion of his mother's estate, including money and property that he could pass on to other individuals, especially his wife, in his own will. After a five-month trial, Marshall was convicted on several offenses, including manipulating Mrs. Astor's will and removing and selling art from her Upper East Side apartment without her consent.[12] The typical middle-class reader's response to frequent the media reports about the Astor trial (as evidenced by comments in interviews, *New York Times* letters to the editor, and web blogs) was that the already extremely wealthy Marshall should have left well enough alone. Had he not been so greedy, the prevailing thinking went, he could have enjoyed a really great life. Readers and viewers avidly followed the trial and media reports of what journalists referred to as "a 19-week drama of family dysfunction and high society."[13] Some people concluded that if they had that kind of money, they would know how to spend it and surely could find happiness with all of the possessions the Astor heirs owned, unlike the maladjusted and dysfunctional individuals so often described in news accounts.

Like media representations of actual superwealthy families, entertainment programming about fictitious rich families also uses sour-grapes framing extensively. Multiple generations of daytime and evening soap operas on television have highlighted the foibles of wealthy families, particularly those with members who steal from them, battle with addictions, or engage in frequent sexual liaisons outside of marriage. Shows ranging from *The Bold and the Beautiful* to *Gossip Girl* enhance their story lines by showing the

contradictions between having the wealth and privilege of the rich and dealing with their foibles. A short-lived evening soap, *Dirty Sexy Money*, which
was cancelled because of a writers' strike, is a classic example. Actor Peter
Krause plays a lawyer who inherits his late father's task of taking care of the
dysfunctional members of New York's wealthy Darling family. The Darlings
include a patriarch (Donald Sutherland) and matriarch (Jill Clayburgh), who
are quirky in their own way but much less so than their overindulged, deca-
dent children. Inheritance of the family's money is a key issue in the series,
and its members' opulent lifestyle is practically a character in its own right.
Shows such as this continually come and go on network television, and many
live in perpetuity through syndication on cable channels such as SOAPnet
and a variety of websites.

Newspaper articles and television entertainment programs about people
who have inherited great wealth and those who are newly rich also use sour-
grapes framing. Unlike old-money families that have had vast wealth for
three or more generations and are considered the old guard in their respective
cities, new-money families have accumulated vast economic resources in
the current generation and may not be considered social elites in their communities.[14] A popular form of sour-grapes framing about old money tells a
cautionary tale about the difficulties faced by heirs to great wealth. Consider
the article "Suddenly Popular," in which inheritor Mark McDonough relays
this story:

> So first of all . . . there's this closet called the Green Closet. It's one of the last
> taboos. This culture tells you, if you have more money, you'll be happier. But
> rich people are in this unique position to say, "You know what? More stuff
> doesn't mean more happiness." But as a rich person, you absolutely cannot tell
> anybody that there's anything wrong with your life because, first, everybody
> knows you should be really happy, and second, they say, "I should have your
> problems!" Then there's the shame component. With inherited wealth, there's
> this little logic chain: I have a lot of money, I should be really happy, but I'm
> not happy, so I must be really bad.[15]

Although it is undoubtedly true that possession of great wealth does not equal
happiness, sour-grapes framing emphasizes the problems rather than the advantages of such wealth. Problems faced by some wealthy inheritors include
low self-esteem and self-discipline, difficulty using power, boredom and
alienation, and guilt and suspiciousness.[16] In addition, articles often point out
how difficult it is for rich people to establish positive relationships with others because they never know whether someone loves them for themselves or
for their money; heirs must fend off "opportunists, speculators, hustlers, and
potential lovers" who only want to get their hands on their wealth.[17] Media

audiences may get the message from such articles that having a large amount of money may be a problem and is not something people should desire. Some readers and viewers respond, "I should be so unlucky," convinced that if they only had the money of the "poor little rich girl (or boy)," they indeed could find happiness.

Aside from suggesting that individuals who earn their own money have higher self-esteem, sour-grapes framing highlights the pitfalls faced by the nouveau riche, particularly in television entertainment programs. The long-running hit series *Dallas* (shown on CBS from 1978 until 1991 and still in worldwide syndication) popularized the story line of the rich, dysfunctional family. This show follows the exploits of lead character J. R. Ewing (Larry Hagman), a ruthless oil tycoon worth nearly $3 billion who is always plotting evil deeds and having bitter battles with his family and business associates. Ewing prides himself on evading federal regulators, taking down anyone who stands in the way of Ewing Oil, and maintaining off-the-books partnerships to boost profits and hide debt. His image as the prototypical rich misfit endures, preserved in such tributes as his 2002 pseudobiography in *Forbes*'s "Fictional Fifteen Richest Americans."[18] Continuing interest in the lifestyle of this fictitious family is evident in the fact that the Ewing family's estate, Southfork Ranch, has become a tourist attraction. Each year several thousand people from around the world visit the large white mansion, pool, barns, and other settings where *Dallas* was filmed. Tourists can relive some of the show's memorable moments and watch video clips from the series. They also can visit the ranch's retail stores, Lincolns and Longhorns and Ranch RoundUp, to buy souvenirs and other Southfork gift items.[19] However unhappy and dysfunctional the sour-grapes framing of this popular series makes the Ewings seem, media audiences continue to show interest in their material possessions and lifestyle.

In the twenty-first century, the story line of the rich, dysfunctional family remains popular in such television shows as FOX's *The O.C.* (now in syndication and available on DVD) and ABC's *Brothers & Sisters*. The dysfunctional rich family has also become a favorite subject for a number of reality television series on cable channels. *The O.C.* aired from 2003 to 2007, when conspicuous consumption and dysfunctional families were popular themes for television series. The show's characters frequently go to charity fund-raisers, which are represented as nothing more than places where the moneyed residents of Newport Beach come together to make catty remarks about each other and occasionally get into brawls. "The O.C." refers to Orange County, California, described as "the largest suburban, affluent, Republican county between Los Angeles and San Diego."[20] Setting up a contrast—and potential conflict—between classes, *The O.C.* portrays the problems of Ryan Atwood

(Benjamin McKenzie), a "smart, poor kid" from the working-class community of Chino, who comes to live with the affluent Cohens in Newport Beach
after getting into trouble with the law. Ryan lives with the family of Sandy
Cohen (Peter Gallagher), a public defender from humble origins who resides
with his wife, Kirsten (Kelly Rowan), in Newport Beach. Kirsten's father
is a wealthy and sometimes unscrupulous real estate developer. The Cohen
family accepts Ryan, and his living arrangements become permanent, but
television audiences receive regular reminders that he comes from a lower-
class, dysfunctional background. They are also reminded, however, that many
Newport Beach residents are dysfunctional snobs who look down their noses
at outsiders but have their own dirty laundry to hide. *The O.C.* portrays the
good life of the rich, showing multimillion-dolllar mansions, luxury vehicles,
and black-tie events, but it also shows the sour-grapes side, emphasizing the
shallowness, drug and alcohol abuse, and rampant consumerism of people
who live in the fictitious version of this area of Southern California. *The O.C.*
incorporates a rags-to-riches story line, but one critic suggested that the series
also illustrates the "slippery slope of wealth" and the empty promise of trying
to have it all.[21]

Part of the constant pattern of one entertainment series about the wealthy
and dysfunctional replacing another that gets cancelled, CW's *Gossip Girl*
aired as a replacement for devotees of *The O.C.* Developed by Josh Schwartz,
creator of *The O.C.*, *Gossip Girl*'s characters—extremely wealthy students at
a prestigious prep school on New York's Upper East Side—are even more
status conscious. Very rich Chuck Bass (Ed Westwick) has a sense of entitle-
ment and believes that everything he wants should be his. Other wealthy
characters include Serena van der Woodsen (Blake Lively), who comes back
from boarding school to take care of her younger brother, and Blair Waldorf
(Leighton Meester), who initially snubs Serena. The wrong side of the tracks
is represented by Dan Humphreys (Penn Badgley), whose dad is a rock
singer. Although the Humphreys live in a large loft, they are poor folks in
comparison to the old-moneyed, ultrarich kids. Even before extensive media
criticism and several suicides involving social media, *Gossip Girl* portrayed
young people in constant texting sessions and sending invasive cell phone
photos to each other. Characters obsessively follow a blog written by "Gossip
Girl," who snoops into everyone's lives. The show emphasizes that the characters are "trust-fund babies and legends in their own minds" because Gossip
Girl covers their every action. According to one *Boston Globe* television
critic, "They're Paristocrats [after Paris Hilton]. And, Lord help me, I loved
spending an hour hating them, their pedigrees, and their unlimited credit
cards. It was like studying the peculiar mating rituals and shopping habits of
the species *Manhattanus Elitus*."[22]

Sour-grapes framing, whether in television entertainment series or news accounts, often elicits ambivalent feelings in media audiences. They can experience pleasure looking at expensive merchandise and luxury residences while at the same time becoming aware of problems associated with having wealth and social prominence. Although television shows about families in various economic classes (such as *Parenthood*, *Two and a Half Men*, and *The Middle*) typically make fun of the seemingly dysfunctional American family, the rich and famous are favorite subjects for stories employing sour-grapes framing: it is easier to laugh at their pretentiousness and conspicuous consumption than to face head-on the problems of the working class and poor.

While sour-grapes framing frequently involves the poor-little-rich-girl (or -boy) scenario or a cautionary tale about having great wealth, bad-apple framing focuses on deviant and criminal behavior among the rich. Even bad-apple framing, however, primarily emphasizes the individual nature of these actions rather than the larger patterns of corruption that may constitute a part of the standard business practices of many "wealthy scoundrels."

BAD-APPLE FRAMING #1:
SOME WEALTHY PEOPLE ARE MEDIA HOGS

The media use a relatively mild form of bad-apple framing to report stories about wealthy individuals who are publicity hogs or have perceived personality flaws; criminal behavior receives stronger forms of bad-apple framing. In both instances, the media provide extensive information not only about individuals' misdeeds but their net worth and costly possessions. According to sociologist Gregory Mantsios, the media send several messages about the wealthy as bad apples:

> On rare occasions, the media will mock selected individuals for their personality flaws. Real estate investor Donald Trump and New York Yankees owner George Steinbrenner, for example, are admonished by the media for deliberately seeking publicity (a very un–upper class thing to do); hotel owner Leona Helmsley was caricatured for her personal cruelties; and junk bond broker Michael Milken was condemned because he had the audacity to rob the rich.[23]

As Mantsios suggests, some of the wealthy can be viewed as bad apples because they seek the media spotlight to further their own causes and financial interests. New York real estate developer Donald Trump is an example. Over the years, Trump has been available to the media for profiles about his empire, including his numerous high-rise buildings and development projects in New York City and his hotels and casinos in Atlantic City, New Jersey.

Despite his billions, Trump at one time appeared in McDonald's ads selling dollar-priced sandwiches,[24] and he hosts reality shows like *The Celebrity Apprentice*, on which candidates vie to win money for their favorite charity, and *The Apprentice*, which pits noncelebrities against each other as they seek to win an at least six-figure prize—a job with the Trump organization. In these reality shows, Trump plays a starring role, personally firing some candidates and leaving others to compete for the big prize in the final round.

Since 2007, the class-based nature of Donald Trump's courting of the media to help serve his own interests has been visible in Scotland, where he is working to install the "world's greatest golf course." Trump spent an extensive amount of time with journalists at a packed press conference discussing a proposed golf resort and the fact that he would build it despite one hold-out resident, Michael Forbes, who refused to sell his land to Trump and instead planned to sell it to Tripping Up Trump, a group formed to oppose the massive resort on the Aberdeenshire coast. On several occasions, Trump called Forbes the "village idiot" and informed the media that the Forbes family home at the Mill of Menie was a "slum and pigsty."[25] Media stories about this encounter emphasized the extent to which media hog Trump seems not to care what he says about other people:

> "We want to build a great hotel," Mr. Trump said. "He [Forbes] doesn't maintain his property. It's a slum. It's a horrible way he maintains it. I don't know if he's doing that on purpose. I think that's just the way he maintains his property. So it's a very sad situation. You have rusted oil tanks all over it. You have tractors that are rotting and rusting into this beautiful sand. You have oil tanks that are leaking into the sand. I think somebody should do something about it."
>
> Warming to his theme, the tycoon continued: "He does have an impact on the hotel because if we build a $300m or $400m hotel, I don't think you want the windows looking down into a slum. I don't think anybody wants to build where your view is obliterated by a slum. . . ." During his wide-ranging press conference, an ebullient Mr. Trump waxed lyrical about everything from the state of the euro to his golf handicap.[26]

According to some analysts, Trump seeks out the media spotlight to maintain his high profile and his business image. In his role as media hog, however, he emphasizes class-based differences among people and often earns a reputation as a bad-but-very-successful apple. But Trump is not alone in being framed by the media in this manner. A *Forbes* magazine article called "The Most Overexposed Billionaires" describes how individuals such as Donald Trump, Cirque du Soleil cofounder Guy Laliberte, investor Warren Buffett, Dallas Mavericks owner Mark Cuban, Virgin Group chief Richard Branson, and Dallas Cowboys owner Jerry Jones have had more than their requisite "fifteen minutes" in the media spotlight.[27]

If Trump and other high-profile wealthy individuals are framed as bad apples because they are media hogs, some other rich people become subject to bad-apple framing due to problematic behavior that suggests they believe their wealth can buy anything.

BAD-APPLE FRAMING #2: SOME WEALTHY PEOPLE BELIEVE THEY CAN BUY ANYTHING

News stories have used bad-apple framing to show how the wealthy buy, or attempt to buy, whatever they want. Of the many possible examples, perhaps the "nursery school scandal" in New York City received the most media attention. What happens when your child is not accepted into a nursery school? Most parents simply find another school. However, this is not what the now discredited $20-million-a-year stock analyst Jack Grubman chose to do when his twin daughters were not accepted at the exclusive Ninety-second Street Y preschool in Manhattan. Instead, Grubman allegedly bargained with Citicorp's Sanford I. Weill (who was also an AT&T director), offering to increase his rating of AT&T stock if Weill would make a few calls to Ninety-second Street Y board members to arrange admission for Grubman's toddlers. Citicorp also pledged $1 million to the school. According to media accounts, Grubman sent Weill an e-mail stating, "There are no bounds for what you do for your children."[28] In the aftermath of the "nursery school scandal," Grubman was later banned from the securities industry for misleading investors who trusted him with their money. According to one telecommunications analyst, "It is one shock that this kind of horse-trading is acceptable within some organizations, yet another that AT&T's investment rating and $1 million of shareholder cash were apparently treated as chips in such an odd game as nursery school poker."[29] This statement epitomizes this form of bad-apple framing: the rich believe that everything and everybody has a price; you only have to find out what that price is and pay it.

This type of behavior did not, however, surprise many other wealthy parents, given the competitiveness of everything in their lives, including the nursery schools their children attend. One journalist summed up the situation as follows:

> To normal people living anywhere else, the news that someone might offer a pledge of $1 million just to get a child into the right nursery school must seem absurd. That an analyst might recommend a particular stock in order to curry favor with a powerful banker who might then help that analyst's child win a coveted spot in a nursery school seems stranger still. But on Manhattan's Upper East Side, the story that Jack Grubman, the former star telecom stock analyst

for Citigroup, attempted to get his twins into the 92nd Street Y nursery school by changing his rating on AT&T stock was greeted with knowing nods rather than disbelief.[30]

Some wealthy parents see rejection by a prestigious nursery school not only as harmful to their children but also as reflecting negatively on their family's social standing. Sociological research bears out the extent to which wealthy elites will pay any price to get the right education for their children, whether in nursery school, high school, or college. In a study of elite private schools, sociologists Peter W. Cookson Jr. and Caroline Hodges Persell concluded,

> To be accepted into a private school is to be accepted into a social club, or more generally speaking, a status group that is defined as a group of people who have a sense of social similarity. People sharing the same status have similar life-styles, common educational background, and pursue similar types of oc-cupations.[31]

Media coverage of a high-society scandal like the Grubman case provides audiences with more than a news account of just the facts—the who, what, when, and where. Media audiences get the message that some wealthy people think they can buy anything, a belief often confirmed by the way others ac-quiesce and do their bidding. Framing of media stories about how the rich buy what they want typically includes information for everyday readers and viewers about the competitive nature of life in the upper classes and how dif-ferent the rich are from everyone else. News articles, television shows, and websites provide lengthy summaries of the wealth of the individuals involved and the value or prestige of the things they desire in their privileged social circles. Consider Grubman, for example. After all of his legal entanglements, journalists estimated his net worth remained between $50 and $70 million, and he owned a luxurious six-story Upper East Side town house in Manhattan and another mansion in East Hampton.[32]

Although bad-apple framing of wealthy people often centers on the pur-chase of some specific consumer service (such as attendance at a prestigious nursery school) or the use of some luxury (such as a corporate expense ac-count and private jet to entertain, and thus curry favor with, important politi-cians), sometimes the media focus on how the wealthy use their resources as hush money to buy the silence of individuals with personal knowledge of their business or family indiscretions. The media have exposed many cases of hush money paid out in business; however, with social media gaining so rapidly in the information marketplace, one common form of framing about the wealthy suggests that the rich and famous believe they can buy anything. A case in point is the global media scandal in which Tiger Woods, one of the world's top professional golfers and highest-paid professional athletes (he earned $110 million in winnings and endorsements in 2008), was accused of having extramarital affairs with a dozen or more women during his marriage to Elin Nordegren. Throughout the separation and divorce, the media framed the issue of the "high price of celebrity divorce" and how much money Woods might have to pay to keep Nordegren from doing interviews and publishing a book about her life with him. Most journalists writing about the family crisis focused on how much money Nordegren might receive: Would it be $100 million or $700 million? Would the prenuptial agreement, allowing her a maximum of $10 million in case of divorce, be set aside if she agreed not to tell all about her marriage? Throughout media stories concerning how Woods might purchase his wife's silence, journalists and bloggers provided audiences with lengthy descriptions of the couple's vast possessions, including an $80 million Florida estate and a $20 million, 155-foot yacht (*Privacy*) with a 6,500-square-foot master suite, six staterooms, a theater, and a gym, to show media audiences that Woods truly lived an enviable life of wealth and luxury.[33]

Given the media emphasis on the good life, it comes as no surprise that even when journalists and other commentators describe the unethical and often criminal conduct of some wealthy elites, many middle- and working-class and poor individuals believe that if they were rich, they would know how to live happily ever after and stay out of the trouble these people have gotten into.

BAD-APPLE FRAMING #3: BAD APPLES WITH GOOD TASTE—WEALTHY WOMEN AND CRIME

Scandals involving wealthy women such as Martha Stewart, the lifestyle expert, or Diana D. Brooks, former chief executive of the famous auction house Sotheby's, are often framed in such a manner as to show that the women have impeccable taste, even when they are accused of committing crimes. Despite the charges of conspiracy, obstruction of justice, and securities fraud against Martha Stewart, most people have forgotten these indiscretions and continue to view her as an icon of good taste and good living. Stewart successfully marketed her products and her lifestyle, referring to herself as "America's most trusted guide to stylish living" and reaching millions of people through her television shows, books, *Martha Stewart Living* magazine, and website.

As business authors Michael J. Silverstein and Neil Fiske write in their popular book *Trading Up*, Martha Stewart "inspired millions of Americans to reach for a richer, more tasteful, more sophisticated lifestyle."[34] According to Silverstein and Fiske, she is one of the leaders in "new luxury" spending on "products and services that possess higher levels of quality, taste, and aspiration than other goods in the category but are not so expensive as to be out of reach" for middle- and upper-middle-income shoppers.[35] For example, new luxury products such as an $8,000 Sub-Zero stainless refrigerator or a $1,199.95 KitchenAid frozen dessert maker for ice cream and frozen margaritas have lower-cost competitors, but the less-expensive products do not have as many features or the same prestige as the more expensive brands.[36] As a wealthy woman convicted of obstruction of justice, Stewart is still seen as having good taste and has remained popular with many of her followers:

> Even during [Martha Stewart's] difficulties . . . involving insider stock trading, her popularity and influence did not decline, although her company's share price did. As one woman said . . . "Martha is one of the first people who said your home is important. She gives the family validity. She is a source of comfort."[37]

Even if many people, including this woman, did not condone Stewart's behavior in the business world, some of them applauded her for the emphasis she placed on home, family, and other positive values. Admiration of Stewart's good taste and comforting nature apparently outstripped the animosity some media audiences might have felt for her behavior.

Throughout Stewart's legal ordeal—including five months served in the Alderson federal prison—the media frequently reminded audiences that she was the icon of good living. Even media reports describing her as a bad apple acknowledged Stewart as a major force in the trading-up phenomenon and as a homemaking icon. Comedians and nighttime television hosts who made seemingly cruel jokes about Stewart's lifestyle and legal problems typically made disclaimers similar to David Letterman's on his *Late Show with David Letterman*: "Now, don't get me wrong. I like Martha Stewart; she's been on our show a number of times, and she makes some really great stuff." Although some journalists focused on the positive aspects of Stewart's good-living empire, some newspaper and magazine headlines told another story. Among these were a *Newsweek* cover story, "Martha's Mess: An Insider Trading Scandal Tarnishes the Queen of Perfection,"[38] and other articles such as "Martha's Dirty Laundry,"[39] "Tarnish, Anyone?"[40] "Martha Stewart's To-Do List May Include Image Polishing,"[41] and "Canapés and Investment Tips Are Served to Well-Heeled."[42]

In the second decade of the twenty-first century, Stewart's reputation as the "doyenne of all things domestic" and "tireless dispenser of advice" has continued unabated. Although she has fallen from the *Forbes* billionaire ranks because of plunging stock prices, Stewart continues to make millions annually from her syndicated *Martha Stewart Show*, MarthaStewart.com website, and branded products at stores ranging from PetSmart and Home Depot to Macy's and Michaels.[43] Despite bad-apple framing in earlier media stories about Stewart, today's coverage typically conveys a positive image of her as the guru of good taste and a wealthy, hardworking businesswoman able to laugh at herself. Her detractors, however, have informed journalists on more than one occasion that this carefully packaged public relations image does not reflect the real person.

The use of bad-apple-with-good-taste framing is not unique, particularly in the coverage of privileged women accused of criminal activity. Another example includes stories accompanying the conviction of Diana D. Brooks, the former chief executive of Sotheby's, for her admitted role in fixing commission rates with Christie's, a rival auction house. As a cooperating witness in the antitrust prosecution of her former boss, A. Alfred Taubman, Brooks received a sentence of three years' probation, a fine of $350,000, a thousand hours of community service, and six months under house arrest. As part of the agreement, Brooks returned her Sotheby's stock options, worth $10 million, plus the approximately $3.25 million she had received in salary after the conspiracy started.[44] Of all these penalties, which some considered too lenient given the magnitude of the charges, journalists were most interested in the idea that she was being punished by house arrest—in her twelve-room, $5 million co-op apartment on the Upper East Side. News stories carried headlines such as "When Home Is a Castle and the Big House, Too"[45] and "You Say House Arrest, I Say Paradise."[46] A photo of Brooks accompanying one of the articles carried the caption "Velvet cuffs: Diana D. Brooks just before she was sentenced to home detention," suggesting that the criminal justice system was treating her as a privileged person. The journalist set the stage by showing how well Brooks lived:

On August evenings, the limestone canyons of Park Avenue and the white-glove streets of the East 70's are quiet, abandoned by the well-to-do for breezier destinations. . . . But last week on East 79th Street, a solitary window emitted a hopeful rectangular glow. The window, on the 10th floor of one of Manhattan's best co-op apartment buildings, belongs to Diana D. Brooks, the former chief executive of Sotheby's, who is four months into a six-month sentence of home detention. . . . She is allowed to leave her 12-room, $5 million apartment for two hours each Friday to go grocery shopping at any store selling food or products related to food preparation. . . . Her forays have included trips to Gristede's and D'Agostino supermarkets and to a Starbucks, according to a friend of Ms. Brooks. . . . [However], Ms. Brooks is not allowed to exercise in Central Park and may not travel to her $4 million oceanfront home in Hobe Sound, Fla., but she may use her telephone and work from home, which is where she has been continuing her volunteer work for troubled girls in public schools.[47]

As this article suggests, aspects of Brooks's elegant lifestyle, including her trips to other exclusive residences or appearances at high-society parties, were prohibited, but she was able to enjoy the luxury of her costly home, which protected her from interactions with "garden-variety criminals." When found guilty, rich-and-famous women often receive seemingly lenient sentences, and media framing of stories about them continues to suggest that they are bad apples with good taste. Some, like Martha Stewart, remain in the media spotlight; others, like Diana D. Brooks, do not resurface except in articles like one newspaper report describing the wedding of her daughter at the Brooks home in Jupiter Island (Hobe Sound), Florida. According to this media account, Brooks's daughter is a hedge fund director in New York, but it makes no mention of the fact that the family has remained close to controversial money issues in the aftermath of the earlier scandal.[48]

Wealthy celebrities accused of offenses such as insider trading, collusion, and even more mundane crimes like shoplifting typically receive extensive media coverage. Two examples of bad-apple-with-good-taste framing for shoplifting involve actress Winona Ryder and Dallas socialite Brooke Stollenwerck Aldridge. The Winona Ryder shoplifting trial became a topic not only of newspaper and magazine accounts but also of such television entertainment shows as *E!*, *Entertainment Tonight*, *Inside Edition*, and *Access Hollywood*. Writers for *Saturday Night Live*, *The Tonight Show with Jay Leno*, and *Late Night with David Letterman* created numerous jokes about "Winona's five-finger discount" and the expensive designer clothing she wore to her trial ("no cheap orange jump suit for Winona," for example). In bad-apple-with-good-taste framing of stories about rich celebrities like Ryder, no detail is spared, particularly when it involves the individual's insatiable desire for expensive goods or the preferential treatment he or she receives in everyday life:

> Probably the biggest gasp in the Winona Ryder shoplifting trial . . . came when two sales clerks in a row testified that the willowy actress had asked them to fetch her Coca-Colas from the Saks Fifth Avenue cafeteria. By the testimony, Ms. Ryder not once, but twice, asked solicitous helpers hovering outside separate dressing rooms to please bring her a Coke on the afternoon of December 12, 2002, when she was in the midst of what authorities say was a $5,560 shoplifting spree. What was unclear was the reason for the gasp. Was it that the audience in the small, crowded Beverly Hills courtroom had caught the prosecutor's intimation that Ms. Ryder had used a need for refreshment to give her more privacy for scissoring security tags from designer clothes and trinkets? Or was it the very notion that a person could actually order up a beverage while trying on clothes—that is, if one is the right sort of person?[49]

Another example of bad-apple-with-good-taste framing involves wealthy Dallas socialite Brooke Stollenwerck Aldridge, convicted of shoplifting: headlines included "An Unfashionable Turn for Stylish HP Socialite,"[50] "Charity Co-chair Steps Down over Shoplifting Charge,"[51] and "Shop Till You Get Caught."[52] In stories about the Aldridge case, journalists typically did more than simply describe the charges against this socially prominent woman, as evidenced by these introductory sentences from a *Dallas Morning News* front-page article:

> It was sure to be another triumphant evening for one of Dallas' society darlings. A good time, a good cause, a good place to see and be seen. As usual, Brooke Stollenwerck Aldridge would be a conspicuous focus of attention—this time, though, as a consummate contradiction to her lofty social status and inspired volunteer work. During the countdown to the big night, some of the city's wealthiest jaws would drop over a shoplifting scandal that shattered the flawless image of a party planner nonpareil, a chic benefactor with a happy, privileged life.[53]

According to numerous articles, Aldridge, heir to part of her mother's East Texas timber and real estate fortune, easily could have paid for the $485 pair of black designer pants, the $1,250 Hermes wallet, and the $120 Kate Spade wallet that she placed in her purse or shopping bag at the Neiman Marcus store. Most news accounts indicated Aldridge's good taste by including the brand names of the stolen merchandise. In 2007, when Aldridge died of non-Hodgkin's lymphoma, her *Dallas Morning News* obituary provided readers with numerous examples of her life as a socialite and civic volunteer but included the following statement: "In the fall of 2003, she drew unwanted publicity after she was arrested on a shoplifting charge at the Neiman Marcus store in NorthPark Center. She pleaded guilty and received probation."[54]

Articles and television accounts about the shoplifting convictions of Ryder and Aldridge utilized bad-apple-with-good-taste framing to depict a few wealthy individuals who could afford anything they wanted but apparently had psychological problems or other complicated reasons for engaging in such deviant conduct. All the same, even when they get caught, privileged elites are described as having the right connections to help them with their plight. Consider, for example, media reports about Aldridge's arrest:

> [Aldridge's] $500 bond was paid in cash by her father, lawyer Henry Stollenwerck. . . . "It's unusual to pay cash if you're poor, but not for somebody of that stature," Sgt. Don Peritz, the Dallas County sheriff's spokesman, said of the bond. "It's probably like walking money for them, I'm reckoning. My guess is Daddy was waiting there with his engine idling."[55]

Of course, such assumptions were confirmed by media reports at Ms. Aldridge's death that she had received probation for her conduct and not the sentence that women of other classes or races might have received under similar circumstances.

Stories about the crimes of wealthy women maintain the rich-and-tasteful-socialite stereotype through the visual images that accompany articles or video segments about their misconduct. As communications scholars have suggested, photographs serve as a form of pictorial stereotyping in the media. Sometimes these representations create or maintain distorted images of individuals and contribute to bias against people based on their ethnicity, gender, age, disability, sexual orientation, or other characteristics.[56] Consider, on the other hand, what kind of media coverage, if any, a working-class woman would receive for shoplifting a $25 pair of shoes and a $49 pantsuit from Walmart or another discount chain. In any case, most media coverage of the rich and famous who commit crimes focuses on the wrongdoings of elite men.

BAD-APPLE FRAMING #4: BAD APPLES WITH MOGUL STYLE—WEALTHY MEN AND CRIME

Wealthy men's high status and the cost of their entertainment and luxury possessions are key components of media coverage about the downfall of corporate CEOs and their companies. Mogul style refers to the idea that some rich corporate executives take less interest in conspicuous consumption for its own sake than in contemptuous consumption—spending money (sometimes not their own) not for the pleasure of ownership or connoisseurship but for the gratification they receive from making other moguls fearful or jealous.[57] According to one journalist,

> The gossip columns and the glossy magazines got it all wrong. For years they've been glorifying the homes and lives of the rich and famous by defining the rich and famous as movie stars, fashion designers and rap music impresarios. But it turns out that the trend they missed was Mogul Style: excessive spending on the chief executive's imperial lifestyle.[58]

Whether in the national news, business, or lifestyle sections of local newspapers or on infotainment TV shows like *Dateline*, *20/20*, or *60 Minutes*, executives' arrests and trials have garnered headlines, giving media audiences opportunities to look at the mogul style these men display, be it at corporate parties or in their private residences. In fact, the lifestyles of some top (and former) CEOs have been described as "more flamboyant and expensive than

Hollywood Style, than anyone on *MTV Cribs* or in the pages of *In Style* magazine. . . . Whereas celebs are trying to impress their fans, moguls are trying to impress each other."[59]

Journalists and news correspondents employed media framing using the bad-apple-with-mogul-style theme in stories about the suicide of Finn M. W. Caspersen, heir to the Beneficial Corporation fortune. At the time of his death, investigators were building a case against Caspersen for federal tax evasion. Mogul-style framing is apparent in articles like "Suicide Victim May Have Harbored a Secret":

> He seemed, in many ways, like a man from another time, a Gatsbyesque figure who glided through a world of old money, private clubs and pedigree horses, his family name emblazoned on Ivy League halls. Then, in an instant, he was gone—his privileged life ended, by his own hand, with a single gunshot to the head.
>
> No one can know exactly what Finn M. W. Caspersen, a prominent philanthropist and the heir to the Beneficial Corporation fortune, was thinking when he decided to take his life on Labor Day. Although Mr. Caspersen, 67, was battling kidney cancer, his suicide shocked his family and friends.[60]

Notwithstanding Caspersen's contributing millions of dollars to charities and to Princeton and Harvard universities (including a $30 million gift to the Harvard Law School), UBS, a giant Swiss bank, exposed him as an American client holding "secret" bank accounts in "offshore" havens to evade U.S. federal income taxes.[61] In the Caspersen case and others like it, bad-apple media framing often describes the problem as an individual pathology, not a structural concern rooted in the larger economic, political, or social inequalities in society. From an individualized perspective, a few bad apples like Caspersen are responsible for all incidences of tax evasion and banking scandals; there is nothing wrong with the system.

The focus of bad-apple framing remains on the individual scoundrel even if that person's illegal activities are embedded in a larger organizational context, such as a megacorporation or the Wall Street banking industry. Consider the scandal in which the Securities and Exchange Commission (SEC) accused Goldman Sachs of securities fraud. One individual's name showed up most often in media coverage: that of Goldman Sachs vice president Fabrice Tourre. Little initial information disclosed the extent to which a number of Wall Street firms were operating in a corporate culture in which anything goes as long as you get rich but don't get caught. Tourre became infamous for helping to create and sell an investment vehicle called Abacus 2007-AC1, which was secretly intended to fail. The idea behind this scheme was as follows: After analyzing the high number of extremely risky home mortgages made in various states, Goldman Sachs officials and some of their clients wanted a financial vehicle for betting against those high-risk loans. The analysts and their clients predicted that many of the risky mortgages would fail and contribute to the collapse of the already overheated housing market, a situation that did indeed occur. Tourre was the fall guy for the scheme because he supposedly

> committed fraud by failing to disclose to investors that a hedge fund that helped choose the mortgage-backed securities going into a Goldman-structured investment was the same hedge fund betting against that deal. The hedge fund involved . . . ultimately reaped a $1 billion profit while the deal's investors lost more than $1 billion.[62]

This type of activity violated a number of laws pertaining to the finance industry.

Why do journalists often focus on one or a few individuals rather than the corporate culture of places such as Goldman Sachs or Enron when they hatch such schemes? Media audiences have an easier time focusing on stories about individuals, for instance, about the role that Fabrice Tourre (nicknamed "Fabulous Fab" by the media) played in that scandal. People not in the financial industry find it difficult to comprehend how such frauds are perpetrated because understanding requires advanced knowledge of accounting principles, the law, and business practices. By contrast, highlighting the alleged wrongdoings and sumptuous lifestyles of one or a few individuals makes it easier for laypersons to point a finger and place blame.

In 2010, the SEC settled its complaints with Goldman Sachs for $550 million. The company agreed to pay $300 million in fines and $250 million in restitution to settle federal claims that it had misled investors in a subprime mortgage product as the housing market began to collapse. Clearly, the settlement made only a small dent in the $13.38 billion in profits that Goldman earned in 2009. In the settlement, the company admitted to no wrongdoing in the Abacus 2007-AC1 scandal but agreed to a judicial order barring it from committing "intentional fraud" in the future under federal securities laws. Many people thought of this as a slap on the hand rather than actual punishment for the wrongs committed.

Prior to the Goldman Sachs complaint and other Wall Street crises, one of the most widely publicized scandals involved Enron Corporation, then the country's seventh-largest company. In the Enron case, the U.S. Department of Labor filed a civil lawsuit against CEO Kenneth Lay and a few other top executives in an effort to recover hundreds of millions of dollars in employees' lost retirement money. Criminal charges were also filed against Lay and CFO Andrew Fastow, who later pleaded guilty to two counts of wire and securities fraud and was sentenced to ten years in prison. According to one media report, "Enron hid billions of dollars in debts and operating losses inside private partnerships and dizzyingly complex accounting schemes that were intended to pump up buzz about the company and support its inflated stock price."[63] Apparently, Enron officials would not have been able to perpetrate their criminal acts had it not been for an accounting firm that looked the other way and for the government's failure to take action when it should have. As one journalist stated,

> It is a failure of government: having greased nearly every campaigner's palm in Washington, Enron worked overtime to keep the regulators from looking too closely at a balance sheet gone bad. And it is a failure of character, especially inside Enron, where managers who knew something was badly wrong did not say anything publicly until the subpoenas began to arrive.[64]

Despite this collective responsibility, worldwide media coverage of the Enron scandal and the corporation's subsequent collapse often employed bad-apple-with-mogul-style framing, regaling audiences with stories about Kenneth Lay's broad influence in business and politics as well as the lavish lifestyle he and other top Enron executives had enjoyed. One journalist described Enron's glory days in terms of its top employees' material possessions: "You could always tell it was bonus time at Enron when the shiny new silver Porches began arriving in the company garage. The $100,000 sports car was the status symbol of choice among the young Masters of the Universe who worked at the global trading company."[65] Even the death notices for Clifford Baxter (a former Enron executive who resigned before the scandal broke and committed suicide after challenging the corporation's secret partnership agreements) provided a laundry list of his mogul-style material possessions, including the Mercedes-Benz S500 sedan in which he died, the seventy-two-foot yacht, *Tranquility Base*, that he used for weekend relaxation, and his family's $700,000 residence in an exclusive Houston suburb.[66]

Media stories about Enron's collapse emphasized the "lavish excess" typical of corporate events as well as the luxury travel and expensive restaurants enjoyed by top executives. Even when the economic tide had shifted at the corporation, officials had set aside $1.5 million for a Christmas party at Enron Field (now Minute Maid Park) in Houston. As one news report stated, "Everything Enron did had to be better and flashier—from the new business ventures it unveiled nearly every year to the way it celebrated Secretaries' Day with gifts of Waterford crystal—and no gesture seemed too lavish, workers and competitors agree."[67]

Media reporting about the fall of former Tyco International CEO L. Dennis Kozlowski serves as another example of bad-apple-with-mogul-style media framing. Kozlowski was charged with enterprise corruption and grand larceny for allegedly stealing $600 million from Tyco. Journalists reported in elaborate detail on the $2 million weeklong party on the island of Sardinia that Kozlowski threw for his wife's fortieth birthday. According to court papers, Kozlowski also used Tyco money to pay $80,000 to American Express and $72,000 to a German yacht builder. For his residences, Tyco money bought a $15,000 umbrella stand, a $6,000 shower curtain, and a $2,900 set of coat hangers, in addition to two sets of sheets costing $5,960.[68] In discussing these expenditures, business journalists (who ordinarily do not describe accessories of interior design) learned that bad-apple-with-mogul-style framing is very popular with audiences. Consider this excerpt from a *Wall Street Journal* article titled "Newest 'Tyco Gone Wild' Video Is Out, and Jurors See $6,000 Shower Curtain":

> Now it can be told: The $6,000 shower curtain was in the maid's bathroom . . . in Mr. Kozlowski's opulent, $18 million apartment on Fifth Avenue in Manhattan. The dimly lit tape [shown during trial] showcased costly china, antiques, oil paintings, and four-poster beds. Prosecutors contend most of the duplex apartment's furnishings, including a $15,000 umbrella stand, were improperly bought with Tyco assets. But it was the famous shower curtain that everyone was waiting to see. When news of the costly fabric first surfaced last year, it became a symbol of corporate excess, the butt of jokes by late-night TV comedians.[69]

The shower curtain and umbrella stand were considered crucial evidence in the Kozlowski trial; however, journalists' and correspondents' story framing highlighted even more the excesses designed to impress other moguls, sometimes at the expense of lower-level employees and shareholders.

Media reports of the alleged crimes of real-life individuals like Kozlowski and Lay occasionally parallel TV crime-drama story lines in a way that reveals for viewers the elegant lifestyles of rich bad apples. The technique also typically suggests that the rich and powerful consider themselves to be above the law or, at the least, feel they should not be bothered by police officers or courts.

BAD APPLES IN TELEVISION CRIME DRAMAS: "WE'RE ABOVE THE LAW"

Bad-apple framing of various forms in media stories about real-life rich men and women in legal trouble are often stranger than fiction. Crime dramas, on the other hand, frequently use fictitious characters to reflect the bad-apple behavior of wealthy people who are victims of homicides or suspects in criminal cases. For example, wealthy people seldom come out looking noble in the syndicated crime series *Law & Order*, which, over many TV seasons and in various spin-offs, has explored numerous crimes involving wealthy and influential individuals. In at least one episode each season, detectives go to the residence of a rich family to investigate a homicide that has been committed. They routinely make unfavorable comments about the person's wealth or affluent residence as they leave the bloodstained premises, such as "Well, I guess the maid forgot to clean up before she left." *Law & Order* story lines involving the wealthy often portray them as above the law, too busy and important to help the detectives, or unconcerned about whether justice is done. In some episodes, the rich and famous make phone calls to higher-ups in the city's administration or the judicial system, resulting in warnings to detectives or prosecutors to be careful in their investigation or prosecution ("you'd better be right, or there'll be hell to pay").

Three examples show how *Law & Order* frames stories about wealthy characters. One episode, "Family Business," focuses on the police investigation of the murder of the president of New York's most popular (and expensive) department store. Detectives are led to the feuding daughters of the store's elderly owner as possible suspects; however, the store owner seeks to outsmart the district attorney.[70] In another episode, "Entitled," the police investigate the "wayward socialite daughter of a wealthy, politically connected—and threatening—grande dame" as a possible suspect in a murder. A third episode, "For Love or Money," tells the story of detectives who investigate the murder of a rich man and come to believe that the victim's widow might have hired a hit man to kill him.

In yet another episode, "Darwinian," the detectives investigate a case in which a homeless, mentally ill person has apparently been killed in a hit-and-run accident. Subsequent investigation reveals that the victim "was trapped inside the car's windshield after the accident and that the driver—a high profile publicist—left the man dying in her garage" before disposing of the body.[71] "Darwinian" uses what *Law & Order* refers to as a "ripped-from-the-headlines" plot that combines two real criminal cases, one in which a woman (of more modest means than in the TV show) left a man to die on her windshield after hitting him with her car and a second involving a well-known society publicist convicted on a felony charge of leaving the scene of an accident after she backed her Mercedes SUV into a group of people going to a night club. This episode is characteristic of the bad-apple messages that *Law & Order* and other crime dramas send to viewers.[72]

When Bernard ("Bernie") Madoff was accused of perpetrating a $65 billion fraud in a Ponzi scheme, set up through Bernard L. Madoff Investment Securities, that cost many investors their life savings, a *Law & Order* episode combined elements of his crimes with the murder of a television reporter:

> While investigating the murder of television reporter Dawn Prescott, detectives Lupo and Bernard discover that she was involved in a love triangle involving

another reporter at the station. This leads them to another suspect, veteran an-chor Joe Delaney, who was threatened by the success of his younger co-workers and may have hacked into their email to gain an advantage. As they search for the killer, the detectives uncover that Dawn was working on a major story sur-rounding a huge hedge fund fraud and there may be a connection with the recent murder of Fred Decker, a whistle-blower who filed an SEC suit against hedge fund owner Fredric Matson and his wife Irene.[73]

Ironically, the true story of Madoff's life is as bizarre as this Hollywood ver-sion. Some media accounts suggest that Madoff has $9 billion stashed away, even though he is serving a 150-year prison sentence. Other articles indicate that Madoff's wealth and notoriety have earned him a privileged place in the prison hierarchy.[74]

After the cancellation of the original *Law & Order* franchise, NBC shifted the venue for this program to Los Angeles, where subsequent episodes, such as "Bling Ring Burglars," portrayed teenagers accused of targeting the residences of wealthy actors like Paris Hilton and Orlando Bloom. Similarly, scenes in the "Pasadena" episode showed posh residences and tree-lined streets in an affluent suburb where the hit-and-run of a pregnant woman was linked to a political scandal inspired by John Edwards's affair.

Whether in true stories about people's lives or in story lines produced by television scriptwriters, framing about the downfall of affluent people has key commonalities. One is that the rich and famous live more glamorous and exciting lives than ordinary people. Even when they are in trouble with the law, their money and position in the community make them likely to avoid the harshest penalties the system might impose. In sum, their wealth provides them with a cushion that others simply do not have.

GILDED CAGES:
EFFECTS OF SOUR-GRAPES AND BAD-APPLE FRAMING

Media framing of stories about the rich and famous influences our thinking about how people in the top economic tiers of society live. It also plays a role in whether audiences see issues of inequality in terms of individual cir-cumstances or larger structural conditions embedded in the social institutions of our nation. In contrast with the framing approaches discussed in chapter 2 (those that suggest the rich are like everyone else, deserve admiration for their achievements, or should be applauded for their virtues and good deeds), sour-grapes and bad-apple framing send divergent messages about wealth and how the rich conduct their lives.

Sour-grapes framing portrays the rich as often unhappy and dysfunctional people. The notion of the poor little rich girl may lead audiences to see the problems of the wealthy as self-inflicted and stemming from individual character flaws. Cautionary tales about inherited wealth or the problems of the nouveau riche suggest that wealth will cause a great deal of pain. At the same time, sour-grapes framing also provides the contradictory message that wealth generates a great deal of pleasure. In entertainment television as well, story lines about corruption and insecurity convey messages similar to the real-world stories of individuals whose riches have not brought them happiness or success to the extent that they would have liked.

As media coverage of the activities of the rich and famous creates the illusion over time that we know these individuals, the frames utilized to tell stories about them may distort our perception of reality. Bad-apple framing frequently includes elaborate discussions of what life is like in the rarified world of luxury estates, yachts, private jets, and $1 million office Christmas parties, perhaps subordinating the message about the evildoing of some of these individuals to descriptions of the good life. The sagas of corporate wrongdoing are often told as stories about individuals, making it appear as though purging one or a few bad apples would fix all problems, and business as usual could resume unimpeded. Only when news of a number of business scandals breaks at once, such as during the first decade of the twenty-first century, does a pattern of financial misconduct and corporate malfeasance actually receive attention in media accounts about the wrongdoings of wealthy business elites.

The milder forms of bad-apple framing merely portray the rich as seeking publicity (media hogs) or acting as if money can buy anything (or anyone). The stronger forms of such framing, however—employed, for instance, when wealthy individuals are accused of crimes—still emphasize the importance of material possessions and characterize the culprit as having either good taste in merchandise (as in the case of women shoplifters) or mogul style (as in the case of CEOs trying to impress other moguls and provide their families with the best of luxury living).

A number of television crime series portray the bad attitudes of the rich as revealed in their conduct toward law enforcement officials and the court system. Although I have focused only on NBC's *Law & Order*, other shows carry similar messages about the elegant lifestyles and arrogance of the rich and famous. Even as some readers and viewers experience schadenfreude, they may also feel a desire to trade up, to own things they really cannot afford, and blame themselves for their failure to reach the American Dream of success and wealth.

When the wealthy commit crimes, we may believe that they should be punished, but we are not surprised to learn of their differential treatment by the criminal justice system or about what their money can buy them in the process. Journalists make media audiences aware of the favorable treatment that some wealthy criminals receive. An article titled "For the Elite, Easing the Way to Prison," for example, describes how A. Alfred Taubman, the (then) seventy-eight-year-old principal owner and former chairman of Sotheby's, received a year-and-a-day sentence and a $7.5 million fine for leading a six-year price-fixing scheme (the same one that brought house arrest for Diana D. Brooks). It explained how high-paid lawyers representing such people attempt to get their clients into the best prisons with the lightest possible sentences if it appears that jail time is inevitable:

> "In these cases, the defense attorney will act almost like an agent in Hollywood, negotiating the perp's rights, wheeling and dealing to get her into the best spot," [security consultant and investigator Bill Stanton] said. "He can say, 'This prison has tennis, this one has nicer rooms.'"
>
> Defense lawyers have some influence over where their clients serve time, legal experts say. . . . And in the last decade, dozens of specialists have begun marketing their services to experts in sentence mitigation. These are the lawyers, criminologists, or former corrections officials known as "postconviction specialists," who—for fees that can reach into tens of thousands of dollars— navigate and cajole the prison and judicial systems, bargaining for the chance at a light, sweet sentence. They are a grim reality in the lives of the criminally convicted elite: counselors as valued in their way as the SAT prep teachers, personal shoppers and chefs who also serve the well-to-do.[75]

Media framing of the treatment of elite criminals typically focuses on hierarchies in the prison system. Madoff was sentenced to Butner Medium I, which the media pointed out is referred to as "Camp Fluffy" because it is filled with "soft" prisoners who might not survive in other institutions:

> The facility had been planned during a brief period of penal optimism and was designed to humanize the prison experience. The physical space resembles a campus, with landscaped yards and hedges shaped by inmates into giant globes. There's flowers and trees; you can lay out on the grass and tan. . . . There's no bars. There are windows. There's a gym, a library, pool tables, a chapel, a volleyball court, and an Indian sweat lodge. But however soft, prison is a hardship.[76]

Media reports also inform audiences that the rich often receive a "soft landing" on leaving prison. For example, elite felons like Diana D. Brooks and A. Alfred Taubman used their wealth to ease their reentry into society. One journalist contrasted the reentry of an "ordinary criminal" with that of Taubman after he had served nine and a half months of his sentence and was released:

Raymond Carter's release from prison followed a familiarly bleak script. After two years at the Wyoming Correctional Facility in upstate New York for sale of a controlled substance, he was granted his freedom on June 23, and given back his personal belongings—a Social Security card and some medication—then handed 40 bucks and a one-way bus ticket to the Port Authority Bus Terminal in Manhattan. He had a little time, so he savored a quiet meal at McDonald's. . . .

A. Alfred Taubman's reintroduction to society went down a little differently. . . . Mr. Taubman . . . learned on June 13 at a halfway house in Detroit that he was a free man. Mr. Taubman's first move was to order his chauffeur to pick him up posthaste. After a quiet night at home in nearby Bloomfield Hills, Mich., with his wife, Judy, amid their collection of Jackson Pollocks and Kandinskys, Mr. Taubman boarded his Gulfsteam IV and headed straight to his sprawling ocean-front estate in the Hamptons. By evening, he was savoring a meal at Mirko's . . . at the best table in the house.[77]

In 2010, Taubman has a net worth of $1.5 billion. He owns twenty-five malls in sixteen states and possesses a vast, world-class contemporary art collection. He shows up each year in *Fortune* and *Forbes* on lists of the wealthiest individuals in the United States. From media reports like this, we learn that even when the wealthy reside in "gilded cages" and experience problems, their lives still have silver linings compared to those of people living in poverty or in the working and middle classes. Moreover, wealthy and powerful individuals may be excused for their conduct even beyond their death. After Enron founder Kenneth Lay, who was convicted of ten counts of fraud, conspiracy, and lying to banks in two separate cases, died of heart disease while vacationing with his wife in Colorado, a federal judge ruled that Lay's death vacated his conviction on fraud and conspiracy charges connected to the downfall of Enron. Consequently, Lay's criminal record is now clean, and the government has had difficulty collecting the $43.5 million it sought from his estate.[78]

While cable channels in the second decade of the twenty-first century still glorify the rich and famous—even the downfallen—network television has reduced the number of programs shown about extremely wealthy people. Many reality shows, however, offer ordinary people a chance to compete for $1 million or more in prize money using their talent, knowledge, or other attributes. Television news media and social-networking sites are full of gossip about wealthy celebrities who go astray, including Lindsay Lohan and Britney Spears. According to a *Wall Street Journal* article titled "Rich People on TV Aren't Really Rich," however,

The real economy may still be in crisis, but the TV economy has never been richer.

We have an entire nation of bling-flashing "Housewives," a seemingly endless spending parade of Kardashians and Joan Rivers asking the Rolls-Royce-owning creator of Wee Wee Pads, "How'd You Get So Rich?"

It goes without saying that most of the wealth on TV isn't real wealth. . . . Most of these characters aren't rich, they just play [rich people] on reality TV— usually in hopes of getting rich. . . .

The problem is that these shows give us all a false impression of wealth. Economic and psychological research has shown time and again that wealth is a relative concept, based on a reference group of our peers. . . . But in our media-saturated age, our "peers" are increasingly the rich people we see on TV. . . . Rich reality-TV, in other words, distorts our own reality of wealth.[79]

And therein lies the central problem discussed in this and the previous chapter: media distortion of reality about the wealthy. Positive media frames and their messages, including the consensus, admiration, emulation, and price-tag frames, create distortions in our thinking about how the rich and powerful live. Negative framing devices used to portray the upper class, such as the sour-grapes and bad-apple frames, may end up glorifying the rich, or at least giving the impression that the upper classes are somehow better than everyone else and, even in their weakest moments, above the law.

Chapter 4

Fragile Frames

The Poor and the Homeless

New York, January 30, 1870:

Down in the squalid environs of —— street this woman lives, whose story we shall tell, having been sought out in the crusade of a *Times* reporter among the haunts of a starving and in the main, ill-used class. Through a foul alley, reeking with noisome odors, lay the approach to a den of a room—odorous of pestilence, one might suppose, intuitively desiring to keep one's mouth shut while waiting. . . . The dingiest of dingy old women threw out a tub of suds as we approached, then conveyed us to the room. A young child was there, begrimed and sooty. These and the mother of the latter were the occupants, and it is of this mother that we shall principally speak. Young she was, and pretty but for the pinched and perished look one sees so often, it is grievous to say, among this class of laborers. . . .

[The mother] was out of work now. Her last situation had paid her $5 per week.

"And you lost it—how?" we asked.

"I will tell you," was the reply. "I was to have reached the place by 7 o'clock in the morning. I told them I would; but as it happened, one or two mornings there was no one to be with my little child, and I was behind time; it might have been forty minutes, at most, but hardly more than half an hour, I think. . . . Next day I was discharged, and here I am—nothing to help myself with, only because I wanted to do a mother's part by my little one. I have sometimes heard of mothers drowning themselves and their children in straits like mine. I couldn't do that, but I oftentimes think could that be much worse than to live as we live?"[1]

The reporter of this early article about poverty in New York City frames the story to show that the poor are to be pitied, particularly if they are willing to work. More than 130 years later, journalists still employ a sympathetic frame in some articles about the poor and homeless, but most articles and stories about those on the bottom rungs of society either treat them as mere statistics or have a critical edge, portraying them as losers, welfare dependents, mentally ill people, or criminals. This approach differs quite a bit from that taken by articles and story lines about the rich and famous. As previous chapters discuss, frames presenting the upper class typically encourage us to believe that what is good for the wealthy and famous is good for everyone else (consensus framing) or that we should admire or emulate them, even if there are a few bad apples in the barrel.

Articles and stories about the upper classes appear frequently in newspapers and on television, but the poor are invisible, except when presented as faceless statistics or as "problems" to be dealt with in a community. This chapter shows how the media have generally ignored the poor, and when they do appear in what we read and watch, they are often portrayed in a negative light that ignores larger community and societal conditions that may have contributed to or exacerbated their condition.

MEDIA FRAMING OF STORIES
ABOUT THE POOR AND HOMELESS

The relative invisibility of the poor in media reporting has been referred to as a case of "benign neglect"[2] that hides the realities of poverty from middle- and upper-class readers and viewers. This neglect may be intentional because media audiences do not want to have the poor in their faces:

> Fear of poverty rests at the very core of the American culture—the "American dream" is precisely the hope of rising from rags to riches. . . . The media offer those who are not poor, especially Whites, little guidance in reconciling the conflicting emotions toward poverty embedded within American culture, with its simultaneously sympathetic and impatient assumption that America offers the promise of escape from poverty to all who work hard.[3]

By providing only a few stories about the poor, journalists do not have to deal often with middle- and upper-class fears about poverty or with the conflicting emotions potentially generated by a greater awareness of poverty, hunger, and homelessness in a nation referred to as the land of opportunity.

How are the words "poor" and "poverty" employed in the media? There is no standard usage. Some journalists use them loosely to refer to people on the bottom rungs of the nation's economic ladder, whereas others use them to specify those living near the official poverty line created by the Social Security Administration to indicate the minimum amount of money required to live at a subsistence level in any particular year. The poverty line is computed by determining the cost of a minimally nutritious diet (a low-cost food budget on which a family could survive nutritionally on a short-term, emergency basis) and multiplying this figure by three to allow for nonfood costs. Based on this method of calculation, about 39.8 million people (more than 13.2 percent of the U.S. population) lived below the official government poverty level of $22,025 for a family of four in 2008. The poverty line increased only slightly, to $22,128, in 2009.

According to critics, however, measuring poverty in terms of cash income and household size does not take into account the increased cost of other basic necessities, such as housing, health care, and child care.[4] When the formula for the official poverty line was created, low-income families spent about one-third of their earnings on food; food today constitutes about one-fifth of low-income budgets, and housing costs have sharply increased. The poverty line also employs a one-size-fits-all logic, operating on the assumption that the same standards for poverty can be applied in New York City as in rural southern communities.[5]

The formulation of news stories based on statistics and trends is often referred to as thematic framing, which in this case means that journalists primarily write about such facts as changes in the poverty rate, government definitions of poverty, and the states with the largest increases in poverty or hunger.[6] In these stories, the object of the coverage is abstract and impersonal,[7] sending a message to media audiences that "the poor are faceless."[8] According to some analysts, thematic framing of poverty is dehumanizing in that it "ignores the human tragedy of poverty—the suffering, indignities, and misery endured by millions of children and adults."[9]

By contrast, episodic framing reveals poverty "in terms of personal experience: the viewer is provided with a particular [episode] of an individual or family living under economic duress."[10] This type of framing gives poverty a human face but often ignores the larger structural factors (such as high unemployment rates) that affect the problem or portrays the poor negatively based on the actions of the few individuals featured in the article. For example, episodic framing of some stories may suggest that most of the poor are undeserving because they are welfare cheats, drug addicts, or greedy panhandlers.[11] It may therefore cause audiences to conclude that the poor have only themselves to blame because of their bad attitudes and behavior.[12] As communications scholars Robert M. Entman and Andrew Rojecki state, media audiences may infer that "inexplicably, some people choose to live in deteriorating neighborhoods where they frequently commit or become victims of crime, or have trouble receiving health care and finding adequate schools."[13]

Such framing also suggests that the poor are an eyesore on the landscape of daily life.[14] Stories about panhandlers disturbing people on city streets or about individuals standing in line outside homeless shelters portray the poor as contributors to urban blight, particularly as viewed by middle-class observers interviewed because of concern about the placement of a homeless shelter or after being accosted on the street by a panhandler. Typically, the voices heard in this type of reporting belong not to the poor but to the middle class expressing disdain for them.[15]

Perhaps the most benevolent message that episodic framing conveys about poverty is that the poor are down on their luck.[16] This type of framing is especially popular in news stories published near holidays like Thanksgiving or Christmas, asking readers to help meet some of the needs of the poor temporarily. Most newspaper coverage of the poor over the past 150 years, however, has seemed more intent on selling newspapers to middle- and upper-class readers than assisting the impoverished.

HISTORICAL FRAMING:
THE POOR YOU WILL HAVE WITH YOU ALWAYS

Framing of early newspaper articles about the poor used vivid terminology to portray their plight, including descriptions such as "squalid environs," a "foul alley reeking with noisome odors," and "begrimed and sooty."[17] Today, the language of newspaper reporting has changed somewhat, but the format for describing the poor has not been modified significantly. It still fails to examine the larger structural issues that perpetuate poverty, such as growing rates of economic inequality, a decline in the number of available jobs, continuing racial and gender discrimination, and other social and technological changes that reduce opportunity.

A systematic examination of the *New York Times* archives between September 1851 and December 1995 reveals 4,126 articles with the word "poverty" in the headline. Many of the early articles linked poverty to other social problems, such as suicide and murder. "Distressing Case of Poverty and Suicide," for example, describes the suicide of John Murphy, a forty-five-year-old Irish immigrant tailor and father of five who had lost his job. According to the article, Murphy's unemployment produced mental illness and ultimately led to his taking his own life: "Finding his family in a starving condition, it affected him so at times he was out of his mind."[18] In the end, "the deceased . . . came to his death by cutting his throat with a razor, while laboring under a temporary derangement of mind, consequent upon his destitute condition."[19] This article is typical of a number of nineteenth-century articles that blamed the suicides of indigent people on derangement resulting from their destitute condition. Other examples include "Melancholy Case of Suicide: Pride and

Poverty the Cause"[20] and "A Sad Case of Poverty: A Woman Commits Suicide, Her Husband at the Point of Death,"[21] both of which tell of residents in tenement houses who took their own lives when they could no longer stand their impoverished condition. People who had once been more affluent and ended up in poverty were believed to be prime candidates for suicide. "A Sad Life Story: Reduced from Wealth to Poverty and Dying Almost without Friends"[22] describes the death of a "remarkable septuagenarian lady, Mary Jane Marquis," who ended her own life after being reduced to penury.

The framing of nineteenth-century articles about the relationship between poverty and suicide was in keeping with the common sociological thought of the day, as found in the works of French sociologist Emile Durkheim. According to Durkheim, fatalistic suicide is likely to occur among "persons with futures pitilessly blocked and passions violently choked by oppressive discipline."[23] Many reports in the *New York Times* told of people overcome by such fatalism, including poor women with children to feed, recent immigrants who were lonely and had no home, merchants whose businesses had failed, and the elderly.[24]

Just as suicide and poverty were often linked in early media reports, so too were crime and poverty. "Down among the Lowly: The Sights That One Sees in the Fourth Ward" describes the "intense, and perhaps undeserved suffering" in New York City's Fourth Ward, where "coarse-looking men and slovenly women stand listlessly in the doorways of the huge tenement houses, or gaze stupidly out of the windows."[25] The reporter focused his article on the relationship between poverty and crime:

> The reputation of the Fourth Ward for crimes of every nature has created a general distrust toward all of its inhabitants, which has prevented or neutralized many efforts for their improvement. Dismal tales of foul outrage and drunken brutality, combined with the loathsome appearance of the place, have given to it a far worse name than it deserves, for Police records will show that though there are none that can equal it in misery, there are several wards in this City that surpass it in criminality. Indeed, almost all of the crimes committed there can be traced directly or indirectly to the common curse of poverty, which has blighted the hopes and aspirations of its inhabitants.[26]

Of all poverty-and-crime stories, journalists took the most interest in cases in which parents killed their children. For instance, "Terrible Tragedy: An Insane Mother Kills Her Daughter"[27] describes how the Elliott family's poverty brought about the insanity of the mother, who murdered her seventeen-year-old daughter. Like most of the poor in news stories of that day, the Elliott family lived in a tenement house; the father had been unemployed for some time, reducing the family to almost abject poverty. Worse yet, according to the journalist, Mr. Elliott had become "addicted to the use of intoxicating liquor, and for the last three weeks he had been on a continual spree." When he left the house one day, Mrs. Elliott strangled their daughter, laid her body out on the bed, and calmly informed her husband when he returned home that the girl was dead.[28] Headlines for articles about parents in poverty who killed their children frequently summarized the entire story, as in this example: "A Father's Awful Crime: Shooting His Three Little Girls. Why John Remmler, of Holyoke, Killed His Children—Poverty and a Fear for Their Future His Reasons."[29]

Linkages between poverty, region, and race were quite evident in the framing of stories about the poor in the South. Northeastern newspapers like the *New York Times* periodically published articles informing urban dwellers how bad off the poor were in the South, particularly in the former slave states,[30] and many contemporary stereotypes of "poor," "black" African Americans can also be found in nineteenth-century news reporting.

From the 1850s to the present, many stories about the poor have been embedded in articles about the charitableness of the wealthy. An 1870 *New York Times* article, "Poverty and Charity," states that acts of public and private charity, particularly by the wealthy will take care of "all God's poor":

> In no other country of the world is public charity dispensed more lavishly or with so tender a regard to the feelings of those whom vice or misfortune [has] compelled to solicit our bounty. . . . And [the poor] do move us, as a community, to deeds of disinterested endeavor and practical succor that should put all other countries under heaven to the blush. In this way, better than any other, is the humanizing influence of our republican form of government made apparent. Here the brotherhood of man is fully recognized. . . . Our rich men may be self-seeking, and even avaricious—they may be worldly and even irreligious—but they are not uncharitable. They pity poverty and are always ready and willing to relieve it.[31]

This article is framed more to praise the generosity of the rich than to explore the condition of the poor. Similarly, "Feeding the City's Poor: Giving Bountiful Dinners to Children and Poverty-Stricken People" tells how the "city's poor, its prisoners, and its other charges had their share yesterday of the good things that are distributed on Thanksgiving" when about "11,000 mouths" were fed at "the various hospitals, prisons, and asylums."[32]

Journalists in the 1800s also reported on the problem of the homeless; the framing of these articles focused on the destitute situation of homeless children. One article, "Walks among the New York Poor: Homeless Children," for example, describes children whose most frequent statement is that they "don't live nowheres!"[33] Another article, "Homeless Children," emphasizes how difficult it is at Christmastime for the more affluent to walk by and see "the number of wretched little children in our streets who have no homes to go to, nor any parents or guardians to provide them."[34] Reporters also praised charitable groups that provided residences for homeless children. "Lodging-House for Homeless Girls a New Project of the Children's Aid Society" describes the Girl's Lodging-House as "a place which is intended to invite to a decent bed and satisfactory meal, she of the unsuccessful search after a situation, or the little pilgrim through the busy streets, attracting purchasers for her basket variety of temptingly arranged wares."[35] Similarly, the News Boy's Lodging-House, a residence for homeless boys and young men, was opened "in view of the terrible destitution and homelessness of the poor this Winter."[36]

CONTEMPORARY FRAMING OF
STORIES ABOUT THE POOR AND HOMELESS

The media serve as important sources of information about the extent and distribution of hardship in the contemporary United States.[37] Some media reports provide causal analysis that demonstrates how political leaders and governmental agencies contribute to, or seek to reduce, poverty, hunger, or homelessness. Other news items focus on the lives of the poor, sometimes portraying them as partly responsible for their plight due to certain actions (such as dropping out of school or taking illegal drugs) or their failure to act (for instance, by not looking for a job or being unwilling to utilize the services of a homeless shelter).

When news stories frame poverty as primarily an individual problem, they assign responsibility to those who are poor. This individualistic perspective makes it possible to blame them both for their own situations and for numerous other community problems. Suggestions that homeless people create disorder on the streets, are bad for business because they discourage shoppers, and are a drain on taxpayers because of the added expense of maintaining law and order are only a few of the ways homeless people might be blamed for other social issues. By contrast, when journalists frame stories in a manner that portrays poverty as a general outcome—meaning they take a systemic perspective that places responsibility on communities and the nation—they characterize poverty, hunger, and homelessness using a structural approach that focuses on such factors as how local and national economic and housing conditions produce homelessness.[38]

As mentioned previously, news reports and articles about poverty and homelessness in the United States use two general categories of framing

devices: thematic framing, which places events in broad context and provides details about trends; and episodic framing, which puts a human face on
poverty by telling true stories about people who are poor and homeless. Episodic framing of poverty has four major subcategories: sympathetic framing,
negative-image framing, exceptionalism framing, and charitable framing.
Before turning to these forms of episodic framing, let us examine thematic
framing in greater detail.

THEMATIC FRAMING:
THE POOR AS STATISTICS, NOT REAL PEOPLE

In a newspaper headline or the title of a television news segment about
poverty or homelessness, words relating to numbers or rates can indicate thematic framing in the accompanying story. For example, the headlines "Last
Year's Poverty Rate Was Highest in 12 Years"[39] and "Nation's Economic
Collapse Triggers Rise in Homeless Families"[40] refer to numbers, in this case
the number of homeless families, or rates, the percentage of poor individuals, families, or households according to some standard, usually the official
poverty line established by the federal government. The newspaper account
of the rise in the poverty rate is an example of a thematically framed article
that views the poor primarily as statistics rather than real people:

> In the recession, the nation's poverty rate climbed to 13.2 percent last year, up
> from 12.5 percent in 2007, according to an annual report released Thursday by
> the Census Bureau. The report also documented a decline in employer-provided
> health insurance and in coverage for adults. The rise in the poverty rate, to the
> highest level since 1997, portends even larger increases this year, which has
> registered far higher unemployment than in 2008, economists said. The bureau
> said that 39.8 million residents last year lived below the poverty line, defined as
> an income of $22,025 for a family of four.[41]

On television, a story like this may be accompanied by video footage of a
poor Latino or African American man shuffling despondently down a city
street. Newscasters typically report this information in a detached manner,
as if there is much more important news to cover—such as war, crime, missing children, and current market trends.[42] Stories about poverty have similar
formats on television and in the newspapers, and they offer virtually identical
information, frequently prepackaged by the Associated Press or other news
organizations that provide news, photographs, and audio and video feeds to
thousands of newspapers and radio and television outlets throughout in the
United States.

Thematic framing is not only used to position stories about poverty; it is frequently used to describe a rise or fall in the number of homeless families in a given period. An example is the following:

> Record job losses and foreclosures helped push more than 170,000 families into homeless shelters in 2009, up 30 percent since 2007 when the recession first gripped the nation, a government report released Wednesday shows. While the total number of homeless people on any given night fell by 5 percent from 2008 to 2009, the number of homeless families increased for the second straight year, according to the 2009 Annual Homeless Assessment Report to Congress prepared by the U.S. Department of Housing and Urban Development. "Throughout the course of a year, approximately 1.56 million people found themselves without a place to call home," said Mercedes Marquez, HUD assistant secretary for community planning and development. The report is the first comprehensive national homeless study to capture the full impact of the economic downturn. It shows how badly the recession has shaken the stability of families nationwide.[43]

The format of this article is typical in that it begins with data from a U.S. Department of Housing and Urban Development (HUD) report, then provides a quote from a spokesperson commenting on that data, which is often followed by statements from experts who hold differing views as to what the figures actually mean. Later in the article cited above, Nan Roman, president of the National Alliance to End Homelessness, points out that statistics about how many people are homeless are misleading because some families without permanent residences move in with other people ("double up"). Eventually, however, many of these doubled-up families become homeless. As some media sources point out, it is difficult to determine how many people actually are homeless in the United States because estimates, such as the one used in the HUD report, are based on a national "snapshot" count of the homeless on a single night along with full-year statistics from shelters across the country.

When journalists report on statistical data issued by government agencies, their articles sometimes reveal political controversies about how the data are gathered, computed, and interpreted. Discussions regarding these data are often contentious topics for politicians, and journalists quickly pick up on these issues as newsworthy. Many of the topics remain in the news year after year, as an examination of the *New York Times* archives shows.

Two recurring issues raised in thematic framing about poverty entail who the poor are and how many people in the United States should be considered poor. The dividing line for identifying them is a contested terrain because many analysts believe that the government's definition of poverty is out-of-date. Headlines in the 1990s reflected articles about these statistics: "In Rising Debate on Poverty, the Question: Who Is Poor?"[44]; "Poverty Rate Is the

Highest in 16 Years, a Report Says"[45]; and "A Proposed Definition of Poverty
May Raise Number of U.S. Poor."[46] These issues remain unresolved in the
2000s, and headlines continue to identify the same issues and to ask similar
questions: "One Number Can't Measure Poverty"[47] and "Who's Poor? Don't
Ask the Census Bureau."[48] Here is one article's description of the problem in
determining the poverty line:

> As soon as the government announced the second straight yearly increase in
> the nation's poverty rate, politicians and special-interest groups began toss-
> ing around the numbers like the political football the poor have become. But
> researchers say the government is not very good at keeping score. There is a
> near-unanimous agreement among experts and politicians that the method used
> to measure poverty—based on the spending habits of the 1950s—is flawed and
> outdated. The current measure of poverty, which takes into account household
> size and income, underestimates the number of poor by as much as 50 percent,
> some experts contend.[49]

Why is the government unable to update its method of identifying the poor?
According to some media reports, changing the current method would have
unpopular political ramifications. Counting the poor more accurately would
add millions of people to the eligibility rolls of antipoverty programs, dramatically increasing the national debt and further sinking states into budget
deficits. Consider this news report, for example:

> Who is poor in America? This is a hard question to answer, and the Obama
> administration would make it harder. It's hard because there's no conclusive
> definition of poverty. Low income matters, though how low is unclear. Poverty
> is also a mindset that fosters self-defeating behavior—bad work habits, family
> breakdowns, out-of-wedlock births, and addictions. Finally, poverty results
> from lousy luck: accidents, job losses, disability. . . .
>   The existing poverty line could be improved by adding some income sources
> and subtracting some expenses (example: child care). Unfortunately, the admin-
> istration's proposal for a "supplemental poverty measure" in 2011—to comple-
> ment, not replace, the existing poverty line—goes beyond that. The new pov-
> erty number would compound public confusion. It also raises questions about
> whether the statistic is tailored to favor a political agenda. . . . It's legitimate
> to debate how much we should aid the poor or try to reduce economic inequal-
> ity. But the debate should not be skewed by misleading statistics that not one
> American in 100,000 could possibly understand. Government statistics should
> strive for political neutrality. This one fails.[50]

This article refers to an effort to create a new way of measuring poverty.
Media reports point out that the plan generated extensive controversy even
before it could be finalized. The new Supplemental Poverty Measure takes

near-cash benefits and taxes into account to supplement conventional poverty measures. It links poverty thresholds to more accurate measures of people's expenditures not only on food but on shelter, clothing, and utilities. It takes into account work-related expenses, such as child-care spending for employed parents. Although some media reports and blogs suggest that these changes will eventually produce more accurate data on poverty, others stress that we are "defining poverty up," which will ultimately create more "poor" in the United States.

As debates continue in the political arena and in newspapers and television reports about how to define poverty and which statistics are most accurate, larger societal issues about the causes of poverty and homelessness and what to do about them are largely ignored. Because controversy sells more newspapers and draws larger TV and website audiences, the media are likely to focus on those issues that bring in revenue.

Like news reports about poverty, stories about hunger frequently use thematic framing. The headline "Hungry Families in U.S. on the Rise"[51] is typical of articles about the growing problem of American families that cannot afford to buy adequate food. Hunger is most often the subject of news stories shortly before holidays like Thanksgiving and Christmas and at times when new statistical data on the problem have been released. On the basis of data from the U.S. Department of Agriculture (USDA) and the Census Bureau, media reports have described an increase in the number of hungry people in the United States, indicating that about 36.2 million Americans, including 12.4 million children, live in households that experience hunger or the risk of it each year. Thematic framing of stories about the USDA's categories of hunger, such as "food insecure" and "food insecure, with hunger," convey to audiences the message that the messy topic of hunger (among the poor) is not the problem of middle- and upper-income readers and viewers. Articles like "Of Fuzzy Math and 'Food Security'"[52] describe the extent to which tabulating hunger "is an inexact science and a political test" rather than a cause for concern about the number of people in this country who are hungry on a specified date.

Media reporting about hunger often increases following the release of data about changes in the number of hungry people in this country. After the U.S. Conference of Mayors (an organization that includes the mayors of 1,204 cities with populations of thirty thousand or more) reported a 26 percent increase in the demand for emergency food and a slight decrease in the number of individuals who were homeless, news sources highlighted the fact that individual homelessness had decreased but deemphasized a sharp increase in the need for food assistance in many cities. Such framing tends to diminish the human face of hunger and reduce the impact of the sharp increase in the need for hunger assistance between October 2008 and September 2009, the latest period for which data are available at the time of this writing.[53]

Thematic framing that focuses on statistics and emphasizes increases or decreases in hunger may deflect people's attention from more pressing issues about the causes and consequences of hunger, particularly for children. "Are some groups exaggerating the numbers of people who are hungry?" is a far different question from "What can be done about the problem of hunger?" Articles about the numbers debate make hunger seem like a numbers game and of little consequence. Consider, for example, one journalist's allegation about the likelihood of service providers, such as soup kitchen operators and food bank administrators, exaggerating in order to sustain contributions to their organizations:

> So what's the real story? Social ills like hunger and need for food assistance are notoriously difficult to measure. In a flagging economy, or even in boom times, those on the front lines—soup kitchen operators and food bank adminis-trators, who must rely on donations and government subsidies—are always in the shadow of a shortfall. So it is not surprising that the mayors' survey, which relies primarily on the collected impressions (and varied record keeping) of these agencies, would consistently report an increase in demand.[54]

The visual images that accompany articles and television news accounts about hunger typically show political leaders like the president helping out at a Washington, DC, food bank or the mayor of a major city serving lunch at a homeless shelter on Thanksgiving Day. This imbues the seemingly dry sta-tistics related to poverty and hunger with empathy and erects a humanitarian façade. Important officials are portrayed as caring individuals who feed the hungry rather than vote-seeking politicians who show up for the occasional photo op with the less fortunate.

Stories about homelessness, like those about poverty and hunger, often describe how counting the homeless is problematic. Since statistics on homelessness are not available from the Census Bureau, news organizations rely on data gathered by the U.S. Conference of Mayors and the National Coalition for the Homeless. According to the latter, there is no easy answer to the question of how many people in the United States are homeless: "In most cases, homelessness is a temporary circumstance—not a permanent condition. A more appropriate measure of the magnitude of homelessness is therefore the number of people who experience homelessness over time, not the number of 'homeless people.'"[55] According to some media reports, the homeless are seriously undercounted because most studies count only those who are on the street or living in shelters on a specific date. As previously mentioned, many homeless people stay with relatives and friends in crowded, temporary arrangements and are not counted if they are not visibly homeless when the data are gathered.[56]

Over the past two decades, media reports about the homeless—often carrying headlines such as "The Real Face of Homelessness"[57] or "Homelessness Grows As More Live Check-to-Check"[58]—have outnumbered those about poverty or hunger. According to legal scholar Gary Blasi, homelessness has won out over poverty in media accounts because both politicians and the general public react more favorably to it.[59] Turning poverty and homelessness into separate issues has shifted the focus of media coverage and public policy: "The homeless" have come to be viewed more favorably, at least temporarily, than "the poor," even when the terms are used to describe the same individuals, perhaps because media audiences and the general public can more easily empathize with the homeless. Moreover, homelessness appears to have an easier short-term solution than poverty. It can be declared an "emergency situation" resolvable by providing individuals with temporary shelter so that they will not freeze to death on a park bench, whereas poverty is a more complex problem. As Blasi states, "We may not be willing to support the kind of massive restructuring that would end poverty, but surely we could provide the homeless poor the same kind of shelter we provide to victims of natural disasters."[60]

Media coverage of homeless statistics, however, has illustrated the short-sighted nature of this solution to the problem. Stories about homeless shelters often refer to these establishments as having revolving doors:

> You don't see homeless people as much as you did in the '80s because the one great policy initiative of the past 20 years has been to move them from grates into the newest form of the poorhouse, the shelter. Even though cities are building shelters as fast as they can, the homeless are pouring out of them again, returning to the grates.[61]

Television news reports particularly have focused on homeless individuals who have given up on shelters, providing local data on the number of beds available, the overcrowded conditions in winter, and individuals who choose not to stay inside regardless of conditions outside.

As we have seen, thematic framing in news reporting emphasizes data and how they are gathered. Although the media may occasionally show audiences the "human face" of the poor, the larger issues associated with poverty, hunger, and homelessness are easily lost in debates over how government statistics are generated, interpreted, disseminated, and employed in social policy decisions. The concern expressed by Gregory Mantsios remains valid: the manner in which the media frame many stories about poverty renders the poor faceless,[62] as does the lack of media attention generally given to this problem. Journalist and author Barbara Ehrenreich stated this best in a *New York Times* opinion piece titled "Too Poor to Make the News":

> The human side of the recession, in the new media genre that's been called "recession porn," is the story of an incremental descent from excess to frugality, from ease to austerity. The super-rich give up their personal jets; the upper middle class cut back on private Pilates classes; the merely middle class forgo vacations and evenings at Applebee's. In some accounts, the recession is even described as the "great leveler," smudging the dizzying levels of inequality that characterized the last couple of decades and squeezing everyone into a single great class, the Nouveau Poor. . . . But the outlook is not so cozy when we look at the effects of the recession on a group generally omitted from all the vivid narratives of downward mobility—the already poor, the estimated 20 percent to 30 percent of the population who struggle to get by in the best of times. . . . The current recession is knocking the working poor down another notch—from low-wage employment and inadequate housing toward erratic employment and no housing at all.[63]

As Ehrenreich suggests, the invisible poor are becoming even more invisible during a recession in which some people claim that everyone has suffered hardship because of the world economic crisis. Some former members of the working poor (discussed further in chapter 5) have joined the hardcore poor, and there is no end in sight to the problems of unemployment, foreclosure, and short-term measures like "doubling up" with relatives in an effort to avoid homelessness. Media accounts of the Great Recession typically devote more attention to the downsizing of elite lifestyles and less to the struggles of the already down and out.

Because television news reporting is often organized around assigned beats, such as medicine/health, crime/police, consumer news, and government/politics, the problem of poverty does not surface unless it arises in connection with one of these areas—for example, a report on infant mortality rates and poverty on the health beat.[64] As media analysts have pointed out, the tacit rule "if it bleeds, it leads" prevails in most television newsrooms, where stories about crime, disaster, and war predominate while topics like poverty receive about 1.8 percent of airtime.[65] Even when social issues such as poverty or hunger are briefly presented, the context is usually absent, and attention focuses on a tragic event (such as the death of a homeless person) rather than on what might have caused the event to occur.

Episodic framing of newspaper and television stories about poverty may provide more insight than thematic framing does regarding what it means to be poor, hungry, or homeless in an affluent society like the United States. By examining the individual's personal experience, reporters provide their audiences with specific examples of individuals or families living under economic duress.[66] The four forms of episodic framing—sympathetic, negative image, exceptionalism, and charitable—are discussed below.

SYMPATHETIC FRAMING:
CHILDREN, THE ELDERLY, AND THE ILL

Episodic framing of media stories about the poor uses the personal experiences of individuals living in poverty to represent those of a larger category of people undergoing extreme economic duress.[67] The impoverished most likely to receive sympathetic media portrayal are children, the elderly, and the chronically ill.

"Locked Out at a Young Age," journalist Bob Herbert's op-ed piece about how poorly some children in low-income Chicago families fare, provides an example of sympathetic framing that does not wag a disapproving finger at the poor. According to Herbert, U.S. involvement in the war in Iraq has drawn attention away from "millions of young people in America's urban centers" who are "drifting aimlessly from one day to the next. They're out of school, out of work, and . . . all but out of hope."[68] Herbert's article discusses data from Chicago, where about 22 percent of all residents between the ages of sixteen and twenty-four were neither in school nor employed at the time of the report. Ridiculing the popular sound bite about disconnected youth, widely employed to describe the situation of young people like those in Chicago, Herbert argues that the difficulties they face will become, in one way or another, "difficulties to be faced by the society as a whole."[69]

A child's death typically produces sympathetic portrayals of the plight of the poor; however, news reports about such an event often question one or both of the child's parents' judgment. For example, a *New York Times* article describes the loss of two children in a residential fire allegedly set deliberately. The journalist paints the scenario as follows:

> Last Sunday, as her night shift neared, Kim Brathwaite faced a hard choice. Her baby sitter had not shown up, and to miss work might end her new position as assistant manager at a McDonald's in downtown Brooklyn. So she left her two children, 9 and 1, alone, trying to stay in touch by phone. It turned out to be a disastrous decision. Someone, it seems, deliberately set fire to her apartment. Her children died. And within hours, Ms. Brathwaite was under arrest, charged with recklessly endangering her children.[70]

Although the children's mother was not a suspect in the arson case that destroyed their residence, law enforcement officials held her responsible for leaving the children unattended—a decision that, according to the journalist, "experts suggest, cuts uncomfortably close to some choices made every day by American families."[71] Such news reports from across the nation briefly call attention to the fact that more than 3 million children under age thirteen, including some as young as five years old, are left alone at least a few hours a week on a regular basis.

Although the journalist attempts to portray the Brathwaite family in a sympathetic light, because many families have no choice but to leave children at home alone, photos accompanying the article show the two smiling children whose lives were cut short by the fire. The journalist comments, "What age is old enough to be left alone? The law rarely specifies." Like many members of the working poor, Ms. Brathwaite found herself in a catch-22 situation: if she did not go to work, she could not support her children, but if she went to work, she had no one to care for them, and her low-wage job at McDonald's made it impossible to afford reliable child care. According to Brathwaite's lawyer, "She is guilty of nothing more than being a single mom working a 12-hour shift."[72]

Sympathetic framing regarding children living in poverty appears in newspaper columns authored by political and social analysts affiliated with think tanks like the Brookings Institution. Consider "Handing Out Hardship" by E. J. Dionne Jr., a senior fellow at Brookings and a *Washington Post* columnist. In this article, Dionne chastises the Bush administration for wanting $87 billion in new spending for Iraq and proposing cutbacks on child care for mothers trying to leave welfare. Using a satirical approach, Dionne writes,

> Not to worry. It may be good for those poor working mothers not to have the child-care money. Warning against the idea of child care as an entitlement, Sen. Rick Santorum, a Pennsylvania Republican, reassured us: "Making people struggle a little bit is not necessarily the worst thing."
>
> You should be inspired by those words the next time you see a mother working behind the counter at an ice cream place or a Burger King with her kids in tow. Just tell her having the kids around is good for family values. Struggle will build character. The kids can always do their homework in the corner.[73]

Like stories about impoverished children, media reports about the elderly poor often employ sympathetic framing that focuses on the problems of individuals deemed representative of a larger category of people. One article, "Golden Years, on $678 a Month," tells the story of Anna Berroa, who is sixty-eight and poor:

> She trudged languorously along the thrumming streets of Elmhurst, Queens, lost in her early evening thoughts. . . . Walking consumes time, and in the awkward caution of her life it drains her of troubled memories. She does this loop from her

apartment every day. She derives comfort from one of the few things she can do that carry no price tag. . . . This is a doleful life that Anna Berroa never anticipated. It seems to catch her unawares. One moment she was middle class, envisioning a placid old age, and then a series of untoward events ambushed her. . . . Poverty is particularly frightful from the lens of old age, when there are few, if any, opportunities to enhance one's prospects and the only escape hatch seems to be death.[74]

Tracing the steps in her life—from Havana, Cuba, to New York—and the road that took her from a relatively comfortable economic status to poverty, the journalist shows the austerity of Berroa's current circumstances. For example, she spent her sixty-eighth birthday alone in her room; a friend had asked her to dinner, but "she felt funny because she knew she couldn't reciprocate, so she declined."[75] Most of this article focuses on Berroa's experiences. The journalist frames her story sympathetically and seeks to show that her situation is not unique among the elderly living in large cities like New York. However, poverty among older people is often invisible because others assume that the elderly can take care of themselves.

Unlike the generally sympathetic journalist of the Berroa article, many news reporters tend to juxtapose the needs of the elderly poor with those of young people and community budgets. "An Aging Population, a Looming Crisis," for example, discusses the problems of older people in upstate New York and quotes officials who state that the bill for caring for the poorest of the state's elderly is beginning to strangle communities, and the problem will only get worse in the future:

> "We are dealing with seniors burning through their financial resources and having to go on Medicaid," County Executive [Mark] Thomas, a Democrat, said in an interview at his office in Mayville, the county seat. "And because of the way the system is financed in New York, their overwhelming health care needs become a burden to the rest of us. These expenses dwarf everything else."[76]

According to this article, the aging population in Chautauqua County and other areas of upstate New York potentially places a great onus on younger area residents, particularly when the older people have limited economic resources. As young residents have relocated to other communities for better jobs, they have left behind the senior members of their families, whose "needs are often overwhelming: the county helps many people pay their heating bills, build wheelchair ramps outside houses, clean up after themselves, get to doctors' appointments and get food."[77] Although it describes the problems of the elderly poor in somewhat sympathetic terms, the story clearly considers these individuals in terms of their potential burden on others and on the budgets of their counties.

Many other articles have been written, with somewhat sympathetic framing, about the health concerns of people of all ages living in poverty. The
cover of a *New York Times Magazine* greets readers with a sepia-toned photo
of a hazy city in the background and a shirtless African American man walk-
ing barefoot, head down, in the foreground. The caption reads, "There's a
killer haunting America's inner cities. Not drugs. Not handguns. But . . .
Stress?" The accompanying article, "Enough to Make You Sick?" describes
"America's rundown urban neighborhoods" and explains how the "diseases
associated with the old are afflicting the young."[78] Beginning with the lived
experiences of a woman residing in a housing project in southwest Yonkers,
the article describes her many medical problems, including asthma, diabetes,
high blood pressure, rheumatoid arthritis, gout, an enlarged heart, and blood
with a dangerous tendency to clot spontaneously. The journalist partly attributes the woman's problems, like those of many other inner-city residents, to
the fact they live in "poor urban minority neighborhoods [that] seem to be
especially unhealthy."[79]

The article characterizes the stress of living in poverty in these neighborhoods as producing "weathering, a condition not unlike the effect of exposure
to wind and rain on houses."[80] The description of these neighborhoods can
evoke in readers a sympathetic or negative response ("thank God, I don't
have to live there"):

> The neighborhoods where Beverly, Monica, Ebony, Dominique and Jo-Scama
> live look like poor urban areas all across the country, with bricked-up aban-
> doned buildings, vacant storefronts, broken sidewalks and empty lots with
> mangy grass overgrowing the ruins of old cars, machine parts and heaps of gar-
> bage. Young men in black nylon skullcaps lurk around the payphones on street
> corners. These neighborhoods are as segregated from the more affluent, white
> sections of metropolitan New York as any township in South Africa under apart-
> heid. Living in such neighborhoods . . . is assumed to predispose the poor to a
> number of social ills, including drug abuse, truancy and the persistent jobless-
> ness that draws young people into a long cycle of crime and incarceration. Now
> it turns out these neighborhoods could be destroying people's health as well.[81]

In this article, journalist Helen Epstein paints a candid portrait of the poor
and their health problems, emphasizing that those who are able to move away
from their troubled neighborhoods feel much better—their health improves
away from the stress brought about by living in deprived conditions. According to Epstein, stress relates not only to the objective condition of poverty
but also to the subjective condition of hopelessness, which is associated with
such factors as rising rates of unemployment, an increase in job loss in many
occupational sectors, a sharp rise in the number of people being added to the

ranks of the poor, and the lack of effective governmental action to reduce these problems. For Epstein, all of these factors produce a psychological miasma that damages people living in poverty and generates many of the stress-related illnesses that afflict the poor.

Like newspaper accounts, television news reports about poverty often focus on interviews that can be turned into brief sound bites and aired along with an accompanying story. Coverage of the poor often involves cut-and-paste interviews with public officials, providers of services (such as the director of a food bank or soup kitchen), and a few poor individuals who benefit from these services. When funding cuts threaten, the poor who are interviewed typically state that they do not know what they would do without the food, clothing, shelter, or other services provided by the organization facing budget cuts.

Sympathetic framing of the poor occasionally surfaces in television news programs, as it did in the *20/20* segment in which Diane Sawyer examined poverty in Appalachia. Sawyer was empathetic toward the people she interviewed because she had family ties to the region that stretched back for decades. According to Sawyer, "I'm always so moved by the bravery and the vitality of these American fighters. And now they've got a battle that they aren't wining." [82] Among the children that Sawyer interviewed were eleven-year-old Erica, who wanted her mother to overcome a drug habit, and Courtney, age twelve, whose family was completely out of food. Sawyer demonstrated a special appreciation for the problems they were facing, and she was familiar with the area because she had covered the Louisville, Kentucky, region as a local television reporter during the late 1960s. This prime-time special, "A Hidden America: Children of the Mountains," was one in a series of ABC programs focusing on poverty. Another looked at the lives of impoverished children in Camden, New Jersey.

When prime-time specials deal with the subject of homelessness, they typically aim to show the homeless and near-homeless sympathetically. As a downside, however, media messages about who is homeless and why can cast them in a negative light without necessarily intending to do so and convey the idea that many poor people are responsible for their own condition.

NEGATIVE-IMAGE FRAMING: DEPENDENCY AND DEVIANCE

Negative-image framing in stories about poverty is often subtle and thus open to a variety of interpretations by readers. Two topics that frequently form the subject of such framing are welfare programs and homelessness.

Although readers might expect partisan publications, produced by politicians, public interest groups, or conservative think tanks, to take moral stands on these issues, they might assume that newspaper and television news reports will be more balanced and less judgmental; however, this is not always the case.

Welfare is one issue that often receives negative-image media framing. Research examining media depictions of welfare in 252 magazine articles published between 1929 through 1996 identified four recurring (but contradictory) themes: welfare helps the needy, provides family support, creates dependency, and undermines families.[83] Although the prevalence of each of these themes shifted over time, each could be identified in magazine articles throughout the twentieth century. The idea that welfare results in dependency and undermines families was most widely found in articles in the 1960s and 1970s, but this theme remains popular in newspaper and television news today.

A keyword search for "welfare dependency" yielded more than thirty-five hundred newspaper articles, television news reports, and Internet blogs on welfare between the early 1990s and 2010. When President Bill Clinton originally signed into law the Personal Responsibility and Work Opportunity Reconciliation Act of 1996, he stated his hope that this welfare-reform legislation would end "welfare as we know it" and bring a new day of hope for former recipients. The new law replaced Aid to Families with Dependent Children—a program that had provided both short- and long-term cash assistance to poor families since 1950—with Temporary Assistance for Needy Families. Now the assistance would be temporary and require women to participate in job-training programs or meet work requirements that would eventually get them off welfare altogether. Some analysts assert that the overhaul of welfare was a success, particularly prior to the economic recession of the early twenty-first century. They cite data showing that hundreds of thousands of people moved from welfare to work, and many had higher incomes. Other analysts believe either that the 1996 reform failed completely or that the Barack Obama administration's stimulus bill passed by Congress in 2009 will undermine any success it had. According to some conservative scholars, the stimulus bill will further increase welfare spending, perhaps by as much as $800 billion over ten years, and the new mechanism will contribute to even more welfare spending than in the past because larger numbers of people will swell welfare rolls in the future.[84] Some media reports take a sympathetic tone toward the plight of individuals living near the poverty line; however, others obscure the problems of people who have fallen through the cracks, ultimately judging some to have slipped because of their own moral failings.

So-called welfare mothers are particularly vulnerable to negative media images. In a 2010 study of television news coverage of welfare reform, sociologist Maura Kelly found that negative stereotyping of poor mothers remained the norm in media coverage and that these images often framed the public debate in terms of welfare recipients' responsibility (or irresponsibility): "[My] analysis demonstrates that the controlling image of the welfare mother was ubiquitous in television news coverage of U.S. welfare reform from 1992–2007. This controlling image consists of racist stereotypes of women on public assistance as childlike, hyperfertile, lazy, and bad mothers."[85] As Kelly emphasizes, negative media stereotypes about poor, single mothers incorporate a number of factors:

1. Race: African American women are overrepresented in news stories about welfare.
2. Childlike nature: These women do not know how to get off welfare because they are unintelligent, naïve, or childlike.
3. Hyperfertility: They have more children than average, have children out of wedlock, have children as teenagers, and have children they cannot afford.
4. Laziness: They have a poor work ethic, do not work, stay on public assistance for a long time, or drop out of school and job training.
5. Bad parenting: They raise children as single parents, set a bad example, and reinforce a "culture of poverty."

When we consider all of these attributes, it becomes obvious that some media representations are glaring indictments of the lives of mothers in poverty, particularly if they receive public assistance. As Kelly further states,

> In the discourse on welfare reform, these stereotypes were deployed to support policies intended to control poor women's reproduction and mothering. The welfare mother image was central to framing the debate in terms of the responsibility of public assistance recipients rather than the structural constraints that lead families to require public assistance.[86]

By using framing that focuses on the lives of individuals, media reports may point a spotlight on the negative attributes of poor people believed to be welfare dependent. Such framing may predispose media audiences to think of the issue primarily in terms of welfare dependency and to ignore larger societal conditions (structural constraints) that contribute to poverty initially. In the aftermath of welfare reform, some journalists cited reports about individual women that suggested welfare reform had been somewhat successful and that many low-income single mothers had left welfare for work. Consider, for example, this description of the problems experienced by Shelly Vaughan:

> Survival keeps getting in the way of Shelly Vaughan's attempts to improve her life.
>   The Garland resident earned an associate's degree in junior college, but it wasn't enough to begin a career in her chosen field. So she ended up working minimum-wage jobs in retail and manufacturing. Later, she studied to become a medical assistant and then missed taking the certification test because she became pregnant. Now, the 38-year-old single mother of two, including one with special needs, has a full-time job and help from relatives, but has trouble making ends meet. She recently separated from her children's father and started receiving housing assistance. But she said she wouldn't consider relying only on welfare to get by. "I'm raising two boys. I don't want them to grow up thinking this is how it should be," she said.[87]

This description tells us not only that Vaughan is optimistic about the welfare-to-work process but that her attempts at education have been fragmented, that pregnancy derailed one of her attempts at a career, that although she holds a full-time job, she cannot make ends meet, and that she is no longer living with the father of her two sons. Single parenthood, whether through out-of-wedlock births or divorce, is one of the key factors raised by critics of welfare programs, who argue that some women seem to enjoy welfare dependency. By contrast, the journalist quotes Vaughan as saying that she does not want to become dependent on welfare; nor does she want her two sons to think "this is how it should be."

Other journalists have focused on the temporary nature of most work found by postwelfare mothers and indicate that these individuals have shifted their reliance from Temporary Assistance for Needy Families to unemployment insurance benefits.[88] The articles typically do not take into account why many of the women have become unemployed. Media framing of these stories omits factors such as layoffs and downsizing, the offshoring of jobs, the lack of affordable child care and transportation, and numerous other structural issues.

One of the subtle judgments sometimes found in articles about welfare has to do with how poor people perpetuate the cycle of poverty and welfare dependency. For example, an article titled "Millions Have Left Welfare, but Are They Better Off? Yes, No and Maybe"[89] provides a generally sympathetic frame in reporting on studies about the overhaul of welfare, but it concludes with the example of one woman whose situation shows the difficulty of breaking the cycle. After comparing the arguments of authorities who believe that welfare reform is a success with studies by the "left-leaning" Urban Institute, the journalist concludes that some former welfare recipients are better off, others are worse off, and still others fall somewhere in between. Families off welfare but unemployed were among the hardest hit, particularly when no one had been employed for three years or more. Cynthia Brown serves as an example of people in this category:

> Cynthia Brown of New Haven is feeling that pinch. Ms. Brown, 31, who says she is healthy, has spent most of her life on welfare. "I just came from that," she said with a shrug.
>
> In 2001, Connecticut denied her benefits, saying she had already hit her lifetime limit. Ms. Brown and her three children did not cope well. They lived with an aunt in public housing until she made them leave, fearing the overcrowding would cause her to lose her lease. They lived in a park for a week and then in a homeless shelter for three months, until Ms. Brown obtained subsidized housing and a year's extension on welfare, the last reprieve she will get under state law.
>
> Two months before the extension will expire, Ms. Brown says she is earnestly looking for work but has not found any. She was briefly employed at Yale as a cook, but says she lost the job after her cutting skills were found wanting. Now, she says, her only chance is that something in her life will go so wrong that she will be exempted from the state's rules. "I am hoping for a disaster," she said.[90]

Although Brown's plight receives a generally sympathetic description, readers may interpret this piece judgmentally based on the snippets presented of her life. Here, it would seem, is a "healthy" woman who "came from welfare" and thus expects others to take care of her and her children. Moreover, she cannot keep a job doing something as simple as cutting up the ingredients for meals.

Like coverage of welfare and laws to reform it, media representations of hunger describe some politicians' concern that low-income families will become dependent on food stamps and subsidized school lunches. Media reports have described, for example, how advocates of revamping these programs argue that they serve too many people who do not need the help and that even those who do need it can become dependent on food stamps. A Heritage Foundation spokesperson quoted in "Welfare Wars: Are the Poor Suffering from Hunger Anymore?" stated, "Food stamps and cash welfare are two halves of a whole. All the things about cash welfare that discouraged work and marriage, and encouraged long-term dependence, apply identically to food stamps."[91] The issue of food stamps is politically charged and provides a hot topic for media coverage because any family with an income that falls below 130 percent of the poverty line is eligible for the program.

By telling the stories of individuals who have recently experienced hunger but are considered by medical standards to be obese, journalists frame stories to suggest a linkage between governmental food handouts and the growing weight problem in the United States. "Welfare Wars" quotes a spokesperson for the conservative American Enterprise Institute's Project on Social and

Individual Responsibility in this regard: "We are feeding the poor as if they are starving, when anyone can see that the real problem for them, like other Americans, is expanding girth."[92] Advocates for the poor deny any causal relationship between food stamps and increasing obesity among low-income individuals but also acknowledge that the nature of hunger has changed in the first decade of the twenty-first century because, although the "food insecure" may occasionally miss meals and feel hungry, hunger is not an epidemic. Media framing of stories about hunger often end with statements like this: "No longer are advocates for the poor discussing 'hunger,' with its dire implications, but 'insecurity,' a more nuanced, less compelling justification for help. If conservatives have got food advocates to concede this much, perhaps they have already won Round 1 of the battle."[93]

Just as articles about poverty and hunger often use negative-image framing, much contemporary media framing of stories about homelessness either directly or indirectly relates to the problem of deviancy. In *Reading the Homeless: The Media's Image of Homeless Culture*, Eungjun Min argues that media images depict the homeless as "drunk, stoned, crazy, sick, and drug abusers."[94] Although he acknowledges that these images may be accurate in some cases, he points out that they create obstacles that limit others' understanding of the homeless and the issues surrounding the larger problem of homelessness. According to Min, media framing of homelessness presents homeless individuals as socially dysfunctional rather than giving them the chance to "describe their conditions in their own discourses to provide a more accurate and balanced depiction of the homeless."[95] In Min's view, "media narrative and image blur and distort the distinction between fact and fiction and between information and entertainment."[96]

Nowhere is the problem Min describes more evident than on some Internet postings about the homeless. "Down and Out in Santa Monica," an Internet article by Eric Olsen, shows a concern with both dependency and deviance on the part of homeless individuals: "The problem with the homeless is the problem with social welfare policies in general: we want to provide for the individual, legitimately needy, but we don't want to encourage dependence upon such help, to foster a 'culture of dependency.'"[97] After describing Santa Monica, California, as having been very liberal until it was "inundated with the homeless, who like all other organisms are drawn to where the living is easiest: it's just gravity," Olsen argues that this group has taken unfair advantage of local residents and is largely to blame for its own problems:

> Not all homeless people have themselves to blame for their homelessness, especially in hard economic times, but many, if not most, do. Besides those legitimately down on their luck and temporarily unable to house themselves—for whom we must do all we can to keep them invested in society—the homeless

also consist of alcoholics, drug addicts, the mentally ill (these three categories often blend together), general misfits . . . sluggards, and miscellany others. Please do not accuse me of lumping them all together because every homeless person has his/her own story to tell, but collectively, past a certain level of density and visibility, the homeless are a blight on a community for all of the obvious reasons: sanitation, petty crime, eyesore, annoyance, all of which lead to downward pressure on property values, and downward pressure on one's beach side property is the fastest way to turn a liberal into a conservative.

Although the presence of large numbers of homeless individuals clearly placed a burden on Santa Monica, causing the city to crack down on the problem, the vitriolic language of Olsen's blog calls attention to the judgmental attitudes often expressed about the homeless. The Internet now makes it possible for people to express their opinions to much larger audiences than they could sitting in the local coffee shop expounding on their beliefs.

Just as Olsen's blog points out negative attributes of the homeless, stories about the homeless in mainstream print and television news typically focus on what the homeless have done wrong. This negative-image framing is often found in articles describing tragedies or crimes for which homeless individuals are deemed at least partly responsible. An example is an Associated Press article about how a homeless couple was charged in the deaths of six firefighters in Worcester, Massachusetts. According to the article, a homeless couple "allegedly knocked over a candle during an argument" on the second floor of an abandoned warehouse where they had lived for several months and, after trying unsuccessfully to extinguish the fire, fled without attempting to report it. The blaze grew rapidly, and when firefighters arrived, two went into the building to rescue the "squatters who had been living there." Lost in the thick smoke, the firefighters called for help, and four others entered the structure. All six firefighters died in the blaze, and the homeless couple was charged with involuntary manslaughter.

Some articles about homeless individuals make them look irresponsible and willing to lie about their actions. Others make them seem desperate or mentally deranged. "Homeless Woman Arrested for Threatening Postal Worker," for example, was the lead story on a San Diego County television station. The homeless woman, who allegedly held a thirteen-inch knife to a postal worker's side and threatened him as he was sorting mail, said she only wanted to secure shelter in jail because she had nowhere else to stay. According to media reports, as a reward for her efforts she was jailed on suspicion of kidnapping and attempted carjacking.[98]

Just as this woman's behavior received widespread media attention, stealing shopping carts has also received much coverage. A Dallas city ordinance makes it illegal to possess a shopping cart off the premises of the business that owns it. One article about this ordinance, "Losing Their Cart Blanche: Police Say Basket Ban Is about 'Safety and Crime,' not Targeting Homeless," begins with episodic framing, telling the story of one homeless person with a shopping cart:

> Darryl Johnson is homeless and doesn't have a car. So he uses an abandoned shopping cart he found near a creek to move around his blankets, clothes and other belongings. Because of a new city ordinance that police will start enforcing today, Mr. Johnson may want to ditch the cart—or face jail or a fine. . . . Police and city officials announced the law in November as part of a crime-fighting initiative. But Mr. Johnson, other homeless people and their advocates say the ordinance unfairly targets the homeless. "We have no place to stay, and we have to move our stuff when they run us off," said Mr. Johnson, 38, who's been homeless for several years and sleeps near downtown Dallas. "It's not hurting anybody."[99]

According to the article, the main purpose of the shopping-cart ordinance is to cut property losses: "Taking a shopping cart from the owner is theft," police officials stated.[100] The article suggests that it is mainly the homeless who steal shopping carts to store their possessions in them on the streets. A homeless-rights advocate quoted in the article asserts that the shopping-cart ordinance punishes and criminalizes this group: "The focus is taken off the more underlying and serious problem of homelessness."[101] However, the article concludes with this statement from Mr. Johnson: "All these people are running around robbing, killing and raping, and they focus on the homeless. That's not right. We're just trying to survive."

Descriptions of the actions and appearance of homeless people, even when objectively stated, may imply a negative judgment when interpreted from a middle-class perspective. A news report on CNN from Phoenix, Arizona, "Treating the Homeless Where They Live," is an example. The report begins as follows:

> Blood was oozing from Joel Holder's scalp and from Shelly Holder's face one recent morning as nurse Kay Jarrell and case manager John Gallagher walked into their trash-strewn campsite near 35th Avenue and the Salt River bed. Jarrell and Gallagher were making their daily rounds on behalf of Healthcare for the Homeless, a program of the Maricopa County Department of Public Health. Shelly sobbed as Jarrell daubed her face. Joel sat in a chair, smiled and drank from a can of Natural Ice. Two other residents of the campsite also downed beer. "We've been drinking pretty steady for two days now, and I'm afraid we had a little violence a few hours ago," Joel said, smiling with as many teeth as he could muster.[102]

The report then describes how another homeless camper became angry and punched Shelly in the face and whacked Joel over the head with a baseball bat. Although the focus of this report is actually Healthcare for the Homeless, a program that helps homeless individuals with their medical needs, its framing, which highlights the Holders' problems, carries a less-than-sympathetic tone, which the reporter follows up with interviews with Gallagher and Jarrell, the health professionals:

> "Most of the people we see don't want to live in a shelter and feel safe in their own little camp. . . . Most have drug and alcohol problems." Such people need more than just a few weeks of drying out, [Gallaher] said. . . . "They get sober and remember that they spent 10 years being sexually abused by Dad," Jarrell said. "All they want is to forget their pain. Drugs and alcohol are their way of doing that."[103]

Alcoholism and drug dependency are recurring themes in stories about the homeless—problems made more vivid by framing that tells the stories of how particular individuals were unable to change their lives. Also apparent in many articles is the fact that a number of homeless individuals dislike shelters so much that they are willing to risk living outdoors or in other undesirable settings to avoid the problems that they believe exist in them.

The writers of many television legal and crime dramas take a "ripped-from-the-headlines" approach to developing story lines, and the portrayal of the homeless in series like the *Law & Order* franchise often conveys a negative message similar to that found in newspaper articles and Internet postings. The relationship between homelessness and mental illness is an especially popular topic on *Law & Order*, in which numerous plots have included characters like the "homeless schizophrenic allegedly killed by a car" (in an episode titled "Darwinian"), the "delusional homeless man" accused of stabbing a man to death in front of a coffee shop ("Asylum"), and the "bloodied and bruised homeless man" accused of murder by a neighborhood-watch group that wanted the transient off their street ("Volunteers").

Homeless characters on medical dramas such as *Grey's Anatomy* and *ER* (now in syndication and on DVD) are brought into the hospital because of drug overdoses, fights, and other injurious conduct or because they have exhibited raving, psychotic behavior. One episode of *ER* featuring Sally Field, playing nurse Abby Lockhart's homeless mother, particularly frustrated a homeless advocate, who posted this summary online:

> This is the show I most often slap my forehead about for its stereotypical and reductive portrayals of homeless characters. On *ER* those characters are always crazy or chronic public inebriates. They're usually violent (e.g., the mad genius student who stabbed Dr. Carter and Lucy the intern) or smelly. . . . Playing intern Abbie's mother, Field arrived at the ER unexpectedly last fall, having been evicted from her apartment and burnt the bridge of connection to her son.

Although she charms the other residents, it doesn't take long to figure out she has bipolar disorder. We watch helplessly, as Abbie does, while Field goes through her cycles. Abbie is alternately seduced and frustrated by her mother's energy, and finally says, "I just can't do this anymore," refusing to let her continue staying at her apartment. Then Abbie relents, and we watch her hold her sobbing mother at an El station. Next episode we hear the mom has had a brainstorm and returned to Florida.[104]

In a number of television series, homeless people witness crimes, and in this context, they are often shown as incapable of providing good eyewitness accounts of what happened at the crime scene. Despite the fact that many eyewitnesses—regardless of class—cannot provide investigating officers with accurate information about events or a good description of perpetrators, homeless individuals in particular are portrayed as incompetent and "off the wall" in their remarks to law enforcement officials. An episode of ABC's *The Practice* is a classic example of this problem. In "Trees in the Forest," a homeless pedestrian is killed in a hit-and-run accident to which the only witness is another homeless man. Mr. Snow, the witness, is able to describe the driver of a Mercedes as having committed the crime, but his statements are dismissed as flippant or bizarre in the courtroom. When Assistant District Attorney Helen Gamble asks Snow if he knew the victim, he replies, "Nope, he's a homeless man, bigger bum than me." Gamble becomes frustrated with every homeless person she sees, including a "squeegee man" who cleans her windshield at a stoplight. However, when Gamble learns that Snow has led a hard life, including having had his throat slit in a fight with another homeless man, she shows empathy in her closing argument to the jury:

> If a man dies in a forest and nobody hears him cry . . . then he doesn't make a sound, does he? The other day I was stopped at a traffic light and some bum came up asking to wash my windshield. I couldn't tell you what he looked like 'cause I never looked at him. I never look at 'em. Do you? Easier not to. But when you run one of these bums over . . . maybe we should stop the car. Take a look. I guess that's the question for you to go back and decide . . . is there any intrinsic value to human life? Or does he have to be somebody? I don't know. It's your call.[105]

After the wealthy Mercedes driver is acquitted, the final scene shows Gamble going home alone, passing homeless men huddled around burn barrels on Boston street corners.

Burn barrels are a central prop in crime dramas that involve homeless characters. Whether in Las Vegas, New York, Boston, or other major cities around the nation, television depiction of homelessness usually includes these items. A typical scenario is described in this Internet summary of "The Hunger Artist," an episode of *CSI*:

We're . . . at a highway underpass outside Vegas; the sight of a man huddled over a burning trash can provides the visual indication that this is where Las Vegas's homeless population lives. We see Brass and Gil met by a shopping cart; they're hemmed in by a perimeter of yellow police tape marking off the area surrounding the cart. Brass . . . tells Gil that the body hasn't been ID'd. The body in question is a woman, blonde, wrapped in a blanket and stuffed into a shopping cart.[106]

This brief description provides many of the key ingredients for story lines involving homeless individuals: the highway underpass, the burning trash can, and the shopping cart. As a result, media audiences may come to see the homeless, warming their hands over barrels, not only as omnipresent on the streets but also as unreliable witnesses because they are deviants—dirty, surly, alcoholic or drug dependent, and often visibly mentally ill.

Like newspaper articles, television news and entertainment programming about the poor and homeless has the potential to make viewers and readers more aware of those who have serious, sustained problems in our society. There is a fine line, however, between a sympathetic portrayal of such individuals and a judgmental approach that perpetuates old stereotypes and introduces new ones as times change.

EXCEPTIONALISM FRAMING:
"IF THIS PERSON CAN ESCAPE POVERTY . . ."

Some media stories focus on people who have lifted themselves out of poverty or left lives of homelessness. These inspirational stories show the importance of the human spirit in rising above adversity; however, they also suggest that others might be able to do likewise if they set their minds to it.

"Bronx Girl Follows Vision: A Future Far from Home" begins with a description of Faile Street in the Hunts Point section of the Bronx:

Its painted women sell themselves at the bodega on the corner. Its ragged men sell bags of dope from cars along the curb. It passes underneath the ruckus of the elevated highway and then dead-ends in the stench of a sewage treatment plant. Faile Street is poor. It is loud. It is often dangerous. Often, it smells.[107]

From these humble origins comes Jenise Harrell, who gets good grades at a private school, where she serves on the student council, participates in many other activities, and hopes to attend a prestigious university like Harvard. According to the journalist, "She is trying to escape. 'I know I have it in me to get out,' [Harrell] says. 'I have to get out. There's nothing for me here.'"[108] After describing the problems in Harrell's life and her hopes for the future, the journalist concludes, "It is nonetheless understood that Jenise's life will not be like her mother's. 'I love my mother . . . but she grew up in Hunts Point and she's still in Hunts Point. I don't want to be like that.'"[109]

While it remains to be seen whether Jenise Harrell will fulfill her dream of rising above poverty and the problems in her neighborhood, the television movie *Homeless to Harvard: The Liz Murray Story* convinces media audiences that just such a move is possible. Based on the true story of a young girl who spent her early years worrying about whether her parents were going out to score drugs and when she would eat her next meal, the movie tells of how Liz Murray survived by sleeping on subway cars and eating from dumpsters. Despite these obstacles, she pursued an education, graduated from high school, and won a scholarship to Harvard University.

Similar success stories are sprinkled through newspaper accounts and "happy-talk" reports typically aired on evening television news programs. Another example is the story of Richie Spagnole, who rose from poverty and homelessness to a life of respectability with a job and an apartment of his own. "Amid Manhattan's Wealthiest, a Beggar Found Open Hearts" describes how, after ten years on the streets of the Upper East Side of Manhattan, Spagnole succeeded in his quest for a decent life:

> To many New Yorkers, the Upper East Side is a clubby, outsiders-beware territory, where immaculately uniformed doormen and snotty co-op boards guard the gates for billionaires and their personal trainers; a sometimes heartless province where poodles get manicures but maids get minimum wages. But for Richie Spagnole, who lived for a decade on the streets of the city's richest neighborhood, the Upper East Side was a place of astonishing generosity.[110]

Merchants gave Spagnole food; residents provided him with contributions of as much as $50 at a time; he slept in the boiler rooms of tenement buildings on cold nights. Growing tired of using crack cocaine and being homeless, Spagnole decided to turn his life around when he was offered a job as a delivery person for Rosedale Fish Market. Attributes that the journalist states helped him to get off the streets include having "an infectious smile and a rat-a-tat-tat speaking style," being a "man of energy and humor," originally "coming from a good family," being "a special homeless guy . . . who wasn't dirty or smelly, and he was helpful," being "clean," and always caring about people. According to the article,

> Being helpful was part of Mr. Spagnole's come-on [when he was homeless]. He told restaurant owners that he would not beg in front of their places during the day and would keep an eye out for thieves at night if they would just donate left-over food. He also did favors like clearing snowy sidewalks with shovels

"borrowed" from local buildings. For the employees of one restaurant he was the lookout, watching for the police while they gambled inside.[111]

Eventually, Spagnole was reunited with a daughter whom he had not seen for a number of years, and this Valentine's Day news article concludes with an apparent "lived-happily-ever-after" ending.

Media reports about poor and homeless individuals who have successfully overcome their problems provide heartwarming stories. This is exceptionalism framing: singling out individuals who have surmounted obstacles, praising their accomplishments—such as leaving the streets, finding a job, and graduating from high school or college—and creating the impression that anyone in a similar situation can do the same thing. "Man Overcomes Homelessness, Will Graduate from ASU" is an example: Chris Newton, who learned that "shaking the image of [being] a homeless kid" was almost as hard as being homeless, completed his college education and received a degree from Arizona State University.[112] The article points out that, by taking charge of his life at an early age and never giving up, Newton attained a better life for himself and his son: "When things are bad, you maintain an image. You keep the rest inside," Newton stated to the reporter.[113]

Individuals like Newton, who improve their living conditions, overcome hardships and addiction, and find happier lives are clear examples of pulling yourself up by your own bootstraps, but exceptionalism framing ignores the more typical experiences of the poor and homeless, leaving media audiences with an individualistic view of poverty and homelessness that does not focus on the larger societal issues associated with these problems. The individualistic approach to framing of news reports is particularly prevalent in fund-raising appeals on television and in "neediest-cases" articles in newspapers.

CHARITABLE FRAMING: HOLIDAYS AND DISASTERS

Although sympathetic framing of media stories about the poor typically shows empathy for those who are down on their luck, it does not suggest that readers or viewers should take action on behalf of individuals in need. By contrast, charitable framing highlights individuals and families in need of financial assistance with the goal of motivating audiences to contribute money or goods to the poor (for instance, through programs like "Coats for Kids" or "Toys for Tots").

Research shows that most forms of media give minimal coverage to the poor and homeless throughout the year; reporting gradually increases over the fall, peaks during the Christmas holiday season and cold-weather months, and then drops sharply through late winter to early spring.[114] During the height of these human-interest stories, members of the press barrage service providers at soup kitchens and homeless shelters for interviews; volunteers are shown serving turkey dinners to the poor at Thanksgiving and preparing baskets of food for indigent families at Christmas. Cartoonist Gary Trudeau captures the essence of media reporting about holiday assistance to the poor by showing how out of place some reporters are when they try to impose their own thinking on the homeless people they are interviewing. In one Doonesbury comic strip, for example, a homeless man stands in line waiting for his free meal on Thanksgiving Day. A journalist says to him, "You're getting a free meal today . . . but afterwards . . . what do you hope for?" The homeless man replies, "Seconds." The journalist counters, "No, no . . . I mean in the long term." The homeless man replies, "Dessert . . . definitely dessert." As this cartoon shows, the homeless man and the journalist are operating under different assumptions about life and what the future should hold for people.

Holiday coverage of the poor and calls for donations appear in reports across the nation. One of the longest-running series is "The Neediest Cases," published in the *New York Times*. People seeking assistance range from families who need medical care or a place to live to individuals who have recently arrived in the United States with no money and no way to escape a life of poverty. Each article employs charitable framing to tell the human-interest story of a person or family seeking financial assistance. A representative example is "Offering a Hand, and Hope, in a Year of Record Homelessness in New York," which describes the problems of Gloria Hernandez:

> Gloria Hernandez tries to be strong for her five children, but strength, like privacy or full stomachs, does not come easily when you and your family live in a shelter for the homeless. "The children say, 'Mommy, when are we going to get out of here?'" Ms. Hernandez, 40, said softly, her eyes downcast. "You see it in their faces: they don't speak, but they show it. They say it's your fault."[115]

A new landlord had purchased the apartment building where Hernandez lived for ten years and told her and her children to move out, claiming that he needed the space for himself and that too many people were living in her unit. The photo accompanying the article shows Hernandez, looking depressed, standing with her nine-year-old son, who wraps his arm protectively around her neck. The article also carries the story of several other families and explains how the Neediest Cases Fund provides temporary assistance for "the homeless, the gravely ill and the down and out."[116]

According to the *New York Times*, publication of stories like the one about Hernandez has been an annual occurrence since Adolph S. Ochs, publisher of the paper from 1896 to 1935, came across a "shabbily dressed beggar" on

Christmas Day 1911, leading Ochs to publish stories about the poor in the hope that readers would show compassion toward them. Newspapers and television news programs across the country replicate the *New York Times*'s "The Neediest Cases" series; journalists and anchors appeal to audiences to send money, toys, food, and clothing to help the less fortunate in their communities. Programs like "Toys for Tots" at Christmas and "Coats for Kids" during the cold winter months have been a big success at many television stations, as the media work cooperatively with local community service organizations to provide at least a minimal level of assistance to those living in poverty.

In the past, researchers have found that charity fund-raising activities publicized in the media typically show more images of minority-group members, particularly African Americans and Latinos, than of white (European) Americans. According to these analysts, even though charity fund-raising through the media is done for a worthy cause, such portrayal of people in need might firmly establish in readers' and viewers' minds the notion that poverty and minority status are synonymous. A 1990s study of news magazines and television news found, for example, that stories about poverty featured African Americans between 62 and 65 percent of the time, although only 29 percent of poor Americans are black. Based on a systematic examination of *Time, Newsweek,* and *U.S. News & World Report,* political scientist Martin Gilens concluded that news magazines exaggerated the number of poor African Americans, with African Americans shown 62 percent of the time in stories about poverty. In weeknight news shows broadcast by ABC, CBS, and NBC, a similar pattern was identified: African Americans represented the poor 65 percent of the time. According to Gilens, media stories framed to show the negative aspects of the underclass, such as welfare dependency or drug abuse, typically presented African Americans, whereas those showing the poor in a more sympathetic manner, such as articles about the elderly poor or poverty-level workers in job-training programs, were more likely to feature white Americans. Gilens argues that overrepresentation of African Americans in stories about poverty perpetuates stereotypes about race and provides white Americans with more reason to express discontent regarding social welfare programs.[117]

In addition to raising much-needed money for charitable organizations and bringing in toys or clothing for children, charitable framing provides media audiences with a way to feel good about themselves. After one series, "Season for Caring," the *Austin American-Statesman,* for example, printed a follow-up about the families that benefited from readers' contributions. One article, "Thanks, Austin!" described the gratitude of Clydia Jones, who "[did]n't know where to begin thanking people. 'It's been a blessing. Just a blessing,' she says." According to the article, Jones's disabled eleven-year-old granddaughter had received an electric wheelchair donated through the Season for Caring campaign.[118]

Although such campaigns perform a valuable service for a few of the poor, Gregory Mantsios suspects that "these 'Yule time' stories are as much about the affluent as they are about the poor: they tell us that the affluent in our society are a kind, understanding, giving people—which we are not."[119] The seasonal nature of charitable framing in the media has also been criticized because the problems of the poor exist throughout the year and not just during holidays. As one *Los Angeles Times* editorial acknowledged,

> The charity of the holiday season is traditional—and welcome. The problem is that so much is seasonal. . . . Come January, when people go back to their normal routines, the hunger and homelessness recognized in the holiday season will remain. It would be nice if most of the spirit of giving remained, too.[120]

As in news stories, charitable framing of the poor in the story lines of television "family" entertainment shows is also seasonal. A representative example is "Here Comes Santa Claus," an episode of the WB's *7th Heaven* (1996–2007) that takes place during the Christmas season, when Rev. Eric Camden (Stephen Collins) encourages his oldest children to do charity work for the community. Mary Camden (Jessica Biel), one of the daughters, is working in a soup kitchen feeding the homeless when her father comes in to volunteer. Reverend Camden sees that his daughter is unusually happy to be doing the charity work that she initially did not want to do, but then he realizes she is flirting with Carlos, a client at the soup kitchen. When she tells her father about Carlos, she states, "That is Carlos. He got hit by a bus. Isn't he cute?" She also tells her father that Carlos is homeless and that she would like for him to stay at the Camden residence for the holidays. Other than Mary's description of Carlos as homeless, viewers would have little indication of his status based on his appearance, described by one reviewer in this way:

> How stupid is Mary to invite a homeless man she barely knows to stay at her house? It's a good thing he's a sanitized, *7th Heaven* version of a homeless guy, with his healthy complexion, perfectly kept hair, sparkling white teeth, and rugged good looks, and not, like, a more realistic depiction of a homeless person.[121]

By the end of the episode, viewers learn that Carlos is not really homeless after all. Such media portrayals of homeless persons as devious contribute to negative public perceptions about them and their attempts to harm or mislead honest, law-abiding citizens.

Like media representations that focus on the need to extend a helping hand to those down on their luck and homeless during the holidays, stories about disasters focus on their effects on the poor. A typical example is the article "At River's Edge, Left with an 'Empty Feeling,'" which describes the devastation wrought by a flood on a formerly homeless person:

> Things were looking up for Robert Gray. After three months in a homeless shelter in Calvert County, he landed a job paying $10 an hour doing ironwork, found a home in the Hallowing Point trailer park along the Patuxent River, and filled it with enough furniture so that he could live comfortably. But in the time it took for the rising flood waters of Hurricane Isabel to crash through the glass storm door, burst through his closet wall and fill his home with three feet of water, Gray was down again.
> "I lost everything," said Gray, who returned Tuesday to sift through his mud-filled quarters for anything salvageable. "I came here with nothing and I pieced it all together, and now it's like, damn, I have to start over."[122]

Although disasters such as floods typically harm people across all socioeconomic, racial, and ethnic categories, the poor are often in greater peril because they lack insurance and do not have the money to purchase replacement items. Describing the differential effects of a hurricane, one journalist stated,

> Hurricane Isabel was an equal-opportunity destroyer, flooding the houses, snapping the trees and cutting the power of rich and poor alike. But the lingering hardships imposed by the storm are not likely to be so democratic, officials from across the region say. People with low or fixed incomes, the elderly and the unemployed are struggling harder to rebuild, the officials say. Many had little or no insurance; many lost everything they owned.[123]

Unlike the widespread media appeals for the poor at the holidays, disaster relief draws only brief coverage, often describing how government agencies and volunteer organizations like the Red Cross are helping the victims. Overall, the recurring framing focuses on how natural disasters spare neither the poor nor the wealthy. This point is emphasized in headlines like "A Great Equalizer: Isabel Was Her Name,"[124] although the poor are harmed more significantly by even moderate losses than are the more affluent in our society.

Some reality television entertainment shows acknowledge that homelessness itself is an ongoing disaster that continually affects the lives of many people. A&E staged a reality show, *House of Dreams*, in which sixteen would-be homeowners who had never before built a house came together for thirteen weeks to build a home that one contestant would ultimately win.

Some of the contestants wanted to win the house for other, less fortunate individuals; for example, a real estate broker wanted to win the house for a family she hoped to rescue from poverty, and a former investment banker wanted to win for an at-risk high school student he was counseling. Another of the contestants, however, was Tony, an out-of-work landscaper who—with tears in his eyes—told his competitors in the first episode that if they did not win the house, they could go back home, but he and his family had no home to return to, only a homeless shelter.[125]

Although reality shows, such as *Extreme Makeover: Home Edition*, focus on homebuilding or rebuilding for less advantaged people, few of the episodes feature home creation for the homeless. Typically, those chosen to receive assistance are families that include a disabled veteran, a seriously ill child or other family member, or a hero, such as a firefighter injured in the line of duty. Occasionally, a television news show, such as *20/20*, will feature humanitarian organizations like Habitat for Humanity to show their good works on behalf of homeless and nearly homeless families, but not homeless single people.

EFFECTS OF MEDIA COVERAGE OF POVERTY AND HOMELESSNESS

How do media representations of poverty affect viewers and readers? Clearly, portrayal of the poor and homeless sends a different message than do depictions of the rich and famous. Whereas the upper classes receive framing based on consensus, admiration, emulation, and the price tag, the poor, at best, are accorded sympathy and applauded when they manage to escape poverty. At worst, the poor are depicted thematically, as "faceless" statistics, or episodically, remaining all but invisible except at holidays or following natural disasters. For the most part, the poor are framed as bearing some degree of responsibility, allowing media audiences to blame the victims if they choose to do so. Over the past 150 years, poor individuals have been considered not only outsiders, or Others, but objects to be observed, commented on, and derided. They have sometimes been represented as neediest cases or the beneficiaries of elaborate charity fund-raising events attended by wealthy patrons who dress up in their finery to eat and dance the night away while patting themselves on the back for raising money for organizations that benefit the less fortunate.

An examination of thematic framing in the media shows the extent to which print and television news reports about poverty, hunger, and homelessness provide audiences with statistics and trends while ignoring the untold stories of millions of people living in poverty in the United States. Reporting about increases and decreases in the poverty rate or in the number of hungry or homeless people gives media audiences a relatively sterile perspective on a major social problem with many systemic causes and large-scale social consequences for everyone in the nation. The media, however, largely ignore macrolevel concerns.

By contrast, episodic framing too often turns exclusively to discussions of individuals and what audiences may perceive as their personal troubles. When the media frame stories in such a way as to emphasize the shortcomings of the poor or homeless, those who are better off may conclude that these less fortunate individuals have created their own problems. The exception, perhaps, is the category known as the working poor, people who typically work long hours for low wages, as discussed in the next chapter. Otherwise, the poor are usually portrayed as violating middle-class values (about cleanliness, hard work, and moral behavior) and as committing crimes that are far less interesting than those of wealthy elites, who engage in stock fraud or other clean, white-collar offenses. As noted in chapter 3, even when convicted of major crimes, the rich may be admired and praised for their good taste and expensive material possessions.

Throughout my research, I was surprised by the consistency of media coverage linking poverty and deviance. Although most people living in poverty do not commit suicide, homicide, or other crimes, articles over the past 150 years have usually focused on how different the poor are from middle- and upper-class people and how much less interesting their lives are. Whether the poor steal food to eat or shopping carts to transport their few worldly goods, their deviant behavior is more pronounced in media representations than their "normal" behavior.

Children, the elderly, and the ill are most likely to receive sympathetic framing in media stories about the poor. In the latter category, however, the illness typically includes a physical health problem or disability; sympathetic framing often does not extend to individuals deemed mentally ill, particularly if they exhibit frightening or threatening behavior. Subtle derision of the mentally ill homeless in television crime shows, for example, may convey the message to viewers that all homeless people are dangerous and should be feared, when the central problem for many is one of economic hardship and deprivation.

When the media need heartwarming or feel-good stories, particularly during holidays and disasters, the poor are good subjects because they are easily accessible to reporters. Of course, some holiday and disaster coverage of the poor results from the efforts of nonprofit agencies and poverty advocates to gain media coverage for their cause in order to raise money to help affected individuals and families.

One of the major problems that my research identifies in regard to media representations of the poor is the shifting of the larger, structural nature of the issues associated with poverty, hunger, and homelessness onto a softer, more humanitarian type of coverage that provides media audiences with only isolated examples that show the problem's immediate effects on individuals at the personal level. I agree with other scholars' assessments of how television news reports, as well as the "professional" behavior of news anchors, influence audiences' perceptions of homelessness:

> The anchor's gaze functions as an ultimate window through which . . . all other views of the world must be relayed, including the public's view of itself. Due to this authoritative, omnipotent and reliable quality of the anchor's position, he is able to comfort the viewer and relieve the tensions accumulated throughout the narrative [about poverty]. His concluding remarks sound as if he were saying to us, "We have some problems out there. But don't worry. I'll take care of them. Everything will be fine. You have a good night."[126]

Perhaps it is this feeling that comes to audiences when they reach the end of other news stories or entertainment shows in which the subject or character has spent several hours serving the poor in a soup kitchen or taken clothing to a homeless shelter. We can easily believe that someone else is looking after the problems of the poor, that we need not worry about these issues or demand political and economic changes to reduce their gravity. Perhaps it is for this reason that some poverty advocates are creating their own media resources, through grassroots efforts and extensive use of the Internet, to get the message out about poverty and homelessness and to provide audiences with the "real" story of the poor rather than the packaged, sanitized sound bites and video clips presented in news reports or the occasional subplot in a television drama.[127]

A number of media analysts, however, including *Wall Street Journal* reporter Jonathan Kaufman, have questioned the extent to which media audiences actually want to know about poverty, hunger, and homelessness:

> Coverage of race or poverty has begun to mirror the intractability of these problems. I sometimes worry we have succeeded too well in communicating the bleak prospects of the inner-city underclass. . . . Have [these stories] had the unintended consequence of making these problems seem beyond solution or hope? Faced with bleak statistics of poverty, single-parent families, dropout rates, and incarceration, most readers throw up their hands. They read these stories the way many of us read about tragedies in distant lands. . . . It's a shame, but it doesn't really affect us and, therefore, it is not news to which we find connections.[128]

Thus, the question remains, Have U.S. media audiences seen too much, or too little, of the true nature of poverty? Regardless of the answer to this question, one fact remains undisputed: how the media cover the poor differs vastly from how they cover the upper and middle classes, which serve as the norm for how things ought to be in this country. The effects of classism in media coverage deserve far more attention and systematic research in the future than they have received in the past.

Chapter 5

Tarnished Metal Frames

The Working Class and the Working Poor

Toronto, Canada:

> Hot, humid weather and no garbage collection for four days had the city of Toronto smelling like rotting food Thursday as [garbage] strike negotiations continued. . . . The key issues are pay raises equal to what was given emergency workers last year, and the city's desire to drop bankable sick days and replace them with short-term disability insurance. Meanwhile, residents sweltered in line-ups to drop off bags of garbage at collection sites where strikers limited the number of people entering, local media said.[1]

> This [strike] is not simply about garbage pickup. Parks, community centers and even the ferry to Toronto Island has been closed. Let's not forget ambulance workers are working at 75% capacity. This strike affects the most vulnerable people in society, children, the elderly and the poor. Without cars the poor cannot transport their garbage to the temporary dumps, they are stuck with festering garbage. With the garbage inside the city, children and the elderly are being exposed to disease.[2]

The framing of the above UPI article and comment on a blogger's posting about a civil strike in Toronto, Canada, suggests that the greed of unionized workers demanding a pay increase and maintenance of their bankable sick days stinks as much as the piled-up garbage. As in this case, the media typically highlight how the labor actions of working-class individuals inconvenience ordinary people. Strikes by sanitation workers and other public servants are framed to describe health risks and the hassles that accompany work stoppages. Although these unionized workers, earning from $10 to $21 an hour, might seem to have little in common with Caroline Payne, a convenience store clerk who earns $8,000 to $12,000 a year, the media often lump both categories of workers into a generic working-class category and frame their stories differently from those of individuals in the economic classes above them.

Here is Caroline Payne's story:

> Muncie, Indiana: Caroline Payne embraces the ethics of America. She works hard and has no patience with those who don't. She has owned a house, pursued an education and deferred to the needs of her child. Yet she can barely pay her bills. Her earnings have hovered in a twilight between poverty and minimal comfort. . . . She is the invisible American, unnoticed because she blends in. Like millions at the bottom of the labor force who contribute to the country's prosperity, Caroline's diligence is a camouflage. At the convenience store where she works, customers do not see that she struggles against destitution.[3]

As is typical of many media stories about the working class, the episodic framing used in this article describes Caroline Payne's economic condition and establishes her as a valid example of millions of other working poor who earn less than a living wage and remain invisible as they "sew clothes, clean offices, harvest fruit, serve Big Macs and stack merchandise at Wal-Mart."[4] Like most individuals who might be considered among this group, Payne earns an income above the official poverty line but cannot afford many basic necessities.[5] In media framing of news articles and entertainment story lines, Payne represents the working poor, whereas labor unions represent the entire working class—despite the fact that most individuals in this socioeconomic category are not union members.

THE WORKING CLASS AND WORKING POOR IN SOCIOLOGY AND THE MEDIA

Media framing generally represents members of the working class as just that—as workers, laborers, or, in Marxian terminology, the proletariat. Like stories about the poor and homeless, news reports about the working class usually employ episodic framing that provides little information about people in this socioeconomic category beyond human interest. As economist Michael Zweig suggests, "Workers are seen, when they are seen at all, as faces in a crowd or in sound bites, rarely as people with thoughtful things to say about their condition and their country. In the media, the working class is truly the silenced majority."[6] Human-interest stories about the working class are usually based on economics or politics. Examples include workers being laid off at a local factory and activists or politicians speaking out on behalf of residents of a working-class neighborhood who feel threatened by economic development, such as the construction of a Walmart supercenter (a type of retail outlet known in media and commercial parlance as "big box"). As with other forms of episodic framing, many of these media representations do not look at the larger structural issues that produce such problems, focusing primarily on the outrage of the unemployed or people displaced by gentrification. By contrast, business articles in major newspapers often refer to the working class as "organized labor," whereas reporters on the political beat describe its members as "blue-collar workers" who live in "working-class neighborhoods." Similarly, television shows that focus on working-class home life emphasize workers' humble origins, lack of taste, proletarian lifestyle, and disgust with their jobs. Characters, often the object of jokes, are portrayed as buffoons who are sloppy in appearance, ignorant, and sometimes racist.

One of the major problems in media representations of the working class is the lack of a clear definition of who constitutes this group, a fact that makes it easier for journalists and television writers to place the working class "comfortably" in the lower tier of the middle class. For example, a *New York Times* editorial describing a strike by grocery workers in Southern California stated that these workers "are the front line in a battle to prevent middle-class service jobs from turning into poverty-level ones."[7] From a sociological perspective, it is questionable whether workers earning Walmart wages, particularly in high-cost-of-living states like California, should be considered middle class. Many media reports, however, place working-class people in a large, undefined middle class where "everybody" belongs.

Sociologists identify the working class by occupation (such as manual, supervised, unskilled, or semiskilled workers), by how people are compensated for their work and how much they are paid, and by the level of education typically required. The "old" working class, primarily made up of semiskilled blue-collar workers in construction and manufacturing, has been shrinking since the 1950s. By contrast, the working class of the twenty-first century also includes low-skill manual workers, people employed in routine white-collar jobs (such as bank clerks, cashiers, and retail sales workers) and in the rapidly growing service sector (for instance, home health-care workers and employees in fast-food restaurants). According to stratification scholars, the primary characteristics of the working class are that its members "do not have much control or authority over the pace or the content of [their] work and they're not a supervisor and they're not the boss."[8] Some analysts believe that about 30 percent of the U.S. labor force should be classified as working class.[9] In the past, a defining characteristic of the working class was union membership, particularly in the era when goods-producing jobs were a major source of employment in the United States. However, as goods-producing jobs have decreased, union membership has dropped to a small fraction of the labor force.[10] Consequently, the power of the working class to influence economic and political decisions has diminished; today, the media frequently characterize the working class as low in political participation.

Some scholars believe that the working poor should be a category separate from the working class, but my examination of media coverage suggests that the working class and working poor are discussed somewhat interchangeably, particularly as more working-class employees are "only a step—or a second family income—away from poverty."[11] As a result, societal lines, like media distinctions, between the working class and working poor have become increasingly blurred. Global shifts in the labor force through outsourcing, downsizing, and plant closings have created more fluidity between the two groups. Some analysts place the working poor at 13 percent of the U.S. population; so, when combined with the working class (30 percent), these two categories together constitute approximately 43 percent of the population.

Even under the best of circumstances, the working poor hold low-wage positions with little job security, few employee benefits, and no chance to save money. Their work conditions are frequently unpleasant and sometimes dangerous.[12] The working poor may include illegal immigrants (known as undocumented workers) who worry that they will be incarcerated or deported if they complain to employers about wages or working conditions. Women make up a large segment of the working poor: females constitute about 60 percent of the low-wage workforce and 70 percent of part-time labor in the United States.[13]

Examining media representation of the working class is challenging because, as Zweig argues, this class is typically invisible.[14] Sociologist Gregory Mantsios agrees that the media portray the working class as "irrelevant, outmoded, and a dying breed." According to Mantsios, the media suggest that "the hardships faced by blue collar workers are inevitable (due to progress), a result of bad luck (chance circumstances in a particular industry), or a product of their own doing (they priced themselves out of a job)."[15] In the 2000s, the focus of media coverage of the working class is unemployment as levels continue to hover in the 9 to 10 percent range nationwide, with higher rates in some regions of the country. An analysis of the historical framing of the working class provides insights into contemporary media framing of this class.

HISTORICAL FRAMING:
THE WORKING CLASS AS LUMPS OF LABOR

Although nineteenth-century newspaper articles typically did not use the term *working class*, articles from the 1800s dealing with the laboring classes and the working poor can be found in the archives of the *New York Times* and other urban newspapers. Framing typically focused on how laborers organized to demand better working conditions and wages and on the problems that emerged as a result of strikes. With the introduction of Labor Day as a federal holiday in the 1880s, parades and other celebrations attracted media attention and positive coverage of the so-called working man for that one day. During the rest of the year, however, articles focused more on workers and their union leaders as greedy and sometimes as "criminal elements" meriting prosecution. One 1806 article, for example, told of the conviction on charges of criminal conspiracy of members of the Philadelphia Journeymen Cordwainers who had gone on strike demanding higher wages. For a number of years thereafter, newspapers reminded readers that this case had set a precedent with which the U.S. government fought unions for many years.

The most common framing of early stories about the working class highlighted laborers' demands for a shorter workday. Typical news reports described the demands of Boston carpenters for a ten-hour workday in 1825 and of children employed in the Paterson, New Jersey, silk mills for an eleven-hour day and a six-day workweek in 1835. By the 1850s, however, the tone of many articles had grown increasingly antagonistic toward organized labor and more positive toward workers who opposed unions. An example of the latter was a *New York Times* article, "Meeting of Front Bricklayers: A Union of Capital and Labor Advocated," praising nonunion bricklayers for their opposition to the Bricklayers Protective Union.[16] Not long thereafter, editorials and news articles reviled labor organizers for demanding strikes, creating conflict, and inconveniencing the general public. For example, an 1868 article argued for the "principle of harmony" in labor relations rather than confrontation:

> We submit this consideration to those cooperative associations which are now striving to upset and revolutionize all the laws of political economy which experience has taught us. These societies do not simply ask Government to regulate the hours of labor. They have ulterior aims. They propose to distract the political parties from the issues which divide them by bringing into prominence the vexed questions between the capitalist and the laborer.[17]

Acknowledging that organizations comprising workers had evolved into a full-fledged social movement, this journalist questioned what the future of such a movement might be:

> Indeed, how far the movement may go, it is impossible to foresee. But it is plain enough to all intelligent observers that the schemes proposed can be productive of mischief only. The operations of political economy will take care

of themselves without the help of these cooperative associations or of Labor Union Conventions.[18]

As newspapers began to question the ulterior motives of unions and their organizers, some reporters argued that the government should not intervene in disputes between workers and owners or managers. Here is an example from 1868: "Government has just as much right to establish religions as it has to regulate the laws which shall obtain between the capitalist and the laborer."[19] Citing the lack of progress made by bricklayers in bringing about changes through their tactics, this article warned other groups that their efforts would also fail:

> The recent strike of the bricklayers has fully exposed the futility of the attempt of workmen to regulate by associated effort either their hours of labor or their wages. The employers, upon whom these bricklayers attempted to impose the most arbitrary conditions, have held their ground, and they are now masters of the situation. And why? Because they knew that the exactions imposed were arbitrary and unreasonable, and that they defied all the laws of political economy.[20]

In keeping with Adam Smith's philosophy that what is good for the economy is good for everyone, some newspaper reporters became advocates of the "laws of the political economy," which typically benefited members of the capitalist class at the expense of the workers. Some articles in the 1860s even suggested that the best role for the trade unions was to send the working poor to the western United States rather than demanding higher wages for them in the Northeast. According to an article titled "Help for the Working Poor," if the "trades' unions would contribute money to send their poor to the West, instead of supporting them in idleness here, they would render a better and more lasting service."[21] In other words, too many of the working poor were sitting idle, and trade unions could reduce the problem not by making demands on employers in the Northeast but by helping relocate these workers to "the fields of the West, free for them and aching to be cultivated."[22]

For many years, media reporters have viewed the working poor and the activities of labor unions as problematic, resulting, according to some scholars, in an antilabor bias deeply embedded in media culture. In his study of media portrayals of unions, labor scholar William J. Puette concludes that the media's antilabor bias is "heavy-handed and deliberate."[23] According to Puette, many newspaper publishers and editors are employers who must negotiate with unionized workers, and these media elites are therefore less willing to report fairly on workers' issues. On rare occasions, newspapers have carried reports about alleged media bias against workers and organized labor, as in this exchange between Senator Henry William Blair of the U.S. Senate Committee on Education and Labor and President John Jarrett of the Amalgamated Association of Iron and Steel Workers:

MR. JARRETT: There is an impression among the working classes that the press ought to be the mouthpiece of the sentiments of the people in general. There is also an impression that the press is subsidized by capital.

SENATOR BLAIR: You will observe, however, that in the press your statement will be suppressed—unless this remark of mine leads to its publication.

MR. JARRETT: Well, there is certainly a general impression among our working people that a large portion of the press is subsidized by certain large corporations. There are a few papers, to be sure, where the working men can have their interests and views fairly presented, but that is not the case with the majority of papers.[24]

Not all newspaper articles in the late nineteenth and early twentieth centuries took a negative attitude toward the working class. Some were nothing more than brief items about union meetings or workers' grievances, such as those of members of the Bakers' Union, who were required to work fifteen to eighteen hours per day, including Sundays[25]; the "sewing women," who earned twenty-five cents per dozen shirts made, leaving them continually impoverished despite working until 2:00 A.M. most nights[26]; and labor leaders who opposed the hiring of convict labor in the belief that "convicts should not be allowed to compete with skilled workmen [but should be] restricted to work of a menial kind."[27] However, the framing of newspaper articles about the working class at the end of the nineteenth century typically did not tell the stories of individual workers or give voice to their concerns; rather, they focused on "organized labor," leaving the workers as faceless employees controlled by their bosses and union leaders.

Although Labor Day was not officially designated a holiday until 1884, the first celebration took place on September 5, 1882, in New York City, when the Central Labor Union organized about ten thousand men to participate in a parade that was "conducted in an orderly and pleasant manner."[28] The headline of a *New York Times* article about that city's celebration of this holiday in 1902 was typical of media coverage at the time: "Big Labor Day Parade: Thirty Building Trade Unions to Be Represented. Forty Bands to Play in the Procession—Preparations to Handle Holiday Crowds."[29] Not all workers were equally celebrated, however. Media conveyed the message that U.S. workers should fear "immigrant, foreign labor" as a threat to their livelihood and a menace to public safety.[30] The *San Francisco Chronicle*, for example, carried lengthy articles in 1904 explaining how Japanese laborers were taking jobs away from U.S. workers, reflecting a pattern of media reporting that continues in the twenty-first century regarding how immigrant labor may be a contributing factor to unemployment among native-born people in the United States.

Some articles in the 1890s and early 1900s portrayed the laboring classes as greedy, dangerous, and causing grave inconvenience for people in other classes. The violence connected with some labor strikes was a recurring theme, such as during the 1892 Homestead Strike, when eighteen people were killed as Pinkerton guards attempted to help scabs break picket lines at a Carnegie Steel mill, and the bloodshed and looting during a strike against the Pullman Palace Car Company in 1893. During the 1920s and 1930s, media representations of workers and the labor movement grew more negative; not only was the violence continuing, but (in the latter decade) political leaders placed blame for the nation's industrial depression and high unemployment rates on organized labor and its leaders.[31] For example, an article titled "Blames Union Labor for Work Shortage" quoted from a speech by Senator Knute Nelson of Minnesota:

> I am getting tired of these strike threats. I do not know but that it would be a good thing for the country if these railroad men should start a strike. Let the people of this country understand once for all what these men mean by their striking. Let the people realize that they will be deprived of their food supply, their fuel and everything else. If the employees ever embark on such a strike, leading to such results, I venture the prediction that the American people will rise in their might and wipe them from the face of the earth.[32]

The tone of Nelson's statement and the news article containing it shows the negative image being painted of workers because of their demands for change. The focus had shifted from workers' issues and why they were threatening to strike to how workers' actions inconvenienced and harmed other people.

Congressional investigations, governmental actions, and violence during labor strikes provided reporters with fodder for numerous articles on the working class and its problems; however, the focus of many stories remained primarily on labor organizers and what Puette refers to as a "cartoon image" of labor unions—one that portrayed the "worthless, unproductive, overpaid blue-collar work force, which is considered the unhappy but inevitable result of unionization."[33] In articles ranging from coverage of the 1920 Palmer Raids (in which federal agents arrested more than five thousand people to break a nationwide strike)[34] to news reports about passage of the Taft-Hartley Labor Act in 1947 (which curbed union strikes),[35] reporters had ample opportunity to inform their readers about key issues facing workers. They typically chose instead to use only a few narrow frames that often told the story from the perspective of politicians and business leaders.

By the 1950s and 1960s, both newspaper and television coverage of the working class focused almost exclusively on walkouts and strikes, the threat of them, and the alleged criminality of some union leaders. Several reporters covering the labor beat sought to expose the involvement of organized crime in labor unions and unions' large, direct contributions to candidates for federal office. One example is Victor Riesel, a well-known New York newspaper columnist and radio commentator whose reports on organized crime and its infiltration of labor unions hit so close to home that he was attacked in 1956; a mob threw acid in his face, blinding him for life. According to his obituary, however, he "never stopped inveighing against gangster infiltration and other corruption in labor unions that had stirred his emotions since his youth."[36]

Some scholars argue that media reporting on organized labor has shifted over time "from incendiary to invisible."[37] Others, including Puette,[38] hold that blatant discrimination against unions and their members still exists in the media, though it has become more subtle:

> The image of labor has not been reduced to invisibility so much as it has been refocused and filtered into more subtle, indirect projections than before. . . . Television portrayals tend to emphasize the pettiness or foolishness of union bargaining goals and take the cinematic portrayals a step further by portraying good unionists out of power and generally suppressed by their local or national leaders, whose power is considered excessive, out of touch, and corrupt. Television and print news share a preference for using employers as sources, which causes them to adopt the employer's perception of the issues as the basic premise of their reports.

Based on an examination of television news programs like *60 Minutes* in the 1970s and 1980s, Puette concluded that the media's portrayal of unions typically was unsympathetic and tended to label union concerns as nothing more than special interests that might be the undoing of the country. Similarly, Puette concluded that in television dramas depicting the working class and labor unions, labor terminology is frequently abused, and unrealistic situations are often dramatized "without respect for realism or the true plight of the union or nonunion labor depicted."[39] According to Puette, basic "lenses" color and distort media portrayals of organized labor and its leaders. Among these media images are stereotypes that labor unions protect unproductive, lazy, and insubordinate workers; that unions undermine the ability of the United States to compete internationally because they have forced employers to pay exorbitant wages; that unions do not represent the best interests of the working class; that union leaders are not from the educated or cultured (privileged) classes and thus are more likely to be corrupted by power than are business or political leaders; that unions are no longer necessary; and that unions create rather than resolve conflict.[40] If Puette's lenses are accurate representations of how the media portray workers and labor unions, these depictions no doubt have contributed to what he describes as a "systematic and relentless disparagement of the most visible effort at collective empowerment by working Americans."[41]

How much of this past framing is still reflected in contemporary media representations of the U.S. working class? In the following sections, I discuss five frames I identified in my research:

• Shady framing: greedy workers, unions, and organized crime
• Heroic framing: working-class heroes and victims
• Caricature framing #1: white-trashing the working class
• Caricature framing #2: TV's buffoons, bigots, and slobs
• Fading blue-collar framing: out of work or unhappy at work

SHADY FRAMING:
GREEDY WORKERS, UNIONS, AND ORGANIZED CRIME

The media today continue to frame the working class primarily as a laboring class. Reports often fail to look at the wide diversity of individuals who might be categorized as working class, focusing instead on labor unions, their members, and their activities. Despite the fact that fewer than one in six American workers belong to a union, news reports about the working class typically emphasize the problematic aspects of these entities. Such stories often portray unionized workers as greedy individuals who engage in behaviors that harm others (such as work stoppages and strikes) and imply that most, if not all, unions have ties to organized crime.

Negotiations between unions and management are a frequent topic in business reporting, where news-analysis framing provides journalists an opportunity to take a side in the controversy. The content of these articles has shifted increasingly toward union subordination to management since the early 2000s because of changing economic conditions in the United States and issues such as immigrant "cheap labor," the offshoring of jobs, and globalization. For example, in the article "Auto Deal or Bust: Was Anyone Taken for a Ride in the U.A.W.–Big 3 Contract Talks?" journalist Danny Hakim describes a meeting of union leaders and representatives of the Big Three U.S. automobile manufacturers (General Motors, Ford, and DaimlerChrysler): "Last week the United Automobile Workers [UAW] offered more concessions to the Big Three than it has in the last two decades of contract talks. Then again, concessions have not really been a feature of the last two decades of contract talks in the American auto industry."[42] Drawing attention to problems the Big Three face with global competition, Hakim writes,

> Of course, many white-collar workers would love such concessions [as those gained by the UAW]—paying $10 for brand name drugs—or salaries. The average Ford assembly worker made $70,206 in 2002, and the average skilled worker made more than $80,000. Such high labor costs have been a chief contributor to an exodus of 2.7 million manufacturing jobs over the last three years.[43]

Statements like this hold blue-collar workers up against white-collar employees, making the working class appear greedy—to be seeking higher wages and better benefits than most middle-class workers enjoy. Although portraying unionized workers as having a most-money-for-the-least-work attitude has been a recurring theme in media reports over the past century, articles and electronic news reports since 2009 have focused on the restructuring of the auto industry and on companies like General Motors being on the verge of bankruptcy. Conciliatory framing such as this is typical: "A Once-Defiant U.A.W. Local Now Focuses on G.M.'s Success." The article describes how many people blame the union for dragging down the Detroit automakers, but the journalist explains that "the [auto] companies' struggles have turned the U.A.W. into one of their strongest allies." The shop chairman for Local 1112, the Lordstown, Ohio, UAW chapter, is quoted as saying, "We were the bad dog on the street at one time. We've got 3,000 lives to worry about. The cockiness and the arrogance that we once portrayed—we definitely got a lot more humble." The president of Local 1112 agreed: "Everyone has come to a realization that management is not the enemy, and the union is not the enemy. The enemy is the foreign competition."[44]

Other media analysts have focused not on how the unions have become more submissive but on how they believe the Barack Obama administration's intervention in the auto crisis amounts to a "plundering of public assets and assault on the working class." From this perspective, the government's quasi-nationalization of the auto industry, by taking control of nearly 75 percent of General Motors, protected the interests not of the workers and the larger society but of the "most powerful sections of the financial elite at the expense of the working class."[45]

When labor considers striking to gain concessions from management, media coverage about workers and their leadership often becomes more visible and more negative. In a study of *New York Times* coverage of strikes and nonstrike wage settlements between 1949 and 1991, management scholars Christopher L. Erickson and Daniel J. B. Mitchell found that among the factors that determine the extent of news coverage about labor are the "occurrence of a strike,

strike duration, number of workers involved, occurrence of federal intervention, key industry status (that is, whether the affected industry was among
those industries identified as exceptionally important for wage-setting), and
proximity to New York City."[46] The presence of one or more of these factors increases the likelihood of extensive news coverage of labor activities.
Erickson and Mitchell note the irony of this finding: "The fact that strikes are
a key attraction for coverage . . . poses a dilemma for unions, since it implies
that perhaps the surest way to claim attention in the papers is to be involved
in bad news."[47]

By focusing on problems brought about by union actions, media coverage
of the working class suggests not only that union members are greedy but
that they harm others. Two important examples include reports on the 2003
Chicago trash haulers' strike and the 2004 California supermarket strike.
News reports of the Chicago strike emphasized how much garbage was piling
up and the inconvenience to residents and business owners. Although some
news reports suggested that the entire city of Chicago was rapidly becoming
one big garbage dump, the strike was against private haulers and primarily affected commercial areas, apartment buildings, and suburban neighborhoods,
not city neighborhoods with single-family residences, which were served
by public garbage crews. According to one article published shortly after
the trash haulers rejected a settlement offer from management, "A group of
private waste haulers and striking workers failed to agree Sunday on a new
contract, assuring millions of Chicagoans and suburbanites that they would
have to endure a fifth day of mounting heaps of refuse and the stench from
overstuffed trash bins."[48] As this statement suggests, ordinary people had
to "endure" problems such as "mounting heaps of refuse" and "the stench"
because the workers could not reach a settlement. Little attention was paid
to the striking workers' grievances or the conditions under which they were
expected to work. According to spokespersons for the trash haulers, their
concerns pertained not only to wages but to the increasing (and, from their
perspective, unreasonable) demands routinely placed on them to haul away
large items such as sofas and king-sized mattresses.[49]

Media framing of articles about the trash haulers' strike was not unique
in its emphasis on the problems caused by striking workers. When members
of the United Food and Commercial Workers International Union (made up
of stock clerks, cashiers, and other grocery workers) walked off their jobs
in Southern California in 2004 and set up picket lines in front of hundreds
of supermarkets, their reason—to protest various chains' plans to reduce
health-care benefits and require that workers pay a greater proportion of their
insurance costs—was a secondary issue in news reports, which emphasized
the disruptive effects of strike supporters' behavior:

A hundred union supporters shut down a Safeway in Santa Cruz for an hour and a half recently, dancing and chanting in a conga line through the store. Others disrupted a golf tournament in Pebble Beach on Friday, shouting slogans at two supermarket board members who were about to tee off. Labor leaders are threatening to harass supermarket executives wherever they vacation, be it on beaches or ski slopes.[50]

As is typical of reports on labor issues, the longer the strike continued, the more negative media coverage became. By the fourth month of the strike, news articles routinely focused on problems that the strike was causing for ordinary people. For example, "Grocery Strike Wearing on Customers, Workers" begins with a narrative about a shopper inconvenienced by the work stoppage:

Encinitas, Calif.—Linda Cugno avoided shopping at her neighborhood Albertson's store for the first month in support of striking grocery workers. She tried to stay away in the second month of the strike, and the third. But as the grocery workers' strike in Southern California enters its fourth month with no end in sight, she can no longer justify driving out of her way to other stores. "I literally live right up the hill," she said, gesturing while loading groceries in an Albertson's parking lot in this San Diego suburb. "I feel bad (for the strikers) . . . but this has been going on long enough." That's what everybody—shoppers, picketers, grocers—seems to be saying about the work stoppage that has dragged on since October 11, affecting 70,000 workers and 860 stores in Southern California and everybody here who needs milk, eggs, and toilet paper.[51]

Clearly, work stoppages and strikes do inconvenience people; however, the media may now give more coverage to this issue than to investigative, behind-the-scenes analysis of what causes strikes in the first place, how they might be resolved, or what their broader implications are. Regarding strikes by workers in the auto industry, for example, media framing of stories often emphasizes how the demands of one group of workers harm not only the corporation's bottom line but also other industry employees. For example, when workers at a parts supplier that provided needed axles for General Motors automobiles downed tools, some journalists focused on how the auto industry's longest strike in nearly half a century "disrupted production at 32 General Motors plants" and affected the livelihoods of thousands of other workers.[52] Because American Axle's unionized workers were striking at their plant, GM was forced to reduce or halt production on many pickup trucks and large sport-utility vehicles and to lay off tens of thousands of workers. One interpretation of media framing of these labor-dispute stories holds that if the unionized workers had been less greedy, other problems, such as lost wages and lost revenues from vehicle sales, would not have occurred.[53] Moreover, strikes such as this have been blamed for nearly putting auto giants into bankruptcy before the government intervened with bailouts.

Media framing of articles about labor unions focuses not only on workers' alleged greed but on labor racketeering. According to the Federal Bureau of Investigation (FBI), labor racketeering entails "the domination, manipulation, and control of a labor movement which affects related businesses and industries."[54] As a result of racketeering, workers' rights are often denied, and businesses, insurers, and consumers suffer great economic losses. Media have reported on how the FBI uncovered the involvement of La Cosa Nostra, the Gambino family, and other crime syndicates in unions, which they run for their own profit, national power, and influence.[55]

Newspaper headlines and leading television news stories like "Union Boss Indicted" reinforce the connection between unions and crime in the thinking of media audiences with little actual knowledge of union labor. In the late 1990s, news reports focused on government investigations of corruption among union leadership. Clear class distinctions between union leaders and rank-and-file workers became a key theme in many reports on these scandals, as shown in the opening statement of one article: "The scandal that swept the president of New York City's janitors' local from his union penthouse earlier this month was the latest in a series of stinging labor setbacks, stemming from an unusual combination of forces, that have made the city the national capital of union excess and corruption."[56] Class distinctions are shown when the article emphasizes that the head of the janitors' union received a $450,000 salary, lived in an extravagant penthouse, and received $1.5 million in severance pay while supposedly representing janitors and other custodial workers in the bottom tier of the working class. The journalist concluded that several factors resulted in New York City's unions being prone to corruption, including the entrenched Mafia presence, the city's many construction projects, the availability of large numbers of immigrant workers, and the juxtaposition of large, powerful unions with small, vulnerable businesses.[57]

Media reports regarding union corruption have highlighted the FBI's efforts to enforce the Racketeer Influenced and Corrupt Organizations Act since the 1970s and bring an end to labor racketeering. According to the FBI, some unions, including the International Brotherhood of Teamsters and the International Longshoremen's Association, have in the past been "completely dominated by men who either have strong ties to or are members of the organized crime syndicate."[58]

Despite extensive media coverage of the FBI's successes in curtailing organized crime's involvement in labor unions, connections between some unions and crime persist. A 2008 *New York Times* article, "Endless Task: Keeping Unions Clean," is framed to highlight the continual task of keeping unions from becoming dirty. This article describes how the Gambino crime family took over two New York unions, one representing cement truck drivers and the other, construction laborers, as federal officials tried to bring the interconnection between crime and labor to a halt for more than a decade. According to New York prosecutors, Teamsters Local 282, the cement truck drivers' union, was a "candy store" for the mob at one time, funneling as much as $1.2 million a year to the Gambino crime family. Other allegations listed in media coverage included mob involvement in embezzling money from Local 282's health and pension funds and bribing union officials to obtain union cards qualifying individuals for employment on construction jobs and for union benefits.[59]

Framing of articles about the working class has primarily focused on corrupt labor leaders and less-than-honorable workers, but media coverage often fails to provide audiences with a balanced picture of life in unions specifically or in the working class generally. Media emphasis on labor corruption ignores the efforts of hard workers and legitimate unions seeking to better workers' conditions. This approach harms organized labor in general: "The high-profile episodes of corruption and skullduggery in New York and elsewhere are unquestionably hurting efforts to revive the labor movement," according to Nelson Lichtenstein, a University of Virginia labor historian.[60] Although in the past the labor movement brought about positive gains for the working class, such as the eight-hour workday, unemployment compensation, pension plans, and safer working conditions in heavy industry and mining,[61] the contemporary labor union has acquired a bad reputation due to the real-life actions of labor leaders and fictionalized television and film portrayals of mob-infiltrated unions.

One widely watched fictional portrayal of mob life and the mob-labor connection is HBO's *The Sopranos*, now in worldwide syndication and available on DVD and via on-demand cable systems. Although at first his socioeconomic status appears to be middle to upper-middle class, based on visible cues such as his luxurious residence in an affluent New Jersey suburb and the cars his family drives, Tony Soprano (James Gandolfini) is portrayed as a slob who fits stereotypical working-class attributes in how he dresses (ambling down his driveway in a bathrobe and floppy slippers to get the morning paper), speaks (in a pronounced ethnic accent with poor grammar and limited communication skills), eats (with a napkin tucked into his collar as he gorges on huge piles of pasta and talks to his cronies with his mouth full of food), and amuses himself (with mistresses or by watching strippers at his club, The Bada Bing).

Some *Sopranos* story lines touch on the relationship between organized crime and labor. One episode, "Do Not Resuscitate," involves a picket line set up by African American joint fitters, led by Rev. Herman James Jr., who supposedly want jobs at the Massarone Brothers construction site. The owner, Jack Massarone, asks Tony to "fix" the problem, not knowing that Tony has a "business arrangement" with Reverend James. As the episode ends, James acknowledges that he is in cahoots with Tony: "I'm lining my pockets with [the picketing joint fitters'] blood."[62] With Tony's encouragement, Massarone agrees to put five no-shows on his payroll; however, unbeknownst to Massarone, Tony collects the proceeds and divides them with Reverend James.

Although the intersection of crime and labor is not a constant theme in *The Sopranos*, the connection crops up often enough in the story lines to keep viewers associating labor with corruption and other mob activities, such as drug dealing, loan sharking, gambling, and hijacking. The program portrays control of even small-time work as an obsession with mob leaders. One episode shows the attempts of Feech LaManna, a recently paroled wiseguy sent to prison during the 1980s crackdown on organized crime, to take over running the yard-maintenance business in certain neighborhoods in order to grab back his old turf.[63] Although many have described *The Sopranos*, like the entire genre of organized-crime dramas on television and in film, as nothing more than entertainment, its portrayals of the working class as corrupt cast a negative light on millions of hardworking Americans on the lower socioeconomic rungs of society.[64]

As *The Sopranos* was cancelled, HBO's crime drama *The Wire* shifted audiences' attention to the Baltimore police force, drug dealers, snitches, and how American labor unions are dying. Some episodes raise the question of whether organized crime syndicates destroyed labor unions or if the decline should be attributed to the lazy American workers, corrupt labor bosses, and global labor conditions. *The Wire* is named for the wiretap, which is important in many mob-related criminal investigations. At first the wiretaps are employed to apprehend drug dealers, but later their use is expanded to include members of union locals, the board of education, and city hall. According to one reviewer,

> Season two captured the death of the Baltimore docks and its unions with exquisitely painful detail and bumptious color. When the ports at last are filled with robots instead of working stevedores, *The Wire* may be as much of a documentary of that vanishing lifestyle—its nicknames and noble labor and boozy camaraderie—as we possess.[65]

As discussed previously, the media have either perpetuated stereotypes about the working class or ignored this group altogether, except when labor issues are involved. According to media analyst Phil Primack, newspaper and television newsrooms adhering to such an approach usually do not report many important working-class stories:

Most of the few labor reporters left today, like most of the new breed of workplace writers, are assigned to their papers' business sections, where space is tight and the investigative approach is not commonly encouraged. If the workplace were treated more as a hard news beat, and if reporters felt that their pieces could more easily make it to page one, coverage might quickly improve. . . . Stories about factory dangers or worker hassles require getting into factories and talking to workers. This means good old-fashioned beat development and reporting, whether it is called labor or workplace or something else. Meanwhile, the nation's workplaces remain a largely untapped gold mine of stories.[66]

According to a *Los Angeles Times* labor reporter, "You get the impression sometimes that [working-class] people just do not count except when they shoot someone."[67] One exception to this general rule is media framing of stories about labor in the aftermath of a major crisis or a natural disaster. A classic example is the working-class hero, depicted for instance in the aftermath of the terrorist attacks on the United States in 2001 and after disasters such as Hurricane Katrina in 2005 and the massive BP oil spill in the Gulf of Mexico in 2010.

HEROIC FRAMING:
WORKING-CLASS HEROES AND VICTIMS

No event in U.S. history did more to popularize the image of working-class heroes and victims than the terrorist attacks of September 11, 2001, and their aftermath. According to media reports issued during the weeks following those attacks, more than one thousand of the victims had belonged to labor unions. Some were praised for their work as firefighters, police officers, and emergency medical technicians who lost their lives in the effort to rescue thousands of other people; others were union members who lost their lives as they went about their daily jobs in the Twin Towers of the World Trade Center. According to one media account published in *The Village Voice* shortly after the attack,

Union members . . . worked throughout the towers. At Windows on the World, the swank restaurant atop One World Trade Center, as many as 79 members of Local 100 of the Hotel Employees and Restaurant Employees International Union perished. Twenty floors below them, at least 39 members of the Public Employees Federation, most of them workers at the Department of Taxation and Finance on the 86th and 87th floors of the south tower, are missing. Some 27 maintenance workers, members of Local 32B-J of the Service Employees International Union are missing, according to union spokesman Bill Meyerson. "They were window cleaners, security officers, elevator starters," said Meyerson.

In addition, at least 50 members of the building trades were killed, union officials estimate. About 17 of them were carpenters assembling office partitions,
another 15 were electricians, five were painters, and four were laborers. . . . In
a harbinger of the rescue efforts their fellow members would make later that
day, union officials believe some tradesmen died trying to help after the attack.[68]

As later news accounts confirmed, many of those described as missing in this
report were confirmed to be among the dead.

Media framing of articles about the working class in this case was extremely positive, emphasizing the heroism not only of police officers, firefighters, and other emergency personnel but of union members across New
York who rushed to the World Trade Center site to help in the wake of the
attack. At the carpenters union headquarters, for example, more than three
hundred members arrived early on the morning of September 12 to volunteer
their services: "We unloaded every pair of gloves we had, gave them goggles,
hard hats, whatever we could find. Then they marched straight down to the
site. Their pass was their union card and their hard hat; they didn't take 'no'
for an answer," according to Steve McInnis of the New York District Council of Carpenters.[69] Furthermore, union rules about trade demarcation (e.g.,
steam fitters are not supposed to drive nails; carpenters do not touch wir-
ing) were ignored during the gritty excavation work.[70] The heroism of these
union workers was celebrated by a journalist who wrote that any message
the terrorists had tried to send by this horrendous act was "effectively refuted
with every shovelful lifted from the pile"—much of it, in this case, by union
workers who (as discussed earlier in this chapter) often serve as the objects
of media criticism rather than praise.

Like media coverage of the heroic actions of workers in the aftermath of
the terrorist attacks of 9/11, journalists' stories positively framed the actions
of both paid workers and volunteers who helped clean up after Hurricane
Katrina in 2005 and the 2010 BP oil spill in the Gulf of Mexico. In Katrina's
aftermath, relief workers and volunteers poured into New Orleans, Louisiana;
Biloxi, Mississippi; and other regions hardest-hit by hurricane-strength winds
and flooding. Many media sources applauded these people for their bravery
and tenacity. The framing of some stories, however, eventually shifted to
alleged misconduct by Federal Emergency Management Agency workers,
hospital personnel, police officers, and firefighters, some of whom were accused of failing to perform their official duties. Articles that initially focused
on heroism began trumpeting headlines such as "Katrina Cover-Up: Cops
May Face Death Penalty" to call attention to wrongdoing, in this case after
four police officers were indicted for shooting and killing two unarmed civilians and injuring four others on a bridge in the days following the hurricane.
According to media reports, the officers initially claimed they had fired in

self-defense, but a U.S. Department of Justice investigation concluded that they shot the civilians without cause and planted a gun at the scene as part of an elaborate cover-up and falsification of police reports.[71] Other stories broke thereafter, indicating that this shooting represented only the tip of the iceberg in regard to police misconduct in New Orleans. Media framing of this type consumes many hours of television coverage, particularly on cable news networks, and diminishes positive coverage of the heroism of police officers and other civil servants in the aftermath of one of this nation's worst natural disasters.

Although little is written or broadcast about the everyday activities of members of the working class and their small acts of kindness or bravery, such as firefighters putting out a residential fire, construction workers digging a ditch in the street without breaking a water main or gas pipe, or an aide helping an elderly person get comfortable in a nursing home bed, there have been some notable exceptions in coverage of disasters like the 2010 BP oil spill. Consider, for example, continuous coverage on cable news channels of behind-the-scenes efforts to clean up the Gulf. Referring to it as the biggest cleanup job in the world, CNN presented various news specials, including "Rescue: Saving the Gulf" to show how paid workers and ordinary people had come together "to help their neighbors, their communities, their fellow man."[72] The framing of these CNN stories focused on the willingness of individuals to step up in a time of need and accomplish a particular goal because they were "amazing people who happily put all of their opinions of this spill aside and [were] compelled to help."[73]

Similar heroic stories about members of the working class have focused on immigrants who have been instrumental in cleaning up damage to beaches, wildlife, and the ocean. These reports emphasize the heroism of immigrants who comprised almost 50 percent of the hurricane-repair workers in New Orleans following Katrina. For example, Latino immigrants, many of them undocumented workers, have been praised for helping New Orleans get back on its feet and for working in hazardous conditions following the BP spill and other disasters to restore some semblance of normalcy.[74]

With the growing popularity of reality TV, working-class heroes have received more attention in the 2000s. According to some media analysts, the advent of shows such as *Dirty Jobs*, *Construction Intervention*, and *Deadliest Catch* is ironic:

> The irony is that TV networks have been out of touch with the working class for years. Blue-collar TV characters used to be routine: Ralph Kramden, Fred Sanford, Laverne and Shirley. TV was the people's medium, after all. But now network dramas and sitcoms have been gentrified. The better to woo upscale viewers, TV has evicted its mechanics and dockworkers to collect higher rents

from yuppies in coffeehouses. Even cop shows have been taken away from beat cops and given to the eggheads on *CSI* and *Numb3rs*. Goodbye, Roseanne. Hello, Liz Lemon [from *30 Rock*]![75]

Similarly, cable television networks have rediscovered the working person and started featuring shows that follow crews of Alaskan crab fishermen fighting storms (Discovery Channel's *Deadliest Catch*), long-haul drivers in the Arctic (History Channel's *Ice Road Truckers*), and concrete finishers, cricket farmers, chicken busters, bologna makers, and abandoned mine pluggers (Discovery Channel's *Dirty Jobs*). These shows have increased in popularity because their media framing brings a feeling of adventure, excitement, and danger to the world of hard, manual, and semiskilled labor. These programs typically attract young male viewers, who are a target audience for media ratings and advertisers. According to one media analyst, these reality shows are "about men, almost exclusively: men sweating and swearing, men powered by coffee and doughnuts, men revving heavy equipment to heavy-metal sound tracks."[76] Many of the jobs shown are well-paid positions; however, workers' attitudes toward money reveal important class differences because everything is mentioned in terms of its price: how much a lost piece of equipment is worth, how much it costs when a worker loses a day's wages, or how expensive it is when a pipe gets jammed. Some of the shows are so committed to reality that they seek to deal with very difficult real-life situations, such as the death of Phil Harris, captain of the crab-fishing vessel featured on *Deadliest Catch*, from a stroke. The captain and some of his family members wanted viewing audiences to know what life truly is like in that type of work, and some media analysts believe that the series actually captured "the reality of a crabber's life."[77]

Crises and tragedies bring to the foreground individual workers rather than images of organized labor that many in the media have deemed either unnewsworthy or blameworthy. Stories of trapped miners, for example, highlight the role that teamwork plays in saving lives. The framing of articles about miners in such situations often emphasizes their heroism, as was the case in a Brookwood, Alabama, disaster—one of the nation's worst mining calamities in decades. Journalists described how some coal miners who escaped the cave-in that followed the initial explosion did not flee but courageously raced to aid their fallen comrades and became victims themselves when caught in a second explosion forty-five minutes later.[78] Even more media coverage occurs when there are happy endings, as after a 2002 mining accident at the Quecreek Mine in Pennsylvania, when all nine of the trapped miners escaped without serious injury and soon appeared on television entertainment programs like *Late Show with David Letterman*. Letterman introduced the miners and interviewed one of them, Blaine Mayhugh, who described the despair that he and the other eight miners felt when trapped for three and a half days in a four-foot-high tunnel with water up to their chins. Seeking a moment of levity, Letterman asked Mayhugh if anything had been said or done to break the tension. According to Mayhugh, one of the trapped miners said, "We'll be getting a lot of overtime for this."

By the time the Letterman show was broadcast, working-class hero and victim framing had reached its peak with news, entertainment programming, and advertisements that focused on the heroic status of blue-collar workers, as one analyst noted:

> The media and advertisers have responded to Americans' post–September 11 need for heroes by elevating firemen and police officers to mythical status and saturating every conceivable communications vehicle with their images. Last month's trapped miners saga was no different: suffocating coverage and a celebration of heroic efforts to liberate the workers. . . . People who get sweaty rather than wear suits (or pantsuits) to work have become the ultimate content marketing ploy. News, entertainment, advertising, whatever. Just trot 'em out and watch 'em grab eyeballs and sell stuff.[79]

This comment was further affirmed by global media coverage of the 2010 mine collapse in Chile, which captured the interest of more than 1 billion people, who watched the dramatic rescue of all thirty-three miners on television. The workers had been trapped for more than two months after a rock collapse blocked the main entryway of the mine. Although some miners appeared on various media outlets after their rescue, perhaps the most famous was Edison Pena, who appeared on Letterman's show to sing an Elvis Presley song and talk (with the help of a translator) about his New York City Marathon run.

Sadly, many of the portrayals of working-class individuals in settings such as mining disasters do not have heroes because of the devastating nature of the event. After a 2010 West Virginia incident, for instance, media reports basically catalogued the number of workers dead and those unaccounted for after an explosion ripped through a coal mine. Family members lamented the loss of their loved ones, but little was said about increasing safety in mines other than in a few "yell-a-thons" on cable news channels, where competing "experts" voiced their opinions about what is right or wrong with today's mining industry.

Although there may be an occasional overload of working-class portrayals in the media, actual heroic framing of news stories about this class appears to be situational, occurring primarily after a tragedy of major proportions has taken place and when rescuers or survivors are able to help others through the disaster. In sharp contrast to the positive framing of the working class that typically focuses on those people who risk their lives for others, media framing of news articles and television entertainment story lines more often employs caricatures that depict working-class women and men less favorably than people in the middle and upper classes.

CARICATURE FRAMING #1:
WHITE-TRASHING THE WORKING CLASS

Although the middle and upper classes may be caricatured in some media representations, people in the working class are particularly vulnerable to media framing that overemphasizes or misrepresents their appearance or behavior to produce an exaggerated or comic effect and turn them into objects of ridicule. This occurs, for instance, when the media brand working-class individuals as inferior to members of the upper classes with derogatory labels like "white trash."

In early usage, the phrase "white trash" typically referred to low-income individuals whom the more privileged members of society judged to be tasteless, uneducated, lazy, and otherwise inferior. As cultural studies scholars Matt Wray and Annalee Newitz have suggested, "White trash is 'good to think with' when it comes to issues of race and class in the U.S. because the term foregrounds whiteness and working-class or underclass poverty, two social attributes that usually stand far apart in the minds of many Americans."[80] According to Wray and Newitz, many people associate whiteness with the middle and upper classes, not realizing that it persists across class lines. With regard to the impoverished class, classic films like *Gone with the Wind* popularized the phrase "po' white trash"; since the 1980s, the media have employed the white-trash caricature to portray blue-collar and lower-income white-collar families.

The term has also been bandied about in television situation comedies like the now-syndicated *Roseanne*, which features a working-class family that prides itself on its "trashy" origins and behavior. In an episode titled "White Trash Christmas," Roseanne Conner (Roseanne Barr), a blue-collar working mother, and her husband, Dan (John Goodman), snub their neighbors by putting up gaudy Christmas decorations outside their house. In another episode, Roseanne sits in the garage on a favorite sofa the family discarded when they purchased a new one. Roseanne is laughing at an episode of *The Beverly Hillbillies*, a "white-trash-made-good" show, which she is watching on the family's discarded TV set. As Dan and Roseanne talk nostalgically about their old furniture, Roseanne jokingly reveals how she sees their family's class location: "We're white trash, and we'll stay white trash until they haul us out to the curb."

Airing from 1988 through 1997 on network television and still available on DVD and via global syndication, *Roseanne* has no doubt influenced viewers' ideas about what it means to be white trash, portraying the working-class lifestyle as a mixture of tasteless behavior and the genuine love and respect that members of the Conner family show toward each other. Over the show's nine-year run, Roseanne held several working-class jobs, including factory worker, hair washer at a beauty salon, magazine telemarketer, and waitress at the local mall. The family's acceptance of its "white-trash" status was made clear to television audiences through comments the Conners made to each other as well as on a website (Roseanneworld.com), which once pictured a small metal house trailer with the door wide open, chairs and flowers out front, giving the general impression that visitors were welcome. In this symbolic gesture, Roseanne aligned herself not only with the concept of white trash but with that of trailer park trash. In 2010, the Roseanneworld .com website was gentrified to include Roseanne's political opinions, appearances on television talk shows, and blogs by other people about her ideas and statements.

As used by the media, the terms *white trash* and *trailer park trash* often have similar meanings, regardless of whether the individuals in question actually live in trailers. Late-1990s media coverage of the Paula Jones sexual-harassment lawsuit against President Bill Clinton serves as a good example of how one comment about a person's being called "trailer park trash" can produce a media wildfire that rages out of control for months. Briefly stated, Paula Jones alleged that in 1991, when she was a low-wage, hourly employee in an Arkansas state office, she was propositioned by then-governor Clinton. Her allegations were not made public, however, until Clinton was elected U.S. president and became embroiled in a sex scandal involving Monica S. Lewinsky, the White House intern who publicly admitted to having sexual relations with him. When Jones's claims were made public in the media, commentators widely discussed a statement by James Carville, a former Clinton campaign adviser and an ardent defender of the president, who accused Jones of being trailer park trash in an effort to discredit her claims. According to various media sources, Carville made the following statement in explaining why he thought Jones had come forward with her allegations: "Drag a hundred-dollar bill through a trailer park and you never know what you'll find."[81]

By using the term *trailer park*, Carville implied that Jones's testimony against the president had been bought and that her humble origins should discredit her testimony.[82] According to one journalist who followed the case closely,

Carville didn't rely on the well-worn femme clichés of sexual opportunist, hysterical harpy or angry woman spurned when he went after Jones. He fingered a crevice of the American psyche that promised to spurt forth all that and more.

She was white trash, part of a subset blamed for everything from garishly bad taste in dress, America's obesity problem and Elvis adulation to incest, child abuse, alcoholism, spouse beatings, the fracturing of the family and out-of-wedlock motherhood, not to mention Roseanne and Tom Arnold. So powerful are those words that the media took up the smear campaign unquestioningly, for a time.[83]

Although Carville later claimed that he never called Jones white trash, he did concede that he had used similar language in reference to Gennifer Flowers, another woman who claimed to have had a long-standing affair with Clinton.[84] Regardless of the intended victim of this class-based attack by Carville, all media outlets, including television, radio, the Internet, newspapers, and magazines, regaled audiences with play-by-play coverage of the ensuing battle of words. By publicizing Carville's use of the white-trash slur, the media kept the stereotype before people much longer than it might otherwise have lingered.

Just as news stories in the mainstream media may amplify negative images of the working class, another genre, called "white-trash culture" by one scholar,[85] also represents working-class whites in a derogatory fashion. The phrase "white-trash culture" refers to media forms such as tabloids (e.g., the *National Enquirer*), low-brow television talk shows, cable sports networks showing prole events such as demolition derbies, tractor pulls, and female mud wrestling, and websites that celebrate "redneck culture." According to sociologist Laura Grindstaff's study of "trashy" television talk shows, "The issue here is not the race or income level of guests per se but the relation of class and trash. ('They're white trash, black trash, Hispanic—any kind of, like, low-caliber people.')"[86] In Grindstaff's interviews, one producer described typical "guests" on this kind of talk show as follows:

> The trailer-park joke is not far from the truth. . . . Not that they necessarily live in trailer parks, but a lot of these people lead very transient lives. I would say their education level is high school for the most part, people who are semi-skilled. It's the crowd that would have been on an assembly line in a major manufacturing plant before all those jobs disappeared. It's a particular type because it satisfies—because we watch these things and it's almost like, "Gee, at least I'm not that bad off."[87]

Bill Maher, host of HBO's *Real Time with Bill Maher*, further demonstrated the extent to which television talk show personalities use terms like *white trash* and *trailer park trash* in his numerous comments about former Alaska governor Sarah Palin, who ran on the 2008 Republican ticket for U.S. vice president. Because her unmarried adolescent daughter, Bristol Palin, was pregnant during Palin's political campaign, Maher and numerous other television commentators and stand-up comedians referred to Palin's family as white trash. In an interview with Wolf Blitzer on CNN, conservative talk show host Glenn Beck referred not only to Palin and her family but also to himself as white trash. Beck stated that Palin had "white-trash family values" and commented that she could represent many "white-trash families in America," including his own.[88] When Levi Johnston, Bristol Palin's former boyfriend and the father of Sarah Palin's first grandchild, was later interviewed on CBS's *The Early Show*, he stated that the biggest misconception about him was "probably that my family's white trash."[89] The issue remained before the public because late-night talk show hosts and comedians continually brought it up. For example, David Letterman maintained a night-after-night monologue about Sarah Palin and why she is white trash. To prove his point, he held up photos of her hunting in Alaska and dressed in a stars-and-stripes bikini while holding an automatic weapon. He joked about her hunting prowess and about what he considered her redneck attitudes and behavior. Letterman was not alone: print media, television, and Web blogs were full of descriptions of Sarah Palin's trailer park lifestyle. According to well-known author Erica Jong, "White trash America certainly has allure for voters. Some people think rednecks are more American than Harvard educated intellectuals of mixed race. God help us in the [2008 presidential] election. The NRA and the oil industry sure won't."[90]

According to some media analysts, comments about white trash are primarily limited to cable network channels known for expressing conservative views, such as Fox News Network. Mainstream media sources, however, have more frequently employed terms like *trailer park* and *white trash* in describing people on reality shows and creating story lines for sitcoms. According to syndicated columnist Cal Thomas, other media outlets are trying to copy Fox News by "doing more tabloid, more big-lipped blonds, and all this kind of stuff," but "there's only so much of that trailer-trash pie to go around."[91]

Whether white-trash framing is meant as a joke or not, some public opposition to the use of this terminology stems from the perception that it is demeaning to hardworking people with very limited financial resources. A fund-raising effort for a girls' softball team in The Colony (a suburb north of Dallas, Texas) received negative media coverage after organizers planned a "white trash party" and promoted it with a flyer showing a scantily clad woman and a picture of Britney Spears on one side and a trailer park on the other. After extensive negative publicity, the party's theme was changed to "softball, hot dogs, and apple pie." Some partiers, however, still planned to dress for the original theme. One woman told a reporter, "I'm going over there and dress the part, with the fake mullet and everything." Another interviewee stated that she would be wearing her "Daisy Dukes" and a cut-off white tank top.[92]

Although media portrayals of working-class people as white trash come and go, they have a persistent power over time and place. They show up in episodes of adult animated TV series like *Family Guy* when Peter attends a redneck comedy show and decides to buy a pickup truck and become a redneck. On the Redneck Comedy Tour (based on Jeff Foxworthy's "You Might Be a Redneck If . . ." routine), comedians make comments such as "You know you're a redneck if you come from a rural area and behave as such." Others refer to "Larry the Guy Who Works for the Department of Water and Power," referring to Larry the Cable Guy, the stage name of Daniel Lawrence Whitney, a stand-up comedian and actor who, along with Foxworthy, starred on the now defunct WB channel's *Blue Collar TV* from 2004 to 2006 and featured in segments such as "White Trash Days of Our Lives," a spoof of the long-running daytime soap opera *The Days of Our Lives*. In the *Family Guy* episode titled "Airport '07" (originally "Keep on Truckin'"), Peter moves his living room couch to the front lawn of his home and paints the entire rear window of his new pickup, causing him to run into his neighbor's car as he backs out of the driveway. In a commentary accompanying the DVD version of *Family Guy*, the show's producer, David Goodman, comments that this episode shows little respect for rednecks.

Media framing that uses words like "redneck" or "trash" to suggest that working-class white Americans are less worthy than others is more acceptable to some when the economy is doing well and middle- and upper-class individuals feel secure about their position in the social hierarchy. Both the political climate and how people perceive themselves influence these images, as does people's need for a scapegoat onto which they can project their own problems. Moreover, some television entertainment shows featuring working-class characters as buffoons or bigots further reinforce media portrayals of working-class people as white trash.

CARICATURE FRAMING #2:
TV'S BUFFOONS, BIGOTS, AND SLOBS

Changes in the economic well-being of many people in the United States and other nations have affected media representations of working-class people as buffoons, bigots, and slobs since the first edition of *Framing Class* was published. However, as this section illustrates, a long history exists to show how the working class has either been absent altogether from media coverage or has been maligned in stories about people in this demographic. In 2010, ABC shifted the framing of one of its sitcoms, *The Middle*, as economic conditions worsened in the United States. According to Kelli Marshall, a film professor at the University of Toledo, this show initially targeted "the middle of the country, middle age, and middle class"; however, a shift occurred during the production and filming of the series:

> So why this shift? Why would *The Middle* move away from the buffoonish male stereotype that the working-class sitcom has perfected over half a century? Why would it bestow traits of the middle-class sitcom father—self-assured, admired, competent—on its blue-collar character? Three words: the current economy. . . . *The Middle* alone signifies familiar life in the Midwest. Now, consider the current unemployment rate: nearly 15 million people, the majority of whom live in blue-collar Michigan (14% jobless) as well as other Midwestern states. . . . If we reconcile these two realities, we might conclude that it would be mighty irresponsible and potentially risky of ABC to depict its sole blue-collar husband/father (and family) in the negative manner of the traditional working-class sitcom.[93]

As Marshall concludes, it is a shame that it takes dismal real-life situations such as the economic crisis of the early twenty-first century to shift some media portrayals of working-class people, particularly men, from unthinking, incompetent bumbler to undervalued blue-collar individual and strength of the country.

How did such negative caricature framing originate? What is the history of the representation of the working class as buffoons, bigots, and slobs? In one well-known study of prime-time television, media scholar Richard Butsch demonstrates how, since their earliest episodes, U.S. television situation comedies have manipulated gender traits (for instance, portraying blue-collar men as incompetent, immature, and irrational husbands and fathers) to suggest the inferiority of the working to the middle class. According to Butsch, media depictions of the working class typically are either absent or biased:

> The working class is not only underrepresented; the few men who are portrayed are buffoons. They are dumb, immature, irresponsible or lacking in common sense. This is the character of the husbands in almost every sitcom depicting a blue-collar (white) male head of house. *The Honeymooners, The Flintstones, All in the Family* and *The Simpsons* being the most famous examples. He is typically well-intentioned, even lovable, but no one to respect or emulate. These men are played against more mature, sensible wives, such as Ralph against Alice in *The Honeymooners*.[94]

The sitcoms Butsch mentions feature male characters in blue-collar jobs, such as bus driver Ralph Kramden in *The Honeymooners*, rock-quarry "crane" operator Fred Flintstone, dockworker Archie Bunker, and low-level nuclear power plant technician Homer Simpson. These characters are typically portrayed as inept bumblers who cannot achieve success because they do not have the necessary drive or smarts. Working-class wives in these shows are typically more intelligent, levelheaded, and in control than their husbands. According to Butsch, "Situation comedy is built around a humorous 'situation' which is resolved during the half hour. In working-class series the character typically caught in the situation, usually of his own making, was the man. Usually his wife had to help him out of the situation."[95] Unlike some middle-class shows that portray the "man of the house" as wise, cooperative, sensible, and mature, working-class sitcoms invert gender status and devalue male characters. Such media portrayals of working-class men preserve the status quo by reinforcing the notion that the male proletariat needs direct supervision at work and at home.

Early representations of the working class in television sitcoms were based on both class location and ethnicity. In NBC's *The Life of Riley*, Irish American Chester A. Riley (played in 1949 and 1950 by Jackie Gleason and from 1953 to 1958 by William Bendix) worked as an airplane riveter and lived in suburban Los Angeles with his nuclear family. Although each episode took place in the family's residence, Riley's job at the factory was a topic of frequent conversation, particularly regarding his frustration with his boss and animosity toward the upper classes, with their "pretentious nature."[96] The stereotype of the working-class buffoon was central to the story line of each episode, as described in one review:

> Each week, Riley first became flustered, then overwhelmed by seemingly minor problems concerning his job, his family, or his neighbors. These small matters—once Riley became involved—escalated to the verge of disaster. Riley's catch phrase—"What a revoltin' development this is!"—expressed his frustration and became part of the national idiom. His patient wife, Peg . . . managed to keep the family in order despite her husband's calamitous blunders.[97]

Following a similar format, CBS's *The Honeymooners* featured Ralph Kramden (Jackie Gleason) as a New York City bus driver who lived in a rundown Brooklyn apartment with his wife, Alice. In most episodes, Kramden was the object of ridicule and tongue-lashings by Alice, who frequently said, "I told you so." Although Ralph expressed ambivalence toward affluent people, he was not above trying one get-rich-quick scheme after another, such as investing in no-calorie pizza and marketing what he thought was Alice's homemade sauce (only to learn that it was dog food).[98] Comments Ralph made to Alice often indicated his working-class background, including "Just you wait, Alice. One of these days, pow, right in the kisser,"[99] alluding to domestic violence, which audiences supposedly understood would not actually happen in the Kramden household. Airing between 1952 and 1970 as *The Honeymooners* or *The Jackie Gleason Show*, this sitcom is still available on the TV Land network and on DVD.

Animated comedy series like *The Flintstones* and the more contemporary FOX shows *The Simpsons* and *Family Guy* also use buffoonery to frame the working class. In each of these series, the leading male character seems inspired by the characters of Chester Riley and Ralph Kramden. Like them, Fred Flintstone, Homer Simpson, and Peter Griffin are loudmouths who often talk before they think. And, like the earlier working-class sitcoms' wives, Peg Riley and Alice Kramden, the animated wives, Wilma Flintstone, Marge Simpson, and Lois Griffin are smarter than their husbands and often get them out of self-inflicted jams. In *Family Guy*, Lois Griffin comes from a family of wealthy socialites, the Pewterschmidts of Newport, Rhode Island; she met Peter, her future husband, when he worked as a towel boy at her family's country club. By contrast, Peter is a working-class Irish American Catholic. In *The Simpsons*, Homer often does something around the house or at work to create a crisis that others must resolve. He often concocts harebrained, get-rich-quick schemes that backfire, and his work ethic is lacking both at the nuclear power plant and at home, where he is largely useless in matters of domestic maintenance and family life. Although kindhearted, Homer generally provides a negative role model for his children, watching television constantly, eating junk food from the refrigerator or a sack, drinking beer and throwing the empties on the floor, belching loudly, talking in blue-collar speech patterns, and hanging out at Moe's, the local blue-collar bar. Like Riley's daughter Babs, Homer's daughter Lisa is studious, talented, and well organized. In *The Simpsons*, Lisa, although only a second grader, beats Homer at Scrabble, while Bart, the son, beats dad in a video boxing game.[100]

The Life of Riley, *The Honeymooners*, *The Simpsons*, and *Family Guy* all reinforce traditional gender roles: the father earns the family's income while the wife maintains the household. Although the creators of *The Simpsons* might argue that their show is nothing more than a parody of the earlier sitcoms mentioned, it fortifies for new generations of television audiences the stereotypes embodied by the leading characters, including the flustered husband, rock-solid wife, and children who are smarter or more conniving than their father. The *Family Guy* flaunts some of these conventions by having a mother, Lois Griffin, who at first glance appears to be the stereotypical TV wife, a stay-at-home mom who teaches piano lessons to supplement the family income; however, Lois has also been a promiscuous drug user, a gambling addict, and a kleptomaniac, as well as one of the stabler members of her dysfunctional family.

The framing of sitcom story lines not only creates and reinforces the image of the working-class buffoon but portrays some members of this group as racist. Archie Bunker (Carroll O'Connor) of *All in the Family* has been referred to as the "quintessential, all-American bigot . . . who was part of the old guard who failed to recognize the melting pot mentality of the modern world."[101] Indeed, Bunker's character is an intolerant, opinionated, and uneducated blue-collar dock foreman who drives a taxi on the side to earn extra money. Eventually, Archie buys a bar, at which point the show was renamed *Archie Bunker's Place*, but Bunker himself remains a narrow-minded proletarian throughout the show's nine seasons. Even though Archie is sometimes kindhearted when dealing with his wife, Edith (Jean Stapleton), or his daughter, Gloria (Sally Struthers), he embodies working-class sexism, for instance, in referring to Edith as a "dingbat" and speaking to her in a demeaning manner. Edith, portrayed as ditzy and subservient but kind to other people, perfectly balances Archie's harsh character.[102]

Much of Bunker's racism surfaces in conversations with his son-in-law, Mike Stivic (Rob Reiner), and verbal battles with his African American neighbor, George Jefferson (Sherman Hemsley). The Jeffersons' son, Lionel (Mike Evans), shares Mike's liberal views, and bitter debates take place with Archie on one side and Mike and Lionel on the other.

Though as intolerant as Archie, George Jefferson is portrayed as a wealthier, opinionated African American, in contrast to Archie's role as a white, working-class bigot. In early seasons of *All in the Family*, Archie's racism is apparent in episodes like the one in which he refuses to donate his blood because he does not want it to be mixed with a black person's. In another episode, "Lionel Moves into the Neighborhood," Archie tries to prevent a black family from buying the house next door, not realizing that the potential buyers, the Jeffersons, are Lionel's parents. Since Lionel has been a frequent visitor to the Bunkers' home in the past, Archie's opposition creates embarrassment for the Bunker family, which is soon overshadowed by the barbs Archie and George exchange.[103] George Jefferson became the lead character in a spin-off series, *The Jeffersons*, after becoming wealthy and moving from Archie's neighborhood to Manhattan's affluent Upper East Side.

By the ninth (and final) season of *All in the Family*, another black family has moved into the Bunkers' neighborhood, but Archie maintains his racist attitude. When Edith prepares sandwiches to welcome the new neighbors, Archie loudly rails at her for desiring to befriend them. Showing how deeply ingrained his attitudes are, he tells Edith, "You know damn well there's certain things about me I ain't never gonna change. But you keep asking me to make out like I'm gonna," to which Edith replies, after a lengthy pause, "That's right."[104] With this conclusion to the show, Archie, the working-class buffoon and bigot, demonstrates that he was either unable or unwilling to change.

Norman Lear, creator and producer of *All in the Family*, has argued that Archie's attitudes throughout the series merely reflect how life really was in the United States: "If a couple thousand years of Judeo-Christian ethic have not solved the problems of bigotry and narrow-mindedness, I'd be a fool to think a little half-hour situation comedy is gonna do the trick."[105] Some media scholars have argued, however, that portrayals of working-class characters as "lovable bigots" may serve as "proof that racism really isn't a dangerous thing. It might be embarrassing, or unsettling, but never dangerous."[106] As one analyst stated after Carroll O'Connor's death in 2001,

> Archie Bunker never led a lynch mob, but the "Bunkerish" attitude allows for modern lynch mobs that target Blacks, whether in police departments, courts or social service agencies. . . . Images do matter. They help to legitimize, uplift and protect or dehumanize, violate and make expendable. So the world may miss Mr. O'Connor, but don't grieve for Archie Bunker, he's alive and well.[107]

Though less likely to portray working-class women as buffoons or bigots, some sitcoms depict them as lacking in class, particularly as compared with their middle- and upper-middle-class counterparts. The character of Roseanne Conner is perhaps the closest female equivalent of Archie Bunker. According to one media scholar, the sitcom *Roseanne* contributed to the "Roseannification" of working-class women in the media by showing these women as violating the "codes of bourgeois respectability and the codes of femininity."[108]

Since the 1990s, some working-class sitcom portrayals have been subtler; however, characters' behavior, the sets on which the episodes are staged, and other telltale signs of characters' proletariat status reinforce earlier stereotypes. Consider, for example, the syndicated sitcom *The King of Queens*, set in the working-class New York City borough of Queens. The show follows Doug Heffernan (Kevin James), a deliveryman for the International Parcel Service, and his wife, Carrie (Leah Remini), who holds down various jobs over the course of the series. Like most other working-class television wives, Carrie is more ambitious than Doug, and her desire to shop far exceeds the family's budget. Consequently, the Heffernans have numerous financial crises intensified by events such as mold damage to their house and Carrie's being laid off. To make matters worse, Carrie's obstinate, opinionated father, Arthur Spooner (Jerry Stiller), lives in the Heffernans' basement, which had previously been Doug's recreation room, where he and his pals watched a large-screen television. Spooner is often the brunt of working-class jokes, as when friends of the Heffernans reluctantly take him to a Mexican food restaurant and let him eat the hot sauce.

In keeping with earlier working-class sitcoms, Doug is portrayed as a kindhearted bumbler with a slob factor evidenced by extensive discussions about his weight and fixation on food. Like his sitcom predecessors, Doug is also a slob when it comes to performing tasks around the house; in one case he cannot even find the scissors and tape to finish a project, and Carrie has to come to his rescue. The slob factor intensifies when Doug hangs out with his friends, Deacon and Spence, and his cousin, all of whom experience male bonding and share "guy" humor. In "Wild Cards," for example, Doug and Deacon (who is also his coworker) are returning from a delivery in Philadelphia when they decide to go to Atlantic City for an evening of gambling. Since Doug had promised Carrie that they would see a Broadway play that night, he tells her that he cannot go because he has to make an unexpected night delivery. Doug loses all his money and gets into a dispute with Deacon; Carrie catches him in the lie and chastises him about his "boys' night out."[109] This episode illustrates a widely held stereotype that working-class men bond with each other over alcohol, at gambling or strip clubs, while leaving their wives and children at home to fend for themselves.

The setting of *The King of Queens* reinforces the working-class slob stereotype. Like the set of *Roseanne*, the Heffernans' living room has an oversized sofa with a shawl draped across the back. The cluttered kitchen contains a small wooden table and chairs and a refrigerator covered with magnets and pictures. Other than his delivery uniform, Doug usually wears a Jets T-shirt or similar attire, while Carrie, who has a shopping problem, sometimes buys expensive clothes at department stores and boutiques, then returns them. If television portrayals of working-class families like the Heffernans have grown somewhat more sophisticated, contemporary sitcoms still employ many of the recurring themes and characterizations of earlier shows, where the working class typically fares less well than the upper classes. In 2010, reruns of *The King of Queens* still aired five nights a week on television, and DVD and Web viewings remained popular despite the fact that the series filmed new episodes from 1998 to 2007.

Other working-class sitcoms, such as *My Name Is Earl*, air for three or four seasons on network and cable television because this type of entertainment appeals to younger males. *My Name Is Earl* abounds with stereotypical portrayals of white trash and slobs: Earl Hickey (Jason Lee) personifies the white-trash thief who makes people want to lock their doors when they drive past. Earl's luck appears to change when he buys a winning scratch-off lottery ticket worth $100,000, but the ticket flies away when he is hit by a car. After he wakes up in a hospital bed, he watches a TV show about karma and decides that he must make amends to all the people he has harmed in his life. As Earl works to be a better person and improve his karma by doing things like picking up trash outside the motel where he lives, the winning lottery ticket miraculously blows into his hand, and his troubles begin all over. Later episodes of *My Name Is Earl* reveal problems he encounters while trying to make up for the bad things he has done. White-trash and blue-collar culture infuse each episode in the appearance and actions of Earl and other characters. Earl's ex-wife, Joy Turner (Jaime Pressly), tries to steal his lottery winnings. Joy usually wears short, short cutoff blue jeans and a very tight sweater that exposes her midriff. With her blond hair piled up on her head, she sports a kind of low-brow headband that shows "attitude."[110]

Although sitcoms reinforce the idea that the working class still exists in the United States, some media framing has focused on creating just the opposite impression—namely, that the kinds of jobs typically considered working class in this country are vanishing.

FADING BLUE-COLLAR FRAMING:
OUT OF WORK OR UNHAPPY AT WORK

Twenty-first-century media representations of the working class have described the diminished political and economic clout of the laboring class as compared to the heyday of unionized blue-collar workers' earning relatively high wages with good benefits and job stability. News reports now focus on the "fading" of blue-collar work due to job loss, the threat of cheap immigrant labor, the outsourcing of jobs to other countries, the downgrading of blue-collar work generally, and the number of working-class families joining the ranks of the working poor or unemployed. A political cartoon summed up the problems of the formerly well-paid union factory worker by showing a man wearing a hard hat and work shirt sitting across a desk from a young woman at a computer. Behind them, a sign reads, "U.S. Job Placement Agency." The man says, "I'm an experienced factory worker." The woman replies, "What's a factory?"

In this visual image, cartoonist Signe Wilkinson captures a major problem facing the working class: blue-collar workers are becoming dinosaurs as their jobs continue to vanish. For example, an article about the closing of a sugar factory tells the story of a worker who had been employed for twenty-eight years at the Domino Sugar plant in Brooklyn, which had been in continuous operation since the 1880s and provided work for thousands of people. However, as Richard Rednour, the laid-off worker, lamented, "I learned this past week that I'm a dinosaur. . . . Having a job for a long time in one place is not necessarily a good thing. It used to mean I was reliable."[111]

Earlier framing of articles about plant closings often focused on the effects of globalization on the U.S. working class. Contemporary framing now highlights how the Great Recession has killed off jobs and the number of weeks many people have been out of work (ninety-nine and up for many). Looking first at the issue of plant closings, one recurring theme in news reports centers on how native-born American workers are pitted against workers in other countries. Another theme involves the negative consequences for the U.S. working class of having so many immigrant workers in the United States. The first of these themes juxtaposes the job losses experienced by American workers following numerous plants closings with the gains of workers in other countries who are hired in similar positions—for much lower wages and fewer benefits—when the factories relocate. An example of this framing is found in articles about the closing of the Levi Strauss plant in San Antonio, Texas, and former employees' frustration at realizing "their" work was being exported to Mexico. Headlines like "As Levi's Work Is Exported, Stress Stays Home"[112] tell this story in few words. When factories close as work is exported to other countries, former employees must bear the stress triggered by being out of work and without a paycheck.

In factories across America, employees have arrived at work one day expecting to do their jobs and instead learned that the factory was closing soon, leaving them unemployed. According to one veteran Levi Strauss employee, "There still probably is an American dream [for workers in other countries]. But what about us? What happens to our American dream?"[113] The photos accompanying such articles typically show longtime employees dejectedly leaving the factory after learning of their impending unemployment. A photo accompanying an article describing the closing of the Syracuse, New York, Carrier plant shows a twenty-five-year employee with his back to the camera so that the writing on his T-shirt is visible: "UTC Carrier: The Un-American Dream."[114] The linkage between working-class job loss and the decline of the American Dream is a key framing device in many media accounts of plant closings.

The framing of reports about job loss since 2007 has emphasized the problem's permanent nature. The writer of an article titled "7.9 Million Jobs Lost—Many Forever" emphasizes that it is "increasingly likely" that many jobs "killed off" in the recession will never reappear. Based on government reports, one pressing problem associated with job loss is that hiring has slowed to a relative trickle. If hiring and job creation started up again at the old rate, analysts estimate, it would take at least three years to recapture the lost jobs, much less to add any new ones. According to one analyst, "We've got the wrong people in the wrong place with the wrong skills." To mitigate this problem, construction workers in states like California and Florida and auto workers in Michigan would have to relocate and retrain to have any hope of ever finding a new job.[115]

Outsourcing has also contributed to the loss of millions of U.S. jobs in manufacturing and service industries: workers in other countries where wages are lower are now filling many of these positions. Media documentaries on outsourcing highlight the movement of jobs to nations such as India or China and show the negative effects on workers in both the United States and the countries where these positions are now located. An NBC sitcom, *Outsourced*, has sought to frame the issue of outsourcing humorously by depicting a supposedly all-American company, Mid-American Novelties, that sells products such as whoopee cushions, foam hands with extended fingers (like those used at sporting events), and plastic molds that look like pools of fake blood. The Mid-American Novelties call center, where customers place orders, has been outsourced to India. When the company sends a manager, Todd Dempsy (Ben Rappaport), from the United States to run the call center, he quickly learns that he must educate his new staff in the ways of American culture so that they can more effectively interact with U.S. callers and make sales. To accomplish this goal, Dempsy requires employees in India to watch old films so that they can learn U.S. popular culture. They must study English, lose their accents, and pretend to live in the United States when talking with callers. This humorous framing downplays the crisis that outsourcing has created for many U.S. workers and their families. It also minimizes the problems faced by people who increasingly must rely on globalized call centers for technology support and to purchase products and services.

In media framing of stories about job loss in the United States, illegal immigration is a key culprit, along with downsizing and outsourcing. Articles and news reports about the "Americano Dream" explain how indigenous workers are pitted against illegal immigrants, sometimes referred to more politely as undocumented workers, who are a source of cheap labor in this country. Frequently, media sources employ this terminology when a major corporation is accused of labor violations, as when Walmart, the nation's largest private employer (with 1.4 million U.S. workers in 2009), was alleged to be using undocumented workers as cleaning personnel in its megastores. Although earlier media coverage of the chain had praised Walmart's economic success and applauded the ingenuity of founder Sam Walton and other members of his family, subsequent news reports focused on the corporation's questionable labor practices, including the use of undocumented workers.[116] According to Walmart officials, the company hired subcontractors to do the janitorial work without knowing that they hired illegal immigrants:

> After federal agents raided 60 Wal-Mart stores in October and found more than 200 illegal immigrants in the cleaning crews, the world's largest retailer was

quick to defend itself from this enormous embarrassment. Wal-Mart's officers said they had no idea those workers were illegal, insisting they knew next to nothing about the workers from Mexico, Mongolia, Russia and elsewhere because they were employed by contractors. Nor did Wal-Mart know, its spokesmen said, that the contractors were cutting corners by not paying overtime or Social Security taxes or by flouting other labor laws, as the investigators claimed.[117]

As the media later reported in articles such as "Wal-Mart Settles Illegal Immigration Case for $11M," the retailer paid up to end the federal probe and escape criminal charges for using illegal immigrants as custodial workers. Twelve businesses that provided contract janitor services to Walmart also agreed to pay $4 million in fines and pled guilty to criminal immigration charges to resolve the matter.[118] Walmart officials emphasized that the chain is a good corporate citizen and does not hire undocumented workers. Walmart's website states that the company provides good wages and benefits for the workers it hires, and these individuals often include college students and retirees who want to earn extra income.[119] In framing media stories such as these, reporters bandy around phrases like "cheap labor" to describe immigrant workers—documented or not—as a potential threat to the indigenous working class. As a source of cheap labor, however, undocumented workers do not have access to many legitimate jobs and are vulnerable to exploitation by labor contractors, unscrupulous immigration officials, and others who prey on their illegal status.

Media framing of news stories about undocumented workers questions the legality of hiring practices and raises the issue of whether these workers take jobs away from U.S. citizens and depress working-class wages. Some journalists have publicized data suggesting that immigrants in the early twenty-first century have fared better in the job market than U.S. citizens. By 2010, however, media framing had shifted to describing the uncertain work status of undocumented immigrant workers. For example, the *New York Times* article "A Slippery Place in the U.S. Work Force" describes the delicate position of immigrant workers who took "the lowest-paying elbow-grease jobs, some hazardous, in chicken plants and furniture factories" and have been hard hit by the spiraling economy and a massive crackdown on illegal immigration. Problems in the U.S. economy have rendered undocumented workers' already tenuous foothold in the workforce even more precarious.[120]

According to 2007 media reports, the flow of immigration has continued to slow as federal and state officials have worked to reduce the number of people illegally crossing the U.S.-Mexican border and as the U.S. economic recession has continued. By sharp contrast, past articles, such as "U.S. Payday Is Something to Write Home About," once described how immigrants working low-paying jobs in the United States sent billions of dollars to families living in Mexico:

> Inside his little Western wear store [in Austin, Texas] . . . Francisco Javier Aceves can't help but feel a kinship with the angular young men who come in to buy jeans, cowboy boots, phone cards and cell phones. As sure as a regular payday, they come in also to wire money to their families back home in Mexico, in places such as Veracruz, Tabasco, Chiapas and Oaxaca. "Sometimes they come three or four in a car," Aceves said about his customers. "Sometimes they just start lining up to wire money."[121]

The men described by this shop owner earned between $200 and $400 per week and sent $100 to $300 to family members in Mexico. To put this figure in perspective, journalists estimated that immigrant workers sent more money back to Mexico annually than that country earned from tourism or foreign investment.[122]

A few years later, media framing of stories about Latino immigrant workers shifted. Articles such as "Fewer Latino Immigrants Sending Money Home" indicated that more than 3 million workers had stopped sending money to families in their home countries and that increasing numbers were considering giving up on U.S. jobs and returning to their countries of origin. As a result, the number of money transfers (such those described above) declined sharply, and people who continued to send money home often reduced the amount because they had less income and job security and needed to spend the money on their own survival.[123] Some media analysts argue that immigration, legal and illegal, continues to put a fiscal strain on state and local governments, depress wages for low-income workers, widen the U.S. income gap, and displace Americans in the job market.[124] By contrast, other analysts assert that foreign workers revitalize cities, contribute to consumer spending, and pay taxes that prop up Social Security and the federal budget.[125] Regardless of which perspective we choose, clearly immigrant workers in the U.S. economy will remain a pressing issue for the foreseeable future, and these workers will continue to receive extensive attention from politicians and journalists alike.

The final theme in fading blue-collar framing is the increasing impoverishment of the working class as more people join the ranks of the working poor or the unemployed. As with many other topics of media interest, journalists and academics have analyzed the issue of the working poor through the lens of people who are employed full-time but cannot make ends meet. The publication of a best-selling or scholarly book often generates reviews and articles in the print media and heated debates on television "news" programs. A number of books have served as the catalyst for stories about the fading nature of blue-collar work and growth of the working poor: *Nickel and Dimed: On (Not) Getting By in America*, by Barbara Ehrenreich[126]; *The Working Poor: Invisible in America*, by David K. Shipler[127]; *The Betrayal of Work: How Low-Wage Jobs Fail 30 Million Americans and Their Families*, by Beth Shulman;[128] and *Broke, USA: From Pawnshops to Poverty, Inc.—How the Working Poor Became Big Business*, by Gary Rivlin.[129]

Shipler and Shulman based their books on interviews with low-wage workers; Ehrenreich took a series of low-wage jobs herself as a waitress, hotel maid, cleaning woman, nursing home aide, and Walmart sales clerk to see if she could make ends meet on the meager wages she earned. The attention the media gave these books through reviews, reprints of excerpts, author interviews, and other commentaries turned the subject of the working poor, at least temporarily, into a hot topic. Journalists played with the phrase "Take this job and . . ." in headlines that proclaimed this demographic's bad fortune: "Take This Job and Starve" was the banner of a *Time* magazine review[130]; a *New York Times* book review declared, "Take This Job and Be Thankful (for $6.80 an Hour)."[131] According to the *Times* review, the fading of the working class into the ranks of the working poor is partly, but not entirely, society's fault:

> Shipler doesn't place all the blame on society. The people he meets often lack the soft skills that employers require, like showing up on time, following directions, even knowing how to comb their hair. To be sure, they need better schools and reliable medical insurance, but they also need to know better than to use their precious tax-refund checks to get tattoos. Sometimes they clip coupons and turn up faithfully at job training. Sometimes they get drunk and disorderly. They go in for ill-advised sex and foolish spending sprees. In other words, the working poor are not so different from Paris Hilton, except that they have less money. And that makes all the difference. When they stumble, low-wage earners have nothing to fall back on.[132]

Although Shipler, author of *The Working Poor*, is credited with "exposing the wretched conditions of these invisible Americans" and thus performing a "noble and badly needed service,"[133] media framing of articles about popular books dealing with this group tends to shape the discussion within the initial framework established by the book's author, an approach that typically does not accrue diverse viewpoints. For example, Shipler's book tends to blame women who are single heads of household for their low-income status, as when he writes, "Married, Ann was in the middle-class. . . . Divorced, she sank rapidly."[134] By contrast, Barbara Ehrenreich's *Nickel and Dimed* provides more anecdotal evidence, based on her personal journey as a low-wage worker, to suggest that corporate greed and other societal factors, rather than the behavior of the working poor, should be blamed for their economic condition. When Ehrenreich reinterviewed several of the individuals she met while writing *Nickel and Dimed*, she found no significant improvement in their financial condition. A woman referred to as "Melissa" in the book was still working at Walmart, where her wages had risen from $7 to $10 an hour in the intervening nine-year period.[135] In his 2010 book, Gary Rivlin emphasizes the exploitation of the working poor by the "poverty industry." According to Rivlin, the recession has not been equally difficult for everyone: the "mercenary entrepreneurs" have enriched themselves by preying on the "credit-hungry working poor" and misleading them about instant tax refunds, payday loans, subprime mortgages, pawnshop specials, and rental furniture and appliances with strings attached.[136]

Were it not for books like these, the mainstream media might not have published as many reports about the growing problems of the working poor. Through media framing of stories about this group and the increasing problem of long-term unemployment, journalists provide media audiences with information and explode myths that have perpetuated and exacerbated economic and social inequalities in this country for many years. In regard to this myth, *Newsweek* states,

> America is a country that now sits atop the precarious latticework of myth. It is the myth that work provides rewards, that working people can support their families. It's a myth that has become so divorced from reality that it might as well begin with the words "Once upon a time. . . ." The American Dream for the well-to-do grows from the bowed backs of the working poor, who too often have to choose between groceries and rent.[137]

And for blue-collar workers and the working poor, being unemployed is an even greater financial and psychological burden. Media framing of stories about unemployment in this sector of the workforce has grown increasingly poignant during the 2000s. Articles like "What Recovery? For the Unemployed, the Pain Gets Worse" point to the anguish of unemployed workers who know that their unemployment benefits are running out. As jobless figures continued to increase in 2010, more media stories emphasized how long some individuals had been on the unemployment rolls and suggested that some had given up trying to find a job. Even those who finally found work were concerned because they had accepted a pay cut or had taken a job that did not utilize their education or prior experience or that was temporary in nature. These included the thousands of temporary workers hired to conduct the 2010 U.S. Census.[138]

Here, we return to where this chapter began, with the individuals who remain largely invisible because they blend in or work without having much say in what they do, individuals who have worked hard for most of their lives only to learn that they cannot find a job and that the "safety net" they presumed would exist if they faced long-term unemployment is shaky indeed.[139] Perhaps these people find their primary voice in the work of analysts who write about their dilemmas and the reports of journalists and television reporters who pick up on their stories, for "human-interest" filler if nothing else.

EFFECTS OF MEDIA FRAMING OF THE WORKING CLASS

The media typically focus on minute details about how the rich and famous live, including how many houses and vehicles they own, but the working class simply does not have the same appeal to most journalists and television entertainment writers. Whereas the upper and upper-middle classes are showcased for their conspicuous consumerism and lavish lifestyles, the working class—which produces many of the goods and provides most of the services enjoyed by the leisure classes—is largely invisible in the media. Frequently, in the past, this invisibility has resulted from journalists' absorbing members of the working class into an all-inclusive "middle-class majority," creating an inaccurate assessment of the actual resources and social status of the working class. Thus, (mis)placing working-class people in the middle class helps to perpetuate the idea of the American Dream, as communications scholar Linda Holtzman states: "The working-class characters [in television shows] do little to challenge the dominant ideology and the myth of the American Dream."[140]

In media representations of the working class, some stories focus on the greed of workers (for better wages, working conditions, and benefits) but say nothing about avaricious owners, managers, and shareholders, whose wealth can be attributed partly to the work of those below them in the class structure. Working-class union members are portrayed at best as greedy, at worst as shysters or criminals. Even nonunion members of the working class are suspect when it comes to honesty and integrity on the job. This stereotype is employed for humor's sake in old television comedies such as *The Help*, one episode of which takes a possible theft by the hired help as its plot. The rich lady of the house, Arlene Ridgeway (Brenda Strong), accuses her maid, cook, nanny, chauffeur, personal trainer, and dog walker of stealing $1,000 from her purse. At the end of the episode, viewers learn that she has misplaced the money herself; in the meantime, however, the help have scrounged to come up with the money so she will not fire them. Although supposed to poke fun at class warfare, sitcoms like this also reinforce negative stereotypes of the working class as untrustworthy. Even when the joke behind the stereotype is understood, such representations may make the middle and upper classes feel superior to the working class. As the rich woman in *The Help* derisively declares, "I wouldn't want to be a maid."

Derogatory depictions of the working class are not limited to issues of trustworthiness and reliability. Stereotypes also highlight the supposed lack of values, taste, and good manners among people in this group. In contrast with their emphasis on the middle class as the backbone of the nation and the standard bearer with respect to values, the media sometimes portray members of the working class as white trash, buffoons, bigots, and slobs. These depictions raise important questions: Are middle- and upper-class audiences laughing with or at the working-class characters? Do working-class people identify with these negative images and see themselves as lacking in values, taste, and refinement? Is the embracing of a proletariat identity by some members of the working class a genuine affirmation of who they believe they are, or does it reflect how the media have popularized and commercialized negative images of the working class so that a T-shirt emblazoned with "Trailer Park Trash" is deemed humorous or stylish?

Perhaps in faded blue-collar framing the media come closest to providing an accurate representation of the working class and the issues that affect people in this segment of the social hierarchy. By presenting real issues important to members of the working class, including escalating job loss, increases in immigrant workers who might threaten employment, the changing nature of available work, and the dramatic growth of the working poor, the media sometimes raise important questions. Perhaps they should reassess the importance of the working class and view its members as the proverbial canaries in the coal mine. In that light, as the gap between the wealthy and the poor continues to widen, the problems of working-class people should signal a warning that trends evident in the early twenty-first century will negatively affect many people—even on other rungs of the class ladder. If the media continue to ignore the concerns of "the silenced majority," they will ignore pressing issues faced by all of us.

Although the working class and working poor often serve as little more than political props for politicians in election years and receive media coverage in that connection, a few journalists see the crucial problems they face. One is *New York Times* columnist Bob Herbert:

> It's like running on a treadmill that keeps increasing in speed. You have to go faster and faster just to stay in place. Or, as a factory worker said many years ago, "You can work 'til you drop dead, but you won't get ahead." American workers have been remarkably productive in recent years, but they are getting fewer and fewer of the benefits of this increased productivity. While the economy, as measured by the gross domestic product, has been strong for some

time now, ordinary workers have gotten little more than the back of the hand from employers who have pocketed an unprecedented share of the cash from this burst of economic growth.[141]

This statement was written in 2004. Six years later, in 2010, Herbert saw the problem as even more pressing when he described a study of the economic security index, which measures the percentage of Americans who experience a decrease in their household income of 25 percent or more in one year without having the financial resources to offset that loss:

> The pain coursing through American families is all too real and no one seems to know what to do about it. A rigorous new analysis for the Rockefeller Foundation shows Americans are more economically insecure now than they have been in a quarter of a century, and the trend lines suggest that things will only get worse. Rampant joblessness and skyrocketing medical costs are among the biggest factors tearing at the very fabric of American economic life so painstakingly put together in the early post–World War II decades.[142]

Herbert believes that many of the problems of the working class, the working poor, and the unemployed can be attributed to megacorporations that continue to make profits but will not employ new workers, policy makers who refuse to deal with the increasing economic insecurity of people in this country, and the lack of a safety net to help people get back on their feet. In the twenty-first century, working-class people are not treated as thoughtful individuals who might have important things to say. Instead, the media tend to view middle- and upper-class opinions as more significant and relevant to audiences' interests. Perhaps the tarnished metal frames (metaphorically speaking) that the media have employed in portraying the working class should be polished to enable more accurate representations of the working class that include the opinions of its members, how they live their everyday lives, and the positive contributions that they make at home, at work, and in the community. Most important, perhaps, would be a more accurate assessment of the class-related issues and realities of social inequality that affect people in this group; their problems should be of greater concern to everyone, rich and poor alike, if the adage "As the working class goes, so goes the nation" is accurate. In Bob Herbert's words, the vast gaps in the condition of groups at the top and bottom of the economic ladder are "unmistakable signs of impending societal instability. This is dangerous stuff. Nothing good can come of vast armies of the unemployed just sitting out there, simmering."[143] If analysts are correct that the working class actually constitutes the majority of people in this nation, perhaps we (and the media) should be looking to them to see the future of the United States.

Chapter 6

Splintered Wooden Frames

The Middle Class

Portland, Maine:

> Matthew Charlebois is spending a lot more time these days worrying about things he once took for granted. He's scared he'll lose his home. He wonders whether he'll be able to afford new clothes for his job search. He wishes he could do more for his daughter's upcoming wedding. . . . "[Before] I wasn't worried about everything. Now I don't know if I'm going to have to squat and live in a tent city in Deering Oaks [Maine] or not."
>
> The recession has Mainers like Charlebois worried about something very basic: falling out of the middle class. Job insecurity, investment losses, declining home values and threats to their health care coverage have these people concerned about some once-fundamental assumptions they held about their quality of life.[1]

The middle class has been considered the backbone of the nation and for good reason: until the turn of the twenty-first century, middle-income Americans had continued to make absolute progress in earnings and managed to endure relative declines in the economy for decades. Since 1999, however, many people in the middle class have not made economic progress, and the economic insecurity of many so-called middle-class families is greater than it has been at any time on record. As politicians and journalists discuss the possible decline of the middle class, it is important to understand the various ways in which terms like *middle class* and *middle income* are used. Let's look at exactly what categories of people media sources typically include in their definition of the middle class and determine how accurate that categorization is.

THE MIDDLE CLASS:
AN AMBIGUOUS BUT POPULAR TERM

In his 1830s work *Democracy in America*, Alexis de Tocqueville stated that the United States had a condition of equality. For Tocqueville, the ideal of democracy was linked with equality, and he asserted that the United States appeared to have melded into one class: the middle class.[2] Yet, the exact meaning of the term with regard to this country—whether in the nineteenth century or today—is unclear. To some people, being middle-class means having an income at least three times the poverty level or within some range of median household income in any given year.[3] Neither of these definitions, however, accurately delineates the U.S. middle class. Since the 1980s, for example, the line between the middle and working classes has become more ambiguous because it is difficult to determine what dollar figures serve as the upper and lower cutoff points for the middle class. This does not, however, keep politicians from proposing plans to help reverse a decade of middle-class decline, as one journalist explains:

> The definition of who is in the middle class is fuzzy, but it's not hard to see why the White House is pitching proposals directly to the kinds of families who work, vote, and traditionally have had opportunities to steadily climb the economic ladder. . . . After rising for generations, living standards have stagnated over the past decade for millions in this group. . . . All this doesn't mean that middle-income America is falling off an economic cliff, or that it has been hit harder by recession than any other groups. . . . But America's middle class represents a large swath of the voting public, a group more politically powerful than the poor and more vulnerable to economic swings than the wealthy. And the goal of an expanding and prospering middle class has long served as a litmus test for the nation's well-being.[4]

Based on this approach, many politicians are less concerned about who is in the middle class. Most important is who thinks they are, and most people in the United States identify with this class category.

According to sociologist Dennis Gilbert, the typical middle-class household income is about $70,000 (in 2008 dollars). Gilbert suggests that we can solve the dilemma of what constitutes the middle class by distinguishing between the terms *middle class* and *middle income*. As Gilbert points out, what is shrinking in the United States is not the middle class per se but rather the middle-income group because of declining earnings in both the middle and working classes and a corresponding dramatic increase in incomes of people at the upper end of the economic distribution.[5] Popular misperceptions about what constitutes the middle class, however, do not keep most Americans from considering themselves members of that demographic. For example, according to a 2010 report issued by the U.S. Department of Commerce's Economics and Statistics Administration, most Americans consider themselves middle class, particularly when that class is defined as a combination of values, expectations, and aspirations, as well as income levels.[6] Similarly, a 2008 Pew Research Center study found that 53 percent of adult Americans referred to themselves as middle class, while an additional 10 percent identified themselves as lower-middle class, even though they actually comprised a more varied lot.[7] Clearly, income levels alone do not define the middle class: the mathematical middle has room for only 20 percent of all U.S. households, not 53 percent or more. Taking just the center 20 percent would place households with earnings between $40,000 and $62,000 in the true middle.

Even sociologists who have spent years studying the U.S. class structure do not agree about what constitutes the middle class or whether such a class actually exists (some assert that there are only two classes: the upper class and the working class). Social analyst Barbara Ehrenreich expresses the problem well when she states that "class is a notion that is inherently fuzzy at the edges"[8]; however, she believes that the middle class, defined somewhat abstractly, consists of people whose economic and social status is based on education rather than their ownership of capital or property.

Some sociologists use occupational categories to identify social classes. One widely used model divides the middle class into two categories: the middle class itself, consisting of people who have some college education and significant skills and work under loose supervision, and the upper-middle class, consisting of highly educated professionals and corporate managers.[9] Some analysts identify a third middle-class category: the lower-middle class. The dividing line between the middle-middle class and the lower-middle class is very blurred, particularly with regard to the exact point at which the middle class ends and the working class begins. Increasingly, sociologists do not distinguish between the lower-middle and working classes, seeing them as one and the same. This category comprises semiskilled workers, many of whom are employed in factories or in the service sector (as clerks and sales associates, for instance), where their responsibilities involve routine, mechanized tasks requiring little skill beyond basic literacy and a brief period of on-the-job training.[10]

Members of the upper-middle class are often thought to have achieved the American Dream; unlike many in the upper class, however, most members of the upper-middle class must work for a living. Early in the twenty-first century, two best-selling books offered new concepts about the upper-middle class. In *Bobos in Paradise*, David Brooks suggests that many people in the upper-middle class are now "the new upper class," a well-educated elite that he calls "Bobos" (bourgeois bohemians).[11] Based in part on information in the *New York Times* wedding section about brides, grooms, and their families, Brooks argues that the "white-shoed, Whartonized, Episcopalian establishmentarians with protruding jaws" are long gone from the ranks of the privileged upper class, having been replaced by "mountaineering-booted overachievers with excellent orthodontia and impressive GRE scores."[12] However, Brooks's description of the future prospects of the so-called Bobos gives them the appearance of being upper-middle class at best:

> But members of today's educated class can never be secure about their own future. A career crash could be just around the corner. In the educated class even social life is a series of aptitude tests; we all must perpetually perform in accordance with the shift in norms of propriety, ever advancing signals of cultivation. . . . And more important, members of the educated class can never be secure about their children's future. The kids have some domestic and educational advantages—all those tutors and developmental toys—but they still have to work through school and ace the SATs just to achieve the same social rank as their parents. Compared to past elites, little is guaranteed.[13]

In another best-selling book on this subject, *The Rise of the Creative Class*, Richard Florida asserts that the United States has a creative class composed of two major occupational categories: the supercreative core, which consists of occupations in computer science; mathematics; architecture; engineering; the life, physical, and social sciences; education; the arts; and the media; and the creative professions, which are occupations in management, business, finance, law, health care, and high-end sales. In Florida's view, these creative occupations stand in sharp contrast to working-class, service-class, and agricultural occupations. About 30 percent of the U.S. workforce would fit into Florida's creative class, which would thus constitute the dominant economic group.

Books such as these influenced media framing of stories about the upper-middle class and produced cartoons such as one in the *New Yorker* showing a man and woman sitting in a restaurant booth and holding hands. The woman says, "It would never work out between us, Tom—we're from two totally different tiers of the upper middle class."[14]

As compared with the upper-middle class, people in the middle-middle class are characterized as possessing a two- or four-year college degree, having more supervision at work, and experiencing less job stability than those in the upper-middle class. Those in the "solid" middle class are typically characterized as most likely to feel the squeeze of layoffs at work, escalating housing prices, lack of affordable health insurance, and economic problems that contribute to overuse of credit cards.

FORMS OF MEDIA FRAMING OF THE MIDDLE CLASS

The media send a variety of messages to readers and television audiences about the middle class based on the framing of articles and story lines. Sociologist Gregory Mantsios has identified three key messages that he believes the media convey about the middle class. The first is that "the middle class is us," meaning that the news media create a universal middle class in which everyone has similar problems, such as high taxes, lack of job security, and fear of crime, while sharing a feeling of intellectual and moral superiority over those in the working and poor classes. In a nation that has embraced the "mythology of classlessness,"[15] thinking of oneself as middle class creates a mental comfort zone, where the individual is in neither the "snobbish" upper class nor the "inferior" lower classes.

The second message that Mantsios believes the media send portrays the middle class as a victim. If the middle class is doing so well, as suggested by the myth that everyone is middle class, how can people in this category be considered victims? According to Mantsios, the media frequently portray the middle class as being victimized by the wealthy (who control prices and get tax breaks), by the working class (who are greedy, demand higher wages, and drive up prices), and by the poor (who, because of their own shortcomings, run up welfare costs and stretch other governmental programs to their limits).

The third message suggests that the middle class is not a working class. According to Mantsios, media stories typically make clear distinctions between the middle class and individuals in the blue-collar, working-class sector. Some television shows, for example, portray working-class people and the poor as lacking manners, middle-class values, and social respectability.

Somewhat along these lines, I have identified three major frames used in stories pertaining to the middle class in newspaper and magazine articles, on websites, and in television news and entertainment story lines. These three frames are middle-class-values framing, squeeze framing, and victimization framing. Middle-class-values framing emphasizes that the core values held by people in the middle class should serve as the model for this country and that these values remain largely intact despite economic, political, and cultural changes. By contrast, squeeze framing indicates that the middle class is perilously caught between the cost of a middle-class lifestyle and the ability to pay for it. Victimization framing suggests that many of the problems that the middle class faces stem from actions by or on behalf of those above and below it in the social-class hierarchy.

Ironically, media framing of stories about the middle class, while suggesting that nearly everyone is in this demographic, often assert that this group is rapidly shrinking and perhaps in danger of disappearing altogether. These seemingly contradictory messages are not recent in their origin. As far back as the 1860s, newspaper articles portrayed middle-class existence as problematic, and some of the issues raised more than a century ago are still raised as concerns by the media today.

THE PAST STILL PRESENT:
HISTORICAL FRAMING OF THE MIDDLE CLASS

The major U.S. newspapers of the 1900s had barely "discovered" the middle class before journalists began using the three forms of framing described above in their discussions of it. An examination of *New York Times* headlines from as early as 1851 shows the popularity of such framing. The middle class, although the backbone of the nation, was being squeezed by its rampant spending habits and lack of savings, and it was being victimized by the capitalist and working classes.

Numerous newspaper articles decried how people in the middle class were overspending. Even in an era when major daily newspapers provided glowing details about the lavish spending and opulent lifestyles of the rich and famous on the society and women's pages (see chapter 2), these same newspapers admonished the middle class to be more frugal. For example, an 1868 *New York Times* article, "Economy among the Middle Classes," described members of this group as being able to make money easily but spending it too readily:

> The greatest of all obstacles to saving is, of course, the scale of living of our middle classes. People live here in a style entirely out of proportion to income. . . . Our middle classes will never accumulate property til they learn to content themselves with more simple furniture, smaller houses, and less display.[16]

The negative tone of this article suggests to readers that people in the middle class (defined at the time as earning $2,500 to $6,000 annually) were acting irresponsibly by spending all of their income and not saving money. The article concluded by noting that lack of savings is a problem for the middle class because its "children are not trained to labor, and their habits will be expensive."[17] This statement draws a distinction between middle-class children and their working-class counterparts, who presumably are trained to work with their hands and have less-expensive habits than children raised in middle-class families.

Squeeze and victimization framing appeared not only in newspaper articles but also in book reviews, as reflected in a 1905 *New York Times* review of Walter G. Cooper's *The Consumers: Fate of the Middle Classes*. The book equated middle-class status with being a consumer ground between an upper and lower millstone—capital (the upper classes) on the top and labor (the working class) on the bottom:

> Combinations of labor and capital are . . . to be feared [since] they can fix a price which the consumer must pay—a price that [should] yield a living wage and a fair return to capital. Having done this, [labor unions and capitalists] become masters of the situation, and all they have to do is raise profits and wages at the consumer's expense. Thus [the consumer] is, as Mr. Cooper said in the beginning [of the book], ground beneath the upper and nether millstone.[18]

Most readers seem to have agreed with such media representations about the plight of the middle class, as reflected in published letters to the editor such as this one sent to the *New York Times* by "Another Middle Classer":

> While the price of houseroom, food, and clothing rises steadily every year, the large army of [people in the middle class] struggle along with no increase of wages. They have no organized unions or sympathetic strikes. If they do not like their pittances, out they go. There is a horde of waiting hungry ones to take their places.[19]

Affordable housing was a major middle-class concern in the first half of the twentieth century. A 1929 *New York Times* article, for example, described how the middle class was losing its housing to the wealthy in Manhattan: the scarcity of affordable housing was intensified by the demolition of old tenements and private residences, many of which were replaced with exclusive new apartment buildings on the Upper East Side.[20] Now known as co-ops, many of these buildings serve as homes for New York's wealthiest citizens today. As older housing was demolished, middle-class residents were forced to find new homes, and many learned that the only housing they could afford would require a commute to the city from the Bronx or Queens.

Unlike accounts suggesting that middle-income people sought housing in the suburbs because they thought the suburbs would be more agreeable to family life, some of these articles suggest the contrary—that members of the urban middle class, particularly in cities such as New York, were pushed out of their original residences and replaced by wealthier occupants. According to the 1929 *New York Times* article, upper-middle-class professionals, such as lawyers, doctors, and businessmen, found that they could no longer afford to live on the Upper East Side of Manhattan. The plight of the middle class is readily apparent in this article:

> The rich and the poor are being provided for, the former in the Yorkville and the Fifth Avenue sections and the latter in the lower east side, where model tenements are projected. The middle class, however, is fast being excluded from the Manhattan homes of the kind that were abundant a decade ago.[21]

In other words, the middle class was being forced out of its homes as members of the upper class solved their own housing problems by constructing new residences that only they could afford. Meanwhile, the middle class was also being victimized by those serving the interests of the poor, who would have "model tenements" in which to reside.

Almost seventy years later, journalists for the *New York Times* still wrote articles using squeeze and victimization framing to describe middle-class housing problems. Consider, for example, a 1998 article titled "For Middle Class, New York Shrinks As Home Prices Soar," which begins,

> Todd Neuhaus, an advertising executive, and his wife, Christina, didn't want much. They wanted to rent a Manhattan apartment for less than $3,000 with a bedroom for themselves and one for their two boys. They wanted it to be near good public schools, because private school was beyond their means. [However, the couple eventually quit looking for a two bedroom apartment because nothing they liked was available in a price range they could afford.] It is one of the crueler paradoxes of the city's economic boom and bright new image [that] even as middle-income families tend to earn more, they are finding themselves priced out of dozens of neighborhoods in and around Manhattan, say real-estate brokers and legions of frustrated apartment seekers.[22]

Reminiscent of the 1929 *New York Times* article, the 1998 article offered this explanation for why the middle-class housing shortage would continue into the twenty-first century:

> Housing experts say the present squeeze reflects a deeper problem [because] builders are creating new housing only for the city's wealthiest residents and, using government subsidies, for a comparatively small number of its poorest. . . . For various reasons—chiefly the high cost of land and construction—the housing supply is not growing and, in fact, may be shrinking, for those in the middle. They are the city's teachers, nurses, civil servants, small-business owners, even mid-level executives, who want basic, affordable housing near their jobs.[23]

Although this analysis is relatively farsighted, the author did not anticipate the economic crisis brought on by dishonest financiers on Wall Street and subprime lending on mortgages.

Over the years, stories in the media have noted other middle-class aspirations in addition to appropriate residences. A 1935 *New York Times* book review titled "What Is the Middle Class and What Does It Want?" sets forth the reviewer's belief that the United States is a "middle-class nation in outlook and aspiration," but it continues,

Exactly what that means you may not be sure, but you are safe in believing that it includes a desire that children shall go to college, that a new automobile be parked in front of the house, that homes be furnished in the approved fashion, that clothes, whatever else they are, shall be in style. More fundamental perhaps are the emotional urges of home and church and country, to which must be added a profound distrust of anything intellectual.[24]

The 1935 book review saw the middle class as "smug in its values" and "unlikely to revolt" against the capitalist class: "'Trim front yards,' [the book's author] suggests, 'petty snobbery, gossip and *The Saturday Evening Post* may be discouraging soil for revolutionary doctrines, but the radicals would have done better not to ignore [the middle class].'"[25] Here again, the middle class is characterized as wanting nice homes with "trim front yards" but also as engaging in "petty snobbery" and "gossip" and having a fondness for the *Saturday Evening Post*, a magazine known for its middle-class values and portrayal of an idyllic lifestyle depicted in nostalgic cover art by Norman Rockwell, which often featured happy, middle-class American families that taught children respect for parents, God, and country.

Despite admonitions to members of the middle class that they should be frugal, popular magazines such as *Saturday Evening Post*, *American Magazine*, *The Delineator*, *Ladies' Home Journal*, *Cosmopolitan*, *Munsey's*, and *McClure's* in the early to mid-1900s featured articles about middle-class families and encouraged consumerism, particularly of goods and services that would make homes more pleasant, children healthier, and family life more "modern." Magazines targeted the "common man" and the "housewife," not only as readers but as consumers. As one analyst has suggested, "At this point . . . the role of the publisher changed from being a seller of [the magazine] to consumers to being a gatherer of consumers for the advertisers."[26]

Class distinctions often were obvious in the framing of ads, which typically portrayed the middle class as being in the know, while those in the lower classes were not. A 1910 Quaker Oats cereal ad with the headline "The Homes That Never Serve Oatmeal" is an example. Showing the slum section of a major city, with tenement houses in the background, the subcaption reads, "In the lowliest sections of our largest cities not one home in twelve serves oats. Among the highest types we breed, seven-eighths are oatmeal homes." The ad asks, "What Does This Mean?" and replies,

This doesn't mean that some can afford oats and others cannot. Quaker Oats—the finest oatmeal produced—costs but one-half cent per dish. And a pound of Quaker Oats supplies the nutrition of six loaves of bread. . . . It means that some know, and others don't know, the food needs of a child. Some know, and some don't know, what the food of youth means in a child's career. . . . Some know, and some don't know, that the highest authorities on foods for the young give the first rank to oatmeal.[27]

This is middle-class-values framing, the other general category of middle-class framing: the middle class is the backbone of the nation, and its values should be encouraged and supported. It is clear from the ad that people in the middle class should know about good nutrition and desire to provide only the best for their families. According to the ad, when the Quaker Oats interviewers

canvassed hundreds of homes of the educated, the prosperous, the competent—the homes of the leaders in every walk in life . . . we find that oatmeal is a regular diet in seven out of eight . . . four-fifths of all college students come from these oatmeal homes.[28]

The ad suggests that, by contrast, working-class families lack the knowledge and sophistication to feed themselves and their children properly.

Food advertisements particularly bound the middle-class woman to particular brands based on images that manufacturers conveyed to potential consumers. Ads for products such as Betty Crocker pie and cake mixes showed the ideal middle-class family enjoying a meal together. Betty Crocker, a fictitious middle-class woman, became the model of the ideal homemaker, even if her store-bought mixes were not as tasty as the made-from-scratch variety. The image of Betty Crocker personified hearth and home, suggesting the importance of family values and supporting the positive role of the homemaker who performed kitchen magic for the benefit of her family.

Over the years, the media generally have supported the American Dream and encouraged their audiences to view themselves as upwardly mobile. The 1935 *New York Times* book review quoted above, for example, describes what the reviewer believed to be the ultimate aspiration of members of the U.S. middle class:

In the United States there is an individualist tradition, a belief in progress, which has made most men unwilling to accept the label of "worker" for more than a short time. One does not need to be a sociologist to know that Americans as a lot live in hope of a lucky break which will place them or their children on Park Avenue. With such sentiments still widely prevalent, it is wasted breath to talk about the "revolutionary working class."[29]

Politicians have long been aware of the tendency of people in the United States to view themselves as members of the middle class and have therefore lavished praise on that group while promising to do more for it than their opponents would. The media have framed their reporting on politics in similar terms. A 1937 *New York Times* article about Congressman Bruce Barton's first speech to the House of Representatives in Washington, DC, for example, highlighted his frequent references to the middle class as the backbone of the nation and as long-suffering and slow to anger, but it also noted his belief that the middle class was beginning to "stir," particularly as it was caught in a squeeze produced by an increase in living costs.[30]

Defining the middle class as "professional men and women, small business men and shopkeepers, white-collar workers and the thrifty who have saved a few hundred dollars by their toil and invested it in the shares of American industries," Barton is quoted as saying,

> Time was when these people were regarded highly; they were referred to as the backbone of the nation. But unorganized, with no lobby, incapable of political pressure, they are currently treated as of little consequence. The idea seems to be that the nation has lost its backbone or needs no backbone.[31]

By quoting both the section of Barton's speech that referred to the middle class as the backbone of the country and the portion asserting that the middle class is "treated as of little consequence," this article uses both middle-class-values and victimization framing: the middle class holds the country together, but it is in peril, a peril not of its own making. Subsequent articles, such as one covering Congressman Barton's 1938 address to the New England Young Republicans, used similar framing, describing the middle class as "bruised and bleeding" and trapped between the "millstones of bad business and high taxes."[32]

Since the early 1900s, speeches by politicians have provided journalists with many opportunities to write about the problems of the middle class. Headlines such as "Says Middle Class Needs Salvation: Martin Asks National Support of Republican Drive to Avert Its 'Ruin' by New Deal" (1939) and "Save Middle Class, Congress Is Urged" (1942)[33] indicate persistent media framing emphasizing the potential downfall of this class. Threatened by the New Deal and by higher taxes (victimization framing), the middle class was often described as needing salvation. The article on saving the middle class quotes Congressman August Herman Andresen of Minnesota as saying, "When the middle class is liquidated, American democracy is destroyed" and as referring to the middle class as the "backbone of the nation."[34]

During World War II, media framing of stories about the middle class typically had a more optimistic tenor than in the past. Articles often focused on positive comments by politicians and other spokespersons. Consider, for example, a 1943 article with the headline "Wallace Sees All in a Middle Class: Picturing Future, He Asserts the 'Horatio Alger' Spirit Will Never Die Here," which focused on Vice President Henry A. Wallace's forecast for the postwar United States and his vision of "an America where all can become members of the middle class—where all can share in the benefits which that class has enjoyed in the past."[35] The article presents a very positive view of this group, highlighting what many Americans wanted to believe at the time—that this class represented the American Dream, which would exist forever.

Although there is less political talk about Horatio Alger in the twenty-first century, politicians continue to focus on the middle class and insist they can do more for it than their opponents during almost every election. The 2000 and 2004 presidential campaigns were no exception. Battling headlines in the *New York Times* introduced articles discussing how the 2000 presidential candidates, Al Gore and George W. Bush, sought to garner middle-class votes: "Bush Says Rival's Tax-Cut Plan Fails Middle Class," "Gore Offers Vision of Better Times for Middle Class," and "Bush Campaign Turns Attention to Middle Class"[36] are only a few of thousands of examples.

Rhetoric about the needs of the middle class continued in speeches and stories during the 2004 presidential election. An example is media coverage of a speech given by Senator John Kerry of Massachusetts, the Democratic candidate, who criticized President Bush's administration for favoring wealthy special-interest groups. Kerry spoke out against a system he believed to be "stacked against" the middle-class family:

> I'm running for President because the American people are calling 911 for help. I think the American people are tired of watching corporate executives on Friday afternoons pile into their airplanes paid for by their corporations . . . going to homes paid for by the corporations, playing golf on the weekend in memberships paid for by the corporations, going to shows on Broadway paid for by the corporations, all of which is subsidized by the American taxpayer while the American taxpayer is struggling to get along.
>
> Middle-class families have an agenda, too. . . . And it's about time someone in the White House held a special meeting for them.[37]

Moving forward to the presidential election of 2008, Barack H. Obama emphasized his middle-class origins throughout his candidacy, and he has clearly focused on his middle-class upbringing during his administration. The White House website states, for example, "His story is the American story— values from the heartland, a middle-class upbringing in a strong family, hard work, and education as the means of getting ahead, and the conviction that a life so blessed should be lived in service to others."[38]

Consequently, and not surprisingly, President Obama has balked when media analysts have tried to place him and his interests anywhere other than with the middle class. When a 2010 *Washington Post* article stated that Obama was "a rare President who comes from the middle class," some readers clamored that Obama was only one of a number of presidents from families in this economic group. National and international media coverage informed audiences that not only President Obama but also former presidents Lyndon Johnson, Harry Truman, Richard Nixon, Ronald Reagan, and Bill Clinton were all products of the middle class.[39]

Class-related media framing of stories about President Obama has focused on the White House Task Force on Middle Class Families, established by his administration and chaired by Vice President Joseph Biden. The task force's findings include the following:

- Middle class families are defined by their aspirations more than their incomes. We assume that middle-class families aspire to home ownership, a car, college education for their children, health and retirement security, and occasional family vacations.
- Families at a wide variety of income levels aspire to be middle class and, under certain circumstances, can put together budgets that allow them to obtain a middle-class lifestyle.
- Planning and saving are critical elements in attaining a middle-class lifestyle for most families. Under the right circumstances, even lower-income families may be able to achieve many of their aspirations if they are willing to undertake present sacrifices and necessary savings.
- However, many families, particularly those with less income, will find attaining a middle-class lifestyle difficult if not impossible. Areas with high housing costs can make even higher-income families feel pinched. . . . And unforeseen expenses can ruin even the best-laid budget plans.
- It is more difficult now than in the past for many people to achieve middle-class status because prices for certain key goods—health care, college, and housing—have gone up faster than income.

The findings of this task force show the progression of several media framing devices used for many years to describe the U.S. middle class. Underlying numerous articles from the mid-1800s to the 2000s are three framing devices I have identified in stories about the middle class: the middle class and its values constitute the backbone of the nation; the middle class is caught in a squeeze between aspiration and anxiety; and the middle class is victimized by other classes. I now examine these devices in greater detail, starting with the most positive of the three: middle-class-values framing.

MIDDLE-CLASS-VALUES FRAMING:
THE BACKBONE OF THE NATION

In *Fear of Falling: The Inner Life of the Middle Class*, social analyst Barbara Ehrenreich offered the following comments on the pervasive nature of middle-class values and their significance even to people who do not think of themselves as being in this class: "[Middle-class] ideas and assumptions are everywhere, and not least in our own minds. Even those of us who come from very different social settings often find it hard to distinguish middle-class views from what we think we ought to think."[40] According to Ehrenreich, "Traits the middle class [likes] to ascribe to itself [include] self-discipline, a strong super-ego, [and] an ability to plan ahead to meet self-imposed goals." People in the middle class use these traits, she asserts, to evaluate not only others in their economic group but those below them in the class structure, making the poor especially vulnerable to criticism. Other analysts have identified other traits or values they believe are associated with the middle class, such as "punctuality, a certain minimum of reliability and accountability (if not responsibility), as well as a minimum of orderliness [and] a certain amount of postponement of instant gratification."[41]

Sociologist Robin M. Williams Jr. developed one of the most comprehensive lists of so-called American values, identifying ten that he believed constituted the bedrock of the U.S. value system.[42] Four are often associated with the middle class: individualism, achievement and success, progress and material comfort, and freedom and liberty. The value of individualism rests on the belief that people are responsible for their own success or failure and that individual ability and hard work are the keys to success. A belief in individualism makes it possible for middle-class people to praise those who do well while at the same time identifying the shortcomings (such as laziness or lack of intelligence) of nonachievers. Individualism is associated with another core value, achievement (success), which rests on a person's ability to compete effectively with others. One of the rewards for success, both individually and collectively as a society, is the progress and material comfort that often follow. Successful individuals and nations have far more than the basic necessities required for survival, and people can enjoy a wider variety of consumer goods and services. As core values, most people esteem freedom and liberty highly—particularly individuals in the middle and upper classes, who believe that among their freedoms are the right to own property and to expect the government to protect them and the "American way of life." These core values are embedded in the media framing of many articles and story lines about the middle class. Even when the term *middle class* is not specifically used, it is often assumed that the people in this portion of the U.S. class structure share these virtues.

The study "Middle Class in America," conducted by the Obama administration's Middle Class Task Force, suggests that a multidimensional approach to identifying the middle class rests on the perception that certain values and expectations, primarily about economic security, safety, and protection, are strongly associated with that demographic. Examples of these middle-class values include

- strong orientation toward planning for the future;
- control over one's destiny;
- movement up the socioeconomic ladder through hard work and education;
- a well-rounded education for one's children;
- protection against hardship, including crime, poverty, and health problems;
- access to home ownership and financial assets such as a savings account;
- respect for the law.

Media framing of news stories about the middle class often includes a discussion of one or more of these values or a perceived threat to them.

Middle-Class-Values Framing in News Stories

Middle-class-values framing is frequently found in reporting about so-called middle-class neighborhoods and communities. In print, broadcast, and electronic media ranging from *USA Today* to CNN and CNN.com, communities that uphold certain values receive widespread publicity for having "middle-class values." A CNN cable television news report and companion statement on CNN.com regarding the high-tech boom of the late twentieth century, for example, described the Midwestern United States providing the "right kind" of communities for the families of information technology professionals:

> Family values, a strong work ethic and friendly folk are all things you think about when someone mentions the Midwest. But one phrase people don't always associate with the region is "high technology." Des Moines, Iowa, and Omaha are welcoming a growing population of information technology professionals as people seek an area where they can not only hone their technical skills, but can also experience an environment conducive to raising a family.[43]

Via interviews with information technology workers, the framing of this article about the high-tech job opportunities then available also conveys a message to viewers and readers about what the journalist calls "American dreamin'." One interviewee said, "The No. 1 draw for a person with a family is that the school systems are wonderful, and the general ethics and morals of the community and area in itself." Another worker told the reporter,

"People believe in a fair day's labor, a fair day's wage. I think the work culture is one that is a participatory culture. They will pitch in to get the job done." Although based on people's perceptions about their own communities, these statements also suggest that individuals living in the region share good middle-class moral values and a belief in the work ethic.

National and regional news coverage about a community's values are not unique. Like the report carried by CNN, articles in local newspapers such as the *Detroit News* extol the virtues of the middle class. Consider, for example, editorial writer George Cantor's story titled "Middle-Class Livonia Turns into Wayne County Power":

> Livonia is a seething hotbed of middle-class values. It has an almost invisible crime rate [and] neat residential streets, many of them looking as if they had been time-warped from 1956 Detroit. . . . But it is Livonia's sheer lack of drama that is its charm. "The American dream writ large," approvingly says an attorney friend of mine who specializes in municipal finance. Because middle-class values do matter. They supply the essential balance of any community. A sense of restraint. Of responsibility. Of work ethic. If someone asked me to pinpoint exactly when Detroit hit the wall, it would be when the city's political leadership dismissed middle-class values.[44]

Whether in Des Moines, Iowa; Livonia, Michigan; or Franklin, Tennessee, journalists tend to be nostalgic for the "good old days" when, supposedly, middle-class values prevailed, family life was stable, and there was less tension and discord.

In a series of articles examining the "values gap" that divided Americans during the 2000 presidential election and shaped the 2004 campaign, journalists for *USA Today* described Franklin, Tennessee, as the prototypical community with middle-class values. Stories like "Values, Points of View Separate Towns—and Nation" referred to the community as "a sprawling Sun Belt suburb with a distinct Bible Belt flavor" where "horse and dairy farms are giving way to subdivisions and strip malls, but its values remain rooted in tradition."[45] This article quotes the president of the Gospel Music Association as saying, "The lifestyle is at that stage where it's still idyllic. There's a small-town feel. It's almost a return to the social and civic values of life in the '50s." The journalist describes the small-town, middle-class-values feel of Franklin as follows:

> Franklin's hallmark is a veneer of Southern graciousness. Much is left unsaid, and privacy is prized. Families stick close to home in neighborhoods they compare to movie fantasies, complete with horse fences and soda shops. The line between personal and public life is clearly drawn. It's a town where gays remain in the closet, race relations go largely undiscussed and a PTA president declines to be interviewed about her school.[46]

By the 2008 presidential race, however, journalists for *USA Today* were typically framing stories to suggest that family values were less important than in previous election years. "'Family Values' Lower on Agenda in 2008 Race" states, "There are signs that family values have lost their punch as a campaign issue." Most voters say family values in general are important to them, but a *USA Today*/Gallup Poll found that they do not care much about candidates' personal lives. Rather, media audiences appear to subscribe broadly to the idea of middle-class family values but have more immediate concerns of their own, such as war, nuclear programs, the threat of terrorism, and "an economy that's putting stress on low- and middle-income people."[47]

Middle-class values have been debated by politicians, framed by media analysts, and visibly dramatized in television sitcoms that first entered the American living room in the 1950s and persist in many modified forms, including various animated series, in the twenty-first century.

Middle-Class-Values Framing in Sitcom Story Lines

The middle class and its values received the most favorable representation in sitcoms during the post–World War II era of the 1950s and 1960s. According to media scholar David Marc, when it emerged as the new entertainment medium, television gave credibility to "suburbia as democracy's utopia realized, a place where the white middling classes could live in racial serenity, raising children in an engineered environment that contained and regulated the twin dangers of culture and nature."[48] This engineered environment was apparent in the settings and story lines of television shows such as *The Adventures of Ozzie and Harriet* (1952–1966), *Father Knows Best* (1954–1963), and *Leave It to Beaver* (1957–1963), in which characters acted out middle-class values in idealized nuclear families composed of happily married couples and their heartwarming children. With the exception of a few shows like *My Three Sons*, whose story line revolved around Steve Douglas (Fred MacMurray), an aeronautical engineer and widower raising his three boys, most sitcoms employed the tried-and-true format of the traditional nuclear family with the occasional addition of an extra member who visited or lived with the family on a temporary basis. Common themes in these shows included the presumed middle-class values of honesty, integrity, and hard work, all believed to enable people to get ahead in life and solve problems as they arose. The problems these families typically confronted, however, were minor, as reflected by an *Ozzie and Harriet* episode in which the crisis of the day entailed dealing with a mistaken delivery of two chairs to the Nelson family. Similarly, shows such as *Father Knows Best* often showed brief children's arguments easily resolved within one episode by Dad's wise counsel.

White Middle-Class Family Values

Middle-class sitcoms such as these were the pictures of civility. According to media scholar Hal Himmelstein, early sitcoms almost universally
portrayed members of the suburban middle class as "upscale, socially conservative, politically inactive, and essentially kind to one another and their
neighbors."[49] Usually, middle-class fathers, such as Jim Anderson (Robert
Young) in *Father Knows Best*, demonstrated wisdom and good judgment,
never losing their patience with their families or raising their voices when
correcting the children. Middle-class status was clearly established through
dialogue that made viewers aware of the father's professional position
(Anderson managed an insurance company) or visual cues such as clothing
(Anderson wore a suit to work each day and replaced his suit coat with a
pull-over sweater when he came home in the evening). In many sitcoms,
the family's residence and the characters' clothing signified more than just
the setting in which the story line unfolded; such visual cues transmitted
ideological codes about middle-class lifestyles as well. The fact that middle-
class children in early sitcoms showed respect for their parents and teachers,
remorse for wrongdoings, and willingness to "shake hands and make up"
formed not only a part of the story line and a significant proportion of the
characters' dialogue but communicated an ideological code about middle-
class values. As some analysts have noted, the middle class was portrayed
as "principled and benign" and therefore deserving of the advantages that
typically accrue to middle-class family life.[50]

Story lines about middle-class families not only entertained viewers and
attracted consumers for advertisers' products but also contributed to an unrealistic view of the middle class. According to media scholars David Croteau
and William Hoynes,

> Network television presented the suburban family as the core of the modern,
> postscarcity society, a kind of suburban utopia where social problems were
> easily solved (or nonexistent), consensus ruled, and signs of racial, ethnic, or
> class differences or conflict were difficult to find. . . . This image of the postwar
> family—and the not-so-subtle suggestion that this was what a "normal" family
> looked like—was a particular story masked as a universal one. Certainly, these
> families were not typical American families, no matter how often they were
> served up as such.[51]

For whatever reason, domestic comedies prevailed in network scheduling and
in popularity with viewers, and these sitcoms offered many representations of
the middle-class family as well as the rights and responsibilities of its members. As one media scholar notes with regard to the middle-class wife-mother
role on sitcoms such as *Ozzie and Harriet*,

[These wife-mothers] understand the cultural and personal significance of the family and work to maintain family stability. Moreover, their failings are not individual failings but family failings; the wife-mother fails intellectually without her husband, the sons fail academically without their father, and the father fails socially and personally without his wife and children. The lesson, here, is that family is fundamental and needs all of its parts to function effectively so that a wife-mother's place and a husband-father's place is in the home.[52]

This functionalist statement suggests the importance of the ideology of "family values" in framing entertainment shows. Family-values framing stresses that the middle-class family is the backbone of the country and that certain values must be upheld and certain rules adhered to if these families, and society as a whole, are to function properly.

Among the strongest of family values is the belief that there is only one appropriate way to establish and maintain a family: young people should marry by a certain age (which varies over time and place), have children only after an appropriate period has elapsed after the wedding, be actively involved parents, and demonstrate a high level of commitment to work, the community, and doing what's right even when tempted to do otherwise. Betty Friedan and other feminist analysts have argued, however, that middle-class family-values framing imposes a limited role—that of housewife-mother—on women, thus transforming motherhood from an option into a mandate. As media analyst William Douglas explains, "That is, the role of women not only was essentially domestic and defined, in the most fundamental way, by motherhood but was articulated by a more elaborate relational code that relegated women to a dependent and, so, subservient status."[53]

Many sitcoms transcended this simple formula, showing women as willing under some circumstances to violate the family-values code. *I Love Lucy* serves as a classic example of a show that seeks to depict women's tension when torn between remaining a housewife and pursuing a career. In numerous episodes, Lucy Ricardo (Lucille Ball) attempts to break into show business while her husband, Ricky (Desi Arnaz), a Cuban American bandleader, attempts to keep her at home, a story line that becomes the show's staple plot. As the series progresses, the Ricardos not only have a child but become upwardly mobile, transforming themselves from a struggling, lower-middle-class family in a New York City apartment into a solid (although slightly inane) suburban family that lives in a well-appointed country home in Connecticut.

The story lines in *I Love Lucy* frequently involve issues such as home economy, child rearing, and postdating checks; however, the undercurrent of activity often questions what constitutes family values and a woman's "appropriate" role in the family. In one episode Ricky states his desire to have "a wife who's just a wife," telling Lucy, "All you have to do is clean the house for me, bring me my slippers when I come home at night, cook for me, and be the mother of my children."[54] Ultimately, Ricky does not win; the episode ends with Lucy accepting a role in a television show. Media messages about middle-class values, family life, and gender issues in this sitcom are not entirely lost on contemporary audiences. In the twenty-first century (sixty years after it first aired in 1951), *I Love Lucy* continues to air on the U.S. cable network TV Land; it is also in syndication worldwide and available on DVD, bringing new generations of viewers the same story lines that in the past both supported and questioned middle-class family values.

The framing of some twenty-first-century sitcom story lines continues to reinforce the importance of family life and middle-class values. For example, ABC's *According to Jim*, a syndicated show billed as a "traditional family comedy," features Jim (Jim Belushi), his wife, Cheryl (Courtney Thorne-Smith), and their family. Jim is a contractor in a design firm with his architect brother-in-law, while Cheryl is a stay-at-home mom who keeps the three kids on the right track when Jim is at work. The story lines of two episodes serve as examples of framing in which a character's actions violate and then restore middle-class values, such as honesty and integrity. In "We Have a Bingo," Jim cheats at the church fund-raising bingo game by stealing the winning card from an elderly woman who has fallen asleep. Jim has to deal with his conscience for being dishonest and claiming the waterbed actually won by Mrs. Meyer. The minister helps Jim confront his problem, and after several more scrapes with dishonesty, Jim finally comes clean with everyone. In another episode, "The Lemonade Stand," Jim tells his two daughters that they should earn their own money (the work ethic) to buy the new scooters they want (consumerism). When the daughters set up a lemonade stand to make money, they get into avid competition with the neighbor's son, and Jim has to deal with his own competitive feelings toward the boy and his father. Plots such as these include messages about family values ("in our family, we don't do that") and reinforcement of such virtues as honesty and kindness to others, even people we do not like.

Some sitcoms bring the issue of middle-class family values to light by depicting characters who oppose, rather than support, those values. Women who stray from customary family values are popular characters in such story lines. Perhaps the earliest example that garnered national media coverage was the long-running series *Murphy Brown* (1988–1998). Episodes relating to the decision of the title character (Candice Bergen), a star television reporter on a Washington, DC, news magazine show, to bear a child without being married generated extensive controversy among some conservative political leaders and newspaper columnists. Vice President Dan Quayle led the criticism of this character's actions, stating that such shows contribute to the moral decline of the nation.

TV shows based on so-called middle-class families, such as *Desperate Housewives*, *Parenthood*, *Friday Night Lights*, and *Brothers & Sisters*, frame white middle-class family values as situational, based on a sliding normative scale, but as coming through strongly when external forces such as violence, evil neighbors, or financial ruin threaten individuals or families. On *Desperate Housewives*, for example, love for their young son and a desire to see him do well in school takes precedence over their frequent squabbles when his parents, Susan Mayer (Teri Hatcher) and her husband, Mike Delfino (James Denton), decide that Susan should take a part-time job to help pay for the boy's private-school tuition. In the ABC series *Brothers and Sisters*, Nora Walker (Sally Field) is supposedly affluent, but her children and other family members have money troubles to the extent that some media analysts place them in the middle- or upper-middle-class instead. Some of Nora's children live relatively prosperous lives and hold positions like head of the family-owned business, OJAI Foods, or practicing attorney; however, the framing of story lines in the series shows that other Walker family members are just one step away from financial disaster. To show family values, the show depicts family members as fighting with each other first and then sticking together through thick and thin, even when they have opposing political and social viewpoints. The plot is framed so that one regular occurrence in the series, a family dinner given by Nora, serves as the site of family "food fights" and loud discord, but also as a place where heartwarming reassurances are given about the importance of family values and solidarity.

Other examples of shows framed around white middle-class family values include *Parenthood*, which focuses on how four siblings and their spouses raise their own children; *Friday Night Lights*, which uses football and a small-town backdrop to address many issues faced by contemporary American families; and *The Middle*, which, although initially a comedy that made fun of middle-class families, now seeks to highlight some positive attributes of people living on the margin between the middle and working classes.

Middle-Class Values and Minority Families

Family values in sitcoms were originally associated with middle-class white families, because these were the only families shown on network shows. Let us look first at the history of African Americans in sitcoms about middle-class families and their values. The few African American characters in early shows were "presented not only in service to middle-class, White families, but, at the same time, absent from any apparent personal family relations."[55]

These African American characters were typically "comforting domestics" or "uneducated handymen [who] provided menial aid to White employers rather than love and support to families of their own."[56]

For a number of years, network television had difficulty producing shows that portrayed intact African American families comparable to the white (European American) families regularly featured in situation comedies. *Julia* portrayed a widowed African American nurse who took care of her daughter. Early episodes of *Good Times* featured an intact African American family, but even it eventually became parentless; the actors who played the father and mother left the series, and the teenage son became the head of the family. Rather than supporting family values like their white counterparts, sitcoms that featured African American families, like *Good Times*, relied on characters and interactions that were comfortable to white viewers.[57]

The first significant shift in sitcoms featuring predominantly African American characters came with the introduction of *The Cosby Show* (1984–1992), which clearly lauded the upper-middle-class family and its values. This highly successful series focused on the everyday adventures of an African American family consisting of the father (a respected gynecologist), the mother (a successful attorney), and their children. As researchers have noted, in such shows "both husband and wife [are] present; [the] spouses interact frequently, equally, and lovingly with each other; and children are treated with respect and taught achievement-oriented values."[58] These achievement-oriented values support a belief in the middle-class way of life and in the importance of family values in fostering harmony and stability. The portrayal of African American male characters as middle-class in situation comedies therefore shows them to be "competent, successful, and able to provide comfortably for their families."[59] In this way, programs seeking to incorporate more African Americans into mainstream television also communicate middle-class values because, like their working-class white counterparts, blue-collar African American males are generally presented as "inept, stupid, emotional, and so on."[60]

Although *The Cosby Show* was extremely popular with viewers, scholars who have examined the representations of African Americans and other people of color in television typically conclude that this show helped cultivate an impression that racism is no longer a problem and that people of color who have not achieved upward mobility have no one to blame but themselves.[61] According to one study, portrayals in *The Cosby Show* incorporated myths about both race and class:

> Television, in the United States, combines an implicit endorsement of certain middle class life-styles with a squeamish refusal to confront class realities or class issues. This is neither inevitable nor natural. Nothing about being working

or lower middle class prevents someone from being funny, proud, dignified, entertaining, or worthy of admiration and respect, even if the social setting of most TV programs would encourage you to believe otherwise.[62]

Despite such criticisms, however, many subsequent sitcoms featured upper-middle-class African American families if they included any African Americans at all. Programs such as ABC's *My Wife and Kids* replaced *The Cosby Show* in portraying successful African American parents living in fashionable residences, wearing nice clothing, and teaching their children solid middle-class values. Michael Kyle (Damon Wayans) of *My Wife and Kids* is described as "a loving husband and modern-day patriarch who rules his household with a unique and distinct parenting style. As he teaches his three children some of life's lessons, he does so with his own brand of wisdom, discipline and humor."[63]

Twenty-first century sitcoms based on supposedly middle-class African American families, such as TBS's *House of Payne*, have attracted millions of African American viewers, even though these series have been criticized for racially stereotyping black families. The characters in *House of Payne* include a stay-at-home mother, Ella Payne (Cassi Davis), who represents the good-natured voice of reason, and an assortment of far less straightlaced family members and outsiders. Ella is the family's religious voice and the spokesperson for values and morality. By contrast, her husband, Curtis Payne (LaVan Davis), tells derogatory jokes, uses profanity, and has a strong desire to get his nephew C. J. out of his home. (C. J.'s wife burned down their own house while under the influence of illegal drugs.) The combination of some characters with a strong sense of morality and others with major vices sets the audience up for contrasts in family values. However, some analysts believe that such shows are framed primarily to stereotype African Americans rather than to reflect positive family values or provide wholesome entertainment for young people.

One series focusing on middle-class African American families is TBS's *Are We There Yet?* based on a movie by the same title. The show depicts a blended family in which newlyweds Nick (Terry Crews) and Suzanne (Essence Atkins) have ten- and fourteen-year-old children who spend most of their time texting their friends and playing on the computer rather than enjoying time together. In one episode, "The Get Together," family members are gathered in the kitchen, but each person is doing his or her own thing and not paying attention to anyone else. Nick, increasingly frustrated that his wife and the children are not talking to each other, suggests that they plan a family get together at which they can hang out, eat, and play games. His son would rather play on his computer, his daughter would rather talk on her cell phone, and his wife, a professional party planner, wants to continue working on an upcoming event instead. Nick talks to them about what he thinks a family should value and why time together is important. The show's website describes Nick's character as possessing "solid family values and a strong work ethic." While some analysts applaud this type of family-oriented values framing of stories on cable networks, they question why major networks, such as NBC, CBS, ABC, and Fox, air so few shows like this one.[64]

If framing of middle-class family values is limited in TV shows featuring African Americans, it is even more limited when it comes to Latinos and Asian Americans, who are neglected in all prime-time television series, particularly situation comedies. A 2002 study by Children Now National Hispanic Foundation for the Arts found that Latino characters comprised only 4 percent of the prime-time television population, as compared to this group's overall portion of the U.S. population (12.5 percent in 2002). Of those Latino characters written into prime-time television shows, 63 percent appeared in drama and science fiction programs, 21 percent in crime or law enforcement series, and 16 percent in sitcoms or comedic dramas. According to this study, the absence of Latino roles on television is a major concern. The dearth of Latinos in sitcoms is problematic for young viewers because children watch sitcoms more often than any other prime-time genre. For this reason, many viewers and media critics were frustrated when ABC cancelled *The George Lopez Show*, the only sitcom featuring a middle-class Latino family. In the show, George Lopez was a father and a manager at a Los Angeles airplane-parts factory, where he had worked his way up from the assembly line. The show included Lopez's wife, children, and mother and showed the love and stress members of an intergenerational family experience. Some media analysts especially applauded *The George Lopez Show*'s emphasis on family values.[65]

Similar studies about Asian American characters in prime-time television have found that actors in this category are more underrepresented when compared to the number of Asian Americans in the U.S. population. According to a National Asian Pacific American Legal Consortium report, "Given that situational comedies generally feature family and domestic settings, the invisibility of Asian Pacific Island American [APIA] actors in this genre may contribute to an image that APIA's do not represent the 'American family.'" Moreover, when an APIA character makes a short-term appearance on a sitcom or other prime-time network program, the script often fails to portray such individuals realistically. In 2005, APIA characters were featured on three sitcoms, ABC's *Hot Properties*, FOX's *That '70s Show*, and UPN's *Half & Half*. Focused on themes such as selling real estate or stories about half-sisters, none of these series followed the typical middle-class family model in its story line.[66]

Changing Values in Middle-Class Sitcoms

The story lines in some sitcoms either overtly or subtly ridicule the middle-class values and lifestyles portrayed in other shows. *Malcolm in the Middle*, which started on the Fox Network and is now shown on such cable channels as Nick at Night and FX, is an example. The show's story line revolves around a middle-class family comprising "four squabbling brothers and their parents who are just trying to 'hold on until the last one turns eighteen.'" The story is told through the eyes of Malcolm (Frankie Muniz), who scores very high on an IQ test and is placed in a gifted-children program at school. Rather than having parents who represent the voice of reason, Malcolm plays the role of parent, serving as the family's peacemaker and stabilizer on some occasions.

Malcolm in the Middle regularly ridicules the frequent plots of past sitcoms regarding family values and the possibility of striking it rich through good fortune or inheritance. Consider the following from the "Family Reunion" episode, as recorded in Malcolm's journal:

> All right, so we've never been close with Dad's side of the family. There's a couple of reasons: First, Dad can't stand them. Second, they all hate Mom. It sucks though because Grandpa is totally rich and if we play our cards right, big inheritance coming our way . . . a boy can dream can't he?
>
> Anyway, it's Grandpa's birthday and we got the call to join the family at his place for a reunion of sorts. Reese [Malcolm's brother] immediately went into "milk Grandpa for all he's worth" strategic-planning mode. Can't say I blame him. I mean, Grandpa's really rich.
>
> [After they arrive at the party] . . . Grandpa is great. He's always laughing, joking, life of the party. He even took me to see all his Civil War memorabilia, which is cool, but I think I feigned more interest in hope of that inheritance money. Shameless, I know. I will say this though, no money is worth me having to dress in Civil War fatigues and reenact battles with the man. Give me some credit, my hypocrisy has limits.[67]

This episode's story line is typical of the plots of many contemporary television sitcoms about middle-class families, whose members are often depicted as desiring upper-class wealth but as ultimately unwilling to "sell out." The "Family Reunion" episode and Malcolm's fictitious journal account of it (as posted on the FOX website) convey the message to viewers that although a big inheritance might be desirable, there are far more important things to take into account. The episode ends with Malcolm's immediate family making his grandfather and other members of the extended family extremely unhappy. Malcolm's mother locks herself in the bathroom and starts crying upon learning that she was intentionally excluded from the family photo; Malcolm and his siblings decide to ruin the party by driving a golf cart through the party table, trampling the birthday cake, and launching the golf cart into the swimming pool. In supposedly middle-class fashion, Malcolm concludes, "So much for that inheritance, but at least we took care of our own, which may come back to us with Mom being a little nicer . . . wait, who am I kidding?"

Malcolm's father, Hal Wilkerson (Bryan Cranston), has been described as "the antithesis of the traditional sitcom dad, bonding with his sons in wonderfully unwholesome ways and in effect becoming one of them instead of maintaining the paternal distance and the platitudes typical of the rest of TV's patriarchs." As one television critic suggests, however, the framing of family values in shows such as *Malcolm in the Middle* may be much more realistic than past portrayals of sitcom families:

> Back when his star was ascendant, Newt Gingrich [then Speaker of the House of Representatives] once called for the nation's families to return to the values embodied by the Nelsons of *Ozzie and Harriet*, seemingly unaware that the family in question was actually quite dysfunctional in real life, unable to live up to its own fiction. The irony of Gingrich's pronouncement was— and remains—that America has been trying to live up to the ideal of TV family life and it is, to a certain degree, our failure to meet these impossible standards that has led to disillusionment. *Malcolm in the Middle* is very much the product of this disillusionment—Art that imitates Life's inability to imitate art—a candid Polaroid of an only slightly exaggerated family rather than the usual Olan Mills glossy of the sitcom family in its perpetual Sunday best.[68]

Even with the increasing prevalence of reality shows on broadcast networks and cable channels, sitcoms have remained popular as a means of framing story lines about families of various social classes. In the 2000s, more children have appeared as characters in sitcoms, shifting the focus to families, many of which are somewhat dysfunctional and do not necessarily illustrate traditional middle-class values. Throughout the history of sitcoms, the framing of story lines has inaccurately reflected the class composition of the United States. Although television entertainment shows typically have assumed the stability and ongoing integrity of the middle class, the framing of many articles in newspapers and on websites focuses instead on the problems it faces—particularly those of being squeezed by economic conditions and victimized by people in other classes. We now turn to how stories are framed to emphasize the vise in which the middle class is caught and the ways in which individuals in this class are being victimized.

SQUEEZE FRAMING:
CAUGHT BETWEEN ASPIRATION AND GROWING ANXIETY

The idea that the middle class is in peril is a key framing device for news stories about politics and the economy. While the United States enjoyed an economic boom in the 1990s, headlines like "Bottom's Up: The Middle Class—Winning in Politics, Losing in Life" were not unusual. The statements made in the accompanying story were not unusual either:

> The great American middle class. Politicians on the left and right court it. Policies, liberal and conservative, are proclaimed on its behalf. Health care reform was to have eased its cares. Tuition subsidies educate its children. . . . Most voters see themselves as members of the middle class. . . . But for all its mythic power, the middle class is finishing last in the race for improvement in the current economic boom.[69]

As this article indicates, people in the middle class, even when the nation is experiencing an economic boom, are often seen as "losing ground to their upper- and lower-earning fellow citizens." In the second decade of the 2000s, however, media framing of stories about the growing problems of this class has intensified, and postings such as "The Middle Class in America Is Radically Shrinking: Here Are the Stats to Prove It" are widespread. Typically, framing of this topic rests on the assumption that the middle class is being wiped out of existence in the United States. Here are some key statistics the media use to prove that the middle class is disappearing:

- Eighty-three percent of all U.S. stocks are in the hands of 1 percent of the people.
- Sixty-one percent of Americans "always or usually" live paycheck to paycheck.
- Sixty-six percent of the income growth between 2001 and 2007 went to the top 1 percent of all Americans.
- Thirty-six percent of Americans say that they do not contribute anything to retirement savings.
- Forty-three percent of Americans have less than $10,000 saved up for retirement.
- Twenty-four percent of American workers say that they have postponed their planned retirement age in the past year.
- Over 1.4 million Americans filed for personal bankruptcy in 2009, a 32 percent increase over 2008.
- Only the top 5 percent of U.S. households have earned enough additional income to match the rise in housing costs since 1975.

- For the first time in U.S. history, banks own a greater share of residential housing net worth in the United States than all individual Americans put together.
- In 1950, the ratio of the average executive's paycheck to that of the average worker was about thirty to one. Since 2000, that ratio has exploded to between three hundred and five hundred to one.
- As of 2007, the bottom 80 percent of American households held about 7 percent of liquid financial assets.
- The bottom 50 percent of income earners in the United States now collectively owns less than 1 percent of the nation's wealth.
- In America today, the average time needed to find a job has risen to a record 35.2 weeks.
- More than 40 percent of Americans who actually are employed are now working in service jobs, which are often very low paying.
- The top 10 percent of Americans now earn around 50 percent of our national income.[70]

Based on such data, media stories about the middle class often refer to a "giant sucking sound" as the U.S. middle class disappears from the stratification system and workers in this country are merged into a new "global" labor poor. Describing families that earn more than the median income for U.S. households, journalists make statements such as, "Once upon a time this was called the American Dream. Nowadays it might be called America's Fitful Reverie."[71]

What has caused the peril faced by the middle class? Newspaper articles and television news shows suggest that a central problem its members struggle with is the gap between their incomes and the cost of providing for their families. As a result, more families are going into bankruptcy or losing their homes to foreclosure. Intensifying the problem is the fact that Americans feel stuck in their tracks because they believe that they either have not moved forward in life or have fallen backward. Real median annual household income peaked in 1999 and has not reached the same level again, much less continued to grow. As framed by the media, even more depressing for many people is the decades-long stagnation of the median wage as the annual incomes of the bottom 90 percent of U.S. families have remained essentially flat since 1973.[72]

According to some media reports, part of the problem stems from chronic excessive spending by middle-class consumers who have consequently not put enough money into savings. Other media reports suggest, however, that we should not blame the middle class because corporate advertisers seeking to expand their consumer base target middle-income individuals heavily, leading to excessive consumerism by many who cannot afford such goods and services. For example, a *Fortune* magazine article, "Getting Malled," describes the extent to which retailers compete for middle-class shoppers: "Big retailers are locked in a bloody battle for the shrinking middle-class pocketbook."[73] Another article, "Shaking the House of Cards," points out that some former members of the middle class are now entering the ranks of the poor. Bob Herbert of the *New York Times* often frames his opinion columns to focus on the problems of the middle class, as in pieces like "Caught in the Credit Card Vise," "Caught in the Squeeze," and "Living on Borrowed Money."[74] His article about the "credit card vise" squeezing the middle class provides this statement by Julie Pickett, a middle-class homemaker who quit her full-time job when her twins were born: "I'm still paying for groceries I bought for my family years ago." Herbert adds, "She meant it literally. Mrs. Pickett and her husband, Jerry, of Middletown, Ohio, are trapped in the iron grasp of credit card debt. Except for the fact that no one is threatening to damage their kneecaps, they're in the same dismal position as the classic victim of loan-sharking."[75] Herbert's article explains that buying on credit used to help the middle-class family stay afloat, at least temporarily, but in the long run, many of these families have actually gone "deeper and deeper into debt, in large part because of the overuse of credit cards."[76] Citing a report titled "Borrowing to Make Ends Meet" (compiled by a nonpartisan public-policy group), Herbert states that "more and more Americans are using credit cards to bridge the difficult gap between household earnings and the cost of essential goods and services."[77] Heightening this predicament are structural problems in the U.S. economy, such as widespread job displacement, declining real wages, and rising housing and health-care costs. As a result, many in the middle class rely on credit cards as "a way of warding off complete disaster," until they exhaust this avenue, and unpaid credit card debt continues to pile up.[78]

The framing of a number of articles, including Herbert's, about the middle-class squeeze reflects the content of published government reports or well-received books that highlight the "gloom and doom" of the middle class. Consider, for instance, the media coverage given to Elizabeth Warren and Amelia Warren Tyagi's *The Two-Income Trap: Why Middle Class Mothers and Fathers Are Going Broke*.[79] The book contains many useful sound bites easily used by commentators and digested by media audiences, adding to the book's popularity. For example, Herbert used information gleaned from the book to inform his readers that home mortgage costs between 1970 and 2000 rose seventy times faster than the average male head of household's income during that same period and that two-income families are not faring well in the early twenty-first century's economy.[80] As Herbert states, "So you end up with two parents working like crazy just to keep the family economically afloat."[81] *The Two-Income Trap* also highlights middle-class families' lack of savings because most today set aside virtually nothing and continue to pile up consumer debt. Based on this book and an application of the ideology of the American Dream, Herbert states, "The American Dream has morphed into a treacherous survival regimen in which the good life—a life that includes a home, family vacations, adequate health coverage, money to provide the kids with a solid education, and a comfortable retirement—is increasingly elusive."[82]

Economic peril is the most prevalent theme framing news stories about the middle class. Headlines lament, "Middle Class Barely Treads Water,"[83] and journalists and television commentators repeat warnings about how middle-class mothers and fathers are going broke.[84] Newspapers, magazines, and Internet and television news reports about the middle-class squeeze typically feature college-educated parents who have purchased a home, then experienced an economic catastrophe, such as a job loss due to illness or disability, that depletes any accrued savings. According to one news account, "The dance of financial ruin starts slowly but picks up speed rapidly, exhausting the dancers before it ends."[85] However, individuals in so-called financial ruin are not those whom most people might expect to be in bankruptcy:

> They are not the very young, tempted by the freedom of their first credit cards. They are not the elderly, trapped by failing bodies and declining savings accounts. And they are not a random assortment of Americans who lack the self-control to keep their spending in check. Rather, the people who consistently rank in the worst financial trouble are united by one surprising characteristic. They are parents with children at home. Having a child is now the single best predictor that a woman will end up in financial collapse.[86]

Based on *The Two-Income Trap*, reporters on NBC's *Today Show* and MS-NBC.com framed a number of their stories using such phrases as "middle-class problems," "financial meltdown," "living from paycheck to paycheck," and "pressing families against the wall."[87] Journalists widely adopted "the two-income trap" sound bite to describe the problems that middle-class families experience when both parents are employed outside the household, but the family cannot make ends meet.

Often implicit in the framing of stories about the middle-class squeeze is the assumption of whiteness, meaning that journalists and media audiences typically associate middle-class problems with the white (non-Hispanic) population. This does not, however, reflect reality, as middle-class families across racial and ethnic categories experience economic problems. In 2010 a new study revealed that the wealth gap between white and African American families has increased more than four times since 1984, from $20,000 to $95,000. Defining wealth as "what you own minus what you owe," the researchers found that middle-income white households have made greater gains in financial assets than high-income African Americans: white households they studied had accumulated an average of $74,000 as compared to only $18,000 owned by the average high-income African American family.[88]

Few media sources discussed this new study, and those that did failed to explain why differences had occurred in the "wealth factor" between African and white Americans. According to the researchers in this study,

> The racial wealth gap results from historical and contemporary factors but the disturbing four-fold increase in such a short time reflects public policies, such as tax cuts on investment income and inheritances which benefit the wealthiest, and redistribute wealth and opportunities. Tax deductions for home mortgages, retirement accounts, and college savings all disproportionately benefit higher income families. At the same time, evidence from multiple sources demonstrates the powerful role of persistent discrimination in housing, credit, and labor markets.[89]

Earlier articles also highlighted the fact that the weakening power of labor unions and job loss affect African Americans more than some white American workers. In 2003, "Blacks Lose Better Jobs Faster As Middle-Class Work Drops" reported on government data showing that African Americans are "hit disproportionately harder than whites" by job loss in the United States. Written by journalist Louis Uchitelle and originally published in the *New York Times*, this article was subsequently reported on CNN TV and CNN.com. It quotes William Lucy, president of the Coalition of Black Trade Unionists, as saying that "the number of jobs and the types of jobs that have been lost have severely diminished the standing of many blacks in the middle class."[90] Although some sociologists might argue that union jobs paying $12 to $13 an hour are properly classified as working-class, journalists typically use the term *middle class* to describe this type of work, based on the widely held myth that most workers fall into this vast demographic. Since this article was written in 2003, the problems of African American workers in all classes have worsened, their sting felt particularly by middle-income and upper-middle-class individuals, some the first in their families to reach high levels of education and income, only to see their earnings diminished by changing economic conditions across the nation and world.

No topic has received greater media attention regarding the middle-class squeeze than the issue of health insurance. Prior to the passage of the Barack Obama administration's health-care legislation, a typical headline framing such a story was "For Middle Class, Health Insurance Becomes a Luxury."[91] Although being uninsured or underinsured is a major problem for millions of people in the United States, many articles focused on how this "health-care crisis" harms the middle class. One typical article states, "The majority of the uninsured are neither poor by official standards nor unemployed. They are accountants, employees of small businesses, civil servants, single working mothers and those working part time or on contract."[92] The journalist's interviewees emphasized the middle-class nature of the health-care crisis. R. King Hillier, director of legislative relations for Harris County, Texas (which includes the city of Houston), stated, "Now [being uninsured] is hitting people who look like you and me, dress like you and me, drive nice cars and live in nice houses but can't afford $1,000 a month for health insurance for their families."[93] Although articles like this do not completely exclude the working class and poor, their framing suggests that the cost of health insurance is primarily a middle-class concern. There is an implicit assumption that charity in public hospitals and government-funded programs take care of the poor.

While the U.S. Congress debated the health-care-reform bill in 2009, media sources referred to one version of the Senate's bill as a "middle-class time bomb"[94] because it would have imposed a 40 percent excise tax on plans that would pay in excess of $23,000 annually for families or $8,500 for individuals.[95] In actuality, the health-care-reform legislation would affect very few in the middle class, particularly during the early years of its implementation. With health-care costs rising rapidly, however, the excise tax could spread to nearly 20 percent of all U.S. workers within three years. Media framing of debates about the Senate's health bill focused on its potentially disastrous effect on the middle class, and Congress eventually passed, and President Obama signed into law, a compromise bill that levied tax increases on high-income households rather than placing an excise tax on health plans.[96]

During the health-care-reform debates, the middle-class squeeze in regard to the high cost of health care was widely discussed on television talk shows, and commentators typically assumed that the middle class had employer-based insurance. The word "hardworking" was used frequently to describe middle-income Americans employed full-time, and media analysts often assumed these hardworking Americans would not experience the same problems as the unemployed or those working without health benefits. As the Great Recession worsened in 2010, media analysts began to shift their discussions to include most people in the middle- and upper-middle class in their squeeze framing of stories.[97]

As we have seen, squeeze framing emphasizes the economic woes of the middle class and points out the resulting danger not only for this group but for the American way of life. The "Middle Class Squeeze," shown on PBS's *Now with Bill Moyers*, summed up this problem as follows: "Some say the broadly middle class society we used to take for granted has unraveled—unraveled to the point where America is no longer the land of widespread economic and social opportunity we believe it to be."[98] That probably is an overstatement; as discussed earlier in this chapter, for more than 150 years news stories have framed articles in terms of how the middle class is being squeezed out of existence—and yet it still exists. In fact, most people still think of themselves as its members. However, victimization framing in news articles, discussed next, points a finger at some of the potential culprits who contribute to the problems that members of the middle class believe they face.

VICTIMIZATION FRAMING:
FEAR FACTOR AND THE MIDDLE CLASS

Victimization framing identifies specific villains or perpetrators—ranging from national political leaders and top corporate executives to individuals designated "ordinary street criminals"—whose actions allegedly threaten the middle class (although possibly members of other classes as well). One form of victimization framing suggests that those who occupy top economic and political leadership positions in the nation have created and are now perpetuating the problems of the middle class, pitting the interests of this group against those of the wealthy and powerful. Another form of victimization framing suggests that the working class and the poor are victimizing the middle class, this time pitting their interests against those of people below them in the social-class hierarchy.

Victimization by the Rich and Powerful

Two recurring themes in the first of these forms of victimization framing include how the rich have benefitted—at the expense of the middle and lower classes—from changes in the tax laws and from the greed of corporate CEOs and wealthy shareholders. Early in the 2000s, a typical headline about U.S. tax laws demonstrated the first of these themes: "Plan Gives Most Benefits to Wealthy and Families."[99] The accompanying story discusses how changes in the tax law during the George W. Bush administration affected households in various income ranges. The article asserted that nearly half of the benefits in that administration's tax cut program would flow to the wealthiest 10 percent of taxpayers. To show that many middle-class people believed the tax cuts left them out in the cold, the reporter included an interview with Robert and Bee Moorhead of Austin, Texas. The article informed readers that the Moorheads were both employed, with a combined income of about $88,000, but still could not accumulate any substantial savings. Mr. Moorhead showed typical middle-class disbelief regarding the proposed change: "They're trying to sell this once again as trickle-down economics. I have my doubts."[100] A photo of the Moorhead family sitting on their porch, looking how most people expect members of the middle class to look, facilitated the story's framing. The general framing of the article focused on the greater benefit wealthy families would receive, as compared with middle-class families like the Moorheads, even though the journalist acknowledged that "President Bush's mammoth tax plan would give something to almost everybody."[101] Another article, "Caught in the Squeeze," stated, "Only the rich have reason to cheer" about the 2003 tax cut President Bush signed into law,[102] while another bore the headline "Tax Analysis Says the Rich Still Win."[103]

Media also used visual framing in the form of political cartoons to inform audiences that the rich were the primary beneficiaries of the Bush tax laws. In 2003, political cartoons throughout the nation showed how the rich benefited from the bill that cut taxes for the wealthy and increased the federal debt limit by nearly $1 trillion. Syndicated cartoonist Ben Sargent portrayed a very obese, wealthy man in a full-length coat wiping tears from his eyes with a large handkerchief while standing in front of a house where two seemingly middle-class parents sit on the front porch staring at a photograph of their son, who is in uniform and evidently serving in the U.S. armed forces in Iraq. The wealthy man says to the parents, "Oh, yeah? Well, now they're talking about cutting my next massive tax cut in half! Don't talk t'me about sacrifice!"[104] Another Sargent cartoon depicts a wealthy, well-dressed (but extremely overweight) man and woman talking to a mother with her child in a stroller. The wealthy man holds a sucker on a stick out to the child. The wealthy man's wife says to the child's mother, "Don't mind Howard. . . . He's just determined to thank the future generations who'll be paying for our lovely tax cut."[105] These cartoons visually reflect the form of victimization framing that suggests to media audiences that many actions benefitting the rich harm the middle class.

By 2010, in the sobering light of trillions of dollars of rapidly growing federal debt and the lingering U.S. economic recession, changes in the framing of stories could be seen in headlines that asked media audiences to consider what would happen when the Bush income tax cuts expired. For example, media reports such as an Associated Press article titled "With Income Tax Cuts Expiring, Rates Could Rise for Wealthy—but What about Middle Class?" emphasized that, although President Obama had repeatedly promised throughout his election campaign and early tenure in office to shield the middle class from higher tax rates, in actuality, many middle- and upper-middle-income families might be hit with much larger tax increases within the next two or three years. With the Bush tax cuts set to expire in

January 2011, elected officials and political party spokespersons were heavily divided over whether to pass legislation to make them permanent or to allow them to expire, in which case tax rates would increase to their previous higher level across most income categories. One proposal called for only allowing the cuts to expire for couples earning more than $250,000 and individuals earning more than $200,000 per year, which would place about 2 percent of U.S. households back in the 39.6 percent tax bracket (up from 35 percent). Although those making more than $200,000 in taxable income were most at risk for having to pay higher taxes, media framing emphasized that, once again, the middle class would likely be victimized by the rich when changes were made in the tax code. Although many Bush tax breaks helped middle-class families because they involved educational allowances and deductions for mortgage interest and charitable donations, as well as tax credits for some families with children, media framing of many stories focused on how much the wealthy or near wealthy benefitted from the tax cuts. After the Republican Party regained control of the U.S. House of Representatives in the 2010 mid-term elections, Congress passed, and President Obama signed into law, the Tax Hike Prevention Act of 2010, which extended all Bush-era income tax rates for two years and established a thirteen-month extension of federal jobless benefits, among other provisions. Media framing of some stories about the so-called tax-cut deal highlighted its negative effect in trillions of dollars on the federal deficit and on middle- and working-class people. Other stories primarily suggested that political partisanship and getting reelected were major factors in political leaders' decisions about temporarily renewing tax cuts that benefit the rich at the expense of the middle class.[106]

The other primary theme of victimization-by-the-wealthy framing is corporate greed. As chapter 3 shows, this issue has intensified in the early twenty-first century. In 2010, *New York Times* columnist Bob Herbert referred to the problem as "a sin and a shame" in an article published under that headline. According to Herbert, corporate America has treated workers much worse than most people realize, and the primary motivation for such actions has been "outright greed by corporate managers." From this perspective, although corporations have "mountains of cash," they are not hiring new workers or increasing employees' paychecks despite the fact that worker productivity has increased dramatically. In Herbert's words, "There can be no robust recovery as long as corporations are intent on keeping idle workers sidelined and squeezing the pay of those on the job."[107] The problem described here is not new: consider earlier articles, such as *Time* magazine's "They're Getting Richer!" describing how several major corporations, including Viacom, Citigroup, and Goldman Sachs, dramatically boosted the stock dividends paid to their top executives and shareholders after the Bush administration's 2003 tax cut went into effect. Supposedly, the tax cut was intended to provide a stimulus to corporations so that they would hire additional employees and help the U.S. economy. According to this article, "Dividends are a clean way for many CEOs to give themselves a big raise—and you have to figure that they will."[108] In hindsight, many things clearly contributed to the boom and bust experienced by giant corporations like Citigroup and Goldman Sachs since 2003. Corporate greed became even more visible to everyday people, however, as the media highlighted the questionable practices of large corporations and financial institutions.

Victimization framing of media stories about the middle class informs audiences of how the decisions of corporate elites harm this group. In the midst of corporate downsizing, layoffs, offshoring, and outsourcing of upper-middle-, middle-, and working-class jobs, one political cartoonist captured the essence of this form of victimization by portraying a bald CEO, wearing a nice suit and tie, shopping at "The Corporate Card Shoppe." The CEO fills his basket with cards from various sections of a rack labeled with greetings like "Congratulations! You've been downsized," "Good-bye! We're moving off-shore," "Sorry about your pension," and "I'm in recovery . . . too bad your job isn't." A *New Yorker* cartoon conveyed a similar idea: a judge sits in his courtroom listening to a well-dressed attorney standing before him with an affluent client by his side. The attorney states, "Your Honor, my client would like to be tried offshore."[109]

Articles such as "Bracing for the Blow"[110] and "The White-Collar Blues"[111] ask, "Who's next out the exit door?" as corporations continue sending jobs offshore. Although the practice of shipping thousands of jobs to lower-paid workers in other nations first hit the manufacturing sector and many so-called blue-collar workers hard, the problem has now extended to higher-paying, middle- and upper-middle-class positions. In "Education Is No Protection," Bob Herbert describes a New York conference titled "Offshore Outsourcing: Making the Journey Work for Your Corporation," offered to help executives make decisions about "the shipment of higher-paying white-collar jobs to countries with eager, well-educated and much lower-paid workers."[112] As the article's headline suggests, the education that middle-class individuals so highly value is not adequate protection against offshoring of jobs; many middle- and upper-middle-class positions formerly located in the United States can be performed less expensively by well-educated, white-collar workers in other countries.

Extensive media coverage followed after IBM, once considered a mainstay of the American economy, announced it was offshoring well-paid jobs such as those belonging to computer technicians. IBM uses the term *global sourcing* for sending jobs to workers in other countries; white-collar workers in the United States see this practice as further eroding their way of life, as middle-class jobs become increasingly difficult to find and those available do not pay as well as in the past.[113]

A news report titled "Guess Which Jobs Are Going Abroad," broadcast on CNN and posted on the CNN/Money website, contained the following statement: "If a tax preparer gets you an unexpected refund this year, you may have an accountant in India to thank. That's because accounting firms are joining the outsourcing trend established years ago by cost-conscious American manufacturers."[114] The movement of jobs out of the country continued in 2010 as articles like "Due Diligence from Afar" explained how "cost-conscious companies" were outsourcing legal work from cities such as New York to New Delhi. An example is Pangea3, a legal outsourcing firm that employs 110 Indian lawyers in New Delhi to review legal documents and do other work previously performed by lawyers in U.S. firms. Outsourcing makes sense to corporate executives because it is cheaper: Indian law firms charge one-tenth to one-third of what a U.S. law firm would bill per hour. Outsourcing means the end of jobs or much tighter competition for the jobs that exist in the United States, and this problem now affects the middle- and upper-middle class as it previously did blue-collar workers and other working-class people in this country. By 2010, India had become a prime location for outsourcing professional work, such as legal and publishing services: that nation has lower wages and a large pool of young, English-speaking professionals described as highly motivated.[115]

Media framing of stories sends a message that middle- and upper-middle-class employees in the United States are being victimized by wealthy corporate elites whose decisions affect the livelihoods of tens of thousands of people in this country when they choose to move jobs, including scientific laboratory analysis, medical billing, accounting, and legal work, to other nations, leaving U.S. workers in the lurch. Such stories pit corporations and their profitability against middle- and upper-middle-class workers. Obviously, most CEOs and corporate shareholders, who frequently benefit from cost-cutting measures such as downsizing, layoffs, offshoring, and outsourcing, do not share the problems of these middle-income workers and upper-middle-class professionals. In summing up the victimization of the middle class and the long-term slump of the U.S. economy, some journalists refer to these issues as the "new normal," in which economic growth is "too slow to bring down the unemployment rate and the government is forced to intervene even more forcefully in a struggling private sector."[116] According to one journalist, "The new normal challenges the optimism that's been at the root of American success for decades, if not centuries. And if it is here, the new normal could force Democrats and

Republicans to rethink their traditional approach to unemployment and other social problems."[117] Many fear that the new normal means that high, long-term unemployment, particularly for the middle class, is now a way of life. Headlines such as "Nation Lost 131,000 Jobs As Governments Cut Back," inform readers that the scale of job layoffs not only in the private sector but also by state and local governments in 2010 surprised economists.[118] Although the official unemployment rate remained at 9.5 percent in mid-2010, government estimates reached as high as 16.5 percent when the broadest definition of unemployment was used. This figure includes people who have given up searching for work even though they want and need a job. In the words of Mary Moore, a former administrative assistant at a publishing company who lost her job more than a year ago, "This economy is absolutely appalling. As an American I did not believe we would see times such as this."[119]

Victimization by the Poor and Homeless

Although some forms of victimization framing emphasize the role of the wealthy and powerful in subordinating the middle class, media also use it to show audiences that the middle class is being victimized by those beneath it in the social-class hierarchy. The theme of victimization of the middle class by the poor and homeless typically surfaces in media stories about middle-class housing and shelters for homeless people. Both of these residential settings are evaluated in terms of the widely held belief that the middle class is entitled to privacy, safety, maintenance of property values, and a feeling of community.

Home ownership is a key ingredient in the American Dream, and many in the middle class have realized this dream in residential settings that provide physical and psychological distance from lower-income people and the poor. According to many urban scholars, the need for this social distance contributed to the growth of suburbs in the past and to the popularity of exurbia and gated communities (residential areas surrounded by walls or fences with a secured entrance). News articles and television reports discussing gated communities and reviewing popular books on the topic, such as *Fortress America: Gated Communities in the United States*[120] and *Behind the Gates: Life, Security, and the Pursuit of Happiness in Fortress America*,[121] have informed media audiences that these communities are popular with middle-class residents who fear for their safety and want to keep out those who might victimize them. Framing of stories in this manner suggests that the gated community not only extends the middle-class American Dream but symbolizes the middle-class fear of violation:

It transforms Americans' dilemma of how to protect themselves and their children from danger, crime, and unknown others while still perpetuating open, friendly neighborhoods and comfortable, safe homes. It reinforces the norms of a middle-class lifestyle in a historical period in which everyday events and news media exacerbate fears of violence and terrorism. Thus, residents cite their "need" for gated communities to provide a safe and secure home in the face of a lack of other societal alternatives.[122]

Extensive media coverage of middle-class gated communities and books such as *Behind the Gates* convey the message that the middle class is not only emulating the upper class in its desire for safe and exclusive residences but participating in a new phase of residential development that will have a long-term effect on other urban problems, such as city planning, crime prevention, and public education. As *Washington Post* columnist Jonathan Yardley explains:

People living in urban high-rises with security systems and doormen have done that for generations, of course, but the suburban walled community is a recent phenomenon and is not, in fact, a suburb as the term has been understood until now. This is "a new phase of residential development," in which "architectural and planning parameters are redefining neighborhoods physically and socially by using walls and guards—not just distance, street patterns, and middle-class norms and mores."[123]

A number of journalists used the titles of books like *Fortress America* and *Behind the Gates* as sound bites in their discussions of urban problems, gated communities, and middle-class fears of victimization. However, as anthropologist Setha Low, author of *Behind the Gates*, states, the middle class may be putting too much hope in these communities:

Architectural symbols such as gates and walls also provide a rationale for the moral inconsistencies of everyday life. For instance, many residents want to feel safe in their homes and argue that walls and gates help keep out criminals, but gated communities are not safer than nongated suburban neighborhoods, where crime rates are already low. Instead, the logic of the symbolism satisfies conventional middle-class understandings of the nature of criminal activity—"it makes it harder for them to get in"—and justifies the choice to live in a gated community in terms of its moral and physical consequences—"look at my friends who were randomly robbed living in a nongated development."[124]

Just as the gated community serves as a source of reassurance for upper-middle- and middle-class residents, many people who do not live in such communities obtain security devices to prevent unauthorized intrusions of every type into their homes. According to "Fortress Home: Welcome Mat Bites," the 2004 annual International Builders Show in Las Vegas featured "all manner of newfangled security devices" ranging from security cameras that can be manipulated from anywhere in the world to protect a home's perimeter to deadbolt locks twenty-eight inches long.[125] According to the article, consumers—many of them middle class—fall into three groups: "the anxious, those whose peers are also arming themselves with alarms and deadbolts, and those who have experienced some kind of violence or violation."[126] Although the middle class is not the only socioeconomic category of people whose concerns about safety and security have been heightened by media reports about crimes like sniper shootings, members of this group have the economic resources to invest in security systems and fortress-building devices for their homes, as the wealthy have done for many years.

Although much media coverage has focused on how more affluent people try to live away from the poor and homeless by moving to the suburbs, security-oriented high-rise buildings, or gated communities, some researchers have also found that the public spaces in major cities are becoming more and more off-limits for poor people. Despite large influxes of recent immigrants into some cities, many neighborhoods have become more segregated. The framing of stories about the use of public space and how it affects the middle class often incorporates issues of race and class. In one incident, police harassed a group of African American friends as they stood on a corner, drinking beer. Another group—white customers at a restaurant with an outdoor patio—were drinking wine, but they were not bothered. According to one analyst, middle- and upper-middle-class gentrification "can redefine some activities. . . . The actual activity is not necessarily changing—people outside drinking alcohol—but the context is different and one is proscribed and one is not."[127]

It may initially appear a wide jump to shift to media framing of articles about homeless shelters, but victimization of the middle class is a recurring theme in this type of story as well. Articles about the infringement of the poor and homeless on private and public spaces that members of the middle class feel entitled to call their own gain salience with audiences because some fear that they too might "fall" and end up living in a shelter themselves. Media framing contributes to this fear with headlines like "From Middle Class to the Shelter Door: In a Trend, New Yorkers Face Poverty after Last Unemployment Check"[128] and "U.S. Offers a Hand to Those on Eviction's Edge."[129] In such articles, the people interviewed have either lost their jobs and unemployment benefits or experienced personal problems that left them destitute. As one article states, "Unemployment benefits have traditionally been a safety net of the middle class, as public assistance has been for the poor," and there is now a widespread fear that this safety net is not secure enough to keep people from falling out of the middle class.[130]

Middle- and upper-middle-class people who once believed they were safe from the worst effects of an economic recession, but have learned otherwise, find stories about home evictions particularly frightening. The framing of one story highlights a two-year "merciless downward spiral" experienced by Antonio Moore, who nearly had to live on the streets after he lost his $75,000-a-year job as a mortgage consultant, his three-bedroom house, and his Lexus sedan. Eventually, he did not have the money to pay for a small studio apartment because he was working as a part-time fry cook earning $10 an hour. A $1.5 billion federal program implemented in 2010 to help middle-class people avoid eviction enabled him to remain in his apartment—at least for the time being. The journalist writes,

> Much like the Great Depression, when millions of previously working people came to rely on a new social safety net for their sustenance, a swelling group of formerly middle-class Americans like Mr. Moore, 30, is seeking government aid for the first time. Without help, say economists, many are at risk of slipping permanently into poverty, even as economic conditions improve.[131]

Another recurring media frame entails the physical proximity of the poor and homeless to the daily paths of those who consider themselves members of the middle and upper-middle classes. For decades, public libraries have been a terrain contested by the middle class and the homeless. In an article titled "Anywhere but Here: Library Tells Homeless to Move Along," we learn that hundreds of homeless people in Dallas, Texas, have congregated in or near the public library; however, the library strictly enforces rules about sleeping on and misusing the premises because of complaints from middle-class citizens who believe the homeless infringe on the rights of library patrons. According to this article, "The recent crackdown is the latest in response to long-standing complaints about homeless people bathing in library restrooms, muttering obscenities, panhandling outside, littering and forming a gauntlet that makes some patrons uncomfortable. But many see it as another round in an endless cycle of dealing unsuccessfully with homelessness."[132] In cities across the nation, including Washington, DC, and San Francisco, California, journalists have described similar library encounters between the middle class and the homeless. The West End Library in Washington, DC, has attempted to welcome the homeless as much as possible; however, "older, richer, and whiter people" have registered complaints about their presence and asked the library to stock *New York Times* bestsellers rather than the self-help books assumed to be a favorite among the poor and homeless. Media framing about the homeless taking over the libraries has contributed to a middle-class fear of victimization in some cities. For example, the media report about Washington's West End Library brought this response from one reader:

> As a former resident of DC (Foggy Bottom) and as someone who works with a variety of libraries, I have to say that allowing libraries to become day-time homeless shelters isn't fair to anyone. Nor is it valid to suggest that those uncomfortable around the mentally ill are just the self-absorbed rich whites. Government agencies (city, state, federal) don't want to pick up the care for the homeless because it costs money so they look the other way when services used by the middle class collapse under the weight. Why shouldn't the needs of the middle class be considered alongside the needs of the homeless?[133]

Headlines regarding the homeless and libraries crop up across the country. For example, a San Francisco newspaper reports that John Banks, a homeless man in a wheelchair, shows up at the main library every day when it opens and stays there until it closes, at which time, he returns to the bus terminal where he spends the night.[134] As discussed in chapter 4, some journalists frame stories in a manner that engenders sympathy for the poor and homeless, asking, for instance, where a person like John Banks is supposed to stay. However, even stories originally intended to produce sympathy for this marginalized group may instead generate hostility from middle- and upper-middle-class people who feel threatened. One media analyst suggests that newspaper articles about the homeless often follow a standard frame:

> Dirty, smelly homeless people are ruining the enjoyment of facility X (in this case, a youth hostel) by upstanding group Y (tourists). City department Z (the Office of Homelessness), while trying to do its best, is just too overwhelmed to make anyone happy. Middle- or working-class citizens are interviewed about the latest dilemma, and lo and behold, out of their mouths pop prejudice and stereotypes about the homeless. A reaction quote from advocates for the homeless rounds out the picture.[135]

Media framing about placing homeless shelters within any particular community often asserts that choosing a particular location potentially threatens the middle class and informs media audiences of the negative responses of middle-class residents to these facilities. Examples include articles from the *San Francisco Chronicle*, "Homeless Shelter Plan Attacked, Potrero Hill Neighbors Worry about Property Values,"[136] and the *San Francisco Examiner*, "Showdown over Shelter: A Gritty Little Neighborhood Fights S.F. Plan for Homeless,"[137] both of which use NIMBY ("not in my back yard") framing and carry the underlying theme of middle-class victimization.

This approach to framing stories about the effects of homeless shelters on the middle class is not unique. "Chicago Looks for Home for Shelter for Homeless" describes Pacific Garden Mission, a shelter in need of a new location because the city wanted the property to build a new gymnasium and library for a high school. As more middle- to upper-middle-class residents moved into the expensive condominiums and town houses built as the area became gentrified, the shelter—at one time considered to be on skid row in "an undesirable neighborhood that people would rather avoid than come to"—was now deemed an eyesore and a threat to middle-class residents living and working nearby.[138]

Consider one final example of the pitting of the middle class against the homeless when it comes to shelters. Articles and letters to the editor published in the Fredericksburg, Virginia, *Free Lance-Star* informed readers that middle-class residents were concerned about their and their children's safety due to plans to move the Thurman Bisben Homeless Shelter to their neighborhood. "Shelter's Plan Not a Popular Move" prominently featured a photo of Theresa Lewis, a twenty-seven-year-old mother of four, expressing her opposition to the shelter at a local civic association meeting. According to the article, Lewis did not want the shelter in her backyard: "I feel badly for the families, but I have to think of my children. How can you guarantee their safety from these strange people?" she asked the approximately fifty people gathered.[139] In the days immediately prior to and after that news report, readers sent sharply contrasting letters to the newspaper's editor: pieces with titles like "Shelter Will Bring Only Crime"[140] and "Please Don't Let Shelter Ruin Our Neighborhood"[141] presented the middle-class-victimization side of the argument; "There's No Reason to Fear the Poor Residents of a Shelter"[142] and "L.A. Confidential: A Well-Run Shelter Suppresses Crime"[143] argued the other side of the debate.

Overall, media framing of articles about homeless shelters and their effect on the middle class may contribute to a sense on the part of members of that group of increasing victimization not only by those above them in the class structure but also by those living in poverty and experiencing homelessness. Although a variety of social problems do harm individuals in the middle class, these problems also hurt people in other demographics as well. For this reason, media framing of stories suggesting that middle-class concerns are more important than those of other people is in itself an important issue to evaluate when considering how media representations of various classes may influence audiences.

EFFECTS OF MEDIA FRAMING ABOUT THE MIDDLE CLASS

When I began my research into how the media frame news articles and television entertainment story lines about the middle class, I assumed that

I would primarily find data to support a representation of the middle class as "us"—the vast category into which almost everyone in the United States supposedly fits. I also expected that the media would focus on positive attributes of the middle class, such as people's values and lifestyles. Based on the popularity of books like Brooks's *Bobos in Paradise* and Florida's *The Rise of the Creative Class*, I anticipated depictions of the middle class as "in charge" and upwardly mobile. Instead, I found that although some journalists and television writers extol the virtues of this group, many others focus on the constant peril it faces, and they have done so for more than 150 years. This type of framing has become more prevalent given the economic climate of the United States in the early twenty-first century, and even more stories are found in all forms social networking and mainstream media.

Media framing of the middle class as the backbone of the nation supports the notion that this class holds the rest of the country together and that middle-class mores are the core values of the United States. News reports and television sitcoms of the past widely used family-values framing, but much of this has given way to a portrayal of the middle class as deeply conflicted, fragmented, and fragile. News articles suggesting that the middle class is in peril—its existence perhaps even in jeopardy—reflects such framing further.

The fragility of the middle class is a recurring theme in media framing. Many articles and news stories depict this demographic as caught in an economic vise. If readers and viewers accept the premise behind squeeze framing, they may see the middle class as continually caught between aspiration and anxiety. As a proliferation of products and services, coupled with high levels of credit card and other types of debt, fuel rampant consumerism, we can either praise the middle class or blame it for its consumer habits.

Media framing of news articles shapes, at least in part, how people think about the middle class and its habits. For example, when the media depict the middle class as overspending and taking out mortgages that they cannot afford, squeeze framing assigns responsibility to those individuals and their families. If, however, the media present these middle-class problems as a form of victimization, the blame shifts to corporations and government officials. Even the poor and homeless may be portrayed as infringing on the rights and property of the middle class. As political scientist Shanto Iyengar states with regard to the media framing of poverty, "While there is as yet no well-developed theory of framing effects, it seems quite likely that these effects occur because the terms or 'frames' embodied by a stimulus subtly direct attention to particular reference points or considerations."[144] Similarly, media framing of stories about the middle class also directs audiences' attention to particular reference points and considerations.

Representing the middle class as victimized by the wealthy can either produce middle-class animosity toward the rich or engender greater resolve to earn more money (or strike it rich playing the lottery) and join the ranks of the rich and famous, thereby gaining their tax breaks and lifestyle advantages. It is hard to explain our fascination with the wealthy if some part of us does not aspire to their status, or at least have a deep-seated interest in how they manage to live "above" everyone else. Rather than systematically opposing laws and policies that benefit the well-to-do, some in the middle classes are content to live vicariously, watching reality shows in which people get rich because they have talent (FOX's *American Idol*, NBC's *America's Got Talent*), correctly answer a number of questions on a quiz show (ABC's *Who Wants to Be a Millionaire?*), or successfully compete against others for a job or other high-value resources (NBC's *The Apprentice*).

By contrast, the more that media coverage shows middle-class people as victimized by the poor and homeless, the more likely some in the former group will be to wish to segregate themselves and their families from individuals in other classes who might do them harm. Media coverage may also encourage people to oppose national, state, or local decisions that bring low-income and homeless individuals into closer proximity with middle-class families. "Not in my backyard" and "I don't want them to take away what I've worked so hard to get" are common reactions to such situations as plans to build new homeless shelters.

Just as fear of others probably constituted one of many factors contributing to the growth of suburbs in the past, the proliferation of exurbs and gated communities in the twenty-first century stems partly from the facts that fear sells; the middle class is a prime target of marketing for security systems and other protection devices. For many years, the upper class fortified itself against encroachment by the poor (and even by the middle class) in its high-security, high-rise urban residences and in its fenced estates with guard dogs. Now the middle class has joined its ranks, seeking to fortify its residences and schools, and even public spaces like streets and city libraries, against those they find threatening. As Edward J. Blakely and Mary Gail Snyder conclude in *Fortress America: Gated Communities in America*, community building has greatly diminished in the United States, and the emphasis has shifted, at least among those with the ability to pay, toward "privatization, increasing atomization, and increasing localism."[145] These authors question whether democracy can long endure under these conditions, and they suggest that perhaps the more media coverage encourages the middle class to "duck and cover," the less focus there will be on community building in this country. According to Blakely and Snyder,

> When privatization and exclusion become dominant, and neighborhood con-
> nectedness and mutual support structures disappear, we must question whether
> an American democracy founded on citizenship and community remains pos-
> sible. . . . All of the walls of prejudice, ignorance, and economic and social in-
> equality must come down before we can rendezvous with our democratic ideals.
> The walls of the mind must open to accept and cherish a more diverse nation.
> Then the walls that separate our communities, block social contact, and weaken
> the social contract will also come down.[146]

Certainly, members of the middle class are not the only ones contributing to the building of the walls of separation in the United States. However, if media representations of this class over the past 150 years are any indica-tion, much of the news reporting and many of the entertainment shows have contributed to a view of the middle class not as the great unifier in society but as part of the great divide, increasingly squeezed by economic conditions, perpetually victimized by the wealthy and the poor, and generally living in fear of its future. Media framing of news reports and entertainment story lines about the middle class may find a vast well of insecurities—economic, political, and social, as well as moral—upon which to prey in the portrayal of this group.

Chapter 7

Framing Class, Vicarious Living, and Conspicuous Consumption

The world leadership qualities of the United States, once so prevalent, are fading faster than the polar ice caps. We once set the standard for industrial might, for the advanced state of our physical infrastructure, and for the quality of our citizens' lives. All are experiencing significant decline. . . . At a time when a college education is needed more than ever to establish and maintain a middle-class standard of living, America's young people are moving in exactly the wrong direction. . . . Instead of exercising the appropriate mental muscles, we're allowing ourselves to become a nation of nitwits, obsessed with the coming and going of Lindsay Lohan and increasingly oblivious to crucially important societal issues that are all but screaming for attention. . . .We no longer know how to put our people to work. We read less and less and write like barbarians. We've increasingly turned our backs on the very idea of hard-won excellence while flinging open the doors to decadence and decline. No wonder Lady Gaga and Snooki from "Jersey Shore" are cultural heroes.[1]

These words from *New York Times* columnist Bob Herbert in a piece titled "Putting Our Brains on Hold" may sound harsh; however, for many years, Herbert has framed his articles and blogs to call attention to numerous pressing social problems worldwide, including vast and growing economic inequality, high rates of un- and underemployment, and massive homelessness and poverty. It is no surprise, therefore, that Herbert's words have become more strident as he has wearied of being a lone voice in the wilderness calling for significant changes before these major economic and social problems overcome us.

The first edition of *Framing Class*, published in 2005, argued that the media often trivialize heavy topics, such as class and social inequality. Clearly, journalists like Herbert are the exception to this statement, and more media have shifted their framing of class-related articles and entertainment programs as the United States has experienced persistent economic problems in the 2000s. The first edition of *Framing Class* also posited that the media encourage overconsumption among people of all classes, particularly those who seek to emulate the rich—whether or not they can afford to do so. Chapter 7 of that edition began with a TV critic's statement that Paris Hilton, a wealthy celebrity and occasional reality TV star, like others who are "famous for being famous," could take "the heaviest of topics and make them weightless as a social X-ray."[2] That critic's point was well made: media representations of inequality frequently make light of the problems of the poor and working class while emphasizing the values and virtues of the middle class and celebrating the luxurious lifestyles and material possessions of those in the top tier of the social hierarchy, regardless of how they may have accumulated these possessions. Previously, I placed most of the blame on journalists, entertainment writers, and Web content providers who seemed insensitive or oblivious to class-based inequality:

> Rather than providing a meaningful analysis of inequality and showing realistic portrayals of life in various social classes, the media either play class differences for laughs or sweep the issue of class under the rug so that important distinctions are rendered invisible. By ignoring class or trivializing it, the media involve themselves in a social construction of reality that rewards the affluent and penalizes the working class and the poor.[3]

Although my newer data largely confirm this statement, the Great Recession of the 2000s, for which there was no end in sight as of 2011, is apparently affecting how some journalists, bloggers, and entertainment writers represent the growing economic problems of individuals and the nation as a whole.

Throughout *Framing Class*, I have provided many examples of how the media frame class and the messages these framing devices may convey to audiences. In this chapter, I look at the sociological implications of how framing contributes to our understanding of class and leads us either to try to emulate other people or to take the ostrich approach, sticking our heads in the sand and ignoring the everyday realities that surround us. First, we look at two questions: How do media audiences understand and act upon popular-culture images or frames? Do we understand class differently today because of these frames?

MEDIA FRAMING AND THE
PERFORMANCE OF CLASS IN EVERYDAY LIFE

In a mass-mediated culture such as ours, the media do not simply mirror society; rather, they help to shape it and to create cultural perceptions.[4] The blurring between what is real and what is not encourages people to emulate the upper classes and shun the working class and the poor. Television shows, magazines, and newspapers sell the idea that the only way to get ahead is to identify with the rich and powerful and to live vicariously through them. From sitcoms to reality shows, the media encourage ordinary people to believe that they may rise to fame and fortune; they too can be the next winner of the lottery or *American Idol.* Constantly bombarded by stories about the lifestyles of the rich and famous, viewers feel a sense of intimacy with elites, with whom they have little or no contact in their daily lives.[5] According to social critic bell hooks, we overidentify with the wealthy because the media socialize us to believe that people in the upper classes are better than we are. The media also suggest that we owe no allegiance to people in our own class or to those who are less fortunate.[6]

Many people's reading and viewing habits and their patterns of consumption reflect vicarious living—that is, the tendency to watch how other individuals live rather than to experience life for ourselves—through media representations of wealth and success. According to hooks, television promotes hedonistic consumerism:

> Largely through marketing and advertising, television promoted the myth of the classless society, offering on one hand images of an American dream fulfilled wherein any and everyone can become rich and on the other suggesting that the lived experience of this lack of class hierarchy was expressed by our equal right to purchase anything we could afford.[7]

As hooks suggests, equality does not exist in contemporary society, but media encourage audiences to view themselves as having an "equal right" to purchase items that will somehow render them equal to people above them in the social-class hierarchy. However, the catch is that we must actually be able to afford these purchases. Manufacturers and the media have dealt with this problem by offering relatively cheap products that buyers can purchase without actually having the money to pay for them.[8]

The media's framing of stories about class does make a difference in how we think about other people and how we spend our money. Media frames constitute a mental shortcut (schema) that helps us formulate our thoughts.

The Upper Classes: Affluence and Consumerism Make People Happy

Although some media frames show the rich and famous in a negative manner, they still glorify the material possessions and lifestyles of the upper classes. Research has found that people who extensively watch television have exaggerated views of how wealthy most Americans are and of the material possessions they own. Studies have also found that extensive television viewing leads to higher rates of spending and lower savings, presumably because television stimulates consumer desires.[9]

For many years, most media framing of stories about the upper classes has been positive, ranging from consensus framing, which depicts the wealthy as being like everyone else, to admiration framing, which portrays them as generous, caring individuals. The frame most closely associated with rampant consumerism is emulation framing, which suggests that people in all classes should reward themselves with a few of the perks of the wealthy, such as a larger house, a more luxurious vehicle, or better jewelry. The writers of television shows like *Platinum Weddings*, *The Fabulous Life*, and *Keeping Up with the Kardashians* rely heavily not only on admiration framing but on price-tag framing, according to which a person's worth is measured by what he or she owns and how many assistants cater to his or her whims. In this world, the people with the most expensive limousines, yachts, and jets are declared the winners in life. Reality shows like *American Idol, America's Got Talent,* and *The Apprentice* suggest that anyone can move up the class ladder and live like the rich if he or she displays the best looks, greatest talent, or sharpest entrepreneurial skills. No wonder economist Juliet B. Schor finds that the overriding goal of children age ten to thirteen is to get rich. In response to the statement "I want to make a lot of money when I grow up," 63 percent of the children in Schor's study agreed, whereas only 7 percent disagreed.[10]

Many adults who hope to live the good life simply plunge further into debt. Many reports show that middle- and working-class American consumers are incurring massive consumer debts as they purchase larger houses, more expensive vehicles, and many other items beyond their means. According to one analyst, media portrayals of excessive consumer spending and bombardment by credit card advertisements encourage people to load up on debt.[11] Consequently, some people with average incomes who aspire to the lives of luxury of the upper classes have instead found themselves spending their way into the poor house, joining members of the impoverished class. According to a Pew Research Center study, "Inside the Middle Class: Bad Times Hit the Good Life," middle-income Americans have spent more and borrowed more since the 1980s, in large part for housing. Many families bought new single-family dwellings, which are about 50 percent larger than in the past, and existing houses were about 60 percent more expensive (in inflation-adjusted dollars) in 2008 than in the mid-1980s.[12] According to this study, increased consumerism, even by those who cannot afford it, relates to the vastly expanding supply of goods to purchase and services to desire:

Goods and services that didn't exist a few decades ago—such as high definition television, high speed internet, and cable or satellite subscriptions—have become commonplace consumer items. And the costs of many of the anchors of a middle class lifestyle—not just housing, but medical care and college education—have risen more sharply than inflation.[13]

As working-class and middle-income people saw the rich grow increasingly wealthy and the income gap between the rich and everyone else continue to grow, until it was the highest it had been in thirty years, they found it extremely tempting to buy houses with adjustable-rate mortgages, which initially made the property affordable; then, monthly payments would spiral upward, making it impossible for owners to keep up with their mortgage payments and all the monthly expenses associated with the property.

As wealthy elites have publicly run afoul of the law and media coverage has intensified about financial tycoons' improprieties and excessive spending, some journalists, late-night talk show hosts, cable TV network talking heads, and social media bloggers have berated these so-called masters of the universe. Despite condemning the actions of unscrupulous individuals, however, many people still hold a grudging admiration for those who manage to accumulate the trappings of wealth and success, regardless of how they do so. Many corporate CEOs and financial executives, such as hedge fund managers accused of civil or criminal offenses, have exited their organizations with golden parachutes—severance packages that amount to millions or billions in cash and stock options. Ironically, people view some scoundrels leaving such parachutes as winners because, in their own perverse way, they have achieved the American Dream, just not in the traditional manner. Media framing of stories about the wealthy and unscrupulous continues to exhibit grudging admiration, mixed in with disdain, for the illegal actions of elites: the media spotlight highlights their prominence in society and vividly describes the lavish trappings of their success. Occasionally, when it looks like getting ahead is a game that only the already-wealthy can play, people in other classes become angry about the exclusionary nature of the winner-takes-all society in which business as usual is an exclusive private club. Secretly, many people wish that they had the wealth and benefits of the upper classes without having to face some of the problems affluent people experience. According to a social analyst quoted in the *New York Times*,

> There's always been envy and hatred toward the rich, but there was also a strong undercurrent of admiration that was holding these people up as a goal. This time it's different because it feels like it's a closed club and the rich have an unfair advantage. . . . But the same people who say that money is bad say that money is connected to their self-worth—and they wished they had it and you didn't.[14]

The Poor and Homeless: "Not Me!"—Negative Role Models in the Media

The sharpest contrasts in media portrayals are between depictions of people in the upper classes and images of those at the bottom of the class structure. In the twenty-first century, social analysts like Barbara Ehrenreich have argued that it is possible to be "too poor to make the news."[15] In the recession of the 2000s, many of the superrich made media headlines when they gave up their private jets; upper-middle-class individuals thought of themselves as the "new poor" because they could not afford a new luxury vehicle every year. According to Ehrenreich, however, the already invisible poor became even more invisible in the recession, partly because they were seen as not having much to lose in the first place.

When the media do provide coverage of the poor and homeless, individuals in these categories are portrayed, at best, as deserving our sympathy on holidays or after disaster has struck. In these situations, those in the bottom classes are depicted as being temporarily down on their luck or as working hard to get out of their current situation but in need of public assistance. At worst, however, the poor are blamed for their own problems, and the homeless are stereotyped as bums, alcoholics, and drug addicts, caught in a hopeless downward spiral because of their individual pathological behavior.

For the most part, people at the bottom of the class hierarchy remain out of sight and out of mind for most media audiences. Thematic framing depicts the poor and homeless as "faceless" statistics in reports on poverty. Episodic framing highlights some problems of the poor but typically does not link their personal situations to such larger societal problems as limited educational opportunities, high unemployment rates, and jobs that pay depressingly low wages.

The poor do not fare well on television entertainment shows; writers typically present them as one-dimensional, bedraggled characters standing on a street corner holding a cardboard sign reading, "Need money for food." When television writers tackle the issue of homelessness, they often portray lead characters (who usually are white and relatively affluent) as helpful people, while they depict the poor and homeless as deviants who might harm themselves or others. Hospital and crime dramas like *Grey's Anatomy*, *House M.D.*, *CSI*, and *Law & Order*, as well as other network and cable series that frequently come and go within one or two seasons, consistently portray the poor and homeless as crazy, inebriated, or otherwise incompetent to provide key information to officials. Television reality shows like *Cops* go so far as to advertise that they provide "footage of debris from the bottom tiers of the urban social order."[16] Such statements say a lot about how television producers, directors, and writers view (or would have us view) the lower classes.

From a sociological perspective, framing of stories about the poor and home-less contrasts starkly with that of stories about upper-class individuals and suggests that we should distance ourselves from "those people." Such framing encourages us to view the poor and homeless as the Other, the outsider; the me-dia show us little commonality between our lives and the experiences of people at the bottom of the class hierarchy. As a result, we find it easy to buy into the dominant ideological construct that poverty is a problem of individuals, not of society as a whole, and we may feel justified in our rejection of the poor.[17]

The Working Class: Historical Relics and Jokes

As we have seen, the working class and working poor do not fare much better than the poor and homeless in media representations. Described as "labor," working-class people are usually nothing more than faces in a crowd on television shows. The media portray those who produce goods and services as much less interesting than the people who excessively purchase them—a problem that can only intensify as more of the workers who make such prod-ucts are thousands of miles away from the typical American consumer, in nations like China and India.[18]

Contemporary media coverage carries little information about the working class or its problems. Low wages, lack of benefits, and hazardous working conditions are considered boring and uninteresting topics, except on the public broadcasting networks or as an occasional segment on television "news shows" like *60 Minutes* or *20/20*, after some major case of worker abuse has been revealed. The most popular portrayal of the working class, caricature fram-ing, depicts these people in negative ways, for instance, as idiots, white trash, buffoons, bigots, or slobs. Many television shows featuring working-class characters play on the idea that their clothing, manners, and speech patterns are inferior to those of the middle or upper classes. For example, working-class characters may compare themselves to the middle and upper classes by saying that they are not as "fancy as the rich people." Sitcom writers have perpetuated working-class stereotypes, and a number of reality shows try to "improve" seemingly "ordinary" working-class people through exercise, surgery, fashion, and makeovers. TLC's *American Chopper* features characters with tattoos—particularly a father and son duo who fight all the time—and participate in the rough-and-tumble blue-collar world of bikers, yet show great creativity when they create a new bike. *American Chopper* illustrates how working-class men may be perceived as macho while, at the same time, they produce custom bikes that sport a unique appearance and elaborate design.

Like their upper-class celebrity counterparts, so-called working-class come-dians like Jeff Foxworthy have ridiculed the blue-collar lifestyle. They have also marketed products that make fun of the working class. Foxworthy's website (www.jefffoxworthy.com), for example, includes redneck figurines ("little statues for inside the house"), redneck cookbooks, *Games Rednecks Play*, and calendars that make fun of the working class generally. Although some people see these items as humorous ("where's yore sense of humor?"), the real message is that people in the lower classes lack good taste, socially acceptable manners, and, above all, middle-class values. If you purchase redneck merchandise, you too can make fun of the working class and clearly distance yourself from it.

Late-night television program *The Tonight Show with Jay Leno* demonstrated the persistence of class-based jokes about rednecks and white trash when host Jay Leno showed pictures of "white trash repairs," described as how white trash might repair broken items in their homes. According to Leno, examples of white-trash repairs include using a stack of old books to prop up a chair with a broken leg, holding a broken belt together with the tines of a fork, and dealing with a broken stove by cooking food on an upside-down clothes iron. Mainstreaming of jokes about white trash on network television legitimizes a culture that mocks people based on class and their assumed lack of education and cultural capital.

In the 2000s, the working class has fared somewhat better on a few reality series that have attempted documentary-style coverage of selected blue-collar occupations. Episodes of shows like *Undercover Boss*, *Dirty Jobs*, *Ice Road Truckers*, *Construction Intervention*, and *Deadliest Catch* illustrate the difficulty of surviving in jobs in which workers face all kinds of hazardous weather and working conditions. Ultimately, however, media framing of disaster stories—such as the vast BP oil spill in the Gulf of Mexico, the aftermath of Hurricane Katrina, and the U.S. economic crisis—overlook many problems confronting the working class and working poor. The media also largely ignore the contributions of the working-class people who are then called on to "fix" these problems, focusing instead on the ideas and concerns of politicians and business executives, many of whom may have contributed to these problems in the first place. We make a mistake when we trivialize or ignore the working class because the nation goes much as the working class does. Media framing of stories about people in this segment of the class hierarchy leaves much to be desired because it provides few insights into problems faced by working people in everyday life.

MIDDLE-CLASS FRAMING AND HIGH-LEVEL WORRYING

Media framing of stories about the middle class tells us that this economic group is the value center and backbone of the nation. Middle-class-values framing suggests that the mores of this class hold the nation together. Even the White House has conducted studies and made extensive lists of common characteristics of middle-income individuals and families to show that certain common threads run through this group. According to these studies, their aspirations more than their incomes define middle-class families. Also, high prices, job insecurity, and the U.S. economic crisis are making it more difficult in the early twenty-first century to achieve and maintain middle-class status. Media framing of stories about the middle class (and the would-be middle class) informs us that many middle-income people are going through a period of great economic and social uncertainty, and neither these families nor officials in federal, state, and local governments know what to do to permanently reverse the problem.

Why have networks framed television shows to appeal to the middle class and emphasize middle-class values? Early television writers knew that their shows needed to appeal to middle-class audiences, the targeted consumers for advertisers' products, and thus framing of the middle-class values of honesty, integrity, and hard work formed an integral ingredient of early sitcoms. However, some contemporary television writers spoof the middle class and poke fun at the values supposedly associated with people in this demographic. Some sitcom writers focus on the dysfunctions of a fictional middle-class family, including conflicts between husbands and wives, parents and children, and family members and outsiders. Media critics have also noticed the absence of Latino and Asian American families in television sitcoms. Characters from these racial/ethnic categories tend to have small roles and to be part of a program's joke. Asian Americans are particularly likely to be depicted as middle class but as having some sort of quirkiness.

If they want to appeal to middle-class viewers, why do some television shows make fun of the middle class? The corporations that pay for advertising want to capture the attention of males between the ages of eighteen and thirty-nine, and individuals in this category, it is believed, enjoy laughing at the uptight customs and ideas of conventional middle-class families. Advertisers also recognize the influence programs have on families. That is why they happily spend billions of dollars on product placements (such as a Diet Coke can sitting on a character's desk) and on ads during commercial breaks.

In *Born to Buy: The Commercialized Child and the New Consumer Culture*, Schor examines why very young children buy into consumer culture and concludes that extensive media exposure to products is a key reason: "More children [in the United States] than anywhere else believe that their clothes and brands describe who they are and define their social status. American kids display more brand affinity than their counterparts anywhere else in the world; indeed, experts describe them as increasingly 'bonded to brands.'"[19] Part of this bonding occurs through constant television watching, Internet use, and participation in social media, as a steady stream of ads and blogs targets children and young people. Schor concludes that we face a greater problem than just excessive consumerism. Consumer culture undermines children's well-being: "High consumer involvement is a significant cause of depression, anxiety, low self-esteem, and psychosomatic complaints."[20] Although no similar studies have determined the effects of the media's emphasis on wealth and consumerism among adults, today's children will likely take these values with them into adulthood if our society does not first reach the breaking point with respect to consumer debt, and some analysts believe we are heading in this direction, given high rates of long-term unemployment, a stalled housing market, high foreclosure rates, and an unsuccessful effort by the federal government to stimulate the economy.

The issue of class in the United States has not been portrayed in the media through a realistic assessment of wealth, poverty, and inequality: rather, it has been shown through superficial patterns of rampant self-interest and consumerism. Among these patterns in media representation are the glorifying of shopping as a major life experience, encouraging individuals to acquire large mortgages they cannot afford and that will soon sour on them, and offering high-risk people seemingly unlimited amounts of credit, but then loudly lamenting the fact that these unsupportable patterns of behavior have contributed to the worst economic meltdown in the United States since the 1930s Great Depression. The general message remains, one article stated, "We pledge allegiance to the mall."[21]

MEDIA FRAMING AND OUR
DISTORTED VIEW OF INEQUALITY

Class clearly permeates media culture and influences our thinking about social inequality. Media framing of stories involving class presents a socially constructed reality that is not necessarily an accurate reflection of the United States. Because of their pervasive nature, the media have the capacity to define the world symbolically for other people. In turn, readers and viewers glean information from the media that they use to construct a picture of class and inequality—one that they come to see as realistically representing where they stand in the class structure, what they should (or should not) aspire to achieve, and whether and why they should view other people as superior, equal, or inferior to themselves.

Because of the media's power to socially construct reality, we must make an effort to find out about the objective nature of class and evaluate social inequality on our own terms. Although postmodern thinkers believe it is impossible to distinguish between real life and the fictionalized version of reality presented by the media, some sociologists argue that we can learn to discern the difference between media images of reality and the actual facts pertaining to wealth, poverty, and inequality. The more we become aware that we are not receiving "raw" information or "just" entertainment from the media, the more we are capable of rationally thinking about how media portrayals represent us and what these depictions encourage us to do (engage in hedonistic consumerism, for example). Print and electronic media have become extremely adept at framing issues of class in a certain manner, but we still have the ability to develop alternative frames that better explain who we are and what our nation is truly like in regard to class divisions.

The Realities of Class

What are the realities of inequality? The truth is that the rich are getting richer, and the gulf between the rich and poor continues to widen in the United States. How do we know this? In the decade between 1996 and 2006, the income of the top one-fifth of U.S. families increased by more than 40 percent; during that same period, the income of the bottom one-fifth increased by only 5.6 percent. By 2009, the rich were no longer getting richer at the same rate as in the past, but they were far from living in poverty. This drop stemmed partly from the recession that started in December 2007, when real median household income declined by 3.6 percent (from $52,163 to $50,303) between 2007 and 2008.

As discussed in chapter 2, sociologist Dennis Gilbert compares the U.S. income distribution to a national pie and shows that the wealthiest 20 percent of households received 50 percent of the total income pie in 2008, while the poorest 20 percent of households received 3 percent. Moreover, the income share claimed by the richest fifth of households is seventeen times that received by the poorest fifth, contradicting the common belief that most income in the United States goes to the middle class.[22] Income distribution also varies by race/ethnicity, and this disparity has continued for many years. Consider the following figures for 2008: The highest median income was for Asian households ($65,637), as compared to white (non-Hispanic) households ($55,530), Hispanic households ($37,913), and African American households ($34,218). As these figures show, African Americans and Latinos are over-represented among those in the bottom income levels. Over half of African American and Latino households fall within the lowest income categories.[23]

Wealth inequality is even more pronounced than income inequality. Wealth includes property such as buildings, houses, land, farms, factories, and cars, as well as other assets such as bank accounts, corporate stocks, bonds, and insurance policies. Wealth is computed by subtracting all debt obligations (what you own minus what you owe) and converting the value of remaining assets into cash. Since the 1970s, the wealth of the richest 1 percent of American families has grown dramatically. In 2007, the wealthiest 1 percent owned about one-third (33.8 percent) of total family wealth in the United States. The next wealthiest 9 percent owned about 37.7 percent, leaving the rest (90 percent of families) with the remaining 26 percent of wealth. For the upper class, wealth often comes from interest income, dividends, and inheritance. Consider, for example, that about half of the individuals on the *Forbes* 400 list of the wealthiest people in the United States had inherited sufficient wealth to put them on the list. As with income, wealth disparities are greatest across racial and ethnic categories. As discussed in chapter 6, the wealth gap between white and African American families has more than quadrupled over the course of a generation. By 2007, the average middle-income white household accumulated $74,000 in wealth, whereas the average high-income African American household owned only $18,000 in wealth.[24] Moreover, in 2008, 39.8 million people lived below the official government poverty level of about $22,000 for a family of four. The official poverty rate for 2008 was 13.2 percent; however, many analysts believe that this number has continued to increase, and more people have found themselves without employment and sometimes without homes.[25]

Data showing how people are faring in the second decade of the twenty-first century highlight the fact that we are not all comfortably located in the middle class; nor is the middle class as comfortable as many politicians would have us believe. In fact, many in the middle- and upper-middle classes, and even in some segments of the upper class, are trying to overcome financial problems that became more pronounced after a period of hedonistic consumerism.

THE HANGOVER AFTER HEDONISTIC CONSUMERISM

Consumerism is a normal part of life; we purchase the things that we need to live. Hedonistic consumerism, however, exceeds all necessary and meaningful boundaries. As the word "hedonism" suggests, some people are so caught up in consumerism that it becomes the main reason for their existence, their primary source of happiness. Such people engage in the self-indulgent pursuit of happiness through what they buy.

When the U.S. economy was soaring, people were encouraged to spend money. When the recession started in the fourth quarter of 2007, families were still encouraged to spend money to help stimulate the faltering economy. As the Great Recession worsened, however, many people began cutting back on spending for some items but not others. The information, entertainment, and advertising media have contributed to the types of products and services for which Americans have increased or decreased consumption. Since the recession began, spending has increased almost 17 percent on mobile devices such as smart phones. Although these phones have many uses and applications beyond simply telephony, they are also widely used and promoted on television, the Internet, and other forms of media. For example, on competitive television shows like *American Idol* and *America's Got Talent*, viewers are repeatedly reminded to call or text in their votes. Communications devices, including cell phones, Kindle readers, and iPads, are widely advertised as the new must-have items.

By contrast, Americans are spending less on moving and storage because they cannot afford to buy newer and bigger houses. They are spending less on motor vehicles and gas and a little less on clothing and travel, particularly to foreign countries. Despite some cutbacks in spending, problems such as job loss, part-time rather than full-time work, owning a house bought at the top of the market and trying to sell after the housing market bottomed out, and an increase in so-called fixed costs, such as utilities and food, have increased the overall debt owed by families. Estimates vary widely on the amount of credit card debt that individuals possess: some estimate the average unpaid credit card balance to be about $3,387. Other estimates place the average credit card debt per household at about $15,788. Despite problems associated with credit cards, some credit card companies run aggressive advertising campaigns to entice potential customers into opening an account. Capital One's "What's in Your Wallet?" uses humor to show that, despite adversity, everything will come out fine for people if they own a credit card from that company. Obviously, credit card advertisements are successful because sponsors pay as much as $5.4 million per month to run them on sports and entertainment shows. Despite ups and downs in the economy, as consumers our expectations for ourselves and our children have risen as the media have continued to portray the good life and bombard us with other products that we must have. The iPhone 3 is not good enough; we must have access to the new applications ("apps") available on iPhone 4, and then iPhone 5, and on it goes.

Are we Americans only interested in getting the economy back on track so that we can continue our consumer habits, or are we actually interested in learning about class and inequality? Although some people prefer to operate in a climate of denial, media critics believe that more people are awakening to biases in the media, particularly when they see vast inconsistencies between media portrayals of class and everyday reality. According to sociologists

Robert Perrucci and Earl Wysong, "It is apparent that increasing experiences with and knowledge about class-based inequalities among the nonprivileged is fostering a growing awareness of and concerns about the nature and extent of superclass interests, motives, and power in the economic and political arenas."[26] Some individuals are becoming aware of the effect that media biases can have on how they interpret what they read, see, and hear. A Pew Research Center poll, for example, shows that working-class individuals do not unquestioningly accept media information and commentary that preponderantly support the status quo.[27]

Similarly, Perrucci and Wysong note that television can have a paradoxical effect on viewers: it can serve both as a pacifier and as a source of heightened class consciousness. Shows that focus on how much money the very wealthy have may provide a source of entertainment for nonelites, but seeing people get paid so much for doing so little (e.g., the actress who earns $17 million per film or the sports star who signs a $100 million, multiyear contract) may also produce antagonism among people who work hard and earn comparatively little. Even more egregious are individuals who do not work at all but have been born into the "right family" and inherited billions of dollars.

Although affluent audiences might prefer that the media industry work to "reinforce and disguise privileged-class interests,"[28] denizens of the United States may become more class conscious as we face tougher economic conditions, which some believe the greed of the wealthy and powerful has exacerbated. In the future people may demand more accurate assessments of the problems we face, particularly if more middle- and working-class families see their lifestyles continue to deteriorate in the twenty-first century.

IS CHANGE LIKELY?
MEDIA REALITIES SUPPORT THE STATUS QUO

Will journalists and entertainment writers become more cognizant of class-related issues in news reports and television shows? Will they more accurately portray those issues in the future? It is possible that the media will become more aware of class as an important subject to address, but several trends do not bode well for more accurate portrayals of class. Among these are the issues of media ownership and control.

Media Ownership

Media ownership has become increasingly concentrated since the 1990s. Massive mergers and acquisitions involving the three major television networks (ABC, CBS, and NBC) have created three media behemoths—General Electric, Walt Disney Company, and CBS—whose news and entertainment divisions now constitute only small elements of much larger, highly diversified corporate structures. Today, these media giants control many outlets of expression, and entertainment and news divisions of major networks are viewed as "just another contributor to the bottom line."[29] As media scholar Shirley Biagi states, "The central force driving the media business in America is the desire to make money. American media are businesses, vast businesses. The products of these businesses are information and entertainment. . . . But American media are, above all, profit-centered."[30]

The top online news companies are Yahoo!, General Electric, Time Warner, Gannet, and AOL. However, these new-media sites are closely related to old-media sources, such as newspaper chains (Gannett, MediaNews Group, McClatchy, Advance Publications, and Tribune Company) and television companies, because new media have limited ability to produce content on their own and often disseminate information from old-media sources such as the Associated Press and United Press International. Concentration of media ownership through chains, broadcast networks, cross-media ownership, conglomerates, and vertical integration (when one company controls several related aspects of the same business) impose major impediments to change in how class is represented in the news and entertainment industry. Social analysts like Gregory Mantsios are pessimistic about the prospects for reform because of the upper-class-based loyalties of media corporate elites:

> It is no wonder Americans cannot think straight about class. The mass media is neither objective, balanced, independent, nor neutral. Those who own and direct the mass media are themselves part of the upper class, and neither they nor the ruling class in general have to conspire to manipulate public opinion. Their interest is in preserving the status quo, and their view of society as fair and equitable comes naturally to them. But their ideology dominates our society and justifies what is in reality a perverse social order—one that perpetuates unprecedented elite privilege and power on the one hand and widespread deprivation on the other.[31]

According to Mantsios, wealthy media shareholders, corporate executives, and political leaders have a vested interest in obscuring class relations not only because these elites are primarily concerned about profits but because—being among the haves themselves—they do not see any reason to stir up class-related animosities. Why should they call attention to the real causes of poverty and inequality and risk generating friction among the classes?

Media executives do not particularly care if the general public criticizes popular-cultural content as long as audiences do not begin to question the superstructure of media ownership and the benefits these corporations derive from corporate-friendly public policies. According to sociologist Karen Sternheimer,

> Media conglomerates have a lot to gain by keeping us focused on the popular culture "problem," lest we decide to close some of the corporate tax loopholes to fund more social programs. . . . In short, the news media promote media phobia because it doesn't threaten the bottom line. Calling for social programs to reduce inequality and poverty would.[32]

Although shareholders and individuals in the top corporate ranks may set the corporate culture of the media industry, day-to-day decisions often rest in the hands of the editor in chief (or a person in a similar role) at a newspaper or a television executive at a local station. Typically, the goals of these individuals reflect the profit-driven missions of their parent companies and the continual need to attract the right audiences (often young males between eighteen and thirty-five years of age) for advertisers. Television commentator Jeff Greenfield acknowledges this reality: "The most common misconception most people have about television concerns its product. To the viewer, the product is the programming. To the television executive, the product is the audience."[33] Television and the Internet derive their profits from advertising, not from producing programs or providing information that accurately reflects social life.

Since the 1996 Telecommunications Act was passed, trends in the media industry—including concentration of ownership, a focus on increasing profits, and a move toward less federal regulation—do not offer reassurance that media representations of class (along with race, gender, age, and sexual orientation) will be of much concern to corporate shareholders or executives at the top media giants—unless, of course, this issue becomes related to the bottom line or there is public demand for change, neither of which seems likely. It does, however, appear that there is a possibility for change among some journalists and entertainment writers.

Old-Media Journalists: Constraints and Opportunities

Some analysts divide journalists into "big-time" players, that is, reporters and journalists who are rich, having earned media salaries in the millions, and "everyday" players, who are primarily known in their local or regional media markets. Elite journalists in the first category typically work for major television networks (ABC, CBS, and NBC), popular cable news channels (CNN and FOX News), or major national newspapers (*Wall Street Journal*, *New York Times*, or *USA Today*). These journalists may be influential in national media agenda setting, whereas the everyday media players, beat reporters, journalists, and middle- to upper-level managers at local newspapers or television stations can at best influence local markets.

Some individuals at both levels are deeply concerned about the state of journalism in this country, as one Pew Research Center for the People and the Press study of 547 national and local reporters, editors, and executives found.[34] One major concern among these journalists was the belief that their companies' economic behavior was eroding the quality of journalism in the United States. By way of example, some journalists believe that business pressures in the media industry are making the news "thinner and shallower."[35] Journalists are also concerned that the news media pay "too little attention . . . to complex issues."[36] However, a disturbing finding by the Pew study was that some journalists believe that news content is becoming shallower because that is what the public wants. This cynical view may become a self-fulfilling prophecy that leads journalists to produce a shallower product, based on the mistaken belief that the public cannot handle anything else.[37] Despite all this, some opportunities do exist in the local and national news for community or civic journalism—for the "belief that journalism has an obligation to public life—an obligation that goes beyond just telling the news or unloading lots of facts."[38] Civic journalism is rooted in the assumption that the profession has the ability either to empower or to help disable a community. Based on a civic-journalism perspective, a news reporter gathering information for a story has an opportunity to introduce other voices beyond those of the typical mainstream spokesperson called upon to discuss a specific issue, such as the loss of jobs in a community or the growing problem of homelessness. Just as more journalists have become aware of the importance of fair and accurate representations of people based on race, gender, age, disability, and sexual orientation, we may be able to improve media representations of class. Rather than pitting the middle class against the working class and the poor, for example, the media might frame stories in such a way as to increase people's awareness of their shared concerns in a nation where members of the upper class typically get portrayed as more important and more deserving than the average citizen.

Civic journalism encourages journalists to rethink their use of frames. Choosing a specific frame for a story is "the most powerful decision a journalist will make."[39] As journalists become more aware that the media are more than neutral storytellers, perhaps more of them will develop alternative frames that look deeply into a community of interest (which might include examining the class-based realities of neighborhoods) to see "how the community interacts with, interrelates to, and potentially solves a pressing community problem." By asking, "What is the essence of this story?" rather than

"What is the conflict value of this story?" journalists might be less intent, for example, on pitting the indigenous U.S. working class against more recent immigrants or confronting unionized workers with their nonunionized counterparts. Stories that stress conflict have winners and losers, victors and villains; they suggest that people must compete, rather than cooperate, across class lines.[40] An exploration of other types of framing devices might produce better results in showing how social mobility does or does not work in the U.S. stratification system—highlighting, for example, individuals' real chances for moving up the class ladder (the possibility of which much of the jargon about the rich and famous promises).

Advocates of civic journalism suggest that two practices might help journalists do a better job of framing in the public interest: public listening and civic mapping. Public listening refers to "the ability of journalists to listen with open minds and open ears; to understand what people are really saying."[41] Journalists engaged in public listening would be less interested in getting "superficial quotes or sound bites" and would instead move more deeply into the conversations actually taking place. They would use open-ended questions in their interviews, by which they could look more deeply into people's hopes, fears, and values, rather than asking closed-ended questions to which the only response choices are yes/no or agree/disagree—answers that, in effect, quickly (and superficially) gauge an individual's opinion on a topic. When journalists use civic mapping, they seek out underlying community concerns through discussions with people. They attempt to look beneath the surface of current public discourse on an issue. Mapping helps them learn about the ideas, attitudes, and opinions that really exist among diverse groups of people, not just "public opinion" or politicians' views of events.

By seeking out "third places"—locations where people gather and often end up talking about things that are important to them—journalists can find other voices, hear different stories, and perhaps learn more about people from diverse backgrounds and what they are actually thinking and experiencing.[42] According to sociologist Ray Oldenburg, the term *third place* describes "a great variety of public places that host the regular, voluntary, informal, and happily anticipated gatherings of individuals beyond the realms of home and work."[43] If the first place is the home, and the second place is the work setting, then the third place includes churches, community centers, cafes, coffee shops, bookstores, bars, and other spots where people gather informally. As journalists join in the conversation, they can learn what everyday people are thinking about a social issue such as tax cuts for the wealthy. They can also discover what concerns people have and what they think contributes to such problems as neighborhood deterioration.

In addition to listening to other voices and seeking out different stories in third places, journalists might look more systematically at how changes in public policies—such as in tax laws, welfare initiatives, or publicly funded child care or housing programs—might affect people in various class locations. What are the political and business pressures behind key policy decisions like these? How do policies affect the middle class? The working class? Others? For example, what part does class play in perceptions about local law enforcement agencies? How are police officers viewed in small, affluent incorporated cities that have their own police departments, as compared to the low-income neighborhoods of bigger cities? While wealthy residents in the smaller cities may view police officers as employees who do their bidding (such as prohibiting the "wrong kind of people" from entering their city limits at night), in some low-income sectors of larger cities, the police may be viewed as oppressors or as racists who contribute to, rather than reduce, problems of lawlessness and crime in the community. Journalists who practice civic journalism might look beyond typical framing devices to tell a more compelling story about how the intersections of race and class produce a unique chemistry between citizens and law enforcement officials. In this way, journalists would not be using the taken-for-granted framing devices previously employed to "explain" what is happening in these communities.

Given constraints on the media, including the fact that much of the new investment in journalism is spent on disseminating rather than collecting news,[44] there is room for only cautious optimism that some journalists will break out of the standard reflexive mode to explore the microscopic realities of class at the level where people live, as well as at the macroscopic level of society, where corporate and governmental elites make important decisions that affect everyone else.

Some media analysts believe that greater awareness of class-related realities in the media would strengthen the democratic process in the United States. According to Mantsios, "A mass media that did not have its own class interests in preserving the status quo would acknowledge that inordinate wealth and power undermine democracy and that a 'free market' economy can ravage a people and their communities."[45] It remains to be seen, however, whether organizations like the Project for Excellence in Journalism and the Committee of Concerned Journalists will be successful in their efforts to encourage journalists to move beyond the standard reflexive mode to use new frames that more accurately reflect class-based realities.

Like journalists, many television entertainment writers could look for better ways to frame stories. However, these writers are also beleaguered by changes in the media environment, including new threats to their economic security from reality and talent competition shows and from new social media sources that often do not use either in-house or freelance writers. As a result, it has become increasingly difficult for writers to stay gainfully employed, let alone bring new ideas into television entertainment.[46]

New Media: Constraints and Opportunities

The Project for Excellence in Journalism and the Pew Internet and American Life Project have conducted extensive studies about the nature of audience behavior in regard to new media, which comprise Internet communications and cell phones. According to these studies, "The Internet and cell phones are changing people's relationship to news,"[47] and so they may also change how we view class-related issues. One change brought about by new media is that social media sites and blogs have helped the news become a social experience rather than a passive one for many consumers: "People use their social networks to filter, assess, and react to news."[48] Another change is that laptops and cell phones provide mobile connectivity, which turns news gathering and news awareness into an "anytime, anywhere affair for a segment of avid news watchers."[49] It also means that people across lines of class, race, and gender can find the kind of news and entertainment that they want, while largely excluding all other information from their life. For example, 21 percent of online news users report that they routinely rely on just one website for their news and information.[50]

Although people get their news from a wider variety of platforms, including broadcast, online, and print media, they may selectively choose their sources. Some may prefer their news from CNN cable television and CNN .com as compared with FOX and FOX.com. A cell phone "app" may quickly retrieve news and entertainment from one network but not the other. Or they may prefer blogs or Tweets bringing specific kinds of information to them because it suits their interests and lifestyle, but they may be completely unaware of other sources of news and entertainment. It is no surprise that online news users are younger than the general adult population: about two-thirds are under age fifty, and 71 percent are white (non-Hispanic).[51] One of the major changes that the unbundling of news—dividing it across a number of different platforms—will bring about for journalists and media consumers alike is fragmentation: consumers are not looking to one news or entertainment source for their full news agenda or for their amusement. They are "grazing" across multiple outlets, and this will have a profound effect on how all news and entertainment are framed and packaged for sampling by potential consumers. Cable television is the only portion of the old-media sector that has growing audiences, and today more than 1 million blogs and social media sites beckon to potential consumers for their time, attention, and money. According to the Project for Excellence in Journalism, "self-interested information providers" are now growing rapidly, and many nonjournalistic players are entering the information and news field. Any further cutbacks in old media, such as the hiring of fewer investigative reporters, will affect what people learn in both old and new media because traditional media have been the source of most Internet and new social media information. It is estimated that only 14 percent of new-media sites actually produce original reportorial content rather than providing commentary on existing media reports.[52]

It remains to be seen what effect these rapid changes in the media, as well as the downturn in the U.S. economy, will have on how the media frame class. In the future, however, we are likely to have even more of "all media, all the time," and it will be up to us to measure the extent to which we are willing to accept ideas about class and inequality set forth in old and new media. The popularity of cell phones and social media indicates that the melding of information and entertainment will only increase, as it seems people cannot get enough media spectacle and are willing to participate in what analysts refer to as a "mediated" life.

We cannot assume that most journalists and television writers are in a position to change media portrayals of class and inequality; however, in the final analysis, the responsibility rests with us to evaluate the media and to treat it as only one limited source of information and entertainment in our lives. For the sake of our children and grandchildren, we must balance the perspectives we gain from the media with our own lived experiences and use a wider sociological lens to look at what is going on around us in everyday life. Some analysts believe that the media amuse and lull audiences into complacency rather than stimulating them or encouraging them to think, but we must not become complacent, believing that everything is all right as our society and world become increasingly divided between the haves and the have-nots.[53] If the media industry persists in retaining the same old frames for class, it will behoove each of us as readers and viewers to break out of those frames and more thoroughly explore these issues on our own.

Notes

CHAPTER 1: CLASS ACTION IN THE MEDIA

1. Kevin Fagan, "Shame of the City: Homeless Island," *San Francisco Chronicle*, November 30, 2003, http://www.sfgate.com (accessed April 11, 2004).

2. Fagan, "Shame of the City."

3. See Diana Kendall, *The Power of Good Deeds: Privileged Women and the Social Reproduction of the Upper Class* (Lanham, MD: Rowman & Littlefield, 2002).

4. David Croteau and William Hoynes, *Media/Society: Industries, Images, and Audiences*, 3rd ed. (Thousand Oaks, CA: Pine Forge, 2003).

5. Herbert Gans, *Deciding What's News* (New York: Pantheon Books, 1979), 61.

6. Croteau and Hoynes, *Media/Society.*

7. Robert Perrucci and Earl Wysong, *The New Class Society*, 2nd ed. (Lanham, MD: Rowman & Littlefield, 2003).

8. Steven Reinberg, "U.S. Kids Using Media Almost 8 Hours a Day," *Bloomberg Businessweek,* January 20, 2010, http://www.businessweek.com/lifestyle/content/healthday/635134.html (accessed June 22, 2010).

9. Amy Porterfield, "Social Media Differences among Teens, Boomers, and Moms: Study Findings," Social Media Examiner, March 5, 2010, http://www.socialmediaexaminer.com/social-media-differences-among-teens-boomers-and-moms-new-study-findings (accessed June 21, 2010).

10. See, for example, Robert M. Entman and Andrew Rojecki, *The Black Image in the White Mind: Media and Race in America* (Chicago: University of Chicago Press, 2000); Todd Gitlin, *The Whole World Is Watching* (Berkeley: University of California Press, 1980); Todd Gitlin, *Media Unlimited: How the Torrent of Images and Sounds Overwhelms Our Lives* (New York: Henry Holt, 2003); Shanto Iyengar, *Is Anyone Responsible? How Television Frames Political Issues* (Chicago: University of Chicago Press, 1991); Pippa Norris, Montague Kern, and Marion Just, *Framing Terrorism: The News Media, the Government, and the Public* (New York: Routledge, 2003); Stephen D. Reese, Oscar H. Gandy Jr., and August E. Grant, eds., *Framing Public*

Life: Perspectives on Media and Our Understanding of the Social World (Mahwah, NJ: Lawrence Erlbaum, 2003).

11. William A. Gamson et al., "Media Images and the Social Construction of Reality," *Annual Review of Sociology* 18 (1992): 373–93.

12. Robert K. Manoff, "Writing the News, by Telling the 'Story,'" in *Reading the News*, ed. Robert K. Manoff and Michael Schudson, 197–229 (New York: Pantheon, 1987).

13. Gaye Tuchman, *Making News: A Study in the Construction of Reality* (New York: Free Press, 1978), 193.

14. Max Horkheimer and Theodor W. Adorno, *Dialectic of Enlightenment*, trans. John Cummings (New York: Continuum International, 2002 [1944]).

15. Jean Baudrillard, *Simulations* (New York: Semiotext[e], 1983).

16. Gitlin, *The Whole World Is Watching*, 1.

17. Peter L. Berger and Thomas Luckmann, *The Social Construction of Reality: A Treatise in the Sociology of Knowledge* (New York: Anchor/Doubleday, 1967), 189.

18. Berger and Luckmann, *The Social Construction of Reality*, 131.

19. Berger and Luckmann, *The Social Construction of Reality*, 151.

20. Rebecca Ann Lind and Colleen Salo, "The Framing of Feminists and Feminism in News and Public Affairs Programs in U.S. Electronic Media," *Journal of Communication* 52 (2002): 211–28.

21. Entman and Rojecki, *The Black Image in the White Mind*.

22. See Robert D. Benford and David A. Snow, "Framing Processes and Social Movements: An Overview and Assessment," *Annual Review of Sociology* 26 (2000): 611–39; Paul D'Angelo, "News Framing As a Multiparadigmatic Research Program: A Response to Entman," *Journal of Communication* 52 (2002): 870–88; Robert M. Entman, "Framing: Toward Clarification of a Fractured Paradigm," *Journal of Communication* 43 (1993): 51–58; Dietram A. Scheufele, "Framing As a Theory of Media Effects," *Journal of Communications* 49 (1999): 103–22.

23. Erving Goffman, *Frame Analysis: An Essay on the Organization of Experience* (Boston: Northeastern University Press, 1974), 10–11.

24. Benford and Snow, "Framing Processes and Social Movements"; Goffman, *Frame Analysis*, 21.

25. Gitlin, *The Whole World Is Watching*, 6–7.

26. Gitlin, *The Whole World Is Watching*; Benford and Snow, "Framing Processes and Social Movements"; David A. Snow et al., "Frame Alignment Processes, Micromobilization, and Movement Participation," *American Sociological Review* 51 (1986): 464–81.

27. Pippa Norris, *Women, Media, and Politics* (New York: Oxford University Press, 1997).

28. Norris, Kern, and Just, *Framing Terrorism*.

29. Benford and Snow, "Framing Processes and Social Movements," 623.

30. Benford and Snow, "Framing Processes and Social Movements," 623.

31. Pippa Norris and Susan J. Carroll, "The Dynamics of the News Framing Process: From Reagan's Gender Gap to Clinton's Soccer Moms," John F. Kennedy School of Government, 1997, ksghome.harvard.edu/~.pnorris.shorenstein.ksg/acrobat/carroll.pdf (accessed August 27, 2003).

32. William A. Gamson, "News As Framing: Comments on Graber," *American Behavioral Scientist* 33 (1989): 157.

33. Entman, "Framing."

34. Entman, "Framing."

35. Gitlin, *The Whole World Is Watching*, 6.

36. Tuchman, *Making News*.

37. Steven Best and Douglas Kellner, *Postmodern Theory: Critical Interrogations* (New York: Guilford, 1991).

38. Jasmin Aline Persch, "'House' Effect: TV Doc Has Real Impact on Care," MSNBC.com, September 9, 2009, http://www.msnbc.msn.com/id/32745079/ns/health-health_care (accessed June 25, 2010).

39. Gina Bellafante, "In Hospitals the Reality Is Real," *New York Times*, June 24, 2010, C1.

40. See Gitlin, *The Whole World Is Watching*; Norris, Kern, and Just, *Framing Terrorism*; Reese, Gandy, and Grant, *Framing Public Life*.

41. William K. Bunis, Angela Yancik, and David Snow, "The Cultural Patterning of Sympathy toward the Homeless and Other Victims of Misfortune," *Social Problems* 43, no. 4 (November 1996): 387–402.

42. Linda Holtzman, *Media Messages: What Film, Television, and Popular Music Teach Us about Race, Class, Gender, and Sexual Orientation* (London: M. E. Sharpe, 2000).

43. Holtzman, *Media Messages*, 32.

44. Douglas Kellner, *Media Spectacle* (New York: Routledge, 2003).

45. Kellner, *Media Spectacle*, 7–8.

46. Jack Lule, *Daily News, Eternal Stories: The Mythological Role of Journalism* (New York: Guilford, 2001), 6.

47. Robert A. Rothman, *Inequality and Stratification: Race, Class, and Gender*, 5th ed. (Upper Saddle River, NJ: Prentice Hall, 2005).

48. Joseph A. Kahl, *The American Class Structure* (New York: Rinehart, 1957); Dennis Gilbert and Joseph A. Kahl, *The American Class Structure: A New Synthesis* (Homewood, IL: Dorsey, 1982); Dennis Gilbert, *The American Class Structure in an Age of Growing Inequality*, 8th ed. (Thousand Oaks, CA: Pine Forge, 2011).

49. Max Weber, *From Max Weber: Essays in Sociology*, ed. H. H. Gerth and C. Wright Mills (New York: Oxford University Press, 1946).

50. Gilbert, *The American Class Structure in an Age of Growing Inequality*.

51. Gilbert, *The American Class Structure in an Age of Growing Inequality*, 245.

52. W. Lloyd Warner and Paul S. Lunt, *The Social Life of a Modern Community* (New Haven, CT: Yale University Press, 1941); Richard P. Coleman and Lee Rainwater, *Social Standing in America: New Dimensions of Class* (New York: Basic, 1978); Kendall, *The Power of Good Deeds*.

53. Andrew Pollack, "Prominent Drug Chief to Sell Abraxis BioScience to Celgene for $2.9 Billion," *New York Times*, June 30, 2010, http://www.nytimes.com/2010/07/01/health/01drug.html (accessed June 30, 2010).

54. Gilbert, *The American Class Structure in an Age of Growing Inequality*.

CHAPTER 2: TWENTY-FOUR-KARAT GOLD FRAMES

1. Robin Pogrebin, "Trustees Find Cultural Board Seats Are Still Highly Coveted Luxury Items," *New York Times*, April 3, 2010, C1, C5.

2. F. Scott Fitzgerald, "The Rich Boy," in *The Short Stories of F. Scott Fitzgerald*, ed. Mathew J. Brucoli, 317–49 (New York: Scribner, 1995 [1926 in *Redbook* magazine]), 318.

3. Robert M. Entman and Andrew Rojecki, *The Black Image in the White Mind: Media and Race in America* (Chicago: University of Chicago Press, 2000).

4. Entman and Rojecki, *The Black Image in the White Mind*, 48–49.

5. Entman and Rojecki, *The Black Image in the White Mind*.

6. Dixon Wecter, *The Saga of American Society: A Record of Social Aspiration, 1607–1937* (New York: Scribner, 1937), 348.

7. Mary Cable, *Top Drawer: American High Society from the Gilded Age to the Roaring Twenties* (New York: Atheneum, 1984).

8. Wecter, *The Saga of American Society*, 349.

9. Wecter, *The Saga of American Society*, 350.

10. Wecter, *The Saga of American Society*.

11. Quoted in Wecter, *The Saga of American Society*, 357.

12. Wecter, *The Saga of American Society*, 358.

13. Wecter, *The Saga of American Society*, 358.

14. Wecter, *The Saga of American Society*, 360.

15. Cable, *Top Drawer*.

16. Wecter, *The Saga of American Society*.

17. Quoted in Wecter, *The Saga of American Society*, 370.

18. Wecter, *The Saga of American Society*, 368.

19. Wecter, *The Saga of American Society*.

20. Cable, *Top Drawer*, 198.

21. Cable, *Top Drawer*; Wecter, *The Saga of American Society*.

22. Lucy Kavaler, *The Private World of High Society* (New York: David McKay, 1960), 77.

23. Kavaler, *The Private World of High Society*, 89.

24. Kavaler, *The Private World of High Society*, 92–93.

25. G. William Domhoff, "The Women's Page As a Window on the Ruling Class," in *Hearth and Home: Images of Women in the Mass Media*, ed. Gaye Tuchman, Arlene Kaplan Daniels, and James Benet, 161–75 (New York: Oxford University Press, 1978).

26. Domhoff, "The Women's Page As a Window on the Ruling Class," 175.

27. Alex Witchel, "Tacos, Stir-Fries and Cake: The Junior League at 102," *New York Times*, October 15, 2003, D1.

28. Witchel, "Tacos, Stir-Fries and Cake," D6.

29. S. Elizabeth Bird and Robert W. Dardenne, "Myth, Chronicle and Story: Exploring the Narrative Qualities of News," in *Social Meaning of News: A Text Reader*, ed. Daniel A. Berkowitz, 333–50 (Thousand Oaks, CA: Sage, 1997).

30. See also Linda Holtzman, *Media Messages: What Film, Television, and Popular Music Teach Us about Race, Class, Gender, and Sexual Orientation* (London: M. E. Sharpe, 2000); Gregory Mantsios, "Media Magic: Making Class Invisible," in *Privilege: A Reader*, ed. Michael S. Kimmel and Abby L. Ferber, 99–109 (Boulder, CO: Westview, 2003).

31. Dennis Gilbert, *The American Class Structure in an Age of Growing Inequality*, 8th ed. (Thousand Oaks, CA: Pine Forge, 2011).

32. Gilbert, *The American Class Structure in an Age of Growing Inequality.*

33. Gilbert, *The American Class Structure in an Age of Growing Inequality.*

34. Gilbert, *The American Class Structure in an Age of Growing Inequality*, 90.

35. Joseph A. Giannone, "Recession, Bear Markets Hit the Rich, Too," Reuters .com, June 25, 2010, http://finance.yahoo.com/news/Recession-bear-markets-hit -rb-4023953240.html.

36. Jan Pakulski and Malcolm Waters, *The Death of Class* (Thousand Oaks, CA: Sage, 1996); Jan Pakulski and Malcolm Waters, "The Reshaping and Dissolution of Social Class in Advanced Society," *Theory and Society* 25 (1996): 667–91.

37. Pakulski and Waters, "The Reshaping and Dissolution of Social Class in Advanced Society," 683.

38. Paul W. Kingston, *The Classless Society* (Stanford, CA: Stanford University Press, 2000).

39. David Croteau and William Hoynes, *Media/Society: Industries, Images, and Audiences*, 3rd ed. (Thousand Oaks, CA: Pine Forge, 2003); Mantsios, "Media Magic."

40. Lawrence Mishell, Jared Bernstein, and John Schmitt, *The State of Working America, 1998–99* (Ithaca, NY: Cornell University Press, 1999), as cited in Croteau and Hoynes, *Media/Society*, 222.

41. Croteau and Hoynes, *Media/Society*, 222.

42. Mantsios, "Media Magic," 103.

43. Mantsios, "Media Magic," 103–4.

44. Allen Salkin, "Homes, Sweet Homes: Michael Bloomberg's Real-Estate Holdings Are Fairly Modest—for a Multibillionaire," *New York Magazine*, April 15, 2002, 23.

45. Jennifer Steinhauer, "Bloomberg's Salon, Where the Powerful Mix over Meatloaf," *New York Times*, May 8, 2002, A1.

46. Steinhauer, "Bloomberg's Salon," A1.

47. Steinhauer, "Bloomberg's Salon," A1.

48. Steinhauer, "Bloomberg's Salon," A29.

49. David Carr, "Condé Nast Redesigns Its Future: Newhouse Plans a Transition but Tightens His Grip," *New York Times*, October 26, 2003, BU1.

50. See Diana Kendall, *The Power of Good Deeds: Privileged Women and the Social Reproduction of the Upper Class* (Lanham, MD: Rowman & Littlefield, 2002).

51. Pierre Bourdieu, *Distinction: A Social Critique of the Judgement of Taste*, trans. Richard Nice (Cambridge, MA: Harvard University Press, 1984), 272.

52. Alan Feuer, "After the Polo Match, in the Tented Pavilion," *New York Times*, June 18, 2009, A28.

53. See Geoffrey Cowley, "They've Given Away $24 Billion. Here's Why. Bill's Biggest Bet Yet," *Newsweek*, February 4, 2002, 44–52.

54. See Karen W. Arenson, "Gates to Create 70 Schools for Disadvantaged," *New York Times*, March 19, 2002, A16.

55. Cowley, "They've Given Away $24 Billion."

56. Domhoff, "The Women's Page As a Window on the Ruling Class."

57. Skip Hollingsworth, "Hi, Society!" *Texas Monthly* (September 2002): 198, 200.

58. Cameron Silver, "Texas Hold 'Em," Style.com, 2007, http://www.style.com/peopleparties/parties/thumb/022207LACR/new (accessed June 25, 2010).

59. See Kendall, *The Power of Good Deeds*.

60. Shonda Novak, Lori Hawkins, and Amy Schatz, "Overheard in Austin," *Austin American-Statesman*, February 22, 2002, D1.

61. Christopher Mason, "Where Everybody Has a Name," *New York Times*, October 26, 2003, ST1.

62. Mason, "Where Everybody Has a Name," ST1.

63. Micheline Maynard, "If a Name Is Tarnished, but Carved in Stone," *New York Times*, December 9, 2001, BU4.

64. Maynard, "If a Name Is Tarnished, but Carved in Stone," BU4.

65. "A. Alfred Taubman Biography," University of California, Irvine, Paul Merage School of Business, http://www.merage.uci.edu/classic/TaubmanBio/ (accessed June 27, 2010).

66. "Philanthropy: Enriching Our Communities through Giving," *Austin American-Statesman*, January 1, 2002, A11.

67. Michael Barnes, "An Inside Look at the New Long Center," *Austin American-Statesman*, February 13, 2001, A1, A9.

68. Stephen Scheibal, "Long Center Asks City for $25 Million," *Austin American-Statesman*, February 1, 2003, A1, A10.

69. "Changing a City: Philanthropist Believes in Building Bridges," Dallas News.com, December 10, 2003, http://www.dallasnews.com/opinion/editorials/stories/121003dnedimcder mott98208.html (accessed December 12, 2003).

70. Jennifer L. Hochschild, *Facing Up to the American Dream: Race, Class, and the Soul of the Nation* (Princeton, NJ: Princeton University Press, 1995).

71. Sheldon Danziger and Peter Gottschalk, *America Unequal* (Cambridge, MA: Harvard University Press, 1995).

72. Hochschild, *Facing Up to the American Dream*, 26–30.

73. "School Cooks Win over $95 Million in Powerball," *Dallas Morning News*, October 28, 2003, 5A.

74. "School Cooks Win over $95 Million in Powerball," 5A.

75. Patricia Sellers, "The Business of Being Oprah," *Fortune*, April 1, 2002, http://www.mutualofamerica.com/articles/Fortune/2002_04_08/Oprah1.asp (accessed March 30, 2002).

76. Sellers, "The Business of Being Oprah."

77. LaTonya Taylor, "The Church of O," *Christianity Today*, April 1, 2002, 38–45.

78. Matthew Miller, "The Wealthiest Black Americans," Forbes.com, May 6, 2009, http://www.forbes.com/2009/05/06/richest-black-americans-busienss-billion aires-richest-black-americans.html (accessed June 27, 2010).

79. Arthur Delaney, "No Recession Special on the D.C. Power Lunch Menu," The Huffington Post, November 30, 2009, http://www.huffingtonpost.com/2009/11/30/no-recession-special-on-t_n_373681.html (accessed June 27, 2010).

80. Jared Paventi, "Expensive New York Restaurants," GolfLink, http://www.golflink.com/list_28775_expensive-new-york-restaurants.html (accessed June 27, 2010).

81. David Carr, "The Powering Up of the Power Lunch," *New York Times*, December 10, 2003, D4.

82. Thorstein Veblen, *The Theory of the Leisure Class*, intro. Robert Lekachman (New York: Penguin, 1994 [1899]).

83. Jan Parr and Ted Shen, "The Richest Chicagoans: Who's Up, Who's Down?" *Chicago* (February 2002): 49.

84. "Most Expensive Gated Communities in America," Forbes.com, 2006, http://www.forbes.com/maserati/cx_bs_1114home.html (accessed June 10, 2010).

85. Andrea Truppin, "How Much Is That View in the Window?" *New York Times*, September 18, 2003, D4.

86. Shonda Novak, "Austin Mansion Sale's a Stunner," *Austin American-Statesman*, September 25, 2003, A1.

87. "Move to the Head of Your Class" (advertisement), *Texas Monthly* (October 2003): 137.

88. "The Christmas Book," Neiman Marcus, 2009, http://www.neimanmarcus.com/store/sitelets/christmasbook/christmasbook.jhtml (accessed June 14, 2010).

89. Robert Janjigian, "A Learjet? You Shouldn't Have!" *Austin American-Statesman*, November 4, 2002, E1.

90. "The Superplexus," Hammacher Schlemmer, http://www.hammacher.com/Product/78372 (accessed June 30, 2010).

91. "80th Anniversary Special Winnie the Pooh," Bornrich.org, http://www.bornrich.org/entry/80th-anniversary-special-winnie-the-pooh (accessed June 30, 2010); "The Luxury Car Lot for Kids," RideToys.com, http://mobileation.stores.yahoo.net/luxurycarlot.html (accessed November 8, 2010).

92. Annelena Lobb, "Gifts for Kids Who Have It All," CNN/Money, 2002, http://money.cnn.com/2002/11/26/pf/saving/holiday_haveitall.index.htm (accessed December 5, 2002).

93. "Robin Leach," Barber and Associates, http://www.barberusa.com/pathfind/leach_robin.html (accessed November 20, 2003).

94. "*Wall Street 2* the Movie," Market Folly, June 2, 2009, http://www.marketfolly.com/2009/06/wall-street-2-movie-february-2010-with.html (accessed June 21, 2010).

95. "Lifestyles of the Rich and Famous Video Slots," IGT, http://www.igtonline.com/megajackpots/new_games/lifestyles.html (accessed November 30, 2003).

96. Quoted in Marc Peyser and B. J. Sigesmund, "Heir Heads," *Newsweek*, October 20, 2003, 54.

CHAPTER 3: GILDED CAGES

1. Paul Sullivan, "All This Anger against the Rich May Be Unhealthy," *New York Times*, October 17, 2009, B6.

2. Paul Sullivan, "Too Rich to Worry? Not in This Downturn," *New York Times*, October 3, 2010, http://www.nytimes.com/2009/10/03/your-money/03wealth.html (accessed October 15, 2010).

3. Eric Dash, "Mortgage Executive Accused in Multibillion-Dollar Fraud," *New York Times*, June 17, 2010, B1, B4.

4. Dash, "Mortgage Executive Accused in Multibillion-Dollar Fraud," B4.

5. Tamara Lush, "Disgraced Financier Stanford's Possessions Auctioned Off," *Waco Tribune-Herald*, June 16, 2009, 3B.

6. Michael Parenti, *Inventing Reality: The Politics of the Mass Media* (New York: St. Martin's, 1986), 109.

7. Parenti, *Inventing Reality*, 109; see also Gregory Mantsios, "Media Magic: Making Class Invisible," in *Privilege: A Reader*, ed. Michael S. Kimmel and Abby L. Ferber, 99–109 (Boulder, CO: Westview, 2003).

8. Aesop, "The Fox and the Grapes," Page by Page Books, http://www.page bypagebooks.com/Aesop/Aesops_Fables/The_Fox_and_the_Grapes_p1.html (accessed December 4, 2003).

9. C. David Heymann, *Poor Little Rich Girl: The Life and Legend of Barbara Hutton* (New York: Random House, 1984).

10. Pony Duke and Jason Thomas, *Too Rich: The Family Secrets of Doris Duke* (New York: HarperCollins, 1996).

11. Customer review of *Poor Little Rich Girl: The Life and Legend of Barbara Hutton*, by C. David Heymann, Amazon.com, 2003, http://www.amazon.com/exec/obidos/search-handle-form/ref=s_sf_b_as/002-5171433-1616062 (accessed December 7, 2003).

12. John Eligon, "Housekeeper Tells How Astor's Son Took Paintings," *New York Times*, June 9, 2009, A20.

13. James Barron, "Brooke Astor's Son Is Sentenced to Prison," *New York Times*, December 22, 2009, A1.

14. See Diana Kendall, *The Power of Good Deeds: Privileged Women and the Social Reproduction of the Upper Class* (Lanham, MD: Rowman & Littlefield, 2002).

15. Quoted in Stephen J. Dubner, "Suddenly Popular," *New York Times Magazine*, June 8, 2003, 68.

16. Dubner, "Suddenly Popular," 68.

17. Dubner, "Suddenly Popular," 68.

18. See Michael Noer and Dan Ackman, "The *Forbes* Fictional Fifteen," *Forbes*, September 13, 2002, http://www.forbes.com/2002/09/13/400fictional_10.html (accessed December 7, 2003).

19. See "About Southfork," Southfork Ranch, 2010, http://www.foreverlodging.com/destination.cfm?PropertyKey=93 (accessed July 4, 2010).

20. Nancy Franklin, "Sunny Money: Fox Heads down the Coast from 90210," *New Yorker*, August 18, 25, 2003, 144.

21. Franklin, "Sunny Money," 144.

22. Matthew Gilbert, "Snarky Rich Kids Make for Fun 'Gossip,'" *Boston Globe*, September 19, 2007, http://www.boston.com/ae/tv/articles/2007/09/19/snarky_rich_kids_make_for_fun_gossip (accessed July 4, 2010).

23. Mantsios, "Media Magic," 105.

24. "McDonald's Features Donald Trump in New Ad Campaign Launching Dollar-Priced Big N' Tasty and McChicken Sandwich," McDonalds.com, October 3, 2002, http://www.mcdonalds.com/countries/usa/whatsnew/pressrelease/2002/10032002_a (accessed December 16, 2003).

25. Frank Urquhart, "Donald Trump Jets In and Fires Off 'Slum and Pigsty' Slur," Scotsman.com, May 27, 2010, http://www.scotsman.com/donaldtrump/Donald-Trump-jets-in-and.6322621.jp (accessed July 5, 2010).

26. Urquhart, "Donald Trump Jets In and Fires Off 'Slum and Pigsty' Slur."

27. Katie Evans, "Most Overexposed Billionaires," Forbes.com, January 21, 2010, http://www.forbes.com/2010/01/21/most-overexposed-billionaires-branson-buffett-business-billionaires-trump.html (accessed July 5, 2010).

28. Quoted in Geoffrey Nunberg, "Keeping Ahead of the Joneses," *New York Times*, November 24, 2002, WK4.

29. Parker, Waichman, Alonso, LLP, "Jack Grubman Takes the Fall for Many," December 24, 2002, http://www.yourlawyer.com/articles/read/3963 (accessed October 17, 2010).

30. Clara Hemphill, "Admissions Anxiety," *New York Times*, November 17, 2002, WK11.

31. Peter W. Cookson Jr. and Caroline Hodges Persell, *Preparing for Power: America's Elite Boarding Schools* (New York: Basic Books, 1985), 22.

32. Janet Guyon, "Jack Grubman Is Back. Just Ask Him," *Fortune*, May 16, 2005, http://www.money.cnn.com/magazines/fortune/fortune_archive/2005/05/16/8260134/index.htm (accessed July 3, 2010).

33. "How Much Will Woods Pay Wife to Keep Quiet?" TODAYshow.com, July 3, 2010, http://today.msnbc.msn.com/id/26184891/vp/38104275#38104275 (accessed July 5, 2010).

34. Michael J. Silverstein and Neil Fiske (with John Butman), *Trading Up: The New American Luxury* (New York: Portfolio, 2003), 166.

35. Silverstein and Fiske, *Trading Up*, 3.

36. Alison Arnett, "Counter Culture," *Austin American-Statesman*, December 18, 2003, E1, E10.

37. Silverstein and Fiske, *Trading Up*, 41.

38. Marc Peyser, "Martha's Mess: An Insider Trading Scandal Tarnishes the Queen of Perfection," *Newsweek*, July 1, 2002, 38–43.

39. Sharyn Wizda Vane, "Martha's Dirty Laundry," *Austin American-Statesman*, April 20, 2002, D1.

40. "Tarnish, Anyone?" *People*, July 8, 2002, 44.

41. Alessandra Stanley and Constance L. Hays, "Martha Stewart's To-Do List May Include Image Polishing," *New York Times*, June 23, 2002, A1.

42. Alex Kuczynski and Andrew Ross Sorkin, "Canapés and Investment Tips Are Served to Well-Heeled," *New York Times*, July 1, 2002, A1, A17.

43. Keren Blankfeld, "Billionaire Convicts and Inmates," *Forbes*, May 28, 2010, http://www.forbes.com/2010/05/28/billionaire-convict-inmate-fugitive-sanford-jail .html?feed=rss_business_billionaires (accessed July 7, 2010).

44. Ralph Blumenthal and Carol Vogel, "Ex-Chief of Sotheby's Gets 3-Year Probation and Fine," *New York Times*, April 30, 2002, A27.

45. Alex Kuczynski, "When Home Is a Castle and the Big House, Too," *New York Times*, August 18, 2002, ST1, ST7.

46. Gerry Shanahan, "You Say House Arrest, I Say Paradise," *New York Times*, May 2, 2002, F1.

47. Kuczynski, "When Home Is a Castle and the Big House, Too."

48. "Weddings/Celebrations: Carter Brooks, Talbott Simonds," *New York Times*, April 9, 2006, http://query.nytimes.com/gst/fullpage.html?res=9F06E6DA1130F93 AA35757C0A9609C8B63&scp=1&sq=weddings%20AND%20elinor%20carter%20 brooks?&st=cse (accessed July 6, 2010).

49. Rick Lyman, "For the Ryder Trial, a Hollywood Script," *New York Times*, November 3, 2002, ST8.

50. Mark Wrolstad, "An Unfashionable Turn for Stylish HP Socialite," *Dallas Morning News*, October 25, 2003, 1A, 10A–11A.

51. Alan Peppard, "Charity Co-chair Steps Down over Shoplifting Charge," DallasNews.com, http://www.dallasnews.com (accessed September 29, 2003).

52. "Shop Till You Get Caught," *D Magazine* (November 2003): 20.

53. Wrolstad, "An Unfashionable Turn for Stylish HP Socialite," 1A.

54. See Peppard, "Charity Co-chair Steps Down over Shoplifting Charge"; Joe Simnacher, "Brooke Stollenwerck Aldridge: Socialite, Civic Volunteer," *Dallas Morning News*, March 22, 2007, http://www.dallasnews.com/sharedcontent/dws/ news/city/parkcities/stories/032307dnmetaldridgeob.326e212.html (accessed August 19, 2010).

55. Wrolstad, "An Unfashionable Turn for Stylish HP Socialite," 10A.

56. See Paul Martin Lester, ed., *Images That Injure: Pictorial Stereotypes in the Media* (Westport, CT: Praeger, 1996).

57. Alex Kuczynski, "Lifestyles of the Rich and Red-Faced," *New York Times*, September 22, 2002, ST1.

58. Kuczynski, "Lifestyles of the Rich and Red-Faced," ST1.

59. Kuczynski, "Lifestyles of the Rich and Red-Faced," ST8.

60. Lynnley Browning, "Suicide Victim May Have Harbored a Secret," *New York Times*, September 16, 2009, B1, B2.

61. William D. Cohan, "The Shot Heard 'Round the Clubs," *Vanity Fair*, January 2010, http://www.vanityfair.com/culture/features/2010/02/caspersen-suicide-201002 (accessed July 2, 2010).

62. Alice Gomstyn, "Goldman Sachs' Fabrice 'Fabulous Fab' Tourre: Wall Street's Fall Guy?" abcNEWS.com, April 21, 2010, http://abcnews.go.com/Business/ goldman-sachs-fabrice-fabulous-fab-tourre-wall-streets/story?id=10429139 (accessed April 21, 2010).

63. Michael Duffy, "What Did They Know and When Did They Know It?" *Time*, January 28, 2002, 17.

64. Duffy, "What Did They Know and When Did They Know It?" 50.

65. Evan Thomas and Andrew Murr, "The Gambler Who Blew It All," *Newsweek*, February 4, 2002, 19.

66. Anne Belli Gesalman, "Cliff Was Climbing the Walls," *Newsweek*, February 4, 2002, 24; Margot Habiby and Jim Kennett, "Ex-Enron Executive Killed Self, Police Say," *Austin American-Statesman*, January 26, 2002, A1, A4; Cathy Booth Thomas, "Enron Takes a Life," *Time*, February 4, 2002, 20–21.

67. Neela Banerjee, David Barboza, and Audrey Warren, "At Enron, Lavish Excess Often Came before Success," *New York Times*, February 26, 2001, C1.

68. "Put It on My Tab," *Austin American-Statesman*, September 22, 2002, H1.

69. Colleen DeBaise, "Newest 'Tyco Gone Wild' Video Is Out, and Jurors See $6,000 Shower Curtain," *Wall Street Journal*, November 26, 2003, C1, C7.

70. "*Law & Order*," NBC.com, 2003, http://www.nbc.com/Law_&_Order/about/index.html (accessed December 22, 2003).

71. "*Law & Order*."

72. Elissa Gootman, "Publicist Gets Jail Sentence and Scolding," *New York Times*, October 24, 2002, A28.

73. Lawrence B. Ebert, "'Law & Order' Plotline Follows Larry Mendte Story and Madoff Scam," IPBIZ, March 25, 2009, http://www.ipbiz.blogspot.com/2009/03/law-order-plotline-follows-larry-mendte.html (accessed October 17, 2010).

74. Steve Fishman, "Bernie Madoff, Free At Last," *New York Magazine*, June 14–21, 2010, 35.

75. Alex Kuczynski, "For the Elite, Easing the Way to Prison," *New York Times*, December 9, 2001, ST1, ST2.

76. Fishman, "Bernie Madoff, Free At Last," 35.

77. Warren St. John, "Advice from Ex-Cons to a Jet-Set Jailbird: Best Walk on Eggs," *New York Times*, July 13, 2003, ST1.

78. Juan A. Lozano, "Judge Vacates Conviction of Kenneth Lay," *Washington Post*, October 18, 2006, http://www.washingtonpost.com/wp-dyn/content/article/2006/10/18/AR2006101800201_pf.html (accessed October 15, 2010).

79. "Rich People on TV Aren't Really Rich," *Wall Street Journal*, June 28, 2010, http://blogs.wsj.com/wealth/2010/06/28/rich-people-on-tv-arent-really-rich (accessed July 8, 2010).

CHAPTER 4: FRAGILE FRAMES

1. "Walks among the Poor," *New York Times*, January 30, 1870, 6.

2. Robert M. Entman and Andrew Rojecki, *The Black Image in the White Mind: Media and Race in America* (Chicago: University of Chicago Press, 2000).

3. Entman and Rojecki, *The Black Image in the White Mind*, 94.

4. Jeff Kunerth, "One Number Can't Measure Poverty," *Austin American-Statesman*, October 5, 2003, E4.

5. Kunerth, "One Number Can't Measure Poverty."

6. Shanto Iyengar, "Framing Responsibility for Political Issues: The Case of Poverty," *Political Behavior* 12 (March 1990): 19–40; Shanto Iyengar, *Is Anyone Responsible? How Television Frames Political Issues* (Chicago: University of Chicago Press, 1991).

7. Iyengar, "Framing Responsibility for Political Issues."

8. Gregory Mantsios, "Media Magic: Making Class Invisible," in *Privilege: A Reader*, ed. Michael S. Kimmel and Abby L. Ferber, 99–109 (Boulder, CO: Westview, 2003), 101.

9. Mantsios, "Media Magic," 101.

10. Iyengar, *Is Anyone Responsible?* 22.

11. Mantsios, "Media Magic."

12. Mantsios, "Media Magic."

13. Entman and Rojecki, *The Black Image in the White Mind*, 97.

14. Mantsios, "Media Magic."

15. Mantsios, "Media Magic."

16. Mantsios, "Media Magic," 102.

17. "Walks among the Poor," 6.

18. "Distressing Case of Poverty and Suicide," *New York Times*, January 1, 1855, 4.

19. "Distressing Case of Poverty and Suicide," 4.

20. "Melancholy Case of Suicide: Pride and Poverty the Cause," *New York Times*, March 20, 1873, 1.

21. "A Sad Case of Poverty: A Woman Commits Suicide, Her Husband at the Point of Death," *New York Times*, July 13, 1874, 5.

22. "A Sad Life Story: Reduced from Wealth to Poverty and Dying Almost without Friends," *New York Times*, August 6, 1883, 5.

23. Emile Durkheim, *Suicide* (New York: Free Press, 1951 [1897]), 276.

24. See, for example, "Poverty Leading to Suicide"; "Cause of Mr. Hilsen's Suicide: His Capital Exhausted and Poverty Staring Him in the Face," *New York Times*, January 25, 1883, 8; "Driven to Suicide by Poverty," *New York Times*, February 25, 1884, 8; "Unable to Endure Poverty," *New York Times*, June 2, 1884, 2; "A Violinist in Despair: Domenico Mariani on the Verge of Suicide, Seized As He Was about to Jump from a Hoboken Dock—Poverty in His Old Age Unbearable," *New York Times*, August 30, 1885, 12.

25. "Down among the Lowly: The Sights That One Sees in the Fourth Ward," *New York Times*, May 7, 1871, 8.

26. "Down among the Lowly," 8.

27. "Terrible Tragedy: An Insane Mother Kills Her Daughter," *New York Times*, July 6, 1872, 2.

28. "Terrible Tragedy," 2.

29. "A Father's Awful Crime: Shooting His Three Little Girls. Why John Remmler, of Holyoke, Killed His Children—Poverty and a Fear for Their Future His Reasons," *New York Times*, June 22, 1879, 7.

30. Headlines such as "Alabama: Mobile a Prostrate City, Alarming Decline in the Value of Real Estate, Two Hundred and Fifty Stores without Occupants. Poverty

and Depression Some of the Causes" (*New York Times*, October 21, 1874, 1) and "Destitution in New Orleans: The Existing Poverty and Its Causes—Lotteries and Beer Shops" (*New York Times*, May 7, 1875, 10) emblazoned stories about poverty in the South. Written by "Occasional Correspondent," who reported on the "decay and dilapidation which everywhere prevails," these articles were framed in such a manner as to suggest that depressed economic conditions were not the only causes of poverty in the South but were exacerbated by the presence of lotteries, beer shops, and other attractions that usurped money from the poor. In the 1870s, the media popularized the category of "poor whites," as evidenced by headlines such as "Poor Whites in the South: Their Poverty and Principles" (*New York Times*, May 13, 1877, 5). The head-note of the article shows the contempt "Occasional Correspondent" held for people in this category: "The most degraded, ignorant, and hopeless class in the South—the poorest of the poor whites—how they live in the mountains—loose notions of moral-ity and utter ignorance their chief characteristics." Although the article is framed in a seemingly sympathetic manner, explaining that poor whites were to be pitied because they had been barred from commerce and other success by the "monopoly of money and power in the planter," the journalist also emphasized that their plight might not have been so dire if they had developed a sense of discipline and subscribed to the work ethic.

31. "Poverty and Charity," *New York Times*, November 8, 1870, 2.

32. "Feeding the City's Poor: Giving Bountiful Dinners to Children and Poverty-Stricken People," *New York Times*, November 28, 1884, 3.

33. "Walks among the New York Poor: Homeless Children," *New York Times*, May 4, 1854, 6.

34. "Homeless Children," *New York Times*, December 22, 1856, 4.

35. "Lodging-House for Homeless Girls a New Project of the Children's Aid So-ciety," *New York Times*, May 25, 1862, 3.

36. "A Lodging-House for the Homeless in the Thirteenth Ward," *New York Times*, February 21, 1868, 5.

37. Oscar H. Gandy Jr. et al., "Race and Risk: Factors Affecting the Framing of Stories about Inequality, Discrimination, and Just Plain Bad Luck," *Public Opinion Quarterly* 61 (spring 1997): 158–82.

38. Iyengar, "Framing Responsibility for Political Issues"; Iyengar, *Is Anyone Responsible?*

39. Erik Eckholm, "Last Year's Poverty Rate Was Highest in 12 Years," *New York Times*, September 11, 2009, A1.

40. Tony Pugh, "Nation's Economic Collapse Triggers Rise in Homeless Fami-lies," McClatchy, June 18, 2010, http://www.mcclatchydc.com/2010/06/17/96074/report-nations-economic-collapse.html (accessed July 10, 2010).

41. Eckholm, "Last Year's Poverty Rate Was Highest in 12 Years," A1.

42. See Wally Dean and Lee Ann Brady, "Local TV News Project—2002: After 9/11, Has Anything Changed?" Journalism.org, 2004, http://www.journalism.org/re sources/research/reports/localTV/2002/postsept11.asp (accessed February 29, 2004).

43. Lynette Clemetson, "Census Shows Ranks of Poor Rose by 1.3 Million," *New York Times*, September 3, 2003, A1.

44. Jason DeParle, "In Rising Debate on Poverty, the Question: Who Is Poor?" *New York Times*, September 3, 1990, A1.

45. Kimberly J. McLarin, "Poverty Rate Is the Highest in 16 Years, a Report Says," *New York Times*, July 14, 1995, B3.

46. Robert Pear, "A Proposed Definition of Poverty May Raise Number of U.S. Poor," *New York Times*, April 30, 1995, A1.

47. Kunerth, "One Number Can't Measure Poverty," E4.

48. Jared Bernstein, "Who's Poor? Don't Ask the Census Bureau," *New York Times*, September 26, 2003, A25.

49. Kunerth, "One Number Can't Measure Poverty," E4.

50. Robert J. Samuelson, "Defining Poverty Up: How to Create More 'Poor,'" *Newsweek*, May 30, 2010, http://www.newsweekinteractive.net/2010/05/30/defining -poverty-up.html (accessed July 10, 2010).

51. "Hungry Families in U.S. on the Rise," MSNBC.com, 2003, http://www.ms nbc.msn.com/id/3341630 (accessed February 10, 2004).

52. Tom Zeller, "Of Fuzzy Math and 'Food Security,'" *New York Times*, January 11, 2004, WK16.

53. U.S. Conference of Mayors, "Hunger and Homelessness at Record Levels in U.S. Cities," City Mayors, December 8, 2009, http://www.citymayors.com/features/ uscity_poverty.html (accessed July 11, 2010).

54. Zeller, "Of Fuzzy Math and 'Food Security.'"

55. "How Many People Experience Homelessness?" Fact Sheet 2, National Coalition for the Homeless, 2002, http://www.nationalhomeless.org/numbers.html (accessed February 14, 2004).

56. "How Many People Experience Homelessness?"

57. Joel Stein, "The Real Face of Homelessness," CNN.com, January 13, 2003, http://www.cnn/2003/ALLPOLITICS/01/13/timep.homelessness.tm/index.html (accessed February 11, 2004).

58. Stephanie Armour, "Homelessness Grows As More Live Check-to-Check," *USA Today*, August 12, 2003, A1.

59. Gary Blasi, "And We Are Not Seen: Ideological and Political Barriers to Understanding Homelessness," *American Behavioral Scientist* 37, no. 4 (February 1994): 563–87.

60. Blasi, "And We Are Not Seen."

61. Stein, "The Real Face of Homelessness."

62. Mantsios, "Media Magic."

63. Barbara Ehrenreich, "Too Poor to Make the News," *New York Times*, June 14, 2009, WK10.

64. Dean and Brady, "Local TV News Project—2002."

65. Jeff Cohen and Norman Solomon, "On Local TV News, if It Bleeds It (Still) Leads," FAIR, Media Beat, December 13, 1995, http://www.fair.org/media -beat/951213.html (accessed February 29, 2004).

66. Iyengar, "Framing Responsibility for Political Issues"; Iyengar, *Is Anyone Responsible?*

67. Iyengar, *Is Anyone Responsible?*

68. Bob Herbert, "Locked Out at a Young Age," *New York Times*, October 20, 2003, A19.

69. Herbert, "Locked Out at a Young Age," A19.

70. Bernstein, "Who's Poor?" A25.

71. Bernstein, "Who's Poor?" A25.

72. Quoted in Bernstein, "Who's Poor?" A25.

73. E. J. Dionne Jr., "Handing Out Hardship," *Washington Post*, September 16, 2003, A19.

74. N. R. Kleinfield, "Golden Years, on $678 a Month," *New York Times*, September 3, 2003, B1.

75. Kleinfield, "Golden Years, on $678 a Month," B1.

76. Lydia Polgreen, "An Aging Population, a Looming Crisis," *New York Times*, November 4, 2003, A25.

77. Polgreen, "An Aging Population, a Looming Crisis," A25.

78. Helen Epstein, "Enough to Make You Sick?" *New York Times Magazine*, October 12, 2003, 75.

79. Epstein, "Enough to Make You Sick?" 77.

80. Epstein, "Enough to Make You Sick?" 76.

81. Epstein, "Enough to Make You Sick?" 76.

82. Matea Gold, "Diane Sawyer Examines Poverty in Appalachia," *Los Angeles Times*, February 11, 2009, http://articles.latimes.com/2009/feb/11/entertainment/et -diane-sawyer11 (accessed October 15, 2010).

83. Joya Misra, Stephanie Moller, and Marina Karides, "Envisioning Dependency: Changing Media Depictions of Welfare in the 20th Century," *Social Problems* 50 (2003): 482–504.

84. "A Return to Welfare Dependency," *Washington Times*, February 23, 2009, http://www.washingtontimes.com/news/2009/feb/23/a-return-to-welfare-dependency (accessed July 15, 2010).

85. Maura Kelly, "Regulating the Reproduction and Mothering of Poor Women: The Controlling Image of the Welfare Mother in Television News Coverage of Welfare Reform," *Journal of Poverty* 14, no. 1 (January 2010): 76.

86. Kelly, "Regulating the Reproduction and Mothering of Poor Women," 76.

87. Kristine Hughes, "Foundation Offers Help to Working Poor: Organizers Say Many Need Mentoring to Quit Welfare Dependency," *Dallas Morning News*, July 3, 2003, 18.

88. "Receipt of Unemployment Insurance among Low-Income Single Mothers," ASPE Issue Brief, Office of the Assistant Secretary for Planning and Evaluation, January 2005, http://aspe.hhs.gov/hsp/05/unemp-receipt/ib.pdf (accessed July 15, 2010).

89. Leslie Kaufman, "Millions Have Left Welfare, but Are They Better Off? Yes, No and Maybe," *New York Times*, October 20, 2003, A16.

90. Kaufman, "Millions Have Left Welfare, but Are They Better Off?" A16.

91. Leslie Kaufman, "Welfare Wars: Are the Poor Suffering from Hunger Anymore?" *New York Times*, February 23, 2003, WK4.

92. Kaufman, "Welfare Wars," WK4.

93. Kaufman, "Welfare Wars," WK4.

94. Eungjun Min, ed., *Reading the Homeless: The Media's Image of Homeless Culture* (Westport, CT: Praeger, 1999), ix.

95. Min, *Reading the Homeless*, ix.

96. Min, *Reading the Homeless*, x.

97. Eric Olsen, "Down and Out in Santa Monica," Blogcritics, January 6, 2003, http://www.blogcritics.org/archives/2003/01/06/200033.php (accessed February 22, 2004).

98. "Homeless Woman Arrested for Threatening Postal Worker," KFMB.com, January 16, 2003, http://www.kfmb.com (accessed February 2, 2004).

99. Kim Horner, "Losing Their Cart Blanche," *Dallas Morning News*, January 14, 2004, 1B.

100. Horner, "Losing Their Cart Blanche," 1B.

101. Horner, "Losing Their Cart Blanche," 1B.

102. William Hermann, "Treating the Homeless Where They Live," CNN.com, August 9, 2000, http://www.cnn.com/2000/LOCAL/pacific/08/09/azc.homeless.med ical/index.html (accessed February 8, 2004).

103. Hermann, "Treating the Homeless Where They Live."

104. Michele Marchand, "On the Air and Outside: Homelessness on TV," Anitra .net, http://www.anitra.net/books/activist/mm_on_the_air.html (accessed February 28, 2004).

105. Quoted in Marchand, "On the Air and Outside."

106. "The Hunger Artist," Television without Pity, http://www.televisionwithout pity.com/story.cgi?show=15&story=3487&page=2 (accessed February 28, 2004).

107. Alan Feuer, "Bronx Girl Follows Vision: A Future Far from Home," *New York Times*, October 4, 2003, A1.

108. Feuer, "Bronx Girl Follows Vision," A1.

109. Feuer, "Bronx Girl Follows Vision," A14.

110. Leslie Kaufman, "Amid Manhattan's Wealthiest, a Beggar Found Open Hearts," *New York Times*, February 14, 2004, A1.

111. Kaufman, "Amid Manhattan's Wealthiest, a Beggar Found Open Hearts," A14.

112. Pat Kossan, "Man Overcomes Homelessness, Will Graduate from ASU," Arizona Republic, May 2, 2003, http://www.azcentral.com (accessed February 28, 2004).

113. Kossan, "Man Overcomes Homelessness, Will Graduate from ASU."

114. David A. Snow and Leon Anderson, *Down on Their Luck: A Case Study of Homeless Street People* (Berkeley: University of California Press, 1993); William K. Bunis, Angela Yancik, and David Snow, "The Cultural Patterning of Sympathy toward the Homeless and Other Victims of Misfortune," *Social Problems* (November 1996): 387–402.

115. Arthur Bovino, "Offering a Hand, and Hope, in a Year of Record Homelessness in New York," *New York Times*, November 2, 2003, A25.

116. Bovino, "Offering a Hand, and Hope, in a Year of Record Homelessness in New York," A25.

117. Martin Gilens, *Why Americans Hate Welfare: Race, Media, and the Politics of Antipoverty Policy* (Chicago: University of Chicago Press, 1999).

118. Ricardo Gándara, "Thanks, Austin!" *Austin American-Statesman*, February 1, 2004, K1, K12.

119. Mantsios, "Media Magic," 102.

120. "If Only the Spirit of Giving Could Continue," *Los Angeles Times*, December 25, 1988, 16.

121. "Here Comes Santa Claus," Television without Pity, http://www.televisionwith outpity.com/story.cgi?show=&&story=5940&page=5 (accessed February 28, 2004).

122. Joshua Partlow, "At River's Edge, Left with an 'Empty Feeling,'" *Washington Post*, September 25, 2003, SM3.

123. James Dao, "Hardships and Damage Linger after Hurricane," *New York Times*, October 2, 2003, A18.

124. David Stout, "A Great Equalizer: Isabel Was Her Name," *New York Times*, September 26, 2003, A17.

125. Pam Harbaugh, "Dreamers Battle for Home in Harmony," *Florida Today*, January 4, 2004, http://www.floridatoday.com/!NEWSROOM/peoplestory P0105DREAM.htm (accessed February 2, 2004).

126. Insung Whang and Eungjun Min, "Blaming the Homeless: The Populist Aspect of Network TV News," in *Reading the Homeless: The Media's Image of Homeless Culture*, ed. Eungjun Min, 121–33 (Westport, CT: Praeger, 1999), 131.

127. Miranda Spencer, "Making the Invisible Visible," *Extra!* (January–February 2003), http://www.fair.org/extra/0301/poverty.html (accessed February 29, 2004).

128. Jonathan Kaufman, "Covering Race, Poverty and Class in the New Gilded Age," *Nieman Reports* 55, no. 1 (spring 2001): 25.

CHAPTER 5: TARNISHED METAL FRAMES

1. "Toronto Stinks on Day 4 of Trash Strike," UPI.com, June 25, 2009, http://www.upi.com/Top_News/2009/06/25/Toronto-stinks-on-Day-4-of-trash-strike/UPI -21471245928472 (accessed July 18, 2010).

2. Claire, July 24, 2009 (12:07 a.m.), comment on Toban Black, "Toronto's 'Garbage Strike' Elicits Public Outrage and Labour Disunity," Waging Nonviolence, July 23, 2009, wagingnonviolence.org/2009/07/torontos-garbage-strike-public-outrage -and-labor-chaos (accessed November 15, 2010).

3. David K. Shipler, "A Poor Cousin of the Middle Class," *New York Times Magazine*, January 18, 2004, 22.

4. Shipler, "A Poor Cousin of the Middle Class," 22.

5. See Barbara Ehrenreich, *Nickel and Dimed: On (Not) Getting By in America* (New York: Metropolitan, 2001); John E. Schwarz and Thomas J. Volgy, *The Forgotten Americans* (New York: Norton, 1992); Shipler, "A Poor Cousin of the Middle Class"; David K. Shipler, *The Working Poor: Invisible in America* (New York: Knopf, 2004); Beth Shulman, *The Betrayal of Work: How Low-Wage Jobs Fail 30 Million Americans and Their Families* (New York: New Press, 2003); Gary Rivlin, *Broke, USA: From Pawnshops to Poverty, Inc.—How the Working Poor Became Big Business* (New York: Harper Business, 2010).

6. Michael Zweig, *The Working Class Majority: America's Best Kept Secret* (Ithaca, NY: Cornell University Press, 2001), 57.

7. "The Wal-Martization of America," *New York Times*, November 15, 2003, A26.

8. Zweig, *The Working Class Majority.*

9. Dennis Gilbert, *The American Class Structure in an Age of Growing Inequality*, 8th ed. (Thousand Oaks, CA: Pine Forge, 2011).

10. Gilbert, *The American Class Structure in an Age of Growing Inequality*, 244.

11. "The Wal-Martization of America."

12. Gilbert, *The American Class Structure in an Age of Growing Inequality.*

13. Shulman, *The Betrayal of Work.*

14. Zweig, *The Working Class Majority.*

15. Gregory Mantsios, "Media Magic: Making Class Invisible," in *Privilege: A Reader*, ed. Michael S. Kimmel and Abby L. Ferber, 99–109 (Boulder, CO: Westview, 2003), 106.

16. "Meeting of Front Bricklayers: A Union of Capital and Labor Advocated," *New York Times*, August 30, 1860, 8.

17. "Labor Unions," *New York Times*, August 26, 1868, 4.

18. "Labor Unions," 4.

19. "Labor Unions," 4.

20. "Meeting of Front Bricklayers," 4.

21. "Help for the Working Poor," *New York Times*, April 22, 1869, 4.

22. "Help for the Working Poor," 4.

23. William J. Puette, *Through Jaundiced Eyes: How the Media View Organized Labor* (Ithaca, NY: ILR, 1992).

24. "The Working Men's Views: President Jarrett before the Senate Committee," *New York Times*, September 8, 1883, 8.

25. "Managing Labor Interests: Harmonizing Rival Unions and Concluding to Do without Prayers," *New York Times*, June 11, 1883, 8.

26. "Not Able to Earn a Living: The Letter of a Sewing Woman to the Central Labor Union," *New York Times*, February 16, 1885, 5.

27. "The Working Men's Views."

28. "Working Men on Parade: An Orderly Labor Demonstration—Ten Thousand Men in Line," *New York Times*, September 6, 1882, 8.

29. "Big Labor Day Parade: Thirty Building Trade Unions to Be Represented. Forty Bands to Play in the Procession—Preparations to Handle Holiday Crowds," *New York Times*, August 31, 1902, 24.

30. Puette, *Through Jaundiced Eyes.*

31. "Blames Union Labor for Work Shortage," *New York Times*, October 2, 1921, 1.

32. "Blames Union Labor for Work Shortage," 1.

33. Puette, *Through Jaundiced Eyes*, 154.

34. "Reds Plotted Country Wide Strike. Arrests Exceeded 5,000, 2,635 Held; 3 Transports Ready for Them," *New York Times*, January 4, 1920, 1.

35. "Senate Vote Voided Veto of Labor Bill," *New York Times*, June 24, 1947, 1.

36. Pete Hamill, "In Defense of Honest Labor," *New York Times*, December 31, 1995, SM18.

37. Maureen Williams, "From Incendiary to Invisible: A Print-News Content Analysis of the Labor Movement," *Labor Center Review* 10 (1988): 23–27, quoted in Puette, *Through Jaundiced Eyes*, 153.

38. Puette, *Through Jaundiced Eyes*, 153.

39. Puette, *Through Jaundiced Eyes*, 58.

40. Puette, *Through Jaundiced Eyes*, 154–55.

41. David Croteau and William Hoynes, *Media/Society: Industries, Images, and Audiences*, 3rd ed. (Thousand Oaks, CA: Pine Forge, 2003), 222.

42. Danny Hakim, "Auto Deal or Bust: Was Anyone Taken for a Ride in the U.A.W.–Big 3 Contract Talks?" *New York Times*, September 23, 2003, C2.

43. Hakim, "Auto Deal or Bust," C2.

44. Nick Bunkley, "A Once-Defiant U.A.W. Local Now Focuses on G.M.'s Success," *New York Times*, January 6, 2010, B1.

45. Jerry White, "Wall Street Throws General Motors into Bankruptcy," *World Socialist*, May 29, 2009, http://www.wsws.org/articles/2009/may2009/pers-m29.shtml (accessed July 20, 2010).

46. Christopher L. Erickson and Daniel J. B. Mitchell, "Information on Strikes and Union Settlements: Patterns of Coverage in a 'Newspaper of Record,'" *Industrial and Labor Relations Review* 49, no. 3 (April 1996): 395.

47. Diane E. Schmidt, "Public Opinion and Media Coverage of Labor Unions," *Journal of Labor Research* 15 (spring 1993): 151–64, cited in Erickson and Mitchell, "Information on Strikes and Union Settlements," 406.

48. Jo Napolitano, "As Garbage, and Smell, Rise in Chicago, Striking Trash Haulers Reject a Raise Offer," *New York Times*, October 6, 2003, A9.

49. Jo Napolitano, "Chicago Strike Leaves Garbage Piling Up," *New York Times*, October 3, 2003, A18.

50. Steven Greenhouse, "Labor Raises Pressure on California Supermarkets," *New York Times*, February 10, 2004, A12.

51. Bob Keefe, "Grocery Strike Wearing on Customers, Workers," *Austin American-Statesman*, February 6, 2004, C1.

52. Nick Bunkley, "Tentative Agreement May End Strike That Disrupted Production at 32 G.M. Plants," *New York Times*, May 18, 2008, B1.

53. Bunkley, "Tentative Agreement May End Strike That Disrupted Production at 32 G.M. Plants," B1.

54. "Organized Crime Section: Labor Racketeering," Federal Bureau of Investigation, http://www.fbi.gov/hq/cid/orgcrime/lcn/laborrack.htm (accessed March 22, 2004).

55. "Organized Crime and the Labor Unions," AmericanMafia.com, 2004, http://www.americanmafia.com/Crime_and_Labor.html (accessed March 22, 2004); "Organized Crime Section."

56. Steven Greenhouse, "Scandals Affirm New York As Union Corruption Capital," *New York Times*, February 15, 1999, B1.

57. Greenhouse, "Scandals Affirm New York As Union Corruption Capital," B1.

58. "Organized Crime Section."

59. Steven Greenhouse, "Endless Task: Keeping Unions Clean," *New York Times*, February 10, 2008, A10.

60. Quoted in Greenhouse, "Scandals Affirm New York As Union Corruption Capital," B1.

61. See James T. Bennett and Jason E. Taylor, "Unions Work Selves Out of Job," *USA Today*, August 28, 2003, A13.

62. Allen Rucker, *The Sopranos: A Family History* (New York: New American Library, 2001).

63. Alessandra Stanley, "TV Weekend—Bullies, Bears and Bullets: It's Round 5," *New York Times*, March 5, 2004, E1.

64. Stanley, "TV Weekend."

65. Richard Byrne, "Bodymore, Murdaland," *American Prospect*, October 22, 2006, http://www.prospect.org/cs/articles?article=bodymore_murdaland (accessed October 17, 2010).

66. Phil Primack, "We All Work, Don't We?" *Columbia Journalism Review* (September–October 1992): 56.

67. Quoted in Primack, "We All Work, Don't We?" 56.

68. Tom Robbins, "Working-Class Heroes: Towering Losses, Towering Deeds," *Village Voice* (September 26–October 2, 2001), http://www.villagevoice.com/issues/0139/robbins.php (accessed March 4, 2004).

69. Quoted in Robbins, "Working-Class Heroes."

70. Robbins, "Working-Class Heroes."

71. Pierre Thomas, "Katrina Cover-Up: Cops May Face Death Penalty," abc NEWS.com, July 14, 2010, http://abcnews.go.com/GMA/orleans-police-face-death-penalty-hurricane-katrina-bridge/story?id=11160077 (accessed October 17, 2010).

72. John Murgatroyd, "Behind the Scenes: The Amazing Folks Cleaning Up the Gulf," CNN.com, July 23, 2010, http://www.cnn.com/2010/US/07/23/rescue.murgatroyd/index.html?section=cnn_latest (accessed October 15, 2010).

73. Murgatroyd, "Behind the Scenes."

74. Andrea Nill, "Immigrants Cleaning Up the BP Oil Spill Is Nothing New," The Wonk Room, June 11, 2010, http://wonkroom.thinkprogress.org/2010/06/11/bp-immigration-louisiana (accessed October 15, 2010).

75. James Poniewozik, "Reality TV's Working Class Heroes," Time.com, May 22, 2008, http://www.time.com/time/printout/0,8816,1808612,00.html (accessed October 15, 2010).

76. Poniewozik, "Reality TV's Working Class Heroes."

77. Matt Zoller Seitz, "'Deadliest Catch': Reality TV's First On-Screen Death," Salon.com, July 13, 2010, http://www.salon.com/entertainment/tv/2010/07/13/deadliest_catch_finale (accessed October 15, 2010).

78. David Firestone, "4 Dead and 9 Missing in a Pair of Alabama Mine Blasts," *New York Times*, September 25, 2001, A14.

79. Jack Feuer, "Miner Chord: Is a Working-Class Hero Still Something to Be?" *ADWEEK Southwest*, August 5, 2002, 9.

80. Matt Wray and Annalee Newitz, eds., *White Trash: Race and Class in America* (New York: Routledge, 1997), 4.

81. Quoted in Susan Eastman, "White Trash: America's Dirty Little Secret," *Ace Magazine*, 1998, http://www.aceweekly.com/acemag/backissues/980916/cb2 _980916.html (accessed March 14, 2004).

82. Melinda Henneberger, "Testing of a President: The Accuser; the World of Paula Jones: A Lonely Place amid Clamor," *New York Times*, March 12, 1998, A1.

83. Eastman, "White Trash."

84. Henneberger, "Testing of a President."

85. Gael Sweeney, "The King of White Trash Culture: Elvis Presley and the Aesthetics of Excess," in Wray and Newitz, *White Trash*, 249–66.

86. Laura Grindstaff, *The Money Shot: Trash, Class, and the Making of TV Talk Shows* (Chicago: University of Chicago Press, 2002), 145.

87. Grindstaff, *The Money Shot*, 145–46.

88. Paul Hooson, "Glen Beck Defends Sarah Palin's 'White Trash' Family Values," Wizbang Blue, September 3, 2008, http://www.wizbangblue.com/2008/09/03/glen -beck-defends-sarah-palins-white-trash-family-values.php (accessed July 26, 2010).

89. Michael Saul, "Levi Johnson Calls Sarah Palin 'Snobby,' Says His Family Is Not 'White Trash' on CBS' 'Early Show,'" NYDailyNews.com, April 8, 2009, http:// www.nydailynews.com/news/politics/2009/04/08/2009-04-08_levi_johnston_calls_ sarah_palin_snobby_says_his_family_is_not_white_trash_on_cbs.html (accessed July 26, 2010).

90. Erica Jong, "The Mary Poppins Syndrome," The Huffington Post, September 3, 2008, http://www.huffingtonpost.com/erica-jong/the-mary-poppins -syndrome_b_123584.html (accessed July 26, 2010).

91. Cal Thomas, "Other Media Trying to Copy Fox's Use of 'Big-Lipped Blondes' and 'Trailer Trash,'" Media Matters for America, July 10, 2006, http://www.media matters.org/mmtv/200606190009 (accessed July 26, 2010).

92. "White Trash Party Sparks Ire in Texas Neighborhood," WCCO.com. June 26, 2010, http://wcco.com/watercooler/White.Trash.party.2.1774551.html (accessed October 20, 2010).

93. Kelli Marshall, "ABC's *The Middle*: Redefining the Working-Class Male," FlowTV, June 3, 2010, http://www.flowtv.org/2010/06/abcs-the-middle-redefining -the-working-class-male (accessed July 25, 2010).

94. Richard Butsch, "Ralph, Fred, Archie and Homer: Why Television Keeps Recreating the White Male Working-Class Buffoon," in *Gender, Race and Class in Media*, ed. Gale Dines and Jean M. Humez, 403–12 (Thousand Oaks, CA: Sage, 1995), 404.

95. Richard Butsch, "A Half Century of Class and Gender in American TV Domestic Sitcoms," *Cercles* 8 (2003): 16–34, http://www.cercles.com/n8/butsch.pdf (accessed October 15, 2010).

96. "*The Life of Riley*: U.S. Situation Comedy," Museum.tv.com, 2004, http:// www.museum.tv/archives/etv/L/htmlL/lifeofriley/lifeofriley.htm (accessed March 13, 2004).

97. "*The Life of Riley*."

98. Butsch, "A Half Century of Class and Gender in American TV Domestic Sitcoms"; "The Honeymooners," TVLand.com, 2004, http://www.tvland.com/shows/ honeymooners (accessed March 20, 2004).

99. Butsch, "A Half Century of Class and Gender in American TV Domestic Sitcoms," 22.

100. Butsch, "A Half Century of Class and Gender in American TV Domestic Sitcoms."

101. "All in the Family," TVLand.com, 2004, http://www.tvland.com/shows/aitf (accessed March 21, 2004).

102. "All in the Family," TVLand.com.

103. "All in the Family," Classicsitcoms.com, 2004, http://classicsitcoms.com/ shows/family.html (accessed March 21, 2004).

104. "All in the Family," Classicsitcoms.com.

105. Quoted in "All in the Family," Classicsitcoms.com.

106. Richard Muhammad, "Archie Bunker Lives!" Blinks.net, 2001, http://www .blinks.net/magazine/channels/issues/doc_page5.html (accessed March 14, 2003).

107. Muhammad, "Archie Bunker Lives!"

108. Grindstaff, *The Money Shot.*

109. "The King of Queens: Wild Cards," TV Tome, February 20, 2004, http:// www.tvtome.com/tvtome/servlet/GuidePageServlet/showid-239/epid-1637 (accessed April 18, 2004).

110. R. J. Carter, "DVD Review: 'My Name Is Earl'—Season One," The Trades, September 22, 2006, http://www.the-trades.com/article.php?id=4806 (accessed July 25, 2010).

111. Quoted in William Yardley, "The Last Grain Falls at a Sugar Factory," *New York Times*, January 31, 2004, A13.

112. Ralph Blumenthal, "As Levi's Work Is Exported, Stress Stays Home," *New York Times*, October 19, 2003, A14.

113. Quoted in Blumenthal, "As Levi's Work Is Exported, Stress Stays Home," A14.

114. Lydia Polgreen, "As Jobs Vanish, the Sweet Talk Could Turn Tough," *New York Times*, October 12, 2003, A26.

115. Chris Isidore, "7.9 Million Jobs Lost—Many Forever," CNNMoney.com, July 2, 2010, http://www.money.cnn.com/2010/07/02/news/economy/jobs_gone_for ever/index.htm (accessed July 27, 2010).

116. Lorrie Grant, "Retail Giant Wal-Mart Faces Challenges on Many Fronts: Protests, Allegations Are Price of Success, CEO Says," *USA Today*, November 11, 2003, B1; Amy Tsao, "The Two Faces of Wal-Mart," *Businessweek*, January 28, 2004, http://www.businessweek.com/bwdaily/dnflash/jan2004/nf20040128_6990_db014 .html (accessed February 2, 2004); "Wal-Mart Settles Illegal Immigrant Case for $11 M," Fox News, March 19, 2005, http://www.foxnews.com/story/0,2933,150846,00 .html (accessed July 27, 2010).

117. Steven Greenhouse, "Middlemen in the Low-Wage Economy," *New York Times*, December 28, 2003, WK10.

118. "Wal-Mart Settles Illegal Immigrant Case for $11M."

119. "Fact Sheets," Walmart.com, March 2010, http://www.walmartstores.com/ pressroom/FactSheets (accessed July 27, 2010).

120. Julia Preston, "A Slippery Place in the U.S. Work Force," *New York Times*, March 22, 2009, A1, A18.

121. Juan Castillo, "U.S. Payday Is Something to Write Home About," *Austin American-Statesman*, December 14, 2003, J1.

122. Castillo, "U.S. Payday Is Something to Write Home About."

123. Julia Preston, "Fewer Latino Immigrants Sending Money Home," *New York Times*, May 1, 2008, A1.

124. Sue Kirchhoff and Barbara Hagenbaugh, "Immigration: A Fiscal Boon or Financial Strain? Debate Heats Up over Impact on Economy," *USA Today*, January 22, 2004, B1.

125. Kirchhoff and Hagenbaugh, "Immigration," B1.

126. Ehrenreich, *Nickel and Dimed*.

127. Shipler, *The Working Poor*.

128. Shulman, *The Betrayal of Work*.

129. Rivlin, *Broke, USA*.

130. Richard Lacayo, "Take This Job and Starve," *Time*, February 16, 2004, 76.

131. Michael Massing, "Take This Job and Be Thankful (for $6.80 an Hour)," *New York Times*, February 18, 2004, B8.

132. Lacayo, "Take This Job and Starve," 77.

133. Massing, "Take This Job and Be Thankful (for $6.80 an Hour)," B8.

134. Quoted in Massing, "Take This Job and Be Thankful (for $6.80 an Hour)," B8.

135. Barbara Ehrenreich, "Too Poor to Make the News," *New York Times*, June 14, 2009, WK10.

136. Rivlin, *Broke, USA*.

137. "A New Kind of Poverty," *Newsweek*, November 22, 2003, http://www.msnbc.msn.com/id/3540672 (accessed April 2, 2004).

138. Alina Tugend, "What Recovery? For the Unemployed, the Pain Gets Worse," *New York Times*, July 3, 2010, B5.

139. Michael Luo, "For Long-Term Unemployed, a Shaky Safety Net," *New York Times*, July 18, 2010, A13.

140. Linda Holtzman, *Media Messages: What Film, Television, and Popular Music Teach Us about Race, Class, Gender, and Sexual Orientation* (London: M. E. Sharpe, 2000), 129.

141. Bob Herbert, "We're More Productive. Who Gets the Money?" *New York Times*, April 5, 2004, A25.

142. Bob Herbert, "Long-Term Economic Pain," *New York Times*, July 27, 2010, A17.

143. Bob Herbert, "The Worst of the Pain," *New York Times*, February 9, 2010, A23.

CHAPTER 6: SPLINTERED WOODEN FRAMES

1. Ann S. Kim, "Bottom Falls Out for Middle Class," *Portland Press Herald*, March 12, 2009, http://www.pressherald.com/archive/bottom-falls-out-for-middle -class_2009-03-16.html?searchterm=bottom+falls+out+for+the+middle+class%3F (accessed October 15, 2010).

2. Harold R. Kerbo, *Social Stratification and Inequality*, 7th ed. (Boston: Mc-Graw-Hill, 2009).

3. Tom Zeller, "The Nation: Calculating One Kind of Middle Class," *New York Times*, October 29, 2000, WR5.

4. Mark Trumbull, "Obama's Challenge: Reversing a Decade of Middle-Class Decline," *Christian Science Monitor*, January 25, 2010, http://www.csmonitor.com/USA/2010/0125/Obama-s-challenge-reversing-a-decade-of-middle-class-decline (accessed July 29, 2010).

5. Dennis Gilbert, *The American Class Structure in an Age of Growing Inequality*, 8th ed. (Thousand Oaks, CA: Pine Forge, 2011), 247.

6. "Middle Class in America," U.S. Department of Commerce, Economics and Statistics Administration, January 2010, http://2001-2009.commerce.gov/s/groups/public/@doc/@os/@opa/documents/content/prod01_008833.pdf (accessed July 24, 2010).

7. "Inside the Middle Class: Bad Times Hit the Good Life," Pew Social Trends, April 9, 2008, http://pewsocialtrends.org/pubs/706/middle-class-poll (accessed July 29, 2010).

8. Barbara Ehrenreich, *Fear of Falling: The Inner Life of the Middle Class* (New York: HarperPerennial, 1990), 13.

9. Gilbert, *The American Class Structure in an Age of Growing Inequality*.

10. Gilbert, *The American Class Structure in an Age of Growing Inequality*.

11. David Brooks, *Bobos in Paradise: The New Upper Class and How They Got There* (New York: Simon and Schuster, 2000).

12. E. J. Graff, *"Bobos in Paradise: The New Upper Class and How They Got There,"* *American Prospect*, May 22, 2000, 52, quoting Brooks, *Bobos in Paradise*.

13. Brooks, *Bobos in Paradise*, 52.

14. "It Would Never Work Out . . ." (cartoon), *New Yorker*, March 25, 2002, 75.

15. Benjamin DeMott, *The Imperial Middle: Why Americans Can't Think Straight about Class* (New York: William Morrow, 1990); Gregory Mantsios, "Media Magic: Making Class Invisible," in *Privilege: A Reader*, ed. Michael S. Kimmel and Abby L. Ferber, 99–109 (Boulder, CO: Westview, 2003).

16. "Economy among the Middle Classes," *New York Times*, November 9, 1868, 4.

17. "Economy among the Middle Classes," 4.

18. *"The Consumers: Fate of the Middle Classes.* By Walter G. Cooper," *New York Times*, November 18, 1905, BR774.

19. "Letter to the Editor: Tribulations of the Middle Class," *New York Times*, November 20, 1906, 8.

20. "Middle Class Finds Homes in Suburbs: Demolition of Private Dwellings in the City Drives Residences to Other Localities," *New York Times*, September 1, 1929, RE2.

21. "Middle Class Finds Homes in Suburbs," RE2.

22. Randy Kennedy, "For Middle Class, New York Shrinks As Home Prices Soar," *New York Times*, April 1, 1998, A1.

23. Kennedy, "For Middle Class, New York Shrinks As Home Prices Soar," A1.

24. Francis Brown, "What Is the Middle Class and What Does It Want?" *New York Times*, December 22, 1935, BR6.

25. Quoted in Brown, "What Is the Middle Class and What Does It Want?" BR6.

26. Charles Goodrum and Helen Dalrymple, *Advertising in America: The First 200 Years* (New York: Harry N. Abrams, 1990), 31.

27. Quoted in Goodrum and Dalrymple, *Advertising in America*, 148.

28. Quoted in Goodrum and Dalrymple, *Advertising in America*, 148.

29. Brown, "What Is the Middle Class and What Does It Want?" BR6.

30. "Living Costs Disturb Middle Class, Barton Cautions House in Speech: Warning Crop Plan Means Higher Food and Clothing Prices, He Asserts New Yorkers Ask: 'Why Do We Always Foot the Bill?'" *New York Times*, December 4, 1937, 7.

31. "Living Costs Disturb Middle Class, Barton Cautions House in Speech," 7.

32. "Barton Sees Crisis for Middle Class," *New York Times*, June 26, 1938, 3.

33. "Says Middle Class Needs Salvation: Martin Asks National Support of Republican Drive to Avert Its 'Ruin' by New Deal," *New York Times*, August 27, 1939, 5; "Save Middle Class, Congress Is Urged," *New York Times*, October 21, 1942, 1.

34. "Save Middle Class, Congress Is Urged," 1.

35. "Wallace Sees All in a Middle Class: Picturing Future, He Asserts the 'Horatio Alger' Spirit Will Never Die Here," *New York Times*, January 25, 1943, 1.

36. Frank Bruni, "Bush Campaign Turns Attention to Middle Class," *New York Times*, September 18, 2000, A1; Frank Bruni, "Bush Says Rival's Tax-Cut Plan Fails Middle Class," *New York Times*, August 25, 2000, A22; Katharine Q. Seelye, "Gore Offers Vision of Better Times for Middle Class," *New York Times*, September 7, 2000, A1.

37. Quoted in Edward Wyatt and David M. Halbfinger, "Clark and Kerry Offering Plans to Help Middle Class," *New York Times*, January 6, 2004, A17.

38. "President Barack Obama," Whitehouse.gov, July 28, 2010, http://www.whitehouse.gov/administration/president-obama (accessed July 28, 2010).

39. Brent Baker, "FNC's Baier Corrects Washington Post's Claim Obama 'Rare' Product of Middle Class," NewsBusters, February 5, 2010, http://www.newsbusters.org/blogs/brent-baker/2010/02/05/fnc-s-baier-corrects-washington-post-s-claim-obama-rare-product-middle (accessed October 15, 2010).

40. Ehrenreich, *Fear of Falling*, 5.

41. Ehrenreich, *Fear of Falling*, 51.

42. Robin M. Williams Jr., *American Society: A Sociological Interpretation*, 3rd ed. (New York: Knopf, 1970).

43. Kim Fulcher Linkins, "Midwest Lures Family-Based IT," CNN.com, 1999, http://www.cnn.com/TECH/computing/9906/11/midwest.idg/index.html (accessed February 17, 2004).

44. George Cantor, "Middle-Class Livonia Turns into Wayne County Power," *Detroit News*, January 26, 2002, http://www.detnews.com/2002/editorial/0201/28/d07-400393.htm (accessed February 18, 2004).

45. Jill Lawrence, "Values, Points of View Separate Towns—and Nation," *USA Today*, February 18, 2002, A10.

46. Lawrence, "Values, Points of View Separate Towns."

47. Jill Lawrence, "'Family Values' Lower on Agenda in 2008 Race," *USA Today*, December 18, 2007, http://www.usatoday.com/news/politics/election2008/2007-12-17-Familyvalues_N.htm (accessed July 30, 2010).

48. David Marc, *Comic Visions: Television Comedy and American Culture*, 2nd ed. (Malden, MA: Blackwell, 1997), 42.

49. Hal Himmelstein, *Television Myth and the American Mind* (Westport, CT: Praeger, 1994), 122.

50. William Douglas, *Television Families: Is Something Wrong in Suburbia?* (Mahwah, NJ: Lawrence Erlbaum, 2003); Nina C. Leibman, *Living Room Lectures: The Fifties Families in Film and Television* (Austin: University of Texas Press, 1995).

51. David Croteau and William Hoynes, *Media/Society: Industries, Images, and Audiences*, 3rd ed. (Thousand Oaks, CA: Pine Forge, 2003), 179.

52. Douglas, *Television Families*, 86.

53. Douglas, *Television Families*, 73–74.

54. Gerard Jones, *Honey, I'm Home! Sitcoms: Selling the American Dream* (New York: Grove Weidenfeld, 1992), 70.

55. Douglas, *Television Families*, 142.

56. Douglas, *Television Families*, 142.

57. Douglas, *Television Families*, 142–43.

58. Bishetta Merritt and Carolyn A. Stroman, "Black Family Imagery and Interactions on Television," *Journal of Black Studies* 23 (1993): 492–98.

59. Douglas, *Television Families*, 147.

60. Douglas, *Television Families*, 147; see also Richard Butsch, "Class and Gender in Four Decades of Television Situation Comedy: Plus ça Change . . . ," *Critical Studies in Mass Communication* 9 (1992): 387–99.

61. See Sut Jhally and Justin Lewis, *Enlightened Racism: The Cosby Show, Audiences, and the Myth of the American Dream* (Boulder, CO: Westview, 1992); Leslie B. Inniss and Joe R. Feagin, *"The Cosby Show*: The View from the Black Middle Class," *Journal of Black Studies* 25 (1995): 692–711.

62. Jhally and Lewis, *Enlightened Racism*, 74.

63. *"My Wife and Kids,"* ABC.com, 2004, http://www.abc.go.com/primetime/mywifeandkids/show.html (accessed January 1, 2004).

64. Megan Angelo, "At TBS, Diversity Pays Its Own Way," *New York Times*, May 30, 2010, http://www.nytimes.com/2010/05/30/arts/television/30tbs.html (accessed July 31, 2010).

65. Al Carlos Hernandez, "ABC Network Has Failed Latinos," LatinoLA, May 15, 2007, http://latinola.com/story.php?story=4123 (accessed October 15, 2010).

66. Asian American Justice Center (AAJC), *Asian Pacific Americans in Prime Time: Setting the Stage*, AAJC, 2006, http://www.advancingequality.org/files/aajc_tv_06.pdf (accessed July 15, 2010).

67. *"Malcolm in the Middle,"* FOX.com, 2004, http://www.fox.com/malcolm/journal/404.htm (accessed January 2, 2004).

68. John G. Nettles, *"Malcolm in the Middle,"* Popmatters, 2003, popmatters.com/tv/reviews/m/malcolm-in-the-middle.html (accessed December 30, 2003).

69. Louis Uchitelle, "Bottom's Up: The Middle Class—Winning in Politics, Losing in Life," *New York Times*, July 19, 1998, WR1.

70. Michael Snyder, "The Middle Class in America Is Radically Shrinking: Here Are the Stats to Prove It," Yahoo! Finance, July 15, 2010, http://finance .yahoo.com/tech-ticker/the-u.s.-middle-class-is-being-wiped-out-here's-the-stats-to -prove-it-520657.html (accessed July 24, 2010).

71. Edward Luce, "The Crisis of Middle-Class America," *Financial Times*, July 30, 2010, http://www.ft.com/cms/s/2/1a8a5cb2-9ab2-11df-87e6-00144feab49a.html (accessed August 3, 2010).

72. "Inside the Middle Class: Bad Times Hit the Good Life."

73. Lee Clifford, "Getting Malled," *Fortune*, November 25, 2001, http://www .fortune.com/fortune/investing/articles/0,15114,373012,00.html (accessed September 29, 2003).

74. Bob Herbert, "Shaking the House of Cards," *New York Times*, October 3, 2003, A27; Bob Herbert, "Caught in the Credit Card Vise," *New York Times*, September 22, 2003, A19; Bob Herbert, "Caught in the Squeeze," *New York Times*, May 29, 2003, A27; Bob Herbert, "Living on Borrowed Money," *New York Times*, November 10, 2003, A23.

75. Herbert, "Caught in the Credit Card Vise," A19.

76. Herbert, "Caught in the Credit Card Vise," A19.

77. Herbert, "Caught in the Credit Card Vise," A19.

78. Herbert, "Caught in the Credit Card Vise," A19.

79. Elizabeth Warren and Amelia Warren Tyagi, *The Two-Income Trap: Why Middle Class Mothers and Fathers Are Going Broke* (New York: Basic Books, 2003).

80. Herbert, "Living on Borrowed Money," A23.

81. Herbert, "Living on Borrowed Money," A23.

82. Herbert, "Living on Borrowed Money," A23.

83. Christine Dugas, "Middle Class Barely Treads Water," *USA Today*, September 14, 2003, http://www.usatoday.com/money/perfi/general/2003-09-14-middle -cover_x.htm (accessed December 31, 2003).

84. "'Why Middle Class Mothers and Fathers Are Going Broke,'" MSNBC.com, 2003, msnbc.msn.com/Default.aspx?id=3079221&p1=0 (accessed December 29, 2003).

85. Warren and Tyagi, *The Two-Income Trap*, as quoted in "'Why Middle Class Mothers and Fathers Are Going Broke.'"

86. Warren and Tyagi, *The Two-Income Trap*, as quoted in "'Why Middle Class Mothers and Fathers Are Going Broke.'"

87. See, for example, Sharon Epperson, "How to Escape the 'Two-Income Trap,'" MSNBC, 2003, msnbc.msn.com/id/3087477 (accessed December 29, 2003).

88. Thomas M. Shapiro, Tatjana Meschede, and Laura Sullivan, "The Racial Wealth Gap Increases Fourfold," Institute on Assets and Social Policy, Research and Policy Brief, Heller School for Social Policy and Management, Brandeis University, May 2010, http://iasp.brandeis.edu/pdfs/Racial-Wealth-Gap-Brief.pdf (accessed October 15, 2010).

89. Shapiro, Meschede, and Sullivan, "The Racial Wealth Gap Increases Fourfold."

90. Quoted in Louis Uchitelle, "Blacks Lose Better Jobs Faster As Middle-Class Work Drops," *New York Times*, July 12, 2003, http://www.nytimes.com/2003/07/12/business/blacks-lose-better-jobs-faster-as-middle-class-work-drops.html (accessed November 3, 2010).

91. Stephanie Strom, "For Middle Class, Health Insurance Becomes a Luxury," *New York Times*, November 16, 2003, A25.

92. Strom, "For Middle Class, Health Insurance Becomes a Luxury," A25.

93. Quoted in Strom, "For Middle Class, Health Insurance Becomes a Luxury," A25.

94. Bob Herbert, "A Less Than Honest Policy," *New York Times*, December 28, 2009, http://www.nytimes.com/2009/12/29/opinion/29herbert.html?_r=1 (accessed July 16, 2010).

95. Jill Lawrence, "Health Reform: A Year-by-Year Rundown of What Happens and When," Politics Daily, March 23, 2010, http://www.politicsdaily/2010/03/23/health-reform-a-year-by-year-rundown-of-what-happens-and-when (accessed July 18, 2010).

96. Lawrence, "Health Reform."

97. "Health Care Reform, At Last," *New York Times*, March 22, 2010, A24.

98. Bill Moyers, "Politics and Economy: Transcript—Middle Class Squeeze," PBS.org, December 13, 2002, http://www.pbs.org/now/transcript/transcript_middleclass.html (accessed December 31, 2003).

99. Edmund L. Andrews, "Plan Gives Most Benefits to Wealthy and Families," *New York Times*, January 8, 2003, A17.

100. Quoted in Andrews, "Plan Gives Most Benefits to Wealthy and Families," A17.

101. Andrews, "Plan Gives Most Benefits to Wealthy and Families," A17.

102. "Caught in the Squeeze," *New York Times*, May 29, 2003, A27.

103. David Cay Johnston, "Tax Analysis Says the Rich Still Win," *New York Times*, July 14, 2002, BU10.

104. Ben Sargent, "Oh, Yeah? Well, Now They're Talking . . . ," *Austin American-Statesman*, March 26, 2003, A16.

105. Ben Sargent, "Don't Mind Howard . . . ," *Austin American-Statesman*, August 29, 2003, A16.

106. Stephen Ohlemacher, "With Income Tax Cuts Expiring, Rates Could Rise for Wealthy—but What about Middle Class?" *Star Tribune*, July 22, 2010, http://www.startribune.com/lifestyle/99034509.html (accessed August 7, 2010).

107. Bob Herbert, "A Sin and a Shame," *New York Times*, July 30, 2010, http://www.nytimes.com/2010/07/31/opinion/31herbert.html (accessed November 15, 2010).

108. Daniel Kadlec, "They're Getting Richer!" *Time*, August 18, 2003, 49.

109. "Your Honor, My Client . . ." (cartoon), *New Yorker*, March 25, 2002, 69.

110. Bob Herbert, "Bracing for the Blow," *New York Times*, December 26, 2003, A35.

111. Bob Herbert, "The White-Collar Blues," *New York Times*, December 29, 2003, A21.

112. Bob Herbert, "Education Is No Protection," *New York Times*, January 26, 2004, A27.

113. Herbert, "Bracing for the Blow," A35.

114. Leslie Haggin Geary, "Guess Which Jobs Are Going Abroad," CNN/Money, January 5, 2004, http://money.cnn.com/2003/12/30/pf/offshorejob (accessed January 25, 2004).

115. Heather Timmons, "Due Diligence from Afar," *New York Times*, August 5, 2010, B1, B2.

116. Nelson D. Schwartz, "Jobless and Staying That Way," *New York Times*, August 8, 2010, WK1, WK2.

117. Schwartz, "Jobless and Staying That Way."

118. Motoko Rich, "U.S. Lost 131,00 Jobs As Governments Cut Back," *New York Times*, August 6, 2010, http://www.nytimes.com/2010/08/07/business/economy/07econ.html (accessed November 15, 2010).

119. Rich, "Nation Lost 131,000 Jobs As Governments Cut Back."

120. Edward J. Blakely and Mary Gail Snyder, *Fortress America: Gated Communities in the United States* (Washington, DC: Brookings Institution Press, 1997).

121. Setha Low, *Behind the Gates: Life, Security, and the Pursuit of Happiness in Fortress America* (New York: Routledge, 2003), 12.

122. Low, *Behind the Gates*, 11.

123. Jonathan Yardley, "Book Review: *Behind the Gates*," *Washington Post*, May 8, 2003, CO2.

124. Low, *Behind the Gates*, 10–11.

125. Bradford McKee, "Fortress Home: Welcome Mat Bites," *New York Times*, January 22, 2004, F1.

126. McKee, "Fortress Home."

127. Sewell Chan, "Is Gentrification Transforming the City's Public Spaces?" *New York Times*, August 14, 2007, http://cityroom.blogs.nytimes.com/2007/08/14/is-gentrification-transforming-the-citys-public-spaces/?scp=1&sq=is%20gentrification%20transforming%20the%20city's%20public%20spaces&st=cse (accessed August 8, 2010).

128. Leslie Eaton, "From Middle Class to the Shelter Door: In a Trend, New Yorkers Face Poverty after Last Unemployment Check," *New York Times*, November 17, 2002, A37.

129. Peter S. Goodman, "U.S. Offers a Hand to Those on Eviction's Edge," *New York Times*, April 19, 2010, A1.

130. Eaton, "From Middle Class to the Shelter Door," A37.

131. Goodman, "U.S. Offers a Hand to Those on Eviction's Edge," A1.

132. Kim Horner, "Anywhere but Here: Library Tells Homeless to Move Along," *Dallas Morning News*, October 8, 2003, 1B.

133. Arin Greenwood, "D.C. Libraries: Not a Homeless Shelter, Especially in the West End," *Washington City Paper*, November 12, 2008, http://www.washingtoncitypaper.com/blogs/citydesk/2008/11/12/dc-libraries-not-a-homeless-shelter (accessed August 2, 2010).

134. Evelyn Nieves, "Libraries Dealing with Homeless Try New Approaches: San Francisco Hires A Social Worker," *San Francisco Examiner,* February 20,

2010, http://www.sfexaminer.com/nation/san-fran-library-hires-social-worker-for-homeless-84849352.html (accessed August 2, 2010).

135. Ben Clarke, "S.F. Daily Papers Pit Middle Class against Homeless," Media Alliance, 2000, http://www.media-alliance.org/mediafile/19-1/homeless.html (accessed October 12, 2003).

136. "Homeless Shelter Plan Attacked, Potrero Hill Neighbors Worry about Property Values," *San Francisco Chronicle*, August 6, 1999, http://articles.sfgate.com/1999-08-06/news/17696660_1_homeless-shelter-neighborhood-homeless-people (accessed October 15, 2010).

137. "Showdown over Shelter: A Gritty Little Neighborhood Fights S.F. Plan for Homeless," *San Francisco Examiner*, August 12, 1999.

138. John W. Fountain, "Chicago Looks for Home for Shelter for Homeless," *New York Times*, May 15, 2003, A26.

139. Elizabeth Pezzullo, "Shelter's Plan Not a Popular Move," *Free Lance-Star*, June 7, 2002, http://www.fredericksburg.com/?News/FLS/2002/062002/06072002/631644 (accessed January 25, 2004).

140. Mike Holmes, "Shelter Will Bring Only Crime," Fredericksburg.com, 2003, http://www.fredericksburg.com/?News/FLS/2003/04182003/936435.html (accessed January 25, 2004).

141. Harold A. Morse, "Please Don't Let Shelter Ruin Our Neighborhood," Fredericksburg.com, 2003, http://www.fredericksburg.com/?News/FLS/911/2003/012003/01072003/834032.html (accessed January 25, 2004).

142. Tawny Browne, "There's No Reason to Fear the Poor Residents of a Shelter," Fredericksburg.com, 2002, http://www.fredericksburg.com/?News/FLS/2002/062002/06192002/637549.html (accessed January 25, 2004).

143. Michael Middleton, "L.A. Confidential: A Well-Run Shelter Suppresses Crime," Fredericksburg.com, 2003, http://www.fredericksburg.com/?News/FLS/2003/042003/04072003/921809.html (accessed January 25, 2004).

144. Shanto Iyengar, "Framing Responsibility for Political Issues: The Case of Poverty," *Political Behavior* 12 (March 1990): 20.

145. Blakely and Snyder, *Fortress America*, 176.

146. Blakely and Snyder, *Fortress America*, 177.

CHAPTER 7: FRAMING CLASS, VICARIOUS LIVING, AND CONSPICUOUS CONSUMPTION

1. Bob Herbert, "Putting Our Brains on Hold," *New York Times*, August 6, 2010, http://www.nytimes.com/2010/08/07/opinion/07herbert.html (accessed August 10, 2010).

2. Choire Sicha, "They'll Always Have Paris," *New York Times*, June 13, 2004, AR31.

3. Diana Kendall, *Framing Class: Media Representations of Wealth and Poverty in America*, 1st ed. (Lanham, MD: Rowman & Littlefield, 2005).

4. Tim Delaney and Allene Wilcox, "Sports and the Role of the Media," in *Values, Society and Evolution*, ed. Harry Birx and Tim Delaney, 199–215 (Auburn, NY: Legend, 2002).

5. bell hooks [Gloria Watkins], *Where We Stand: Class Matters* (New York: Routledge, 2000), 73.

6. hooks, *Where We Stand*, 77.

7. hooks, *Where We Stand*, 71.

8. hooks, *Where We Stand*, 72.

9. Juliet B. Schor, *Born to Buy: The Commercialized Child and the New Consumer Culture* (New York: Scribner, 2004).

10. Schor, *Born to Buy*.

11. Joseph Nocera, *A Piece of the Action: How the Middle Class Joined the Money Class* (New York: Simon and Schuster, 1994).

12. "Inside the Middle Class: Bad Times Hit the Good Life," Pew Social Trends, April 9, 2008, http://pewsocialtrends.org/pubs/706/middle-class-poll (accessed July 29, 2010).

13. "Inside the Middle Class: Bad Times Hit the Good Life."

14. Paul Sullivan, "All This Anger against the Rich May Be Unhealthy," *New York Times*, October 17, 2009, B6.

15. Barbara Ehrenreich, "Too Poor to Make the News," *New York Times*, June 13, 2009, http://www.nytimes.com/2009/06/14/opinion/14ehrenreich.html (accessed November 8, 2010).

16. Karen De Coster and Brad Edmonds, "TV Nation: The Killing of American Brain Cells," Lewrockwell.com, March 5, 2003, http://www.lewrockwell.com/decoster/decoster78.html (accessed July 7, 2004).

17. Judith Butler has described gender identity as performative, noting that social reality is not a given but is continually created as an illusion "through language, gesture, and all manner of symbolic social sign" (see Judith Butler, "Performative Acts and Gender Constitution: An Essay in Phenomenology and Feminist Theory," in *Performing Feminisms: Feminist Critical Theory and Theatre*, ed. Sue-Ellen Case [Baltimore: Johns Hopkins University Press, 1990], 270). In this sense, class might also be seen as performative, in that people act out their perceived class location not only in terms of their own class-related identity but in regard to how they treat other people, based on their perceived class position.

18. See Thomas Ginsberg, "Union Hopes to Win Over Starbucks Shop Workers," *Austin American-Statesman*, July 2, 2004, D6.

19. Schor, *Born to Buy*, 13.

20. Schor, *Born to Buy*, 167.

21. Louis Uchitelle, "We Pledge Allegiance to the Mall," *New York Times*, December 6, 2004, C12.

22. Dennis Gilbert, *The American Class Structure in an Age of Growing Inequality*, 8th ed. (Thousand Oaks, CA: Pine Forge, 2011).

23. Gilbert, *The American Class Structure in an Age of Growing Inequality*.

24. Thomas M. Shapiro, Tatjana Meschede, and Laura Sullivan, "The Racial Wealth Gap Increases Fourfold," Institute on Assets and Social Policy, Research and

Policy Brief, Heller School for Social Policy and Management, Brandeis University, May 2010, http://iasp.brandeis.edu/pdfs/Racial-Wealth-Gap-Brief.pdf (accessed October 15, 2010).

25. Carmen DeNavas-Walt, Bernadette D. Proctor, and Jessica C. Smith, *Income, Poverty, and Health Insurance Coverage in the United States: 2008*, U.S. Census Bureau, Current Population Reports, P60-236 (Washington, DC: U.S. Government Printing Office, 2009).

26. Robert Perrucci and Earl Wysong, *The New Class Society*, 2nd ed. (Lanham, MD: Rowman & Littlefield, 2003), 199.

27. Perrucci and Wysong, *The New Class Society*.

28. Perrucci and Wysong, *The New Class Society*, 284.

29. Project for Excellence in Journalism, "The State of the News Media 2010," The State of the News Media, http://www.stateofthemedia.org/2010/overview_major_trends.php (accessed October 15, 2010).

30. Shirley Biagi, *Media Impact: An Introduction to Mass Media* (Belmont, CA: Wadsworth, 2003), 21.

31. Gregory Mantsios, "Media Magic: Making Class Invisible," in *Privilege: A Reader*, ed. Michael S. Kimmel and Abby L. Ferber, 99–109 (Boulder, CO: Westview, 2003), 108.

32. Karen Sternheimer, *It's Not the Media: The Truth about Pop Culture's Influence on Children* (Boulder, CO: Westview, 2003), 211.

33. Quoted in Biagi, *Media Impact*, 170.

34. "Finding Third Places: Other Voices, Different Stories," Pew Center for Civic Journalism, 2004, http://www.pewcenter.org/doingcj/videos/thirdplaces.html (accessed July 6, 2004).

35. Bill Kovach, Tom Rosenstiel, and Amy Mitchell, "A Crisis of Confidence: A Commentary on the Findings," Pew Research Center for the People and the Press, 2004, http://www.stateofthenewsmedia.org/prc.pdf (accessed July 6, 2004), 27.

36. Kovach, Rosenstiel, and Mitchell, "A Crisis of Confidence," 29.

37. Kovach, Rosenstiel, and Mitchell, "A Crisis of Confidence."

38. "Finding Third Places."

39. Steve Smith, "Developing New Reflexes in Framing Stories," Pew Center for Civil Journalism, 1997, http://www.pewcenter.org/doingcj/civiccat/displayCivcat.php?id=97 (accessed July 3, 2004).

40. Richard Harwood, "Framing a Story: What's It Really About?" Pew Center for Civic Journalism, 2004, http://www.pewcenter.org/doingcj/videos/framing.html (accessed July 3, 2004).

41. Smith, "Developing New Reflexes in Framing Stories."

42. "Finding Third Places."

43. Ray Oldenburg, *The Great Good Place: Cafés, Coffee Shops, Bookstores, Bars, Hair Salons and Other Hangouts at the Heart of a Community* (New York: Marlowe, 1999), 16.

44. "The State of the News Media 2004," Committee of Concerned Journalists, http://www.journalism.org (accessed June 17, 2004).

45. Mantsios, "Media Magic," 108.

46. "So You Wanna Be a Sitcom Writer?" SoYouWanna, 2004, http://www.so youwanna.com/site/syws/sitcom/sitcom.html (accessed July 7, 2004).

47. Project for Excellence in Journalism, "The State of the News Media 2010."

48. Project for Excellence in Journalism, "The State of the News Media 2010."

49. Project for Excellence in Journalism, "The State of the News Media 2010."

50. Project for Excellence in Journalism, "The State of the News Media 2010."

51. Project for Excellence in Journalism, "The State of the News Media 2010."

52. Project for Excellence in Journalism, "The State of the News Media 2010."

53. Sternheimer, *It's Not the Media.*

Bibliography

"80th Anniversary Special Winnie the Pooh." bornrich.com. www.bornrich.org/entry/80th-anniversary-special-winnie-the-pooh (accessed June 30, 2010).

"A. Alfred Taubman Biography." University of California, Irvine, Paul Merage School of Business. www.merage.uci.edu/classic/TaubmanBio/ (accessed June 27, 2010).

"A New Kind of Poverty." *Newsweek*, November 22, 2003. www.msnbc.msn.com/id/3540672 (accessed April 2, 2004).

"About Southfork." Southfork Ranch. 2010. www.foreverlodging.com/destination.cfm?PropertyKey=93 (accessed July 4, 2010).

Aesop. "The Fox and the Grapes." Page by Page Books. www.pagebypagebooks.com/Aesop/Aesops_Fables/The_Fox_and_the_Grapes_p1.html (accessed December 4, 2003).

"Alabama: Mobile a Prostrate City, Alarming Decline in the Value of Real Estate, Two Hundred and Fifty Stores without Occupants, Poverty and Depression Some of the Causes." *New York Times*, October 21, 1874, 1.

"All in the Family." Classicsitcoms.com. 2004. http://classicsitcoms.com/shows/family.html (accessed March 21, 2004).

"All in the Family." TVLand.com. 2004. www.tvland.com/shows/aitf (accessed March 21, 2004).

Andrews, Edmund L. "Plan Gives Most Benefits to Wealthy and Families." *New York Times*, January 8, 2003, A17.

Angelo, Megan. "At TBS, Diversity Pays Its Own Way." *New York Times*, May 30, 2010. www.nytimes.com/2010/05/30/arts/television/30tbs.html (accessed July 31, 2010).

Archibold, Randal C. "A Nation Challenged: St. Patrick's: City Celebrates Its Heroes and Grieves over Their Loss." *New York Times*, September 18, 2001, B8.

Arenson, Karen W. "Gates to Create 70 Schools for Disadvantaged." *New York Times*, March 19, 2002, A16.

Armour, Stephanie. "Homelessness Grows As More Live Check-to-Check." *USA Today*, August 12, 2003, A1.

Arnett, Alison. "Counter Culture." *Austin American-Statesman*, December 18, 2003, E1, E10.

Asian American Justice Center (AAJC). *Asian Pacific Americans in Prime Time: Setting the Stage*. AAJC. 2006. www.advancingequality.org/files/aajc_tv_06.pdf (accessed July 15, 2010).

Baker, Brent. "FNC's Baier Corrects Washington Post's Claim Obama 'Rare' Product of Middle Class." NewsBusters. February 5, 2010. www.newsbusters.org/blogs/brent-baker/2010/02/05/fnc-s-baier-corrects-washington-post-s-claim-obama-rare-product-middle (accessed October 15, 2010).

Banerjee, Neela, David Barboza, and Audrey Warren. "At Enron, Lavish Excess Often Came before Success." *New York Times*, February 26, 2001, C1, C6.

Barnes, Michael. "An Inside Look at the New Long Center." *Austin American-Statesman*, February 13, 2001, A1, A9.

Barron, James. "Brooke Astor's Son Is Sentenced to Prison." *New York Times*, December 22, 2009, A1.

"Barton Sees Crisis for Middle Class." *New York Times*, June 26, 1938, 3.

Baudrillard, Jean. *Simulations*. New York: Semiotext(e), 1983.

Bellafante, Gina. "In Hospitals the Reality Is Real." *New York Times*, June 24, 2010, C1.

Benford, Robert D., and David A. Snow. "Framing Processes and Social Movements: An Overview and Assessment." *Annual Review of Sociology* 26 (2000): 611–39.

Bennett, James T., and Jason E. Taylor. "Unions Work Selves Out of Job." *USA Today*, August 28, 2003, A13.

Berger, Peter L., and Thomas Luckmann. *The Social Construction of Reality: A Treatise in the Sociology of Knowledge*. New York: Anchor/Doubleday, 1967.

Bernstein, Jared. "Who's Poor? Don't Ask the Census Bureau." *New York Times*, September 26, 2003, A25.

Best, Steven, and Douglas Kellner. *Postmodern Theory: Critical Interrogations*. New York: Guilford, 1991.

Biagi, Shirley. *Media Impact: An Introduction to Mass Media*. Belmont, CA: Wadsworth, 2003.

"Big Labor Day Parade: Thirty Building Trades Unions to Be Represented. Forty Bands to Play in the Procession—Preparations to Handle Holiday Crowds." *New York Times*, August 31, 1902, 24.

Bird, S. Elizabeth, and Robert W. Dardenne. "Myth, Chronicle and Story: Exploring the Narrative Qualities of News." In *Social Meaning of News: A Text Reader*, edited by Daniel A. Berkowitz, 333–50. Thousand Oaks, CA: Sage, 1997.

Blakely, Edward J., and Mary Gail Snyder. *Fortress America: Gated Communities in the United States*. Washington, DC: Brookings Institution Press, 1997.

"Blames Union Labor for Work Shortage." *New York Times*, October 2, 1921, 1.

Blankfeld, Keren. "Billionaire Convicts and Inmates." *Forbes*, May 28, 2010. www.forbes.com/2010/05/28/billionaire-convict-inmate-fugitive-sanford-jail.html?feed=rss_business_billionaires (accessed July 7, 2010).

Blasi, Gary. "And We Are Not Seen: Ideological and Political Barriers to Understanding Homelessness." *American Behavioral Scientist* 37, no. 4 (February 1994): 563–87.

Blumenthal, Ralph. "As Levi's Work Is Exported, Stress Stays Home." *New York Times*, October 19, 2003, A14.

Blumenthal, Ralph, and Carol Vogel. "Ex-Chief of Sotheby's Gets 3-Year Probation and Fine." *New York Times*, April 30, 2002, A27.

"Bottom-Line Pressures Now Hurting Coverage, Say Journalists." Pew Research Center for the People and the Press. May 23, 2004. www.stateofthenewsmedia.org/prc.pdf (accessed July 6, 2004).

Bourdieu, Pierre. *Distinction: A Social Critique of the Judgement of Taste*. Translated by Richard Nice. Cambridge, MA: Harvard University Press, 1984.

Bovino, Arthur. "Offering a Hand, and Hope, in a Year of Record Homelessness in New York." *New York Times*, November 2, 2003, A25.

Brooks, David. "The Americano Dream." *New York Times*, February 24, 2004, A27.

———. *Bobos in Paradise: The New Upper Class and How They Got There*. New York: Simon and Schuster, 2000.

Brown, Francis. "What Is the Middle Class and What Does It Want?" *New York Times*, December 22, 1935, BR6.

Browne, Tawny. "There's No Reason to Fear the Poor Residents of a Shelter." Fredericksburg.com. 2002. www.fredericksburg.com/?News/FLS/2002/062002/06192002/637549.html (accessed January 25, 2004).

Browning, Lynnley. "Suicide Victim May Have Harbored a Secret." *New York Times*, September 16, 2009, B1, B2.

Bruni, Frank. "Bush Campaign Turns Attention to Middle Class." *New York Times*, September 18, 2000, A1.

———. "Bush Says Rival's Tax-Cut Plan Fails Middle Class." *New York Times*, August 25, 2000, A22.

Bunis, William K., Angela Yancik, and David Snow. "The Cultural Patterning of Sympathy toward the Homeless and Other Victims of Misfortune." *Social Problems* 43, no. 4 (November 1996): 387–402.

Bunkley, Nick. "A Once-Defiant U.A.W. Local Now Focuses on G.M.'s Success." *New York Times*, January 6, 2010, B1.

———. "Tentative Agreement May End Strike That Disrupted Production at 32 G.M. Plants." *New York Times*, May 18, 2008, B1.

Butler, Judith. "Performative Acts and Gender Constitution: An Essay in Phenomenology and Feminist Theory." In *Performing Feminisms: Feminist Critical Theory and Theatre*, edited by Sue-Ellen Case, 270. Baltimore: Johns Hopkins University Press, 1990.

Butsch, Richard. "Class and Gender in Four Decades of Television Situation Comedy: Plus ça Change . . ." *Critical Studies in Mass Communication* 9 (1992): 387–99.

———. "A Half Century of Class and Gender in American TV Domestic Sitcoms." *Cercles* 8 (2003): 16–34. www.cercles.com/n8/butsch.pdf (accessed October 15, 2010).

———. "Ralph, Fred, Archie and Homer: Why Television Keeps Recreating the White Male Working-Class Buffoon." In *Gender, Race and Class in Media*, edited by Gale Dines and Jean M. Humez, 403–12. Thousand Oaks, CA: Sage, 1995.

Byrne, Richard. "Bodymore, Murdaland." *American Prospect*. October 22, 2006. www.prospect.org/cs/articles?article=bodymore_murdaland (accessed October 17, 2010).

Cable, Mary. *Top Drawer: American High Society from the Gilded Age to the Roaring Twenties*. New York: Atheneum, 1984.

Cantor, George. "Middle-Class Livonia Turns into Wayne County Power." *Detroit News*, January 26, 2002. www.detnews.com/2002/editorial/0201/28/d07-400393 .htm (accessed February 18, 2004).

Carr, David. "Condé Nast Redesigns Its Future: Newhouse Plans a Transition but Tightens His Grip." *New York Times*, October 26, 2003, BU1, BU12.

———. "The Powering Up of the Power Lunch." *New York Times*, December 10, 2003, D1, D4.

Carter, R. J. "DVD Review: 'My Name Is Earl'—Season One." The Trades. September 22, 2006. www.the-trades.com/article.php?id=4806 (accessed July 25, 2010).

Castillo, Juan. "U.S. Payday Is Something to Write Home About." *Austin American-Statesman*, December 14, 2003, J1.

"Cause of Mr. Hilsen's Suicide: His Capital Exhausted and Poverty Staring Him in the Face." *New York Times*, January 25, 1883, 8.

Chan, Sewell. "Is Gentrification Transforming the City's Public Spaces?" *New York Times*, August 14, 2007. http://cityroom.blogs.nytimes.com/2007/08/14/is-gentrification-transforming-the-citys-public-spaces/?scp=1&sq=is%20gentrification%20transforming%20the%20city's%20public%20spaces&st=cse (accessed August 8, 2010).

"Changing a City: Philanthropist Believes in Building Bridges." DallasNews.com. December 10, 2003. www.dallasnews.com/opinion/editorials/stories/121003dnedimcder mott98208.html (accessed December 12, 2003).

"The Christmas Book." Neiman Marcus. 2009. www.neimanmarcus.com/store/site lets/christmasbook/christmasbook.jhtml (accessed June 14, 2010).

Clarke, Ben. "S.F. Daily Papers Pit Middle Class against Homeless." MediaAlliance. 2000. www.media-alliance.org/mediafile/19-1/homeless.html (accessed October 12, 2003).

Clemetson, Lynette. "Census Shows Ranks of Poor Rose by 1.3 Million." *New York Times*, September 3, 2003, A1.

Clifford, Lee. "Getting Malled." *Fortune*, November 25, 2001. www.fortune.com/fortune/investing/articles/0,15114,373012,00.html (accessed September 29, 2003).

Cohan, William D. "The Shot Heard 'Round the Clubs." *Vanity Fair*, January 2010. www.vanityfair.com/culture/features/2010/02/caspersen-suicide-201002 (accessed July 2, 2010).

Cohen, Jeff, and Norman Solomon. "On Local TV News, If It Bleeds It (Still) Leads." FAIR, Media Beat. December 13, 1995. www.fair.org/media-beat/951213.html (accessed February 29, 2004).

Coleman, Richard P., and Lee Rainwater. *Social Standing in America: New Dimensions of Class*. New York: Basic, 1978.

Cookson, Peter W., Jr., and Caroline Hodges Persell. *Preparing for Power: America's Elite Boarding Schools*. New York: Basic Books, 1985.

"*The Consumers: Fate of the Middle Classes.* By Walter G. Cooper." *New York Times*, November 18, 1905, BR774.

Cowley, Geoffrey. "They've Given Away $24 Billion. Here's Why. Bill's Biggest Bet Yet." *Newsweek*, February 4, 2002, 44–52.

Croteau, David, and William Hoynes. *Media/Society: Industries, Images, and Audiences.* 3rd ed. Thousand Oaks, CA: Pine Forge, 2003.

Customer review of *Poor Little Rich Girl: The Life and Legend of Barbara Hutton*, by C. David Heymann. Amazon.com. 2003. www.amazon.com/exec/obidos/search -handle-form/ref=s_sf_b_as/002-5171433-1616062 (accessed December 7, 2003).

D'Angelo, Paul. "News Framing As a Multiparadigmatic Research Program: A Response to Entman." *Journal of Communication* 52 (2002): 870–88.

Danziger, Sheldon, and Peter Gottschalk. *America Unequal.* Cambridge, MA: Harvard University Press, 1995.

Dao, James. "Hardships and Damage Linger after Hurricane." *New York Times*, October 2, 2003, A18.

Dash, Eric. "Mortgage Executive Accused in Multibillion-Dollar Fraud." *New York Times*, June 17, 2010, B1, B4.

De Coster, Karen, and Brad Edmonds. "TV Nation: The Killing of American Brain Cells." Lewrockwell.com. March 5, 2003. www.lewrockwell.com/decoster/ decoster78.html (accessed July 7, 2004).

Dean, Wally, and Lee Ann Brady. "Local TV News Project—2002: After 9/11, Has Anything Changed?" Journalism.org. 2004. www.journalism.org/resources/ research/reports/localTV/2002/postsept11.asp (accessed February 29, 2004).

DeBaise, Colleen. "Newest 'Tyco Gone Wild' Video Is Out, and Jurors See $6,000 Shower Curtain." *Wall Street Journal*, November 26, 2003, C1, C7.

Delaney, Arthur. "No Recession Special on the D.C. Power Lunch Menu." The Huffington Post. November 30, 2009. www.huffingtonpost.com/2009/11/30/no -recession-special-on-t_n_373681.html (accessed June 27, 2010).

Delaney, Tim, and Allene Wilcox. "Sports and the Role of the Media." In *Values, Society and Evolution*, edited by Harry Birx and Tim Delaney, 199–215. Auburn, NY: Legend, 2002.

DeMott, Benjamin. *The Imperial Middle: Why Americans Can't Think Straight about Class.* New York: William Morrow, 1990.

DeNavas-Walt, Carmen, Bernadette D. Proctor, and Jessica C. Smith. *Income, Poverty, and Health Insurance Coverage in the United States: 2008.* U.S. Census Bureau, Current Population Reports, P60-236. Washington, DC: U.S. Government Printing Office, 2009.

DeParle, Jason. "In Rising Debate on Poverty, the Question: Who Is Poor?" *New York Times*, September 3, 1990, A1.

"Destitution in New Orleans: The Existing Poverty and Its Causes—Lotteries and Beer Shops." *New York Times*, May 7, 1875, 10.

Dionne, E. J., Jr. "Handing Out Hardship." *Washington Post*, September 16, 2003, A19.

"Distressing Case of Poverty and Suicide." *New York Times*, January 1, 1855, 4.

Domhoff, G. William. *The Higher Circles.* New York: Random House, 1970.

——. "The Women's Page As a Window on the Ruling Class." In *Hearth and Home: Images of Women in the Mass Media*, edited by Gaye Tuchman, Arlene Kaplan Daniels, and James Benet, 161–75. New York: Oxford University Press, 1978.

"Double Dutch." *Joan of Arcadia* episode 1.16. TV Tome. February 20, 2004. www .tvtome.com/tvtome/servlet/EpisodeReviewPage/showid-17466/epid-282012/bl (accessed February 29, 2004).

Douglas, William. *Television Families: Is Something Wrong in Suburbia?* Mahwah, NJ: Lawrence Erlbaum, 2003.

"Down among the Lowly: The Sights That One Sees in the Fourth Ward." *New York Times*, May 7, 1871, 8.

"Driven to Suicide by Poverty." *New York Times*, February 25, 1884, 8.

Dubner, Stephen J. "Suddenly Popular." *New York Times Magazine*, June 8, 2003, 68–71.

Duffy, Michael. "What Did They Know and When Did They Know It?" *Time*, January 28, 2002, 16–22.

Dugas, Christine. "Middle Class Barely Treads Water." *USA Today*, September 14, 2003. www.usatoday.com/money/perfi/general/2003-09-14-middle-cover_x.htm (accessed December 31, 2003).

Duke, Pony, and Jason Thomas. *Too Rich: The Family Secrets of Doris Duke*. New York: HarperCollins, 1996.

Durkheim, Emile. *Suicide*. New York: Free Press, 1951 [1897].

Eastman, Susan. "White Trash: America's Dirty Little Secret." *Ace Magazine*. 1998. www.aceweekly.com/acemag/backissues/980916/cb2_980916.html (accessed March 14, 2004).

Eaton, Leslie. "From Middle Class to the Shelter Door: In a Trend, New Yorkers Face Poverty after Last Unemployment Check." *New York Times*, November 17, 2002, A37.

Ebert, Lawrence B. "'Law & Order' Plotline Follows Larry Mendte Story and Madoff Scam." IPBIZ. March 25, 2009. www.ipbiz.blogspot.com/2009/03/law-order -plotline-follows-larry-mendte.html (accessed October 15, 2010).

Eckholm, Erik. "Last Year's Poverty Rate Was Highest in 12 Years." *New York Times*, September 11, 2009, A1.

"Economy among the Middle Classes." *New York Times*, November 9, 1868, 4.

Ehrenreich, Barbara. *Fear of Falling: The Inner Life of the Middle Class*. New York: HarperPerennial, 1990.

——. *Nickel and Dimed: On (Not) Getting By in America*. New York: Metropolitan, 2001.

——. "Too Poor to Make the News." *New York Times*, June 14, 2009, WK10.

Eligon, John. "Housekeeper Tells How Astor's Son Took Paintings." *New York Times*, June 9, 2009, A20.

Entman, Robert M. "Framing: Toward Clarification of a Fractured Paradigm." *Journal of Communication* 43 (1993): 51–58.

Entman, Robert M., and Andrew Rojecki. *The Black Image in the White Mind: Media and Race in America*. Chicago: University of Chicago Press, 2000.

Epperson, Sharon. "How to Escape the 'Two-Income Trap.'" MSNBC. 2003. msnbc .msn.com/id/3087477 (accessed December 29, 2003).

Epstein, Helen. "Enough to Make You Sick?" *New York Times Magazine*, October 12, 2003, 75–81, 98, 102–106.

Erickson, Christopher L., and Daniel J. B. Mitchell. "Information on Strikes and Union Settlements: Patterns of Coverage in a 'Newspaper of Record.'" *Industrial and Labor Relations Review* 49, no. 3 (April 1996): 395–407.

Evans, Katie. "Most Overexposed Billionaires." Forbes.com. January 21, 2010. www.forbes.com/2010/01/21/most-overexposed-billionaires-branson-buffett-business-billionaires-trump.html (accessed July 5, 2010).

"Fact Sheets." Walmart.com. March 2010. www.walmartstores.com/pressroom/Fact Sheets (accessed July 27, 2010).

Fagan, Kevin. "Shame of the City: Homeless Island." *San Francisco Chronicle*, November 30, 2003. www.sfgate.com (accessed April 11, 2004).

"A Father's Awful Crime: Shooting His Three Little Girls. Why John Remmler, of Holyoke, Killed His Children—Poverty and a Fear for Their Future His Reasons." *New York Times*, June 22, 1879, 7.

"Feeding the City's Poor: Giving Bountiful Dinners to Children and Poverty-Stricken People." *New York Times*, November 28, 1884, 3.

Feuer, Alan. "After the Polo Match, in the Tented Pavilion." *New York Times*, June 18, 2009, A28.

———. "Bronx Girl Follows Vision: A Future Far from Home." *New York Times*, October 4, 2003, A1, A14.

Feuer, Jack. "Miner Chord: Is a Working-Class Hero Still Something to Be?" *ADWEEK Southwest*, August 5, 2002, 9.

"Finding Third Places: Other Voices, Different Stories." Pew Center for Civic Journalism. 2004. www.pewcenter.org/doingcj/videos/thirdplaces.html (accessed July 6, 2004).

Firestone, David. "4 Dead and 9 Missing in a Pair of Alabama Mine Blasts." *New York Times*, September 25, 2001, A14.

Fishman, Steve. "Bernie Madoff, Free At Last." *New York Magazine*, June 14–21, 2010, 35.

Fitzgerald, F. Scott. "The Rich Boy." In *The Short Stories of F. Scott Fitzgerald*, edited by Mathew J. Brucoli, 317–49. New York: Scribner, 1995 [1926 in *Redbook* magazine].

Florida, Richard. *The Rise of the Creative Class: And How It's Transforming Work, Leisure, Community and Everyday Life*. New York: Basic, 2002.

Fountain, John W. "Chicago Looks for Home for Shelter for Homeless." *New York Times*, May 15, 2003, A26.

Franklin, Nancy. "Sunny Money: Fox Heads down the Coast from 90210." *New Yorker*, August 18–25, 2003, 144–45.

Gamson, William A. "News As Framing: Comments on Graber." *American Behavioral Scientist* 33 (1989): 157–61.

Gamson, William A., David Croteau, William Hoynes, and Theodore Sasson. "Media Images and the Social Construction of Reality." *Annual Review of Sociology* 18 (1992): 373–93.

Gándara, Ricardo. "Thanks, Austin!" *Austin American-Statesman*, February 1, 2004, K1, K12.

Gandy, Oscar H., Jr., Katharina Kopp, Tanya Hands, Karen Frazer, and David Phillips. "Race and Risk: Factors Affecting the Framing of Stories about Inequality, Discrimination, and Just Plain Bad Luck." *Public Opinion Quarterly* 61 (spring 1997): 158–82.

Gans, Herbert. *Deciding What's News*. New York: Pantheon Books, 1979.

Geary, Leslie Haggin. "Guess Which Jobs Are Going Abroad." CNN/Money. January 5, 2004. http://money.cnn.com/2003/12/30/pf/offshorejob (accessed January 25, 2004).

Gesalman, Anne Belli. "Cliff Was Climbing the Walls." *Newsweek*, February 4, 2002, 24.

Giannone, Joseph A. "Recession, Bear Markets Hit the Rich, Too." Reuters .com. June 25, 2010. http://finance.yahoo.com/news/Recession-bear-markets-hit -rb-4023953240.html (accessed June 26, 2010).

Gilbert, Dennis. *The American Class Structure in an Age of Growing Inequality*. 8th ed. Thousand Oaks, CA: Pine Forge, 2011.

Gilbert, Dennis, and Joseph A. Kahl. *The American Class Structure: A New Synthesis*. Homewood, IL: Dorsey, 1982.

Gilbert, Matthew. "Snarky Rich Kids Make for Fun 'Gossip,'" *Boston Globe*, September 19, 2007. www.boston.com/ae/tv/articles/2007/09/19/snarky_rich_kids_ make_for_fun_gossip (accessed July 4, 2010).

Gilens, Martin. *Why Americans Hate Welfare: Race, Media, and the Politics of Antipoverty Policy*. Chicago: University of Chicago Press, 1999.

Ginsberg, Thomas. "Union Hopes to Win Over Starbucks Shop Workers." *Austin American-Statesman*, July 2, 2004, D6.

Gitlin, Todd. *Media Unlimited: How the Torrent of Images and Sounds Overwhelms Our Lives*. New York: Henry Holt, 2003.

———. *The Whole World Is Watching*. Berkeley: University of California Press, 1980.

Goffman, Erving. *Frame Analysis: An Essay on the Organization of Experience*. Boston: Northeastern University Press, 1974.

Gold, Matea. "Diane Sawyer Examines Poverty in Appalachia." *Los Angeles Times*, February 11, 2009. http://articles.latimes.com/2009/feb/11/entertainment/et-diane -sawyer11 (accessed October 15, 2010).

Gomstyn, Alice. "Goldman Sachs' Fabrice 'Fabulous Fab' Tourre: Wall Street's Fall Guy?" abcNEWS.com. April 21, 2010. http://abcnews.go.com/Business/goldman -sachs-fabrice-fabulous-fab-tourre-wall-streets/story?id=10429139 (accessed April 21, 2010).

Goodman, Peter S. "U.S. Offers a Hand to Those on Eviction's Edge." *New York Times*, April 19, 2010, A1.

Goodrum, Charles, and Helen Dalrymple. *Advertising in America: The First 200 Years*. New York: Harry N. Abrams, 1990.

Gootman, Elissa. "Publicist Gets Jail Sentence and Scolding." *New York Times*, October 24, 2002, A28.

Graff, E. J. "*Bobos in Paradise: The New Upper Class and How They Got There.*" *American Prospect*, May 22, 2000, 52.

Grant, Lorrie. "Retail Giant Wal-Mart Faces Challenges on Many Fronts: Protests, Allegations Are Price of Success, CEO Says." *USA Today*, November 11, 2003, B1.

Greenhouse, Steven. "Endless Task: Keeping Unions Clean." *New York Times*, February 10, 2008, A10.

———. "Labor Raises Pressure on California Supermarkets." *New York Times*, February 10, 2004, A12.

———. "Middlemen in the Low-Wage Economy." *New York Times*, December 28, 2003, WK10.

———. "Scandals Affirm New York As Union Corruption Capital." *New York Times*, February 15, 1999, B1.

Greenwood, Arin. "D.C. Libraries: Not a Homeless Shelter, Especially in the West End." *Washington City Paper*, November 12, 2008. www.washingtoncitypaper .com/blogs/citydesk/2008/11/12/dc-libraries-not-a-homeless-shelter (accessed August 2, 2010).

Grindstaff, Laura. *The Money Shot: Trash, Class, and the Making of TV Talk Shows.* Chicago: University of Chicago Press, 2002.

Guyon, Janet. "Jack Grubman Is Back. Just Ask Him." *Fortune*, May 16, 2005. www .money.cnn.com/magazines/fortune/fortune_archive/2005/05/16/8260134/index .htm (accessed July 3, 2010).

Habiby, Margot, and Jim Kennett. "Ex-Enron Executive Killed Self, Police Say." *Austin American-Statesman*, January 26, 2002, A1, A4.

Hakim, Danny. "Auto Deal or Bust: Was Anyone Taken for a Ride in the U.A.W.– Big 3 Contract Talks?" *New York Times*, September 23, 2003, C2.

Hamill, Pete. "In Defense of Honest Labor." *New York Times*, December 31, 1995, SM18.

Harbaugh, Pam. "Dreamers Battle for Home in Harmony." *Florida Today*, January 4, 2004. www.floridatoday.com/!NEWSROOM/peoplestoryP0105DREAM.htm (accessed February 2, 2004).

Harwood, Richard. "Framing a Story: What's It Really About?" Pew Center for Civic Journalism. 2004. www.pewcenter.org/doingcj/videos/framing.html (accessed July 3, 2004).

"Health Care Reform, At Last." *New York Times*, March 22, 2010, A24.

"Help for the Working Poor." *New York Times*, April 22, 1869, 4.

Hemphill, Clara. "Admissions Anxiety." *New York Times*, November 17, 2002, WK11.

Henneberger, Melinda. "Testing of a President: The Accuser; the World of Paula Jones: A Lonely Place amid Clamor." *New York Times*, March 12, 1998, A1.

Herbert, Bob. "Bracing for the Blow." *New York Times*, December 26, 2003, A35.

———. "Caught in the Credit Card Vise." *New York Times*, September 22, 2003, A19.

———. "Caught in the Squeeze." *New York Times*, May 29, 2003, A27.

———. "Education Is No Protection." *New York Times*, January 26, 2004, A27.

———. "A Less Than Honest Policy." *New York Times*, December 28, 2009. www .nytimes.com/2009/12/29/opinion/29herbert.html?_r=1 (accessed July 16, 2010).

———. "Living on Borrowed Money." *New York Times*, November 10, 2003, A23.

———. "Locked Out at a Young Age." *New York Times*, October 20, 2003, A19.

———. "Long-Term Economic Pain." *New York Times*, July 27, 2010, A17.

———. "Putting Our Brains on Hold." *New York Times*, August 6, 2010. www.ny
times.com/2010/08/07/opinion/07herbert.html (accessed August 10, 2010).

———. "Shaking the House of Cards." *New York Times*, October 3, 2003, A27.

———. "We're More Productive. Who Gets the Money?" *New York Times*, April 5,
2004, A25.

———. "The White-Collar Blues." *New York Times*, December 29, 2003, A21.

———. "The Worst of the Pain." *New York Times*, February 9, 2010, A23.

"Here Comes Santa Claus." Television without Pity. televisionwithoutpity.com/story
.cgi?show=&&story=5940&page=5 (accessed February 28, 2004).

Hermann, William. "Treating the Homeless Where They Live." CNN.com. August
9, 2000. www.cnn.com/2000/LOCAL/pacific/08/09/azc.homeless.medical/index
.html (accessed February 8, 2004).

Hernandez, Al Carlos. "ABC Network Has Failed Latinos." LatinoLA, May 15, 2007.
http://latinola.com/story.php?story=4123 (accessed October 15, 2010).

Heymann, C. David. *Poor Little Rich Girl: The Life and Legend of Barbara Hutton.*
New York: Random House, 1984.

Himmelstein, Hal. *Television Myth and the American Mind.* Westport, CT: Praeger,
1994.

Hochschild, Jennifer L. *Facing Up to the American Dream: Race, Class, and the Soul
of the Nation.* Princeton, NJ: Princeton University Press, 1995.

Hollingsworth, Skip. "Hi, Society!" *Texas Monthly* (September 2002): 164–67,
194–204.

Holmes, Mike. "Shelter Will Bring Only Crime." Fredericksburg.com. 2003. www
.fredericksburg.com/?News/FLS/2003/04182003/936435.html (accessed January
25, 2004).

Holtzman, Linda. *Media Messages: What Film, Television, and Popular Music Teach
Us about Race, Class, Gender, and Sexual Orientation.* London: M. E. Sharpe, 2000.

"Homeless Children." *New York Times*, December 22, 1856, 4.

"Homeless Shelter Plan Attacked, Potrero Hill Neighbors Worry about Property Values." *San Francisco Chronicle*, August 6, 1999. http://articles.sfgate.com/1999-08
-06/news/17696660_1_homeless-shelter-neighborhood-homeless-people (accessed October 15, 2010).

"Homeless Woman Arrested for Threatening Postal Worker." KFMB.com. January
16, 2003. www.kfmb.com (accessed February 2, 2004).

"The Honeymooners." TVLand.com. 2004. www.tvland.com/shows/honeymooners
(accessed March 20, 2004).

hooks, bell [Gloria Watkins]. *Where We Stand: Class Matters.* New York: Routledge,
2000.

Hooson, Paul. "Glen Beck Defends Sarah Palin's 'White Trash' Family Values."
Wizbang Blue. September 3, 2008. www.wizbangblue.com/2008/09/03/glen-beck
-defends-sarah-palins-white-trash-family-values.php (accessed July 26, 2010).

Horkheimer, Max, and Theodor W. Adorno. *Dialectic of Enlightenment.* Translated
by John Cummings. New York: Continuum International, 2002 [1944].

Horner, Kim. "Anywhere but Here: Library Tells Homeless to Move Along." *Dallas
Morning News*, October 8, 2003, 1B.

———. "Losing Their Cart Blanche." *Dallas Morning News*, January 14, 2004, 1B.

"How Many People Experience Homelessness?" Fact Sheet 2. National Coalition for the Homeless. 2002. www.nationalhomeless.org/numbers.html (accessed February 14, 2004).

"How Much Will Woods Pay Wife to Keep Quiet?" TODAYshow.com. July 3, 2010. http://today.msnbc.msn.com/id/26184891/vp/38104275#38104275 (accessed July 5, 2010).

Hughes, Kristine. "Foundation Offers Help to Working Poor: Organizers Say Many Need Mentoring to Quit Welfare Dependency." *Dallas Morning News*, July 3, 2003, 1S.

"The Hunger Artist." Television without Pity. televisionwithoutpity.com/story .cgi?show=15&story=3487&page=2 (accessed February 28, 2004).

"Hungry Families in U.S. on the Rise." MSNBC.com. 2003. www.msnbc.msn.com/ id/3341630 (accessed February 10, 2004).

"If Only the Spirit of Giving Could Continue." *Los Angeles Times*, December 25, 1988, 16.

Inniss, Leslie B., and Joe R. Feagin. "*The Cosby Show*: The View from the Black Middle Class." *Journal of Black Studies* 25 (1995): 692–711.

"Inside the Middle Class: Bad Times Hit the Good Life." Pew Social Trends. April 9, 2008. http://pewsocialtrends.org/pubs/706/middle-class-poll (accessed July 29, 2010).

Isidore, Chris. "7.9 Million Jobs Lost—Many Forever." CNNMoney.com. July 2, 2010. www.money.cnn.com/2010/07/02/news/economy/jobs_gone_forever/index .htm (accessed July 27, 2010).

"It Would Never Work Out . . ." (cartoon). *New Yorker*, March 25, 2002, 75.

Iyengar, Shanto. "Framing Responsibility for Political Issues: The Case of Poverty." *Political Behavior* 12 (March 1990): 19–40.

———. *Is Anyone Responsible? How Television Frames Political Issues*. Chicago: University of Chicago Press, 1991.

Janjigian, Robert. "A Learjet? You Shouldn't Have!" *Austin American-Statesman*, November 4, 2002, E1.

Jhally, Sut, and Justin Lewis. *Enlightened Racism: The Cosby Show, Audiences, and the Myth of the American Dream*. Boulder, CO: Westview, 1992.

Johnston, David Cay. "Tax Analysis Says the Rich Still Win." *New York Times*, July 14, 2002, BU10.

Jones, Gerard. *Honey, I'm Home! Sitcoms: Selling the American Dream*. New York: Grove Weidenfeld, 1992.

Jong, Erica. "The Mary Poppins Syndrome." The Huffington Post. September 3, 2008. www.huffingtonpost.com/erica-jong/the-mary-poppins-syndrome_b_123584.html (accessed July 26, 2010).

Kadlec, Daniel. "They're Getting Richer!" *Time*, August 18, 2003, 49.

Kahl, Joseph A. *The American Class Structure*. New York: Rinehart, 1957.

Kaufman, Jonathan. "Covering Race, Poverty and Class in the New Gilded Age." *Nieman Reports* 55, no. 1 (spring 2001): 25.

Kaufman, Leslie. "Amid Manhattan's Wealthiest, a Beggar Found Open Hearts." *New York Times*, February 14, 2004, A1, A14.

———. "Millions Have Left Welfare, but Are They Better Off? Yes, No and Maybe." *New York Times*, October 20, 2003, A16.

———. "Welfare Wars: Are the Poor Suffering from Hunger Anymore?" *New York Times*, February 23, 2003, WK4.

Kavaler, Lucy. *The Private World of High Society*. New York: David McKay, 1960.

Keefe, Bob. "Grocery Strike Wearing on Customers, Workers." *Austin American-Statesman*, February 6, 2004, C1, C3.

Kellner, Douglas. *Media Spectacle*. New York: Routledge, 2003.

Kelly, Maura. "Regulating the Reproduction and Mothering of Poor Women: The Controlling Image of the Welfare Mother in Television News Coverage of Welfare Reform." *Journal of Poverty* 14, no. 1 (January 2010): 76–96.

Kendall, Diana. *Framing Class: Media Representations of Wealth and Poverty in America*. 1st ed. Lanham, MD: Rowman & Littlefield, 2005.

———. *The Power of Good Deeds: Privileged Women and the Social Reproduction of the Upper Class*. Lanham, MD: Rowman & Littlefield, 2002.

Kennedy, Randy. "For Middle Class, New York Shrinks As Home Prices Soar." *New York Times*, April 1, 1998, A1.

Kerbo, Harold R. *Social Stratification and Inequality*. 7th ed. Boston: McGraw-Hill, 2009.

Kim, Ann S. "Bottom Falls Out for Middle Class." *Portland Press Herald*, March 12, 2009. www.pressherald.com/archive/bottom-falls-out-for-middle-class_2009-03-16.html?searchterm=bottom+falls+out+for+the+middle+class%3F (accessed October 15, 2010).

"The King of Queens: Wild Cards." TV Tome. February 20, 2004. www.tvtome.com/tvtome/servlet/GuidePageServlet/showid-239/epid-1637 (accessed April 18, 2004).

Kingston, Paul W. *The Classless Society*. Stanford, CA: Stanford University Press, 2000.

Kirchhoff, Sue, and Barbara Hagenbaugh. "Immigration: A Fiscal Boon or Financial Strain? Debate Heats Up over Impact on Economy." *USA Today*, January 22, 2004, B1.

Kleinfield, N. R. "Golden Years, on $678 a Month." *New York Times*, September 3, 2003, B1.

Kossan, Pat. "Man Overcomes Homelessness, Will Graduate from ASU." Arizona Republic. May 2, 2003. www.azcentral.com (accessed February 28, 2004).

Kovach, Bill, Tom Rosenstiel, and Amy Mitchell. "A Crisis of Confidence: A Commentary on the Findings." Pew Research Center for the People and the Press. 2004. www.stateofthenewsmedia.org/prc.pdf (accessed July 6, 2004).

Kuczynski, Alex. "For the Elite, Easing the Way to Prison." *New York Times*, December 9, 2001, ST1, ST2.

———. "Lifestyles of the Rich and Red-Faced." *New York Times*, September 22, 2002, ST1, ST8.

———. "When Home Is a Castle and the Big House, Too." *New York Times*, August 18, 2002, ST1, ST7.

Kuczynski, Alex, and Andrew Ross Sorkin. "Canapés and Investment Tips Are Served to Well-Heeled." *New York Times*, July 1, 2002, A1, A17.

Kunerth, Jeff. "One Number Can't Measure Poverty." *Austin American-Statesman*, October 5, 2003, E4.

"Labor Unions." *New York Times*, August 26, 1868, 4.

Lacayo, Richard. "Take This Job and Starve." *Time*, February 16, 2004, 76–77.

"*Law & Order.*" NBC.com. 2003. www.nbc.com/Law_&_Order/about/index.html (accessed December 22, 2003).

Lawrence, Jill. "'Family Values' Lower on Agenda in 2008 Race." *USA Today*, December 18, 2007. www.usatoday.com/news/politics/election2008/2007-12-17 -Familyvalues_N.htm (accessed July 30, 2010).

———. "Health Reform: A Year-by-Year Rundown of What Happens and When." Politics Daily. March 23, 2010. www.politicsdaily/2010/03/23/health-reform-a -year-by-year-rundown-of-what-happens-and-when (accessed July 18, 2010).

———. "Values, Points of View Separate Towns—and Nation." *USA Today*, February 18, 2002, A10.

Leibman, Nina C. *Living Room Lectures: The Fifties Families in Film and Television.* Austin: University of Texas Press, 1995.

Lester, Paul Martin, ed. *Images That Injure: Pictorial Stereotypes in the Media.* Westport, CT: Praeger, 1996.

"Letter to the Editor: Tribulations of the Middle Class." *New York Times*, November 20, 1906, 8.

"*The Life of Riley*: U.S. Situation Comedy." Museum.tv.com. 2004. www.museum .tv/archives/etv/L/htmlL/lifeofriley/lifeofriley.htm (accessed March 13, 2004).

"Lifestyles of the Rich and Famous Video Slots." IGT. www.igtonline.com/mega jackpots/new_games/lifestyles.html (accessed November 30, 2003).

Lind, Rebecca Ann, and Colleen Salo. "The Framing of Feminists and Feminism in News and Public Affairs Programs in U.S. Electronic Media." *Journal of Communication* 52 (2002): 211–28.

Linkins, Kim Fulcher. "Midwest Lures Family-Based IT." CNN.com. 1999. www .cnn.com/TECH/computing/9906/11/midwest.idg/index.html (accessed February 17, 2004).

Lipton, Michael A., and Steve Barnes. "Just How Real Was the Simple Life? Take a Gander." *People*, December 15, 2003, 68.

"Living Costs Disturb Middle Class, Barton Cautions House in Speech: Warning Crop Plan Means Higher Food and Clothing Prices, He Asserts New Yorkers Ask: 'Why Do We Always Foot the Bill?'" *New York Times*, December 4, 1937, 7.

Lobb, Annelena. "Gifts for Kids Who Have It All." CNN/Money. 2002. http://money .cnn.com/2002/11/26/pf/saving/holiday_haveitall.index.htm (accessed December 5, 2002).

"Lodging-House for Homeless Girls a New Project of the Children's Aid Society." *New York Times*, May 25, 1862, 3.

"A Lodging-House for the Homeless in the Thirteenth Ward." *New York Times*, February 21, 1868, 5.

Low, Setha. *Behind the Gates: Life, Security, and the Pursuit of Happiness in Fortress America*. New York: Routledge, 2003.

Lozano, Juan A. "Judge Vacates Conviction of Kenneth Lay." *Washington Post*, October 18, 2006. www.washingtonpost.com/wp-dyn/content/article/2006/10/18/AR2006101800201_pf.html (accessed October 15, 2010).

Luce, Edward. "The Crisis of Middle-Class America." *Financial Times*, July 30, 2010. www.ft.com/cms/s/2/1a8a5cb2-9ab2-11df-87e6-00144feab49a.html (accessed August 3, 2010).

Lule, Jack. *Daily News, Eternal Stories: The Mythological Role of Journalism*. New York: Guilford, 2001.

Luo, Michael. "For Long-Term Unemployed, a Shaky Safety Net." *New York Times*, July 18, 2010, A13.

Lush, Tamara. "Disgraced Financier Stanford's Possessions Auctioned Off." *Waco Tribune-Herald*, June 16, 2009, 3B.

"The Luxury Car Lot for Kids," RideToys.com. http://mobileation.stores.yahoo.net/luxurycarlot.html (accessed November 8, 2010).

Lyman, Rick. "For the Ryder Trial, a Hollywood Script." *New York Times*, November 3, 2002, ST1, ST8.

"*Malcolm in the Middle*." FOX.com. 2004. www.fox.com/malcolm/journal/404.htm (accessed January 2, 2004).

"Managing Labor Interests: Harmonizing Rival Unions and Concluding to Do without Prayers." *New York Times*, June 11, 1883, 8.

Manoff, Robert K. "Writing the News, by Telling the 'Story.'" In *Reading the News*, edited by Robert K. Manoff and Michael Schudson, 197–229. New York: Pantheon, 1987.

Mantsios, Gregory. "Media Magic: Making Class Invisible." In *Privilege: A Reader*, edited by Michael S. Kimmel and Abby L. Ferber, 99–109. Boulder, CO: Westview, 2003.

Marc, David. *Comic Visions: Television Comedy and American Culture*. 2nd ed. Malden, MA: Blackwell, 1997.

Marchand, Michele. "On the Air and Outside: Homelessness on TV." Anitra.net. www.anitra.net/books/activist/mm_on_the_air.html (accessed February 28, 2004).

Marshall, Kelli. "ABC's *The Middle*: Redefining the Working-Class Male." FlowTV. June 3, 2010. www.flowtv.org/2010/06/abcs-the-middle-redefining-the-working-class-male (accessed July 25, 2010).

Mason, Christopher. "Where Everybody Has a Name." *New York Times*, October 26, 2003, ST1, ST2.

Massing, Michael. "Take This Job and Be Thankful (for $6.80 an Hour)." *New York Times*, February 18, 2004, B8.

Maynard, Micheline. "If a Name Is Tarnished, but Carved in Stone." *New York Times*, December 9, 2001, BU4.

"McDonald's Features Donald Trump in New Ad Campaign Launching Dollar-Priced Big N' Tasty and McChicken Sandwich." McDonalds.com. October 3, 2002.

www.mcdonalds.com/countries/usa/whatsnew/pressrelease/2002/10032002_a (accessed December 16, 2003).

McKee, Bradford. "Fortress Home: Welcome Mat Bites." *New York Times*, January 22, 2004, F1.

McLarin, Kimberly J. "Poverty Rate Is the Highest in 16 Years, a Report Says." *New York Times*, July 14, 1995, B3.

"Meeting of Front Bricklayers: A Union of Capital and Labor Advocated." *New York Times*, August 30, 1860, 8.

"Melancholy Case of Suicide: Pride and Poverty the Cause." *New York Times*, March 20, 1873, 1.

Merritt, Bishetta, and Carolyn A. Stroman. "Black Family Imagery and Interactions on Television." *Journal of Black Studies* 23 (1993): 492–99.

"Middle Class Finds Homes in Suburbs: Demolition of Private Dwellings in the City Drives Residences to Other Localities." *New York Times*, September 1, 1929, RE2.

"Middle Class in America." U.S. Department of Commerce, Economics and Statistics Administration. January 2010. http://2001-2009.commerce.gov/s/groups/public/@doc/@os/@opa/documents/content/prod01_008833.pdf (accessed July 24, 2010).

Middleton, Michael. "L.A. Confidential: A Well-Run Shelter Suppresses Crime." Fredericksburg.com. 2003. www.fredericksburg.com/?News/FLS/2003/042003/04072003/921809.html (accessed January 25, 2004).

Miller, Matthew. "The Wealthiest Black Americans." Forbes.com. May 6, 2009. www.forbes.com/2009/05/06/richest-black-americans-busienss-billionaires-richest-black-americans.html (accessed June 27, 2010).

Min, Eungjun, ed. *Reading the Homeless: The Media's Image of Homeless Culture.* Westport, CT: Praeger, 1999.

Mishell, Lawrence, Jared Bernstein, and John Schmitt. *The State of Working America, 1998–99.* Ithaca, NY: Cornell University Press, 1999.

Misra, Joya, Stephanie Moller, and Marina Karides. "Envisioning Dependency: Changing Media Depictions of Welfare in the 20th Century." *Social Problems* 50 (2003): 482–504.

Morse, Harold A. "Please Don't Let Shelter Ruin Our Neighborhood." Fredericksburg.com. 2003. www.fredericksburg.com/?News/FLS/911/2003/012003/01072003/834032.html (accessed January 25, 2004).

"Most Expensive Gated Communities in America." Forbes.com. 2006. www.forbes.com/maserati/cx_bs_1114home.html (accessed June 10, 2010).

"Move to the Head of Your Class" (advertisement). *Texas Monthly* (October 2003): 137.

Moyers, Bill. "Politics and Economy: Transcript—Middle Class Squeeze." PBS.org. December 13, 2002. www.pbs.org/now/transcript/transcript_middleclass.html (accessed December 31, 2003).

Muhammad, Richard. "Archie Bunker Lives!" Blinks.net. 2001. www.blinks.net/magazine/channels/issues/doc_page5.html (accessed March 14, 2003).

Murgatroyd, John. "Behind the Scenes: The Amazing Folks Cleaning Up the Gulf." CNN.com. July 23, 2010. www.cnn.com/2010/US/07/23/rescue.murgatroyd/index.html?section=cnn_latest (accessed October 15, 2010).

"My Wife and Kids." ABC.com. 2004. www.abc.go.com/primetime/mywifeandkids/ show.html (accessed January 1, 2004).

Napolitano, Jo. "As Garbage, and Smell, Rise in Chicago, Striking Trash Haulers Reject a Raise Offer." *New York Times,* October 6, 2003, A9.

———. "Chicago Strike Leaves Garbage Piling Up." *New York Times,* October 3, 2003, A18.

Nettles, John G. *"Malcolm in the Middle."* PopMatters. 2003. popmatters.com/tv/ reviews/m/malcolm-in-the-middle.html (accessed December 30, 2003).

Nieves, Evelyn. "Libraries Dealing with Homeless Try New Approaches: San Francisco Hires A Social Worker." *San Francisco Examiner,* February 20, 2010. www .sfexaminer.com/nation/san-fran-library-hires-social-worker-for-homeless-84849352 .html (accessed August 2, 2010).

Nill, Andrea. "Immigrants Cleaning Up the BP Oil Spill Is Nothing New." The Wonk Room. June 11, 2010. http://wonkroom.thinkprogress.org/2010/06/11/bp-immigra tion-louisiana (accessed October 15, 2010).

Nocera, Joseph. *A Piece of the Action: How the Middle Class Joined the Money Class.* New York: Simon and Schuster, 1994.

Noer, Michael, and Dan Ackman. "The Forbes Fictional Fifteen." *Forbes,* September 13, 2002. www.forbes.com/2002/09/13/400fictional_10.html (accessed December 7, 2003).

Norris, Pippa. *Women, Media, and Politics.* New York: Oxford University Press, 1997.

Norris, Pippa, and Susan J. Carroll. "The Dynamics of the News Framing Process: From Reagan's Gender Gap to Clinton's Soccer Moms." John F. Kennedy School of Government. 1997. ksghome.harvard.edu/~.pnorris.shorenstein.ksg/acrobat/car roll.pdf (accessed August 27, 2003).

Norris, Pippa, Montague Kern, and Marion Just. *Framing Terrorism: The News Media, the Government and the Public.* New York: Routledge, 2003.

"Not Able to Earn a Living: The Letter of a Sewing Woman to the Central Labor Union." *New York Times,* February 16, 1885, 5.

Novak, Shonda. "Austin Mansion Sale's a Stunner." *Austin American-Statesman,* September 25, 2003, A1, A17.

Novak, Shonda, Lori Hawkins, and Amy Schatz. "Overheard in Austin." *Austin American-Statesman,* February 22, 2002, D1.

Nunberg, Geoffrey. "Keeping Ahead of the Joneses." *New York Times,* November 24, 2002, WK4.

Ohlemacher, Stephen "With Income Tax Cuts Expiring, Rates Could Rise for Wealthy—but What about Middle Class?" *Star Tribune,* July 22, 2010. www.star tribune.com/lifestyle/99034509.html (accessed August 7, 2010).

Oldenburg, Ray. *The Great Good Place: Cafés, Coffee Shops, Bookstores, Bars, Hair Salons and Other Hangouts at the Heart of a Community.* New York: Marlowe, 1999.

Olsen, Eric. "Down and Out in Santa Monica." Blogcritics. January 6, 2003. www .blogcritics.org/archives/2003/01/06/200033.php (accessed February 22, 2004).

"Organized Crime and the Labor Unions." AmericanMafia.com. 2004. www.ameri canmafia.com/Crime_and_Labor.html (accessed March 22, 2004).

"Organized Crime Section: Labor Racketeering." Federal Bureau of Investigation. www.fbi.gov/hq/cid/orgcrime/lcn/laborrack.htm (accessed March 22, 2004).

Pakulski, Jan, and Malcolm Waters. *The Death of Class*. Thousand Oaks, CA: Pine Forge, 1996.

———. "The Reshaping and Dissolution of Social Class in Advanced Society." *Theory and Society* 25 (1996): 667–91.

Parenti, Michael. *Inventing Reality: The Politics of the Mass Media*. New York: St. Martin's, 1986.

Parker, Waichman, Alonso, LLP. "Jack Grubman Takes the Fall for Many." December 24, 2002. www.yourlawyer.com/articles/read/3963 (accessed October 17, 2010).

Parr, Jan, and Ted Shen. "The Richest Chicagoans: Who's Up, Who's Down?" *Chicago* (February 2002): 48–55, 76–81.

Partlow, Joshua. "At River's Edge, Left with an 'Empty Feeling.'" *Washington Post*, September 25, 2003, SM3.

Paventi, Jared. "Expensive New York Restaurants." GolfLink. www.golflink.com/list_28775_expensive-new-york-restaurants.html (accessed June 27, 2010).

Pear, Robert. "A Proposed Definition of Poverty May Raise Number of U.S. Poor." *New York Times*, April 30, 1995, A1.

Peppard, Alan. "Charity Co-chair Steps Down over Shoplifting Charge." Dallas News.com. www.dallasnews.com (accessed September 29, 2003).

Perrucci, Robert, and Earl Wysong. *The New Class Society*. 2nd ed. Lanham, MD: Rowman & Littlefield, 2003.

Persch, Jasmin Aline. "'House' Effect: TV Doc Has Real Impact on Care." MSNBC .com. September 9, 2009. www.msnbc.msn.com/id/32745079/ns/health-health_care (accessed June 25, 2010).

Peyser, Marc. "Martha's Mess: An Insider Trading Scandal Tarnishes the Queen of Perfection." *Newsweek*, July 1, 2002, 38–43.

Peyser, Marc, and B. J. Sigesmund. "Heir Heads." *Newsweek*, October 20, 2003, 54–55.

Pezzullo, Elizabeth. "Shelter's Plan Not a Popular Move." *Free Lance-Star*, June 7, 2002. www.fredericksburg.com/?News/FLS/2002/062002/06072002/631644 (accessed January 25, 2004).

"Philanthropy: Enriching Our Communities through Giving." *Austin American-Statesman*, January 1, 2002, A11.

Pogrebin, Robin. "Trustees Find Cultural Board Seats Are Still Highly Coveted Luxury Items." *New York Times*, April 3, 2010, C1, C5.

Polgreen, Lydia. "An Aging Population, a Looming Crisis." *New York Times*, November 4, 2003, A25.

———. "As Jobs Vanish, the Sweet Talk Could Turn Tough." *New York Times*, October 12, 2003, A26.

Pollack, Andrew. "Prominent Drug Chief to Sell Abraxis BioScience to Celgene for $2.9 Billion." *New York Times*, June 30, 2010. www.nytimes.com/2010/07/01/health/01drug.html (accessed June 30, 2010).

Poniewozik, James. "The New Class Action." *Time*, September 29, 2003. www.time .com/time/magazine/article/0,9171,1005792,00.html (accessed October 17, 2010).

———. "Reality TV's Working Class Heroes." Time.com. May 22, 2008. www.time
.com/time/magazine/article/0,9171,1808612,00.html (accessed October 15, 2010).

"Poor Whites in the South: Their Poverty and Principles." *New York Times*, May 13, 1877, 5.

Porterfield, Amy. "Social Media Differences among Teens, Boomers, and Moms: Study Findings." Social Media Examiner. March 5, 2010. www.socialmediaexam iner.com/social-media-differences-among-teens-boomers-and-moms-new-study -findings (accessed June 21, 2010).

"Poverty and Charity." *New York Times*, November 8, 1870, 2.

"Poverty Leading to Suicide: Another Body of a Woman Found at New Haven." *New York Times*, September 3, 1881, 2.

"President Barack Obama." Whitehouse.gov. July 28, 2010. www.whitehouse.gov/ administration/president-obama (accessed July 28, 2010).

Preston, Julia. "Fewer Latino Immigrants Sending Money Home." *New York Times*, May 1, 2008, A1.

———. "A Slippery Place in the U.S. Work Force." *New York Times*, March 22, 2009, A1, A18.

Primack, Phil. "We All Work, Don't We?" *Columbia Journalism Review* (September–October 1992): 56.

Project for Excellence in Journalism. "The State of the News Media 2010." The State of the News Media. www.stateofthemedia.org/2010/overview_major_trends.php (accessed October 15, 2010).

Puette, William J. *Through Jaundiced Eyes: How the Media View Organized Labor.* Ithaca, NY: ILR, 1992.

Pugh, Tony. "Nation's Economic Collapse Triggers Rise in Homeless Families." McClatchy. June 18, 2010. www.mcclatchydc.com/2010/06/17/96074/report-nations -economic-collapse.html (accessed July 10, 2010).

"Put It on My Tab." *Austin American-Statesman*, September 22, 2002, H1.

"Receipt of Unemployment Insurance among Low-Income Single Mothers." ASPE Issue Brief. Office of the Assistant Secretary for Planning and Evaluation. January 2005. http://aspe.hhs.gov/hsp/05/unemp-receipt/ib.pdf (accessed July 15, 2010).

"Reds Plotted Country Wide Strike. Arrests Exceeded 5,000, 2,635 Held; 3 Transports Ready for Them." *New York Times*, January 4, 1920, 1.

Reese, Stephen D., Oscar H. Gandy Jr., and August E. Grant, eds. *Framing Public Life: Perspectives on Media and Our Understanding of the Social World.* Mahwah, NJ: Lawrence Erlbaum, 2003.

Reinberg, Steven. "U.S. Kids Using Media Almost 8 Hours a Day." *Bloomberg Businessweek*, January 20, 2010. www.businessweek.com/lifestyle/content/health day/635134.html (accessed June 22, 2010).

"A Return to Welfare Dependency." *Washington Times*, February 23, 2009. www .washingtontimes.com/news/2009/feb/23/a-return-to-welfare-dependency (accessed July 15, 2010).

Rich, Frank. "When You Got It, Flaunt It." *New York Times*, November 23, 2003, AR1, AR34.

Rich, Motoko. "Nation Lost 131,000 Jobs As Governments Cut Back." *New York Times*, August 7, 2010, A1, A3.

"*Rich Girls*: Welcome to the World of the Rich Girls." MTV. 2003. www.mtu.com/onair/rich_girls (accessed October 22, 2003).

"Rich People on TV Aren't Really Rich." *Wall Street Journal*, June 28, 2010. http://blogs.wsj.com/wealth/2010/06/28/rich-people-on-tv-arent-really-rich (accessed July 8, 2010).

Rivlin, Gary. *Broke, USA: From Pawnshops to Poverty, Inc.—How the Working Poor Became Big Business*. New York: Harper Business, 2010.

"Robin Leach." Barber and Associates. www.barberusa.com/pathfind/leach_robin.html (accessed November 20, 2003).

Robbins, Tom. "Working-Class Heroes: Towering Losses, Towering Deeds." *Village Voice*, September 26–October 2, 2001. www.villagevoice.com/issues/0139/robbins.php (accessed March 4, 2004).

Rothman, Robert A. *Inequality and Stratification: Race, Class, and Gender*. 5th ed. Upper Saddle River, NJ: Prentice Hall, 2005.

Rucker, Allen. *The Sopranos: A Family History*. New York: New American Library, 2001.

"A Sad Case of Poverty: A Woman Commits Suicide, Her Husband at the Point of Death." *New York Times*, July 13, 1874, 5.

Salkin, Allen. "Homes, Sweet Homes: Michael Bloomberg's Real-Estate Holdings Are Fairly Modest—for a Multibillionaire." *New York Magazine*, April 15, 2002, 23.

Samuelson, Robert J. "Defining Poverty Up: How to Create More 'Poor.'" *Newsweek,* May 30, 2010. www.newsweekinteractive.net/2010/05/30/defining-poverty-up.html (accessed July 10, 2010).

Sargent, Ben. "Don't Mind Howard . . ." *Austin American-Statesman*, August 29, 2003, A16.

———. "Oh, Yeah? Well, Now They're Talking . . ." *Austin American-Statesman*, March 26, 2003, A16.

Saul, Michael. "Levi Johnson Calls Sarah Palin 'Snobby,' Says His Family Is Not 'White Trash' on CBS' 'Early Show.'" NYDailyNews.com. April 8, 2009. www.nydailynews.com/news/politics/2009/04/08/2009-04-08_levi_johnston_calls_sarah_palin_snobby_says_his_family_is_not_white_trash_on_cbs.html (accessed July 26, 2010).

"Save Middle Class, Congress Is Urged." *New York Times*, October 21, 1942, 1.

"Says Middle Class Needs Salvation: Martin Asks National Support of Republican Drive to Avert Its 'Ruin' by New Deal." *New York Times*, August 27, 1939, 5.

Scheibal, Stephen. "Long Center Asks City for $25 Million." *Austin American-Statesman*, February 1, 2003, A1, A10.

Scheufele, Dietram A. "Framing As a Theory of Media Effects." *Journal of Communications* 49 (1999): 103–22.

Schmidt, Diane E. "Public Opinion and Media Coverage of Labor Unions." *Journal of Labor Research* 15 (spring 1993): 151–64.

"School Cooks Win over $95 Million in Powerball." *Dallas Morning News*, October 28, 2003, 5A.

Schor, Juliet B. *Born to Buy: The Commercialized Child and the New Consumer Culture.* New York: Scribner, 2004.

Schwartz, Nelson D. "Jobless and Staying That Way." *New York Times*, August 8, 2010, WK1, WK2.

Schwarz, John E., and Thomas J. Volgy. *The Forgotten Americans.* New York: Norton, 1992.

Seelye, Katharine Q. "Gore Offers Vision of Better Times for Middle Class." *New York Times*, September 7, 2000, A1.

Seitz, Matt Zoller. "'Deadliest Catch': Reality TV's First On-Screen Death." Salon .com. July 13, 2010. www.salon.com/entertainment/tv/2010/07/13/deadliest_ catch_finale (accessed October 15, 2010).

Sellers, Patricia. "The Business of Being Oprah." *Fortune*, April 1, 2002. www .mutualofamerica.com/articles/Fortune/2002_04_08/Oprah1.asp (accessed March 30, 2002).

"Senate Vote Voided Veto of Labor Bill." *New York Times*, June 24, 1947, 1.

Shanahan, Gerry. "You Say House Arrest, I Say Paradise." *New York Times*, May 2, 2002, F1, F7.

Shapiro, Thomas M., Tatjana Meschede, and Laura Sullivan. "The Racial Wealth Gap Increases Fourfold." Institute on Assets and Social Policy, Research and Policy Brief. Heller School for Social Policy and Management, Brandeis University. May 2010. http://iasp.brandeis.edu/pdfs/Racial-Wealth-Gap-Brief.pdf (accessed October 15, 2010).

Shipler, David K. "A Poor Cousin of the Middle Class." *New York Times Magazine*, January 18, 2004, 22–27.

———. *The Working Poor: Invisible in America.* New York: Knopf, 2004.

"Shop Till You Get Caught." *D Magazine* (November 2003): 20.

"Showdown over Shelter: A Gritty Little Neighborhood Fights S.F. Plan for Homeless." *San Francisco Examiner*, August 12, 1999.

Shulman, Beth. *The Betrayal of Work: How Low-Wage Jobs Fail 30 Million Americans and Their Families.* New York: New Press, 2003.

Sicha, Choire. "They'll Always Have Paris." *New York Times*, June 13, 2004, AR31, AR41.

Silver, Cameron. "Texas Hold 'Em." Style.com. 2007. www.style.com/peopleparties/ parties/thumb/022207LACR/new (accessed June 25, 2010).

Silverstein, Michael J., and Neil Fiske (with John Butman). *Trading Up: The New American Luxury.* New York: Portfolio, 2003.

Simnacher, Joe. "Brooke Stollenwerck Aldridge: Socialite, Civic Volunteer." *Dallas Morning News*, March 22, 2007. www.dallasnews.com/sharedcontent/dws/news/ city/parkcities/stories/032307dnmetaldridgeob.326e212.html (accessed August 19, 2010).

Smith, Steve. "Developing New Reflexes in Framing Stories." Pew Center for Civil Journalism. 1997. www.pewcenter.org/doingcj/civiccat/displayCivcat.php?id=97 (accessed July 3, 2004).

Snow, David A., and Leon Anderson. *Down on Their Luck: A Case Study of Homeless Street People.* Berkeley: University of California Press, 1993.

Snow, David A., E. Burke Rochford, Steven K. Worden, and Robert D. Benford. "Frame Alignment Processes, Micromobilization, and Movement Participation." *American Sociological Review* 51 (1986): 464–81.

Snyder, Michael. "The Middle Class in America Is Radically Shrinking: Here Are the Stats to Prove It." Yahoo! Finance. July 15, 2010. http://finance.yahoo .com/tech-ticker/the-u.s.-middle-class-is-being-wiped-out-here's-the-stats-to -prove-it-520657.html (accessed July 24, 2010).

"So You Wanna Be a Sitcom Writer?" SoYouWanna. 2004. www.soyouwanna.com/ site/syws/sitcom/sitcom.html (accessed July 7, 2004).

Spencer, Miranda. "Making the Invisible Visible." *Extra!* (January–February 2003). www.fair.org/extra/0301/poverty.html (accessed February 29, 2004).

St. John, Warren. "Advice from Ex-Cons to a Jet-Set Jailbird: Best Walk on Eggs." *New York Times*, July 13, 2003, ST1, ST2.

Stanley, Alessandra. "Focusing on Residents of Gilded Cages." *New York Times*, October 27, 2003, B8.

———. "TV Weekend—Bullies, Bears and Bullets: It's Round 5." *New York Times*, March 5, 2004, E1.

———. "With a Rich Girl Here and a Rich Girl There." *New York Times*, December 2, 2003, B1, B5.

Stanley, Alessandra, and Constance L. Hays. "Martha Stewart's To-Do List May Include Image Polishing." *New York Times*, June 23, 2002, A1, A24.

"The State of the News Media 2004." Committee of Concerned Journalists. www .journalism.org (accessed June 17, 2004).

Stein, Joel. "The Real Face of Homelessness." CNN.com. January 13, 2003. www .cnn/2003/ALLPOLITICS/01/13/timep.homelessness.tm/index.html (accessed February 11, 2004).

Steinhauer, Jennifer. "Bloomberg's Salon, Where the Powerful Mix over Meatloaf." *New York Times*, May 8, 2002, A1, A29.

Sternheimer, Karen. *It's Not the Media: The Truth about Pop Culture's Influence on Children.* Boulder, CO: Westview, 2003.

Stout, David. "A Great Equalizer: Isabel Was Her Name." *New York Times*, September 26, 2003, A17.

Strom, Stephanie. "For Middle Class, Health Insurance Becomes a Luxury." *New York Times*, November 16, 2003, A25.

Sullivan, Paul. "All This Anger Against the Rich May Be Unhealthy." *New York Times*, October 17, 2009, B6.

———. "Too Rich to Worry? Not in This Downturn." *New York Times*, October 3, 2010. www.nytimes.com/2009/10/03/your-money/03wealth.html (accessed October 15, 2010).

"The Superplexus." Hammacher Schlemmer. www.hammacher.com/Product/78372 (accessed June 30, 2010).

Sweeney, Gael. "The King of White Trash Culture: Elvis Presley and the Aesthetics of Excess." In *White Trash: Race and Class in America*, edited by Matt Wray and Annalee Newitz, 249–66. New York: Routledge, 1997.

"Tarnish, Anyone?" *People*, July 8, 2002, 44–45.

Taylor, LaTonya. "The Church of O." *Christianity Today*, April 1, 2002, 38–45.

"Terrible Tragedy: An Insane Mother Kills Her Daughter." *New York Times*, July 6, 1872, 2.

Thomas, Cal. "Other Media Trying to Copy Fox's Use of 'Big-Lipped Blondes' and 'Trailer Trash.'" Media Matters for America. July 10, 2006. www.mediamatters .org/mmtv/200606190009 (accessed July 26, 2010).

Thomas, Cathy Booth. "Enron Takes a Life." *Time*, February 4, 2002, 20–21.

Thomas, Evan, and Andrew Murr. "The Gambler Who Blew It All." *Newsweek*, February 4, 2002, 24.

Thomas, Pierre. "Katrina Cover-Up: Cops May Face Death Penalty." abcNEWS.com. July 14, 2010. http://abcnews.go.com/GMA/orleans-police-face-death-penalty -hurricane-katrina-bridge/story?id=11160077 (accessed October 17, 2010).

Timmons, Heather. "Due Diligence from Afar." *New York Times*, August 5, 2010, B1, B2.

"Toronto Stinks on Day 4 of Trash Strike." UPI.com. June 25, 2009. www .upi.com/Top_News/2009/06/25/Toronto-stinks-on-Day-4-of-trash-strike/UPI -21471245928472 (accessed July 18, 2010).

Trumbull, Mark. "Obama's Challenge: Reversing a Decade of Middle-Class Decline." *Christian Science Monitor*, January 25, 2010. www.csmonitor.com/ USA/2010/0125/Obama-s-challenge-reversing-a-decade-of-middle-class-decline (accessed July 29, 2010).

Truppin, Andrea. "How Much Is That View in the Window?" *New York Times*, September 18, 2003, D4.

Tsao, Amy. "The Two Faces of Wal-Mart." *Businessweek*, January 28, 2004. www .businessweek.com/bwdaily/dnflash/jan2004/nf20040128_6990_db014.html (accessed February 2, 2004).

Tuchman, Gaye. *Making News: A Study in the Construction of Reality*. New York: Free Press, 1978.

Tugend, Alina. "What Recovery? For the Unemployed, the Pain Gets Worse." *New York Times*, July 3, 2010, B5.

U.S. Conference of Mayors. "Hunger and Homelessness at Record Levels in U.S. Cities." City Mayors. December 8, 2009. www.citymayors.com/features/uscity_pov erty.html (accessed July 11, 2010).

Uchitelle, Louis. "Blacks Lose Better Jobs Faster As Middle-Class Work Drops." *New York Times*, July 12, 2003, A1.

———. "Bottom's Up: The Middle Class—Winning in Politics, Losing in Life." *New York Times*, July 19, 1998, WR1.

———. "We Pledge Allegiance to the Mall." *New York Times*, December 6, 2004, C12.

"Unable to Endure Poverty." *New York Times*, June 2, 1884, 2.

Urquhart, Frank. "Donald Trump Jets In and Fires Off 'Slum and Pigsty' Slur." Scotsman.com. May 27, 2010. www.scotsman.com/donaldtrump/Donald-Trump-jets-in -and.6322621.jp (accessed July 5, 2010).

Vane, Sharyn Wizda. "Martha's Dirty Laundry." *Austin American-Statesman*, April 20, 2002, D1, D13.

Veblen, Thorstein. *The Theory of the Leisure Class*. Introduction by Robert Le-kachman. New York: Penguin, 1994 [1899].

"A Violinist in Despair: Domenico Mariani on the Verge of Suicide, Seized As He Was About to Jump from a Hoboken Dock—Poverty in His Old Age Unbearable." *New York Times*, August 30, 1885, 12.

"Wal-Mart Settles Illegal Immigrant Case for $11 M." Fox News. March 19, 2005. www.foxnews.com/story/0,2933,150846,00.html (accessed July 27, 2010).

"The Wal-Martization of America." *New York Times*, November 15, 2003, A26.

"Walks among the New York Poor: Homeless Children." *New York Times*, May 4, 1854, 6.

"Walks among the Poor." *New York Times*, January 30, 1870, 6.

"*Wall Street 2* the Movie." Market Folly. June 2, 2009. www.marketfolly.com/2009/06/wall-street-2-movie-february-2010-with.html (accessed June 21, 2010).

"Wallace Sees All in a Middle Class: Picturing Future, He Asserts the 'Horatio Alger' Spirit Will Never Die Here." *New York Times*, January 25, 1943, 1.

Warner, W. Lloyd, and Paul S. Lunt. *The Social Life of a Modern Community*. New Haven, CT: Yale University Press, 1941.

Warren, Elizabeth, and Amelia Warren Tyagi. *The Two-Income Trap: Why Middle Class Mothers and Fathers Are Going Broke*. New York: Basic Books, 2003.

Weber, Max. *From Max Weber: Essays in Sociology*. Edited by H. H. Gerth and C. Wright Mills. New York: Oxford University Press, 1946.

Wecter, Dixon. *The Saga of American Society: A Record of Social Aspiration, 1607–1937*. New York: Scribner, 1937.

"Weddings/Celebrations: Carter Brooks, Talbott Simonds." *New York Times*, April 9, 2006. http://query.nytimes.com/gst/fullpage.html?res=9F06E6DA1130F93AA35757C0A9609C8B63&scp=1&sq=weddings%20AND%20elinor%20carter%20brooks?&st=cse (accessed July 6, 2010).

Whang, Insung, and Eungjun Min. "Blaming the Homeless: The Populist Aspect of Network TV News." In *Reading the Homeless: The Media's Image of Homeless Culture*, edited by Eungjun Min, 121–33. Westport, CT: Praeger, 1999.

White, Jerry. "Wall Street Throws General Motors into Bankruptcy." *World Socialist*. May 29, 2009. www.wsws.org/articles/2009/may2009/pers-m29.shtml (accessed July 20, 2010).

"White Trash Party Sparks Ire in Texas Neighborhood." WCCO.com. June 26, 2010. http://wcco.com/watercooler/White.Trash.party.2.1774551.html (accessed October 20, 2010).

"'Why Middle Class Mothers and Fathers Are Going Broke.'" MSNBC.com. 2003. msnbc.msn.com/Default.aspx?id=3079221&p1=0 (accessed December 29, 2003).

Wilkinson, Signe. "The Corporate Card Shoppe" *Austin American-Statesman*, September 16, 2003, A11.

Williams, Maureen. "From Incendiary to Invisible: A Print-News Content Analysis of the Labor Movement." *Labor Center Review* 10 (1988): 23–27.

Williams, Robin M., Jr. *American Society: A Sociological Interpretation*. 3rd ed. New York: Knopf, 1970.

Witchel, Alex. "Tacos, Stir-Fries and Cake: The Junior League at 102." *New York Times*, October 15, 2003, D1, D6.

"Working Men on Parade: An Orderly Labor Demonstration—Ten Thousand Men in Line." *New York Times*, September 6, 1882, 8.

"The Working Men's Views: President Jarrett before the Senate Committee." *New York Times*, September 8, 1883, 8.

Wray, Matt, and Annalee Newitz, eds. *White Trash: Race and Class in America*. New York: Routledge, 1997.

Wrolstad, Mark. "An Unfashionable Turn for Stylish HP Socialite." *Dallas Morning News*, October 25, 2003, 1A, 10A–11A.

Wyatt, Edward, and David M. Halbfinger. "Clark and Kerry Offering Plans to Help Middle Class." *New York Times*, January 6, 2004, A17.

Yardley, Jonathan. "Book Review: *Behind the Gates*." *Washington Post*, May 8, 2003, C02.

Yardley, William. "The Last Grain Falls at a Sugar Factory." *New York Times*, January 31, 2004, A13.

"Your Honor, My Client . . ." (cartoon). *New Yorker*, March 25, 2002, 69.

Zeller, Tom. "The Nation: Calculating One Kind of Middle Class." *New York Times*, October 29, 2000, WR5.

———. "Of Fuzzy Math and 'Food Security.'" *New York Times*, January 11, 2004, WK16.

Zweig, Michael. *The Working Class Majority: America's Best Kept Secret*. Ithaca, NY: Cornell University Press, 2001.

Index

About the Author

Diana Kendall is professor of sociology at Baylor University, where she was named "Outstanding Professor" for her research. Dr. Kendall's research and teaching interests include social theory, stratification, sociology of media, and sociology of law. She is the author of *The Power of Good Deeds: Privileged Women and the Social Reproduction of the Upper Class* (2002), *Member's Only: Elite Clubs and the Process of Exclusion* (2008), and several widely used textbooks, including *Sociology in Our Times* and *Social Problems in a Diverse Society.*